PUBLIC POLICIES
TOWARD BUSINESS

PUBLIC POLICIES TOWARD BUSINESS

William G. Shepherd
Professor of Economics
University of Massachusetts at Amherst

EIGHTH EDITION

Homewood, IL 60430
Boston, MA 02116

Senior sponsoring editor: Gary L. Nelson
Project editor: Karen J. Murphy
Production manager: Ann Cassady
Cover and interior designer: Stuart Patterson
Compositor: Weimer Typesetting Co., Inc.
Typeface: 10/12 Times Roman
Printer: R. R. Donnelley & Sons Company

© RICHARD D. IRWIN, INC., 1955, 1960, 1966, 1971, 1975, 1979, 1985, and 1991

Library of Congress Cataloging-in-Publication Data

Shepherd, William G.
    Public policies toward business / William G. Shepherd.—8th ed.
        p.   cm.
    Includes indexes.
    ISBN 0-256-08464-5
    1. Industry and state—United States.   I. Title.
HD3616.U47S38   1991
338.973–dc20   90–41261

Printed in the United States of America
1 2 3 4 5 6 7 8 9 0 DO 7 6 5 4 3 2 1 0

To Theodora B. Shepherd
and to the memory of Geoffrey S. Shepherd,
peerless scholar and fearless critic.

PREFACE

For about 90 years, from 1888 to 1978, the United States developed a unique set of policies toward business. Antitrust and regulation covered most markets in ways that this book describes. Since then, the policies have been altered drastically, and American industry is still absorbing the aftershocks. The 1980s' merger boom, the divestiture of the Bell Telephone System, the de-regulation of airlines, railroads, and banking—these and other changes have transformed much of this book's subject.

Accordingly, this edition has been revised extensively to reflect the changes. The new material includes the free-market doctrines of the Chicago-UCLA school, which were applied by the Reagan administration during the 1980s. Part One, "The Setting for Policies," covers the contending economic schools more thoroughly than previous editions.

Part Two gives extended coverage of antitrust policies, even though they have been cut back drastically during the Reagan/Chicago-UCLA years. De-regulation and regulation are recast in Part Three to reflect the major experiments in de-regulation and the reduced scope of traditional utility regulation. Public enterprise and special cases have been condensed in Part Four to two chapters.

As before, the aim of this book is to develop the skill of analyzing complex economic issues with an independent mind. Concepts, facts, and cases are provided, but they are only the raw material. Long after you may have forgotten the details, I hope you will retain the method of objective evaluation that this book encourages.

Throughout, you are taken beneath the surface details to the economic effects of policies. They are controversial, of course, but the economic questions must be asked nonetheless. What are these actions really doing? Are they worth their costs? What alternatives might be better?

The book is designed to fit a one-semester or two-quarter treatment of business and government at the upper college level. It is also intended to be useful in law and business courses that deal with competitive issues and with the economic content of antitrust and regulatory law. Although the book's format gives a natural sequence, it can be used flexibly.

The book was started by Clair Wilcox of Swarthmore College, going through four editions during 1955–71. On Wilcox's death, I provided a form of joint authorship for two editions. Wilcox's spirit lives on in the present edition, though I am listed as the sole author.

The text is an outgrowth of many years of teaching by Wilcox at Swarthmore College and by myself at the University of Michigan, the University of Massachusetts, Yale University, and Williams College. It also reflects our service in various public agencies and our research on many issues, sectors, and policy effects, in all parts of the subject.

I owe debts to many people for help in preparing this volume. Richard Hellman and Alan Nichols provided helpful detailed advice about needed revisions throughout the book. Many colleagues' advice and support over many years have also shaped the book. They include Walter Adams, William J. Adams, William J. Baumol, Maxwell Blecher, Kenneth D. Boyer, Richard E. Caves, William S. Comanor, Henry de Jong, Donald J. Dewey, Kenneth Elzinga, Alfred E. Kahn, H. Michael Mann, Charles E. Mueller, Takeo Nakao, James R. Nelson, Richard R. Nelson, Eli Noam, Shorey Peterson, Almarin Phillips, F. M. Scherer, Leonard G. Schifrin, John B. Sheahan, Harry M. Trebing, Don C. Waldman, Leonard W. Weiss, and Oliver E. Williamson. Their generosity and skill are a continuing source of pleasure.

At Irwin, I have benefited from the thoughtful supervision and fine editing of Elizabeth Murry and Karen J. Murphy.

Accordingly, the book's limitations are entirely my responsibility. As always, I invite your help in improving further editions. Your advice will be warmly welcomed.

William G. Shepherd

CONTENTS

P·A·R·T O·N·E   **THE SETTING FOR POLICIES**

C·H·A·P·T·E·R 1   Introduction

For a century, the United States has employed a unique pair of public policies to deal with market power in its economy: antitrust and regulation. In contrast, other countries have relied mainly on mixtures of government support, informal influence, and ownership in various sectors.

By using its complex and evolving set of antitrust policies, the United States has sought to promote competition as the guiding force in most markets. The Sherman Act of 1890 serves as a magna carta of economic freedom, and it has deeply affected the American economy by maintaining greater competition and economic progress.

Toward certain basic utility sectors, the United States has applied the second type of policy: regulation. Unique by world standards, regulation (1) permits monopolies to exist in certain "natural monopoly" industries, but then (2) seeks to restrain their pricing and profits to reflect competitive patterns. Most other countries have put their utilities under government ownership.

The United States also has developed several other lesser policies toward business, including public enterprise (instead of private control), patents for inventions, "social regulation" of safety and pollution, and methods of buying military weapons.

Market power is the main problem that all of these policies try to solve. As economists have long analyzed, market power tends to reduce efficiency, retard innovation, cause unfairness, and introduce other distortions. Monopoly has many forms and effects that arise in a variety of market settings, and so the policies to constrain monopoly need to be adapted carefully, case by case.

The policies are important and fascinating in themselves, dealing with the central character of free market, competitive capitalism. If the policies are well designed and wisely applied, then the economy will be more efficient, innovative, and fair. But the actual policies are hammered out in the rugged political process, rather than calmly perfected, and so they often turn out to be quite imperfect.

How imperfect, and in what ways, is intensely controversial. Antitrust, regulation, and the other policies have always been both denounced and defended, and the debates are often bewildering. Moreover, the policies frequently change and go through swings between strictness and leniency.

The task in this book is to learn (1) the economic criteria of "good" policies, and then (2) the policies' actual design, history, and economic effects, as they have developed since the 1880s. From that basis, you can then judge for yourself how effective the policies, with their specific strengths and faults, have been.

FROM 1890 TO THE RADICAL 1980s

During the nine decades from 1890 to 1980, the policies toward business evolved into the U.S. government's unique approach, combining strong antitrust toward most of the economy with the direct regulation of prices of certain utilities.[1] No other country had these policy tools, and they seemed to work well and to promote long-term growth and innovation in the United States.

Then came a dramatic break during 1975–85. Several regulated industries were briskly de-regulated, especially airlines, railroads, and trucking. During 1981–89, the Reagan administration sharply reduced the scope and strength of antitrust enforcement, and it extended de-regulation even further to telephones, broadcasting, finance, and other sectors. After 1980, America's distinctive policies—particularly the deeply rooted reliance on antitrust policies to curb monopoly—were cut back deeply, amid intense controversy.

---

[1] On antitrust's early history, see Hans Thorelli, *The Federal Antitrust Policy* (Baltimore: Johns Hopkins Press, 1954); William Letwin, *Law and Economic Policy in America* (New York: Random House, 1965); and A. D. Neale and D. G. Goyder, *The Antitrust Laws of the United States of America*, 3d ed. (Cambridge: Cambridge University Press, 1980). More recent summaries include F. M. Scherer and David Ross, *Industrial Market Structure and Economic Performance*, 3d ed. (Boston: Houghton Mifflin, 1990); Richard A. Posner, *Antitrust Policy* (Chicago: University of Chicago Press, 1976); and Harry First, Eleanor M. Fox, and Robert Pitofsky, eds., *Antitrust for Its Second Century* (Westport, Conn.: Greenwood Press, 1990).

On regulation, see Alfred E. Kahn, *The Economics of Regulation*, 2 vols. (Cambridge, Mass.: MIT Press, 1989); and Richard Schmalensee, *The Control of Natural Monopolies* (Lexington, Mass.: D. C. Heath, 1979).

Reagan officials candidly favored big business. They argued that large enterprises are superior in efficiency and innovation to small firms; any dangers of monopoly power would be restrained by the power of competition from little rivals and the entry of new competitors; most of the antitrust restraints on monopoly were no longer necessary in the new, tough global markets where foreign firms applied tight pressures; and antitrust would merely interfere with the rising competition.

This shift in thought and policy was similar to a change in the 1920s, when the Harding-Coolidge administrations favored big business and cut back deeply on antitrust enforcement. But the 1980s' views also reflected a range of "new" economic doctrines, particularly what is called "Chicago-school" economic analysis (actually they are Chicago-UCLA ideas, because some leading members of the school are at the University of California in Los Angeles).[2]

Chicago-UCLA doctrines hold that virtually all markets are effectively competitive already and that government actions tend only to interfere with competition. They say that state actions cause harm even when trying to do good. Therefore, laissez-faire is the correct course; markets should be trusted and government policies ought to be dismantled, according to free market, Chicago-oriented economists and legal scholars.

They found enthusiastic acceptance in the Reagan administration. In virtually all policies covered in this book, the 1980s brought cut-backs toward minimal levels of policy action. In some cases, such as the deregulation of the savings and loan industry, the results are universally recognized to have been disastrous. But in most others, Chicago-UCLA-school economists and officials still believe that their minimalist policies have been successful. The previous moderate antitrust and regulatory policies are said to have been mistaken and extreme.

---

[2]Leading Chicago-UCLA writings include George J. Stigler, *The Organization of Industry* (Homewood, Ill.: Richard D. Irwin, 1968); Yale Brozen, *Concentration, Mergers and Public Policy* (New York: Macmillan, 1982); John S. McGee, *In Defense of Industrial Concentration* (Seattle: University of Washington Press, 1971); McGee, *Industrial Organization* (Englewood Cliffs, N.J.: Prentice-Hall, 1988); and chapters by John S. McGee and Harold Demsetz in Harvey J. Goldschmid, H. Michael Mann, and J. Fred Weston, eds., *Industrial Concentration: The New Learning* (Boston: Little, Brown, 1974).

Less moderate versions are in Robert H. Bork, *The Antitrust Paradox: A Policy at War with Itself* (New York: Basic Books, 1978); Dominick T. Armentano, *Antitrust and Monopoly: Anatomy of a Policy Failure* (New York: John Wiley & Sons, 1982); and William J. Baumol and Janusz Ordover, "Use of Antitrust to Subvert Competition," *Journal of Law and Economics* 28 (May 1985), pp. 247–65. For a parallel criticism of antitrust, see also Franklin M. Fisher, John J. McGowan, and Joen E. Greenwood, *Folded, Spindled and Mutilated: Economic Analysis and U.S. vs. IBM* (Cambridge, Mass.: MIT Press, 1983).

For perceptive comparisons of the Chicago-UCLA and mainstream approaches, see Eleanor M. Fox and Lawrence A. Sullivan, "Antitrust—Retrospective and Prospective: Where Are We Coming From? Where Are We Going?" *New York University Law Review* 62 (November 1987), pp. 936–88.

The new Bush administration officials promised during 1989–90 to temper these changes by reviving antitrust to some degree and avoiding further hasty de-regulation. However, the Reagan patterns remained largely intact through 1990, and the many judges appointed by Reagan officials during the 1980s make it likely that judicial decisions will continue to reinforce the minimalist antitrust and regulatory approaches.

The readers of this book are entering the field at a particularly fascinating time, when the Reagan legacy is widespread and also ripe for reassessment. The actions of the Reagan administration were often stark, and some of them had clear effects. The debates are sharp and wide-ranging, and they provide unusually clear contrasts between the established policies and the new treatments.

Indeed, the policies merely reflect the larger debates between mainstream economists on the one hand and Chicago-UCLA-school economists and other related "new" theorists on the other. This book will present those debates and policy changes since 1900. Within that broad framework, it will focus on the dramatic 1980s' changes and their lessons. Contrasting views and schools will be presented and compared so that you can learn to make your own judgments. To illustrate the main issues, only the most important leading cases will be covered.

The focus of this book is on the policies' economic content. This content can be different from the legal forms of the policies and official rulings. For example, antitrust law continues to prohibit all price fixing among competitors. However, since the enforcement agencies have limited resources, they are able to discover and prosecute only some of the price fixing that occurs. Moreover, the officials can choose to go lightly on some offenses, using their "prosecutorial discretion" just as a local police officer decides whether to arrest all speeders or jaywalkers. In addition, the courts may punish the offenders only mildly or possibly, instead, too harshly.

As you can see, the intensity of actual enforcement is often highly variable and difficult to assess, and the exact economic effects of what has been done are not certain and are inevitably controversial. Is most price fixing stopped, or only a little of it? Should more resources be applied to enforcement? How much more? What are the yields to the economy?

Every public policy deserves such skeptical analysis, where attempts are made to judge its effects and yields. This book prepares you to do that by developing your ability to identify and judge the actions and their effects. In each case, the analysis is on two levels: (1) What is the underlying economic problem, and (2) how well do the actual policies fit economic criteria? Actual policies, regrettably, often reflect economic mistakes or calculated deceptions. Occasionally, they are quite excellent in design and details. By sifting complex arguments and evidence, this book equips you to judge the policies for yourself.

DIAGNOSIS AND TREATMENT

There are parallels between the study of public policy and the study of medicine. Medical students first learn how the healthy human body functions. Likewise, you will learn here how healthy, competitive markets function. Medical students then learn how to *diagnose* what is wrong when there is disease or injury; likewise, you will learn how to assess the causes and effects of monopoly.

After diagnosis, medical students turn to *treatment*, learning how to fit the methods of treatment to the specific disease, for each patient. For economists, the best policy solution for each situation depends on the market's specific conditions. There is usually a range of alternative methods and controversy about the choices as illustrated by the following two examples.[3]

Should AT&T have been split up in 1984? Should AT&T still be regulated in long-distance telephone service markets? It had 70 percent of the market in 1990, while MCI had only 12 percent and US Sprint had 8 percent. AT&T urged immediate de-regulation of itself so that it could set any prices it chose. The rivals and many outside observers insisted instead on the need to wait until competition was more balanced and widespread.

Another good example is the airlines; they were de-regulated during 1978–83 and were intensely competitive. But then a series of major mergers made them more concentrated after 1984. Some say monopoly power is again a serious problem; others disagree. Should the airlines be re-regulated? If so, how much, and in what ways? In each case, Chicago-UCLA-school economists favored less regulation, while other experts called for more restraints on dominant firms.

These two cases will actually be given extensive coverage in later chapters, because they pose two of the most interesting and important current policy controversies. The two industries are probably familiar to you already to some degree from personal experience in telephoning and traveling. The discussions will extend that initial understanding and fill it out with technical detail. Many of the other cases also deal with familiar products and companies, such as breakfast cereals, automobiles, computers, and newspapers.

THE FORMAT

The subject is "real," not just theoretical, but it involves a number of general concepts. The next two chapters set the stage by reviewing the

---

[3]More details and references about them are given in Chapter 3 and later in the book.

Figure 1–1   Policies Act upon Markets
(But Are Also Acted upon)

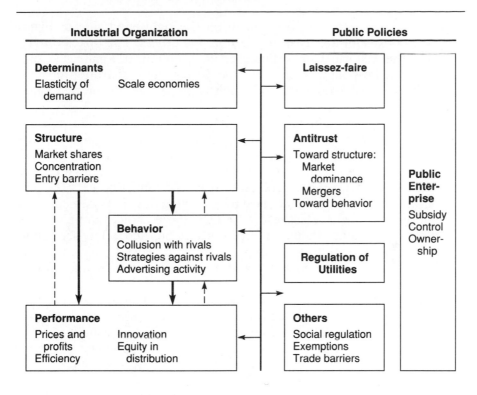

nature of competition and monopoly. This subject is usually called "industrial organization" (IO) and its main format is illustrated in Figure 1–1. Briefly summarized here, it is presented more fully in the next chapter.

Each market has a *structure* at any given moment that may range between pure competition and pure monopoly; in between is oligopoly and the dominant-firm situation. The structure tends to influence the firms' *behavior:* How do they set their prices? By fighting each other or settling into cozy collusion? Structure and behavior influence *performance:* Are the firms efficient and innovative, or slack and stagnant? The degree of monopoly may affect the outcome.

In competitive markets, the competitive process usually gives good results, while monopoly impairs them. However, monopoly comes in many degrees and forms, and, in some cases, it can be justified by economies of scale or superior efficiency, as Chapter 2 will discuss in more detail. The economist needs to consider those market conditions in deciding whether any policy treatment should be applied and, if so, which one and in what ways.

The policy alternatives are shown on the right-hand side of Figure 1–1, with boxes for antitrust, regulation, and others. The boxes roughly indicate the historical importance of each policy. If Figure 1–1 only reflected public policy since 1980, the Reagan-administration changes would make the laissez-faire box much larger, while all the rest would be smaller.

These boxes oversimplify somewhat, because the policies can and often do overlap each other. Antitrust policies can be applied to regulated firms and public enterprises. It is often thought, instead, that each of the main policies (antitrust, regulation, and public enterprise) is mutually exclusive with the others. And, it is said, antitrust gets the mild cases, while the most difficult ones are given the drastic treatment, public enterprise, only as a last resort. In fact, these choices are along two different dimensions. Public enterprises can be, and often are, under antitrust and regulation; an example is the U.S. Postal Service. A free economy (which is also energetic and innovative) can have a lot of public enterprise in it.

Though partly substitutable for each other, the policy treatments are also complementary over wide ranges. Public firms often need a degree of antitrust and regulatory treatment. Regulated firms usually do best when they face a degree of competition. And private firms are often constrained by public policy or subsidized by the government.

The present coverage of the policies seems traditional and even natural to many observers. But (1) it has changed since 1900–30, with major shifts occurring since 1960; (2) it may not be working well; and (3) it will evolve and perhaps change markedly in the future. Moreover, it differs from the policies used in most other countries. American policies are a unique set of experiments. The United States makes much more use of antitrust and utility regulation and much less use of public enterprise than is common in many other advanced industrial economies. It is an open question how well these U.S. polices have worked and how (if at all) they could be improved. Is the United States an eccentric case with dubious policies, or is it the best model for the rest of the world?

The basic U.S. approach has been to prefer open, arm's-length, formal dealings between policymakers and enterprises. Even so, there is much informal negotiation behind the scenes, but less than in Western European economies and Japan. In those countries, by contrast, informal controls and public enterprise are more routine, with little pretense at formal antitrust or regulation.

COMPARING NEEDS AND TREATMENTS

In assessing policies, it is necessary to compare what is done with the need for action. When problems are extensive, extensive policies may be needed, whereas mild problems require only mild actions.

Textbooks have traditionally ignored the adequacy of treatment as a whole, focusing instead on the individual cases in order to illustrate specific policy tools. Here, we will draw the larger picture by showing the main points of the monopoly and collusion problems. The candidates for action can then be compared with what was actually done, to indicate how effective the policies were.

This task is controversial, of course, because economists often disagree on the seriousness of the monopoly problem. For example, Chicago-UCLA-school analysts say that monopoly is weak or even beneficial, and so they call for little or no policy action. In contrast, those economists who see serious harms from monopoly naturally call for stricter cures. No school or view has a monopoly on truth, and so the student must weigh the contrasting views and facts. Therefore, this book first presents those differing views and reviews the scope of market power in actual markets, so that students can judge the facts for themselves. That task occupies chapters 1–4.

In chapters 5–18, we survey the policies actually applied, both in their details and in their larger patterns. The wise student constantly assesses the quality and adequacy of the policies as a whole as well as in their specific parts. Only by doing this can you intelligently judge whether, for example, stronger merger policies would be suitable now, or more de-regulation of the telephone sector, or a doubling of efforts to catch and penalize price fixers.

HOW POLICIES ARE SET

Beginning students often have the naive idea that policies are decided and set by officials, who merely impose them on the companies and markets that are under their authority. The Congress merely "writes" laws that, after testing in the courts (if that is necessary), are applied to private firms by executive agencies. That would be like doctors diagnosing their patients and ordering them to take the correct treatments.

Reality is more complicated and interesting. Policies evolve through the interactions of firms and other interest groups operating through the political process. The policy setting has two basic elements. One element is a political process that carries out the evolving "will" of the people. This process is parallel to the second element, the economic process. The two processes interact and shape each other. Moreover, the political process is not perfect. It has pockets of political monopoly, ignorance, and delay. To some extent, the political process reflects the underlying structure of power and wealth, rather than strictly equal voter power.

Furthermore, democracy and policy choices usually move slowly and openly; this usually gives time for firms to have an influence over the outcomes. In the typical case, policies toward firms A and B are shaped by those firms as well as by firms C . . . H, and perhaps by others. Industries influence policies, and vice versa, in varying degrees. As companies interact with agencies and the public, the resulting policy actions reflect ongoing struggles and adjustments. For instance, if a company faces a possible antitrust suit, it will often work vigorously to persuade the officials not to sue, to get the White House and/or Congress members to intervene, and to argue its case to the general public. Firms commonly have incentives to spend (on experts, legal defenses, lobbying, advertisements, and other forms of persuasion) up to the dollar amounts that are at stake in order to get their desired outcomes (Chapter 4 presents more details on this process).

More broadly, a period of aggressive antitrust enforcement will often trigger a backlash. The targets of the action turn to pressuring the White House and Congress to rein in the officials and reduce their budgets. They may even try to amend the antitrust laws themselves.

Therefore, the arrows in Figure 1–1 point in both directions, showing how influence goes both ways. In some periods and in many cases, the industries may influence the officials more heavily than the other way around. Accordingly, policy actions usually tend to be compromises rather than representative of logical extremes. Actions are taken only after the firms involved have had ample opportunities to influence, if not actually control, the outcome.

Yet, despite all these uncertain struggles and possible errors, it is important for the observer to develop judgments about what the efficient policy choices *would be* in each case. Then these judgments can be compared to the actual decisions to assess the wisdom of what was done. *Was* the AT&T split-up in 1984 wise? Has regulation of electricity been effective? Economic analysis can provide a guide for appraising policies and revising them where appropriate.

THE GOALS FOR POLICIES

Good economic performance has several elements, including efficiency, technological innovation, fairness, competition itself, and wider benefits. These elements or policy goals are briefly summarized here; they will be given more extensive coverage in Chapter 2.

Efficiency has two components. One is *internal business efficiency,* reached by managing the firm tightly so as to avoid waste and inspire maximum effort by employees. It is sometimes called *X-efficiency*. The second component is *allocational efficiency:* Resources are allocated among alternative uses so that their values equal their costs at the margin. The entire market process maximizes the total value of production from the economy's resources. Efficiency also requires an avoidance of wasteful advertising.

Technological innovation raises the productivity of resources by creating new goods and methods of production. *Fairness* involves the distribution of wealth, income, and opportunity. There are several ethical criteria defining what is fair, and no single guideline is universally accepted. Nonetheless, the society may have reasonable compromise standards of fairness.

Other elements include *competition* itself, which provides an open process for the development of excellence through mutual striving. *Freedom of choice* is an important value; so are *personal security* and *cultural diversity*. Though they are less precise, such broad social goals may be affected by competition and monopoly, and they may ultimately be as important as the more technical economic goals.

On the whole, ever since Adam Smith and Alfred Marshall, mainstream economic analysis has shown that competition usually induces or compels firms to perform in line with these goals. Competition enforces efficiency and stimulates innovation. It usually distributes the rewards relatively fairly in line with effort and skill, and it encourages an open, free society and a democratic political process.

Chicago-UCLA-school analysis has developed a different, narrower focus on efficiency goals. It argues that efficient allocation is the only appropriate goal for economists to analyze and for antitrust to promote. Whatever generates efficient allocation is best, as Chapter 2 will discuss more fully. If monopolies deliver results that are as efficient as those due to competition, then monopoly is acceptable to many Chicago-UCLA-school analysts.

This debate may seem like hair splitting over dry topics, but it can affect the policy choices quite deeply. For example, the narrower Chicago-UCLA-school goals justify the deep 1980s' cutbacks in both antitrust and regulation. Therefore, even the goals are open to debate, though the Chicago-UCLA efficiency view is still distinctly in the minority in the profession. Most economists accept some or all of the wider variety of mainstream goals, particularly the importance of innovation as stimulated by competition.

BUSINESSES AND POLICIES

The business enterprises affected by public policies possess certain important features.

There are conflicting interests among firms and sectors, rather than a homogeneous "business community." There is strife among firms, among industries, among sectors, big versus small, local versus international, Main Street versus Wall Street. Firm A's gain usually causes a loss to some firm $B, C, H,$ or $Z,$ or to all of them. Good public policy recognizes these natural conflicts, and it often puts such opposed private interests to work.

Industries differ greatly in their ages and styles. Examples: steel and meat packing are old, while cable television and personal computers are young. The differences in industry ages can strongly influence structure and performance.

Enterprises include many versions: the conventional private firms and banks, plus (1) public firms of many types and degrees; (2) partnerships (lawyers, doctors, small businesses); (3) nonprofit and charitable units (hospitals, universities); and (4) cooperatives, mutuals, and other hybrid forms. They all produce and sell under some form of financial constraint. All of them can monopolize, or conspire, or compete, and can innovate or stagnate. Public policies need to deal with them all, not just the standard private corporation.

Private firms often have deep public effects. Large firms commonly use the capital of thousands of investors, and they have thousands or millions of customers. They affect jobs, prices, local prosperity, future resources, national security, and often the quality of life. The behavior of many private firms is properly a matter of public concern.

Private firms are usually resilient. Their managers and legal advisers can often devise ways through—or around— almost any limit. This flexibility often frustrates public policies; if tactic A is prohibited or limited, the firm can try similar tactics B through G instead. By the same token, business firms can often respond quickly and effectively to almost any treatments, even "radical" ones.

Because of these complexities, the common phrases *probusiness* and *antibusiness* often have little meaning. Each policy affects certain firms relative to others; the identification of these specific effects is simply part of the technical task.

THE HISTORICAL ROOTS AND TRENDS

All of the modern policies have important roots and antecedents in the past.[4] The current policies are often merely more detailed and cover

---

[4]Excellent references include Fritz Machlup, *The Political Economy of Monopoly* (Balti-

bigger industries, and, in some cases, they are *less* sophisticated than policies applied decades or even centuries ago. Tariffs, limits on monopoly, regulations, public ventures, and others are part of the continuing experiments in policies.

A concise review can help to clarify (1) the nature of present treatments, and (2) where the trends in policies are heading. (More detailed histories are given in chapters 5, 12, and 15). Is the regulation of the economy on the rise? Is antitrust—or regulation, or public enterprise—an experiment or a fixture?

Early Origins

Struggles over monopoly power go back to the most ancient times, and the roots of modern policies reach back well before the Renaissance, to three early areas in which policy came to be important: usury, guilds, and food supply.

Usury was the practice of charging high interest rates on loaned capital. It often touched closely on royal power and finance, as well as on the wider use of capital throughout society. Therefore, there was a chronic struggle, with religious and ethnic overtones, over the rate of interest and other terms of loans. From scripture were derived rules limiting the interest that could be charged.

Guilds were the cartels set up by master craftsmen to control their trades and the entrance of trainees. This, too, was important to the structure of power and wealth, for guild membership was widespread and the use of the guilds' products was virtually universal. As the Middle Ages blended into the preindustrial growth period, the power of the guilds to control competition receded.

The third policy area dealt with agricultural supply (especially of grains) to the towns. It was natural for the suppliers or middlemen to try to restrict the supply and raise the prices of grain, profiting at the expense of the townspeople. In various forms, this was called *forestalling, engrossing,* and *regrating.* It, too, involved basic social struggles, affecting the well-being and power of social groups.

To 1890

By the 16th century, early industrial development was stirring in Western Europe. There were too many pockets of monopoly, some stemming from powers of the nobility to exact tolls or other privileges. While the early economic growth was beginning to dissolve and bypass

---

more: Johns Hopkins University Press, 1952); J. M. Clark, *Social Control of Business* (Chicago: University of Chicago Press, 1926); and Joseph Schumpeter, *History of Economic Analysis* (New York: Oxford University Press, 1954).

some of these powers, monarchs were—on the contrary—resorting to grants of monopoly as devices to foster new industrial growth (and to fill the royal purse). This technique reached extensive scope under the Tudor monarchs of England and under Louis XIV in France.[5] In addition, these royal promoters often used public enterprises of various sorts to manage key parts of the economy and to start others. During this "mercantilist" period, statecraft was deeply involved in the deliberate restriction of competition in various directions in order to foster new industries. The restrictions affected not only production but also trade, imports, and other sectors.

It was against this that Adam Smith and other classical economists strove, in order to remove barriers and controls so private interests could operate freely to maximize true national wealth. Tariffs, controls on movement of goods, and monopoly grants were the main targets. This effort coincided with the main eruption of industrial growth in Britain during 1780–1840, which is now called the Industrial Revolution. Whether the reduction of controls helped to cause the growth or vice versa (or neither) is a matter of continuing debate.

Yet, even at the peak of free enterprise classical liberalism, there was much state promotional activity. In addition, there was a growing willingness to designate some markets as "affected by the public interest."

The ascendancy of the Manchester School, the assertion of unfettered power of those with capital, began to wane by 1890 in England. But its legacy was strong: Private enterprise had become the basis for most of the economy in both the United States and Britain by 1860. Other European countries remained more willing to create economic capital directly by the state.

From 1860 to 1900, the beliefs of social Darwinism crested in the United States: The survival of the fittest was said to occur in industrial markets as well as in nature. Out of the ferment of this period grew most of those policies that now prevail. Modern markets were widening and deepening so that the range of structures and constraints on them offered a wide area of choice. Turbulent events were creating not only industrial unrest but also large changes in the structure of industry.

The period from 1860 to 1900 was a watershed for industrial policies in the United States. The policies themselves took concrete form in the decades from 1900 to 1920 as decisive choices about antitrust, regulation, and public enterprise occurred.

Table 1–1 shows concisely the parallel developments in the study of monopoly, in the economy itself, and in the policies. The three sides interacted as changes in ideas and facts led to changes in policies.

---

[5]See W. H. Price, *The English Patents of Monopoly* (Cambridge, Mass.: Harvard University Press, 1913); and Charles W. Cole, *Colbert and a Century of French Mercantilism* (New York: Columbia University Press, 1939).

Antitrust and Regulation Are Established
in the United States

In the United States, there were two decisive changes: *Antitrust* (under Theodore Roosevelt, Taft, and Wilson before 1916) was applied with some strictness, and private utilities were franchised under *regulation*, rather than being converted to public enterprise. By contrast, in Europe, the reliance on public enterprise increased, both in industry and utilities, while antitrust did not develop.

The U.S. move toward antitrust and regulation was primarily a conservative shift, a choice against taking more radical actions.[6] Antitrust enforcement was sharp in several directions: Price fixing was outlawed in 1899, and a spectacular "trust-busting" campaign came to a climax in 1911–15. The Federal Trade Commission was created in 1914. But with the onset of World War I, antitrust activity was virtually halted after 1915. Likewise, the creation of state commissions to regulate utilities seemed to be a progressive move. But it, too, was a conservative step, often sought by the utilities themselves as a way of heading off public ownership (and excluding competition). The 1920s brought a growth of federal regulation in a few utility sectors, but a sharp drop in antitrust activity.

In the 1930s, the Great Depression imposed extreme pressure for action. There resulted several varieties of policy activity. The basic American patterns of antitrust and regulation were hardened and extended during this decade. There was a massive cleaning up of financial abuses in electricity, gas, banking, and securities markets. There was the experiment in industry cartels under the National Recovery Administration during 1933–35. The Reconstruction Finance Corporation, a large public banking agency, restored credit to some farms, banks, and industries. Basic new agricultural policies were created. The Tennessee Valley Authority (TVA) was begun as a major symbol of public enterprise. Perhaps most important, antitrust policies were revived under Thurman Arnold during 1938–44.

The 1940s brought the rise of large new special areas in which the now-conventional policy controls were blurred and weak. The purchasing of military weapons was a prime case, but the oil industry, insurance, and shipbuilding also posed new problems. Antitrust was ripe for reassessment, and utility regulation was just becoming effective toward electric power. By 1950, there was a need for basic review and revision of U.S. policies.

However, despite the need for change, the main policies stayed largely unchanged well into the 1960s when events began to force large

---

[6]See Donald J. Dewey, *Monopoly in Economics and Law* (Chicago: Rand McNally, 1959); and Hans Thorelli, *The Federal Antitrust Policy* (Baltimore: Johns Hopkins University Press, 1954).

Table 1–1   Time Line of the Field, the Economy, and Policies

1880	1890	1900	1910	1920	1930
The industrial organization field					
Early economists denounce monopoly, favor regulation.	Conservative economists defend the trusts.	Intense debate ensues over monopoly, scale economies, and "the trust question." Extensive studies are done on actual industries.	Factual studies of trusts and industries continue.		Chamberlin and Robinson launch the study of oligopoly. Berle and Means say large firms have uncontrolled power. Quantitative studies begin, showing the prevalence of oligopoly.
The U.S. economy					
Railroad and oil monopolies are formed. Telephone and electric utilities begin.	Industrial merger wave, 1897–1901, forms hundreds of dominant firms.	World War I.		Merger boom occurs, peaking in 1929.	Economy collapses. There is apparent rise of market power in industry. Scandals occur in utility sectors and banking.
Policies toward market power					
Supreme Court approves regulation in "the public interest."	Sherman Antitrust Law is enacted, 1890.	Price fixing is flatly prohibited, 1899.	Roosevelt-Taft trust-busting wave affects Standard Oil, American Tobacco, and many others. States begin forming commissions to regulate utilities.	World War I cuts off antitrust. Clayton Act (1914) imposes limits on market power. Federal Trade Commission is formed as the second antitrust agency (1914).	Antitrust lapses during 1920–37.	Strict banking laws and regulations are applied. Regulation spreads to electric, telephone, trucking, and airline sectors. NRA briefly supports price fixing.

Public enterprise is largely rejected in favor of regulated private utilities.

1940	1950	1960	1970	1980	1990

Many indus-
try studies
are done.
Bain devel-
ops study
of entry
barriers.

Theory of
games
raises in-
terest in
oligopoly
as the cen-
tral topic.

Large-scale econometric
studies of concentration,
innovation, economies of
scale, advertising, and
profits are done.

The field contains great
variety among theorists,
statistical studies, industry experts, conserva-
tives, radicals, and the
main stream.

Chicago-UCLA-school
economists assert the
prevalence of competi-
tion and futility of regulation; gain rising
acceptance.

Mathematical
modeling
gains
popularity.

World War II causes boom,
followed by long postwar
growth. Confidence in
private industry revives.

Economies of scale begin
substantial shrinkage,
with new technology re-
placing "smokestack"
industries.

A general rise in competition occurs, caused by
imports, antitrust, and
de-regulation.

Concentration rises both in
industries and in total
shares of large firms.

Vietnam War
stirs attacks
on corporate
power.

A merger
boom
occurs
1981–89.

Merger boom occurs,
peaking in 1969.

Antitrust is
revived
1937–52.
Major
cases are
brought to
court and
won.

Antitrust
recedes,
1952–60.

Several big antitrust cases
go to court: IBM, AT&T,
Xerox, cereals.

The AT&T case
brings large
changes, 1984.

New public
enterprises
are devel-
oped in
electric
sector:
TVA, New
York, Ne-
braska, the
West.

Merger rules are tightened:
New law is passed in
1950; first cases brought
to court in 1950; tightest
landmark case occurs in
1966.

De-regulation begins, in
stock markets, airlines,
railroads, banking, tele-
phones, broadcasting,
trucking, etc.

Reagan officials
sharply reduce
antitrust actions.
They also extend
de-regulation
further.

revisions. During 1952–68, the treatment of dominant firms largely ceased as cases against IBM and AT&T were ended with little result. Merger policy was tightened sharply during 1958–66 to prevent nearly all substantial horizontal and vertical mergers, which would combine over 15 percent of the market. Efforts to stop price fixing remained relatively strict, and most regulated sectors were immune from antitrust.

The regulation of most utilities continued in a relatively passive, co-operative stance until the 1960s. Then the tribunals regulating electricity (the Federal Power Commission) and telephones (the Federal Communications Commission) developed somewhat stricter and more complex actions. Spending on defense and space exploration reached high levels, and these two activities remained virtually untouched by antitrust or other policies to promote competition or restrain monopoly. Public enterprise continued in some sectors, such as parts of the electricity industry and the postal service, and it began to spread in urban transit systems.

By the 1965–75 period, the mainstream field of industrial organization had amassed a wide range of research suggesting the strong impact of monopoly and the limited scope of economies of scale.[7] The research basis for moderate efforts to restrain monopoly in a number of major sectors and to prevent monopoly-creating mergers was now persuasive. In fact, mainstream research during the 1970s led to a widely applauded de-regulation of several important sectors (including airlines and railroads).

Since 1970: "New IO Theories"

Some Chicago-UCLA-school economists were stirred after 1968 to a lively effort to avert what they imagined as a radical antitrust crusade to deconcentrate many industries. Though only moderate suggestions had been made to seek lower concentration in some seven industries, the Chicago-UCLA supporters claimed to fear a wholesale "atomization" of U.S. industry. Stirred by this supposed threat, they developed ideas that claimed to justify virtually all instances of market dominance. These were the "superior efficiency" doctrines that will be discussed in the next chapter. Chicago-UCLA advocates also restated the goals of policy to exclude all but allocational efficiency.

The net effect of this new crusade was a defense of bigness much like those that were mounted in the 1890s, 1920s, and 1950s. But now

---

[7]See First, Fox, and Pitofsky, *Antitrust for Its Second Century;* Henry W. de Jong and William G. Shepherd, eds., *Mainstreams in Industrial Organization,* 2 vols. (Dordrecht: Kluwer Academic Publishers, 1986); and William G. Shepherd, *The Economics of Industrial Organization,* 3d ed. (Englewood Cliffs, N.J.: Prentice-Hall, 1990).

the pro-bigness points were stated more technically and categorically. Harold Demsetz suggested that some dominant firms might reflect superior efficiency. Others changed that "might" to say "may usually" and then "probably," and by 1978 Robert Bork and others were saying that all dominance presumptively reflects only superior efficiency. The Chicago-UCLA supporters did little empirical work to test their insights and assertions about monopoly, but their younger members spread the antipolicy message.

After 1975, economists also turned more toward abstract modeling of oligopolies (more precisely, duopolies), rather than the study of real industries.[8] These models assumed that firms would not collude; their basis was noncooperative game theory. Whatever their solutions, this direction of analysis tended to turn away from real oligopoly markets where firms often do collude.

A third new IO theory strand was the rise of "contestability" theory after 1980.[9] The AT&T company employed staff economists and consultants to explore concepts which might help it fend off the legal challenges to the Bell System. These theorists eventually developed the idea that free entry and exit (which they called *perfect contestability*) might guarantee that even a pure monopolist would be forced to behave like a pure competitor. The idea made the AT&T monopoly seem harmless.

All three new IO directions tended to make monopoly appear harmless or actively beneficial. They declared that the burden of proof was reversed, the presumption now being that monopoly was innocent. Therefore, presumably, no policy actions should be taken to reduce or restrain it. Antitrust was not only unnecessary but actually harmful as an interference in free markets (the one exception was to stop price fixing). And most regulation was also said to be unnecessary and anti-efficient.

Many mainstream economists had been urging since the 1960s that regulation was no longer appropriate in railroads and airlines.[10] Their

---

[8]For summaries of this "new IO theory," see Jean Tirole, *The Theory of Industrial Organization* (Cambridge, Mass.: MIT Press, 1988); Michael Waterson, *Economic Theory of Industry* (Cambridge: Cambridge University Press, 1984); William Sharkey, *The Theory of Natural Monopoly* (Cambridge: Cambridge University Press, 1982); Lester Telser, *Theories of Competition* (Amsterdam: North Holland, 1988); Joseph E. Stiglitz and C. Frank Mathewson, *New Developments in the Analysis of Market Structure* (Cambridge, Mass.: MIT Press, 1986); and Alexis Jacquemin, *The New Industrial Organization* (Cambridge, Mass.: MIT Press, 1987).

[9]William J. Baumol, John C. Panzar and Robert D. Willig, *Contestable Markets and the Theory of Industrial Structure* (San Diego: Harcourt Brace Jovanovich, 1982).

[10]See John R. Meyer, Merton J. Peck, John Stenason, and Charles Zwick, *The Economics of Competition in the Transportation Industries* (Cambridge, Mass.: Harvard University Press, 1959); Richard E. Caves, *Air Transport and Its Regulators* (Cambridge, Mass.: Harvard University Press, 1962); Paul W. MacAvoy, *The Economic Effects of Regulation: The*

research and urgings did lead to de-regulation of railroads starting in 1976 and airlines starting in 1977.[11] But de-regulation became more like a crusade after 1980, as Reagan appointees moved to enact it in many other sectors. Again, the new IO ideas fed an optimism that monopoly merely reflects efficiency and that strong potential competition would prevent any abuses.

In perspective, the new IO revolution has been much narrower than its proponents have urged.[12] Theory has advanced, but the limitations of the modeling have been narrow. Contestability theory has been shown to apply to virtually no important real markets, and the success of the Chicago-UCLA-school has occurred mostly among its own members, conservative think tanks (such as the American Enterprise Institute, the Heritage Foundation, and the Cato Institute), and the upper officials of the Reagan administration. The matter is controversial, however, and Chicago-UCLA supporters assert that they have in fact "won" the intellectual competition.

Policy Changes

In any event, the policy effects have been sharp. Antitrust resources were cut by nearly half, and enforcement was totally withdrawn from several directions. The relaxation of merger constraints helped to stimulate the huge merger boom of the 1980s, leading to higher concentration in a number of markets such as airlines. Actions against dominant firms were halted once the AT&T case was completed by the divestiture of 1984. Antitrust officials sought actively to reverse legal precedents against price discrimination, resale price maintenance, and other actions to be discussed in chapters 9 and 10.

Reviving antitrust enforcement would take time, even if there is a willingness to restore staffing and to appoint judges less conservative than those added during the 1980s.

Deregulation also was pressed far, particularly in broadcasting, the telephone sector, electricity and gas, and financial markets. By 1990, deregulation was even being urged and adopted by some states in local telephone service, where natural monopoly still clearly exists.

Trunk-Line Railroad Cartels and the Interstate Commerce Commission before 1900 (Cambridge, Mass.: MIT Press, 1965); Alfred E. Kahn, *The Economics of Regulation,* 2 vols. (New York: John Wiley & Sons, 1970; reissued by MIT Press, 1988); William A. Jordan, *Airline Regulation in America* (Baltimore: Johns Hopkins Press, 1970); and Almarin Phillips, ed., *Promoting Competition in Regulated Markets* (Washington, D.C.: Brookings Institution, 1975).

[11]See Leonard W. Weiss and Michael W. Klass, eds., *Deregulation: What Really Happened?* (Boston: Little, Brown, 1986); and Theodore E. Keeler, *Railroads, Freight, and Public Policy* (Washington, D.C.: Brookings Institution, 1983).

[12]The "revolution" is approvingly described in John E. Kwoka, Jr., and Lawrence J. White, eds., *The Antitrust Revolution* (Glenview, Ill.: Scott, Foresman, 1989).

In short, the 1980s were similar to the 1920s in the triumph of faith in big business and unfettered markets. Government was said to be the source of harm. Its cures were not needed and would, instead, merely harass efficient businesses.

To put these U.S. changes in perspective, it can be noted that there were some parallel moves in several countries abroad, particularly Britain. After 1979, the Thatcher government developed radical policies to sell most of the public enterprises to the private sector. These public firms included utilities that had been created during 1945–50 and later in a number of manufacturing industries. This "privatization" was pressed far, even to natural monopolies such as the postal service, telephone service, and electricity. The results may have been decidedly mixed (see Chapter 17), but the effort reflected the same Chicago-UCLA-school views which gained influence in the United States. Other European countries took much smaller steps toward privatization, but substantial shifts were made in Japan and numerous less-developed countries such as Brazil and Mexico.

The peaceful political revolutions in Eastern Europe during 1989–90 were thought to usher in a broad shift toward private markets. That would inevitably reduce the state controls and ownership that had been enforced through state monopolies in those socialist countries. But the evolution toward open markets would require developing genuine competition, and that may be a far more complex problem, even more complex than it is in industrialized Western economies.

Therefore, during 1989–90, the subject of this textbook was broadened dramatically to include new ranges of countries and problems. At a time when these countries needed sophisticated guidance for complex shifts of hundreds of industries from state monopoly to private competition, Western leaders and analysts were guided by simple free market notions. They argued that the mere removal of all government policies would assure efficient outcomes and efficiency was all that mattered. But this laissez-faire thinking was an uncertain basis for accomplishing complex tasks. And its role in U.S. policy agencies was likely to evolve toward more balanced and complex ideas.

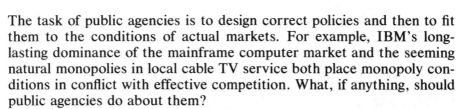

C·H·A·P·T·E·R 2

Concepts of Competition and Monopoly

The task of public agencies is to design correct policies and then to fit them to the conditions of actual markets. For example, IBM's long-lasting dominance of the mainframe computer market and the seeming natural monopolies in local cable TV service both place monopoly conditions in conflict with effective competition. What, if anything, should public agencies do about them?

"Reduce or restrain the monopoly" is the simple answer, but actual policies usually must deal with complicated conditions and entrenched interests. IBM and cable TV have certainly posed complex specific problems, as we will see. And more generally, monopoly's true nature and impacts are still sharply debated, even after more than a century of research. Some Chicago-UCLA-school analysts welcome dominant firms (such as IBM, Eastman Kodak, AT&T, and newspapers in one-newspaper cities), saying that the dominance merely reflects superior efficiency.

To set the stage for wise policy choices, we must now probe the nature of competition and monopoly, drawing on the mainstream literature and new IO concepts. This chapter presents the most important ideas and the debates surrounding them. Chapter 3 turns to evidence; it reviews information about actual markets in the U.S. economy: the degrees and trends of market power, of scale economies, and of the mergers and other forces shaping them. The evidence in Chapter 3 will show the forms that market power takes and the relative importance of monopoly conditions in the U.S. economy.

Chapter 2 explores the nature of the firm first, because it is the building block of markets. Then we turn to the concepts of competition and market power. The effects of monopoly are shown in the third section. The degree of monopoly is usually embodied in market structure, which is analyzed next. Finally, the different types of partial monopoly (dominance, oligopoly, and monopolistic competition) are discussed.

From these basic concepts, Chapter 3 will turn to actual conditions in the economy, showing the business population, the extent and trend of competition since the 1930s, and the causes and effects of the competitive conditions. Readers who have taken a course in industrial organization may be able to review Chapters 2 and 3 quickly. Other students will find that a careful reading is valuable, because the concepts recur throughout the rest of the book. Your understanding of them will shape your judgments about the best ways to design policies toward markets.

I. THE FIRM[1]

Markets are composed of firms, and these firms determine the structure, behavior, and performance of each market. Not only do the firms generate whatever policy problems may exist; they also are the decision units to which policies are applied. They will try to influence those policies as they are applied, and they will adapt their actions to the policies. The following basic features of firms are essential to designing effective policies.

Firms exist in many varieties throughout the sectors of the economy, ranging from local groceries and gas stations to AT&T and IBM. These enterprises often have highly complex forms, goals, production choices, incentives, and patterns of behavior. But the basic organizing motive is simple: maximizing profits.

1. The Basic Flows and Decisions

The firm acquires inputs, uses them in some production process, and then sells the outputs. The inputs are bought at their market prices; the firm's costs are the sum of the physical quantities times the prices paid for the various inputs. The outputs are sold at *their* prices; the firm's

---

[1]Among leading writings on the nature of the firm, see especially Ronald H. Coase, "The Nature of the Firm," *Economica* 4 (November 1937), pp. 386–405; Kenneth J. Arrow, "Control in Large Organizations," *Management Science* 10 (April 1963), pp. 397–408; Kenneth J. Arrow, *The Limits of Organization* (New York: Norton, 1974); and Alfred D. Chandler, Jr., *The Visible Hand: The Managerial Revolution in American Business* (Cambridge, Mass.: Belknap Press, 1977).

For reviews of the literature, see Richard E. Caves, "Corporate Strategy and Structure," *Journal of Economic Literature* 18 (March 1980), pp. 64–92; and Oliver E. Williamson, "The Modern Corporation: Origins, Evolution, Attributes," *Journal of Economic Literature* 19 (December 1981), pp. 1537–68.

sales revenues are the sum of the physical amounts of the various outputs sold, times their prices. Profit (the excess of revenues over costs) is maximized by arranging the best possible physical flows of inputs and outputs, while trying to pay low prices for inputs and (if possible) raise the prices of the outputs. Each firm's profits will reflect both its production efficiency and its pricing policies.

The managers' decisions are on two planes. The first is *production,* the conversion of inputs into outputs using a given capacity. The other is *owning, financing, and managing the firm's assets.* The second set of decisions include investment choices, which change the firm's capacity in line with long-run strategies. The pursuit of profit links these two planes of activity.

Firms are organized and changed by their managers and owners in processes of adjustment, which permit great variety. The ongoing firm's internal structure may range from one extreme, a single unified chain of command, to the other extreme, great diversification among a host of separate, dissimilar divisions. The firm as a whole can also be changed by adding new branches or even merging it into a larger firm. Firms are routinely bought, sold, reorganized, divided, added to, terminated, or absorbed into other firms as part of the normal stuff of business life.

In theory, the firm's managers function strictly to maximize the total profits of the shareholders. That ideal is often closely achieved in small owner-managed firms. But in larger corporations, the *ownership* by thousands of shareholders is divorced in some degree from the *management* by hired executives.[2] Therefore, the managers' motives may become more complex and diverge from the owners' sole interest in profits. In certain policy choices, especially involving mergers (Chapter 8) and regulated utilities (Chapter 13), this separation between owners' and managers' interests can become important.

Managers are the pivotal group. They make the firm's choices about prices, outputs, investment, competitive strategies, and the rest. The top echelon is a small group, with a brief tenure—perhaps three to five years—in the highest positions. Authority is delegated in varying degrees, and often there are layers of bureaucracy between the executive suite and the factory floor. In diversified firms, the upper managers are more remote, dealing mainly with financial matters and the allocation of investment funds.

---

[2]The divorce of ownership from control was first noted in 1932 by A. A. Berle and Gardiner C. Means in *The Modern Corporation and Private Property* (New York: Macmillan, 1932), reissued with additional material in 1968 by Harcourt Brace Jovanovich. Yet the degree of divorce and its effects are controversial. See Philip H. Burch, Jr., *The Managerial Revolution Reassessed* (Lexington, Mass.: Heath, 1972); Edward S. Herman, *Corporate Control, Corporate Power* (Cambridge: Cambridge University Press, 1981); and Gordon Donaldson and Jay W. Lorch, *Decision Making at the Top* (New York: Basic Books, 1983).

These managers' decisions involve public policies as well as strictly economic factors, as Chapter 4 will note in some detail. Maximizing profit often requires brilliant strategies toward antitrust challenges or regulators, as well as optimal business choices about inventory and pricing. The managers not only seek to influence public officials' choices, they also adjust so as to minimize or deflect the impacts of the policies.

2. Profitability

Profit is the direct index of the private firm's degree of success. Profit needs explanation here, because (1) the evaluation of excess profits caused by monopoly power is a central task in applying policies and (2) policies affect profits in ways which need to be understood.

The firm's degree of profitability is measured by taking profit (after taxes) as a percentage rate of return on the capital invested in the business. In simple form:

$$\text{Profitability} = \text{Rate of return} = \frac{\text{Total revenue} - \text{Total cost}}{\text{Invested capital}}$$

$$= \frac{\text{Net income}}{\text{Invested capital}}$$

The most common applied version uses stockholders' equity in the firm as the measure of invested capital, thus:

$$\text{Rate of return} = \frac{\text{Net income}}{\text{Investors' equity}}$$

The calculation is illustrated in Table 2–1.

The rate of return must be a least as high as the cost of capital it uses, which is the return available to investors on other, comparable investments. A deficient rate of return will deter investors, so that the capital needed to maintain or enlarge the firm cannot be attracted. The cost of capital varies with the degree of risk, being higher for riskier firms. For most firms, the cost of capital is in the range of 8 to 15 percent. (However, it cannot be measured precisely for complex reasons that are noted in the discussion of regulation in Chapter 14.) Therefore, the "normal," or "competitive," or "minimum" rate of return is in that range; effective competition usually prevents profit rates from being sustained at higher levels.

Higher profit rates usually contain an element of "excess" profits, which is an excess over the cost of capital. For example, if a firm's profit rate is 15 percent while its cost of capital is 10 percent, then the

Table 2–1   Basic Financial Statements for a Large Firm
($ Billions)

AMERICAN TELEPHONE AND TELEGRAPH COMPANY
Income Statement

Revenues	$69.8
Expenses	
Operating	36.3
Depreciation, etc.	12.7
Net income	$20.8
Taxes and related	9.8
Net income after taxes	$(11.0)

Balance Sheet

Assets		Liabilities	
Plant and property	$158.0	Equity	
Depreciation	30.0	From issuing shares	$ 33.0
Net plant and property	128.1	Retained earnings	28.9
Investments, etc.	5.7	Total equity	(61.9)
Current assets	14.4	Debt	44.1
Total assets	$148.2	Current and others	42.2
		Total liabilities	$148.2

Return on equity capital = 17.7%

Note: Figures may not sum to totals due to rounding.
Source: Annual report of the company.

5 percent difference is excess profit. In general, a sustained 15 percent rate of return is excellent, 18 percent is highly unusual, and over 20 percent is extremely profitable.

Any extra profit can reflect one or more of the following six possible causes:

1. *Monopoly power,* which is exercised by raising some or all of the prices of the firm's outputs. (Monopsony power, in which the firm is a large buyer and can force its suppliers to set lower prices on the inputs it buys, may also exist.)
2. Better *internal efficiency,* with managers holding the physical quantities of inputs below the levels needed by other firms.
3. *Innovation,* which has given the firm superior production techniques or products, or both.
4. A reward for *assuming risks* in its business activities and strategies. Risky actions often lead to better profit results, but the risks must be compensated by giving the investors higher degrees of profitability.

5. *Random luck,* such as from being in a rapidly growing market or from other unforeseeable external events.
6. *Public policies* can also affect profits by changing the firm's opportunities and incentives. The policies may be outside the firm's control; or the firm may manipulate the policies.

All of these causes can affect the prices and quantities of inputs and outputs, resulting in higher profits. Conversely, poor performance or adverse luck can cause profits to be low or negative. The successful firm will not only organize its internal activities well but also (or instead) exert influence externally on the prices it pays for inputs or receives for its outputs.

3. Capitalized Value as Embodied in the Price of the Firm's Stock

Profits are a yearly flow arising from managerial decisions. This flow is capitalized by investors' decisions in line with their expectations about the firm's future profits. A rising profit flow makes the shares more valuable to hold as assets, because the profits will provide greater dividends or capital gains, or both, to their owners. Maximizing long-run profits is, therefore, identical to maximizing the present value (the share price) of the firm at each point.

Investors operating in financial markets are constantly reevaluating each firm's expected future profits, and their choices drive the firm's stock price up or down. The market value of the firm, then, is the going share price times the number of shares outstanding. This value reflects both (1) real factors, such as the firm's market position, capacity, product design, and management caliber and (2) expectations about the firm's future prospects. The share price is not a perfect guide to the firm's present or future conditions; yet it is the best single approximation, based on "the market's" judgment.

Moreover, the stock price applies very real pressure to the firm's managers. They must reach the expected future levels, or the stock price will fall. A sharp fall may so anger investors that it endangers the managers' jobs. The stock market anticipates and discounts performance ahead of time. Therefore:

1. Managers are on a form of treadmill in order to meet the expectations of investors in the market, and

2. Excess profits are capitalized immediately as stock prices rise at the new prospect of future extra profits. The original owners will cream off the excess value of a monopoly (or innovation or a bit of luck) in the form of capital gains. The firm's market value rises above the book value of actual investments made by the firm.

In short, each firm's profitability influences its stockholders' wealth. Both profitability and wealth can be affected by monopoly and by public policies. These effects stimulate the firm's managers to try to control the policies themselves (in ways presented in Chapter 4).

II. DEFINING MARKETS AND COMPETITION

Since firms function within markets, we turn now to define those markets and consider the basic nature of competition. Economists have developed six main categories of markets, ranging from pure competition to pure monopoly:

Pure competition	Monopolistic competition	Loose oligopoly	Tight oligopoly	Dominant firm	Pure monopoly

←——→

Each market type has distinctive features which affect the firms' decisions in specific ways. Those varieties are shown in Sections II and IV.

First, we will discuss the pivotal concept of the market. Nearly every competitive situation—and therefore nearly every public policy—can be correctly understood only by first determining the true extent of the market.

1. Defining the Market

Each market is a grouping of buyers and sellers of a good in which supply and demand interact to set the good's price and quantity. The market's extent is defined by the zone of consumer choice among substitutable goods. An ideal market has well-defined boundaries. Within the boundaries is one homogeneous good over which all consumers exercise choice within a clear range. There is full communication and knowledge among all buyers and sellers. Outside the market's boundaries are all other goods, none of which is substitutable for this good.

Consumers enforce competition by being able to choose among alternative suppliers of the good. If one supplier raises the price, buyers can effortlessly shift to other sellers. That tends to yield just one price in equilibrium.

In practical cases, substitutability is only partial, in some degree (with intermediate values of cross-elasticity). Such markets have indistinct edges. These cases are debatable, often testing the judgment of learned experts and Supreme Court justices.

We save such cases for detailed treatment later, especially in Chapters 7 and 8. For now, the reader can recognize that markets exist, often with indistinct edges, containing varying degrees of competition and monopoly. Chapter 6 will present the detailed methods for defining market edges.

2. Effective Competition Is a Robust Condition

Models of pure competition assume the existence of swarms of competitors, each of which has a negligible share of the market.[3] Each firm has a horizontal demand curve and acts as a *price taker* at the current market price. The firm merely chooses its profit-maximizing output in line with that price. The analysis of those choices clarifies the efficiency properties of competitive markets within the whole market system.

Effective competition in real markets is a much richer phenomenon than that. The main results of competition occur over a wide range of less-than-perfect conditions, including roughly loose oligopoly and monopolistic competition. Even where competition is often ineffective, including tight oligopoly and dominant firms, the pressure of some competition can be strong, either occasionally or frequently. Indeed, even if there are just two rivals, there may be intense rivalry some of the time.

There is a basic unity among all competitive processes, so that the problem of market power is one of degree, not of a binary yes-no character. Generally, as a firm's market share rises, its degree of market power will rise. Pure competition and pure monopoly are only polar cases; in between them, there is a general scaling up of market power in line with market share. Chapter 3 will show the evidence that confirms the general importance of market shares.

Competitive Parity is Needed. Competition is a process that occurs in a series of episodes. At each point, there needs to be a reasonable degree of competitive parity among the rivals. A contest between unequals is not genuine competition. If one competitor has sharp advantages, then the "competition" is not meaningful. The different weight classes in wrestling and boxing recognize this: A bout between a heavyweight and a bantamweight is punishment, not competition.

Also, true competition is a continuous process. A foot race or a game of Monopoly will end; the competition is over once the prizes are gained. In real life, by contrast, competition in markets means a continuous mutual striving among more-or-less equal firms. If, instead, one competitor gains dominance over the market, then effective competition is replaced by a degree of monopoly.

---

[3]See Alfred Marshall, *Principles of Economics,* 8th ed. (London: Macmillan, 1920); Tibor Scitovsky, *Welfare and Competition* (Homewood, Ill.: Richard D. Irwin, 1952); and George J. Stigler, "Perfect Competition, Historically Contemplated," *Journal of Political Economy* 65 (February 1967), pp. 1–17.

Yet competition often poses the following paradox: Each contestant strives to win, but if one of them wins completely, then monopoly occurs. That outcome is the opposite of competition. Effective competition requires an enduring balance of power, so many competitors will continue. Therefore, each competitor must win enough to reward its best efforts, but not enough to eliminate the other competitors. *In so doing, the firms all try to gain dominance, but they mutually neutralize one another's individual efforts to dominate.* When competition is effective, no one competitor is permitted to win most or all of the rewards. Instead, competition rewards all reasonably competent competitors, some more than others. Effective competition contrasts with the usual tournament, which yields one "champion" who has eliminated all the others, the "losers."

One cannot simply count the number of firms in judging the degree of competition, because a large number of tiny firms are not as strong as one or two firms with high market shares. Thus, a market with 20 firms is not effectively competitive if one firm has 90 percent while the rest have less than 1 percent each. Also, if there are only a few firms in the market, they will often try to collude with one another, rather than to compete vigorously. Then 3 (or 5, or 10) supposedly competitive firms may, in fact, exert monopoly power much as a single monopolist would.

The Chicago-UCLA School Dissent. A contrasting *Chicago-UCLA-school* view came to prominence during the 1970s.[4]

At first, they merely argued that any observed monopoly is rare, weak, and transient, quickly fading away.[5] Then, in 1973, they offered the "superior efficiency" hypothesis: Structure merely reflects perform-

---

[4]The history is complex and ironic. Members of the *original* Chicago school in the 1920s and 1930s were deeply opposed to monopoly of every kind, which they saw as widespread, strong, and harmful. The leaders were Frank H. Knight, Henry C. Simons, and Jacob Viner. See especially Simons, *Economic Policy for a Free Society* (Chicago: University of Chicago Press, 1948).

Then in the 1950s, George J. Stigler arrived at Chicago and led a complete reversal of the school, toward optimism: competition was seen as ubiquitous, while monopoly was said to be limited, transient, and weak. In the 1960s and 1970s, his followers, led by Harold Demsetz and J. Fred Weston at UCLA, John McGee at the University of Washington, and Yale Brozen, Richard A. Posner, and Sam Peltzman at Chicago, carried the points further, saying that any monopoly *probably* reflected superior efficiency.

Still other disciples then carried the argument to the extreme, saying that *all* monopoly can be assumed to reflect superior efficiency. They include Robert H. Bork, Dominick T. Armentano, and M. Bruce Johnson.

[5]Leading writers include Stigler, *The Organization of Industry* (Homewood, Ill.: Richard D. Irwin, 1968); Yale Brozen, *Concentration, Mergers and Public Policy* (New York: Macmillan, 1982); John S. McGee, *In Defense of Industrial Concentration* (Seattle: University of Washington Press, 1971); and McGee's *Industrial Organization* (Englewood Cliffs, N.J.: Prentice-Hall, 1988).

ance.[6] It is each firm's relative efficiency which determines its market share, rather than any abuses or monopolizing actions. Markets usually function so smoothly as to prevent such abuses. If the firm has lower costs and is more innovative, it will gain a higher market share and higher profits. But those profits are a well-deserved reward for excellence, not merely monopoly profits.

These suggestions soon were converted into strong assertions and then hardened into near certainties by some Chicago-UCLA writers.[7] The confidence that dominance merely reflects superior performance is the decisive feature of Chicago-UCLA analysis.

The argument reverses the direction of causation. Now performance causes structure; that is the opposite of the mainstream hypothesis that structure influences performance. Accordingly, high market shares are positively welcomed by many Chicago-UCLA analysts in the belief that dominance merely reflects superiority. Demsetz's insight into possible beneficial monopoly has been converted into a certainty about virtually all cases.[8]

If monopoly is presumed to be good rather than harmful, then the policy lessons are important and drastically different. Antitrust to reduce monopoly would be harmful, not valuable. The regulation of monopolies would be unnecessary. The stronger the Chicago-UCLA view, the sharper would be the reversal of public policies. Reagan officials held strong Chicago-UCLA views, and they acted accordingly, cutting antitrust deeply and pressing de-regulation further than it had already gone.

Potential Competition. In 1982, Baumol led another new school of theorists who reinforced the Chicago-UCLA lessons from a different direction.[9] They stressed that entry from outside the market may be

[6]Harold Demsetz, "Industry Structure, Market Rivalry, and Public Policy," *Journal of Law and Economics,* April 1973, pp. 1–9; and Demsetz, "Two Systems of Belief about Monopoly," in *Industrial Concentration: The New Learning,* ed. Harvey J. Goldschmid, H. Michael Mann, and J. Fred Weston (Boston: Little, Brown, 1974).

[7]The most prominent is Robert H. Bork, in *The Antitrust Paradox: A Policy at War with Itself* (New York: Basic Books, 1978). See also Dominick T. Armentano, *Antitrust and Monopoly: Anatomy of a Policy Failure* (New York: John Wiley & Sons, 1982).

[8]One of the few Chicago-UCLA attempts at empirical verification of the basic position is in Sam Peltzman, "The Gains and Losses from Industrial Concentration," *Journal of Law and Economics* 20 (October 1977), pp. 229–63. See also Richard A. Posner, *Antitrust Law* (Chicago: University of Chicago Press, 1976); and Posner, "The Social Costs of Monopoly and Regulation," *Journal of Political Economy,* August 1976, pp. 807–27.

[9]See especially William J. Baumol, John C. Panzar, and Robert D. Willig, *Contestable Markets and the Theory of Industrial Structure* (New York: Harcourt Brace Jovanovich, 1982); and Baumol and Willig, "Contestability: Developments since the Book," *Oxford Economic Papers,* Special Supplement, November 1986.

For critical reviews, see W. G. Shepherd, " 'Contestability' versus Competition,"

decisive, rendering irrelevant any monopoly power inside the market. They discussed "contestable" markets, a situation in which both entry and exit are perfectly free. Potential competition is then so powerful that the incumbent firms must keep prices down to the competitive levels or risk being evicted from the market.

This contestability approach is optimistic, like the Chicago-UCLA view, because it regards monopolists as powerless and harmless. But little practical research has been done so far to test the extent of contestable markets.

Together these schools provide a strong theoretical defense of monopoly. Each approach can be valid for a few, for many, or even for all markets. The question is: Do important actual cases of market power fit the theories or are they merely interesting theories of little practical value? This question is considered in Chapter 3. First we review the main effects of competition and monopoly.

III. THE THEORY OF COMPETITION AND MONOPOLY

1. Results under Competition

Consider a well-defined market with a swarm of sellers in it, all of them with insignificant market shares. Each form has cost curves like those in Figure 2–1. Average costs first decline, reflecting economies of scale. They reach a minimum at optimum size or capacity and then rise as diseconomies of scale set in. In this market, optimum size is only a tiny share of the market. Being so tiny, each firm is a price taker (like a Kansas wheat farmer, who merely finds out what the current price is), not a price maker. Also the firm must be well run internally in order to survive.

With its flat demand curve, the firm's only task is to choose its level of output. This it does where its marginal cost equals the going price (this is the firm's demand curve that, being flat, is also its marginal revenue curve). The firm's profits are at a maximum, given the cost and price conditions. And the suppliers' marginal cost curves sum up to give the market supply curve.

Meanwhile, the many buyers make choices that maximize their welfare. Their actions set the demand curve for the market. The process' yields a market-clearing equilibrium, with demand equalling supply at the going price. In the long run, this brings the firms to or near their lowest average cost so that their marginal cost is just equal to price.

American Economic Review 74 (September 1984), pp. 572–87; and Marius Schwartz, "The Nature and Scope of Contestability Theory," *Oxford Economic Papers*, Special Supplement, November 1986.

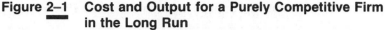

Figure 2–1 Cost and Output for a Purely Competitive Firm in the Long Run

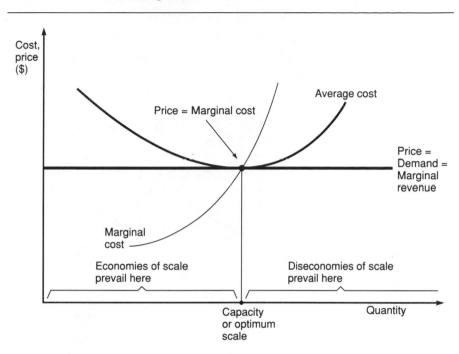

The profound lesson of this is that in a well-functioning competitive system, *marginal cost*—the social sacrifice necessary to produce another unit of input—*equals price*, which measures how valuable that output is believed to be. *Social sacrifice is brought into line with value, and so a social optimum is reached.* This is the familiar efficiency condition, in which consumers, input suppliers, and producers interact to reach the best allocation of resources among diverse uses. Behind each of the individual demand and supply curves lie equilibria in individual choices, so that each of the economic actors is maximizing its own welfare. This all adds up to the "invisible hand" metaphor of Adam Smith, whereby the entire economy reaches an economic optimum.

Limits. There are limits to attaining the social optimum. *First,* there may be external effects in production or consumption. If these are large, the private choices will diverge far from the social optimum. *Second,* dynamic efficiency is not assured. Innovation and other forms of technical progress may lie outside the pure competitive equilibrium result. *Third,* efficiency does not assure equity. The efficient outcome may yield something close to utopia or, instead, gross unfairness.

Figure 2–2   The Monopolist Reduces Output and Raises Price

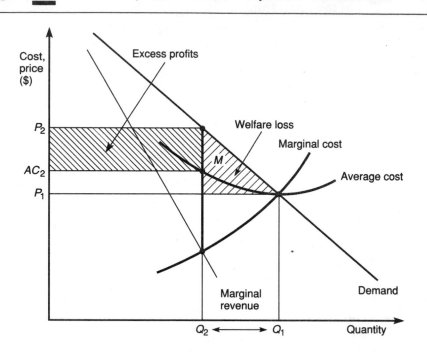

There may occur severe inequality, or equality, or any other distribution of income, wealth, and opportunity. Competition does tend toward equality because of the wide breadth of participation by atomistic firms. Yet there is no assurance that distribution will be fair.

2. Monopoly's Effects

Monopoly changes the efficient competitive outcome. Suppose that all competitive firms in a market are merged together, to create a pure monopoly. This new monopolist now faces the total industry demand curve as the sum of all the former competitive firms' demand. Because the monopolist's demand curve slopes down, the associated marginal revenue curve is separate from it and below it, as illustrated in Figure 2–2. That marginal revenue curve now is crucial to the monopolist's decisions, for it helps to determine the profit maximizing point. The new choice is at point *B*, where marginal revenue equals marginal cost. The monopolist's marginal cost curve is the sum of the marginal cost curves of all the former independent competitive firms.

Point *B* is well below the initial efficient competitive output at point *A*. Output is cut, price is raised, and excess profits are earned. Since price now exceeds marginal cost, people are willing to pay more than the true cost of added output in the range between Q_1 and Q_2, *but the monopolist will not let them do it*. That is the crux of inefficient allocation.

Also, the monopolist cuts back on inputs, so that the values of their marginal products are well above their wages. To this degree, the inputs are exploited; they produce more value than they are paid for. Others of them are now out of work; they will have to try for other jobs at lower wages in other industries.

The monopolist gains excess profits, shown by the shaded rectangle. They can be large, as is illustrated here; to obtain such prizes, firms strive relentlessly to gain monopoly power.

The *burden of misallocation* caused by monopoly is shown by the shaded "welfare triangle" in Figure 2–2. It is the consumer surplus lost by the shift from the competitive result at A to the monopoly outcome at B.[10] This economic loss may be large or small. If demand is inelastic and marginal cost is relatively flat, then the triangle will be large. When people urgently need an item (a necessity, for example), a monopolist can severely exploit them. In contrast, if demand is more elastic and the marginal cost curve is steeply sloped, the effects (and the triangle) will be small.

Monopoly also affects the *internal management efficiency of the firm,* often called *X-efficiency* to distinguish it from allocative efficiency among firms.[11] Being free from the pressures of competition, the monopoly firm's management may lose some of its tightness and vigilance. Cost controls may not be as strict and productivity may decline because everyone working in the firm knows that the firm is profitable and that it won't go out of business if costs rise.

This internal slack is often called X-inefficiency. It differs from *allocative* inefficiency among firms and markets (which the welfare triangle shows). *In a monopoly firm, X-inefficiency may cause a simple rise of the cost curves above their lowest possible levels*. Such X-inefficiency can range from small to large.

---

[10]*Producer* surplus may also be eliminated by the monopoly pricing. That loss is illustrated by the rounded triangular area between the marginal cost curve and the P_1 price line, between quantities Q_2 and Q_1. It can be large, as shown here, but if costs are constant (flat), the loss will be zero. In fact, average costs do tend to be constant in this range in most real industries, and economists have therefore usually regarded the producer-surplus loss as small. The consumer-surplus loss (the "welfare triangle") has been the main focus of debate. But that view does run a risk of underestimating the total impact on efficiency.

[11]The phrase *X-inefficiency* was coined by Harvey J. Leibenstein; see his *Beyond Economic Man* (Cambridge, Mass.: Harvard University Press, 1976) for a full analysis. Slack and sluggishness have long been recognized as possibilities in monopolies. Thus, Adam Smith long ago wrote of "the negligence, profusion and malversation" of workers for monopolies (*Wealth of Nations*, p. 712).

Table 2–2   The Main Effects of Monopoly

I.   Monopoly *harms* economic performance:

    1.   *Efficiency in resource use* is reduced by changes in output and price:

        a.   X-inefficiency may occur, raising average costs.

        b.   Misallocation may occur, eliminating consumer surplus.

    2.   *Equity in distribution* is reduced by monopoly profits (price discrimination may enlarge those profits). Wealth and income are shifted from the many to the few.

    3.   *Technical progress* (invention and innovation) is probably reduced. It becomes optional to the monopolist, and perhaps unprofitable because it reduces the value of the monopolist's assets.

    4.   *Broader values* may be harmed:

        a.   Freedom of choice is reduced.

        b.   Democracy is undermined.

II.   There may be offsetting *benefits* from monopoly:

    1.   *Economies of scale* in production and innovation may be achieved.

    2.   Large innovations may be made more rapidly.

III.   The *net effects* may go either way, in general and in each case. They require careful study, not mere slogans or assertions.

These effects of monopoly are included in the summary of monopoly's effects in Table 2–2. They are defined in a static context: comparing two contrasting outcomes. Monopoly can also have effects in a dynamic context (involving changes *over time*), altering the rates of invention and innovation.

Invention and Innovation. A monopoly is usually not under pressure to *invent* new products or methods. Nor does it have strong incentives to *innovate:* to apply those new inventions in practice and bring new products to the market. *The monopoly may choose to invent and innovate, but it will do so only at its own pace.* Because the new product cuts the value of its existing products, the monopoly will tend to hold back on innovation. Typically, it innovates only when a smaller competitor forces its hand. Even if its capital is outdated or its products mediocre, a monopolist may prefer to protect and continue them rather than to replace them with better ones.

Other Effects of Monopoly. Monopoly restricts *freedom of choice* for everyone involved except the monopolist. Buyers cannot try other suppliers; they are stuck with this one monopolist, for good or ill. Only those goods that the monopolist offers are available in this market, and they carry higher prices to boot. The former competitors are out of business, or working for the monopolist. Newcomers may be unable to enter the market. If entry barriers are high, only the strongest entrants may have a chance; or perhaps no entrant can survive so that the choices of former and potential competitors are reduced.

Suppliers also have less choice. Not only are their sales cut back by the monopolist, but they also have less opportunity to offer new products to a variety of firms—there is only the monopolist to sell to in this market. Workers also have fewer choices. They must deal with only the one monopolist in the industry. Everyone—buyers, suppliers, workers, and would-be competitors—loses freedom of choice.

Unfair Redistribution. The monopoly may also provide *monopoly profits* in excess of the normal profits gained by competitive firms.

The excess profits usually represent a degree of unfairness. They redistribute income, transferring money from the pockets of ordinary consumers into the monopolist's till. The consumers usually have lower incomes than the monopoly's owners. *Therefore, monopoly tends to tilt the income distribution toward greater inequality.* These income flows are capitalized into wealth. A monopoly's stock price will rise to reflect the flow of monopoly profits, and the owners can sell out immediately and put their wealth into other investments. Thus, monopoly creates family fortunes, enriching a few at the expense of many.

Democracy is also affected by monopoly. There are fewer firms, with less diversity of interests. The monopolist is now a power bloc, with a valuable advantage—and perhaps excess profits and market power—to protect. By supporting friendly candidates, by seeking favorable laws and rulings, and by advertising its interests via the media, a monopoly can use the political process to protect and improve its economic position. Even when its actions are mainly subtle, monopoly is likely to undermine democracy.

Culture and society can also be affected. When many markets are monopolized, the economic and social order becomes tight and closed. Society is more stratified and rigid, less open to outsiders and new ideas. Fascism and feudalism, for example, grew partly out of societies that had market power in many key parts of the economy. In another vein, monopolists can often influence consumers' preferences without challenge from others. An economy of monopolies provides a distinctive and unattractive social content, going against many traditional American values.

Chicago-UCLA Modifications. These mainstream points concerning the effects of monopoly would be changed by Chicago-UCLA proponents as follows: The degree of monopoly is likely to be low, with demand being highly elastic even if market shares are large; scale

Figure 2–3   Several Alternative Market Structures

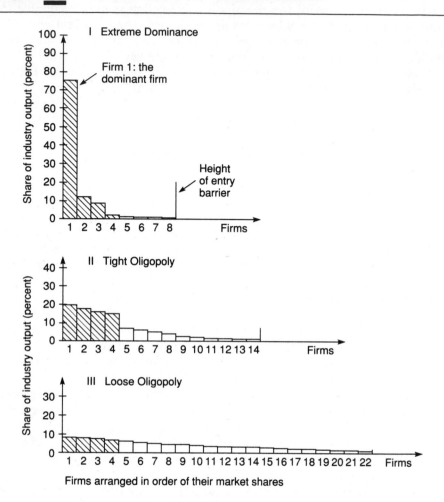

Firms arranged in order of their market shares

economies may be large, so that the market has room for only one or a few firms; the monopoly harms may be smaller than the cost savings from economies of scale; and finally, the firm's superior performance may have benefits larger than any monopoly harms.

IV. THE ELEMENTS OF MARKET STRUCTURE

Structure has several elements, namely market share, concentration, and entry barriers. These elements are portrayed in Figure 2–3 for three different market structures; structure is in fact determined by the distribution of market shares.

An analysis of market structures gives insight into concepts such as market power, demand elasticity, and degree of monopoly. Market power exists, ultimately, in the inelasticity of the firm's demand. Lower elasticity means a wider range of prices from which the firm can choose. It also opens the possibility of setting different prices for specific customers and groups that can create price discrimination, which reflects differences among elasticities of demand.

Inelasticity can rarely be measured, so structural evidence is commonly used to indicate the degree of monopoly. Such evidence is most reliable when comparing conditions within markets: Thus, a market share of 60 percent usually involves much more market power than a share of 15 percent. But also, a share of 60 percent is likely to involve substantial market power in almost any market.

1. Market Share

The firm's market share is simply its share of total sales revenue in the market. It ranges from near zero up to 100 percent.

It is the most important single indicator of market power and has always been recognized in common usage and actual markets. Firms regularly struggle to gain a greater market share as a means to high profitability. Table 2–3 presents some familiar cases of high market shares in the U.S. economy.

Mainstream economists expect market power to become significant as market shares rise above 20 percent and to become substantial as market shares reach and exceed 50 percent. In contrast, many Chicago-UCLA analysts see only weak market power, even when market shares rise above 70 percent. The remaining rivals, according to them, pose strong competition, even when there are only two or three firms.

2. Concentration

Concentration is the sum of the market shares of the four largest firms in the market.[12] It suggests the ability of the leading oligopoly firms to control prices by direct or indirect collusion.

The crucial distinction is between tight and loose oligopoly. In tight oligopoly (four-firm concentration above roughly 60 percent), collusion is often relatively easy and effective. The few leading firms control enough of the market to enforce compliance with their prices, and they can monitor each other relatively well to detect and punish price cutting. Firms in loose oligopolies (concentration below roughly 40 percent) are usually unable to make price collusion stick, because their control over market output is limited. Too many firms are able to cut

---

[12]An alternative is the Hirschman-Herfindahl index, which is explained in Chapter 6.

Table 2–3   A Selection of Leading Instances of Dominant Firms, Oligopolies, and Monopolistic Competition

	Markets	The Firm's Average Market Share (percent)	Entry Barriers
Dominant firms			
IBM Corporation	Mainframe computers	60%	High
Eastman Kodak Company	Photographic supplies	75	Medium
Proctor & Gamble Company	Detergents, toiletries	50	Medium
Boeing Corporation	Aircraft	55	High
Campbell Soup Company	Canned soups	75	Medium
Gillette Corporation	Razors, toiletries	60	Medium
The Wall Street Journal	Business newspapers	65	High
Washington Post	Washington, D.C., area newspapers	80	High

Oligopolies	Estimated 4-Firm Concentration Ratio in Relevant Markets (percent)	**Monopolistic competition**	Estimated 4-Firm Concentration Ratio in Relevant Markets (percent)
Artificial fibers	80%	Movie theaters	30%
Automobiles	84	Poultry	16
Flat glass	90	Yarns	19
Batteries	87	Commercial printing	18
Glass bottles	54	Knit fabrics	20
Cereal breakfast foods	89	Sheet metalwork	10
Newspapers	90+	Costume jewelry	23
Chewing gum	93	Retail shops	6
Cigarettes	95	Restaurants	24
Steel	55	Wood millwork	14
Oil refining	55	Dresses	8
Bearings	56		
Beer	64		
Cement	56		
Fabric weaving	42		

prices without easy detection, and so collusion is likely to collapse quickly.

Chicago-UCLA economists agree that oligopolists do try to collude and that such price fixing is certainly harmful. However Chicago-UCLA supporters also believe that collusion tends to collapse quickly, even when concentration is high—indeed, even when there are only two firms.

3. Barriers to New Competition[13]

A barrier is any condition that makes it difficult for new firms to enter the market. The "height" of the barrier gives the existing firms a limit to which they can raise prices without triggering new competition. Prices may be raised because of the barriers, even if the market's internal structure is not highly monopolistic.

Barriers can arise from two main types of conditions, as summarized in Table 2–4. *Exogenous* causes of barriers are fundamental economic conditions that are outside the influence of the firms already in the market; examples are economies of scale and large absolute size, which force entrants to raise large, costly volumes of capital. *Endogenous* causes can be manipulated by the firms already in the market so as to keep out newcomers. Some barriers are caused by government actions and give existing firms outside protection. Examples include licensing laws and patents. In any event, several barriers may exist in a market, combining to give the total barrier height.

High barriers tend to interact with concentration, each one helping to cause the other. Some analysts find it difficult to separate them, because they are so closely related. Generally, barriers are a peripheral element of structure, because potential entry is literally a peripheral matter to actual competitors already in the market. Typically, a dominant firm worries more about impacts from its actual rivals than about some possible entrant at some uncertain future time.

Actual barriers range in height, as indicated by the estimates in Table 2–3. They cannot be precisely measured, because the barriers' factors are hard to estimate and to combine in a single index of height. Still,

---

[13]The seminal discussion of them is Joe S. Bain, *Barriers to New Competition* (Cambridge, Mass.: Harvard University Press, 1956). For another attempt to measure barriers, see H. Michael Mann, "Seller Concentration, Barriers to Entry, and Rates of Return in Thirty Industries, 1950–1960," *Review of Economics and Statistics* 48 (August 1966), pp. 296–307. See also Steven C. Salop, "Strategic Entry Deterrence," *American Economic Review* 69 (May 1979), pp. 335–38; George S. Yip, *Barriers to Entry: A Corporate-Strategy Perspective* (Lexington, Mass.: Heath, 1982); Robert T. Masson and Joseph Shaanan, "Optimal Oligopoly Pricing and the Threat of Entry," *International Journal of Industrial Organization* 5 (September 1987), pp. 323–39; and Robert Smiley, "Empirical Evidence on Strategic Entry Deterrence," *International Journal of Industrial Organization* 6 (June 1988), pp. 167–80.

Table 2–4   Common Causes of Entry Barriers

Exogenous: Economic (intrinsic) causes of barriers

1. Capital requirements. Are related to the optimal sizes of firms and plants, as well as to the degree of capital intensity.

2. Economies of scale. Arise from both technical and pecuniary causes.

3. Product differentiation. Occurs naturally among products, most strongly in final consumer goods.

4. Absolute cost advantages. May arise from many possible causes, including differences among wage rates.

5. Diversification. Gives the possibility of massing and redeploying resources among branches.

6. Research and development intensity. Makes it necessary to assemble large R&D groups and generate new products before entry is attempted.

7. High durability of firm-specific capital. Gives rise to significant sunk costs, which make entry more costly and risky.

8. Vertical integration. May require entry to occur on two or more levels at once, raising costs and risks.

Endogenous: Voluntary and strategic causes of barriers

1. Retaliation and preemptive actions. Occurs by the use of price or other devices; this category is large and varied.

2. Excess capacity. The scope for expanding production quickly raises the ability to mount effective retaliation or to issue effective threats of retaliation.

3. Selling expenses, including advertising. Can increase the degree of product differentiation.

4. Patents. Provide exclusive control over technology.

5. Control over other strategic resources. Strategic resources include superior ores, locations, and specific talents.

6. "Packing the product space." In industries with high product differentiation, this policy can deter entry.

they do reinforce dominance and concentration in a number of important markets.

Chicago-UCLA analysts are little impressed with barriers, which they regard as a distraction from the conditions inside the market.

4. Other Elements

Other secondary elements of structure include *vertical* conditions. Powerful suppliers or buyers may be able to exert pressure upon firms with high market shares. As Galbraith noted, a monopsonist buyer may play off oligopoly sellers against each other, and it can threaten to integrate vertically by merging or creating its own capacity at the previous stage of production.[14] Also, a dominant firm with its own supply may raise the level of risk for its smaller nonintegrated competitors.

Chicago-UCLA economists generally deny that vertical conditions matter for competition.[15] According to them, only horizontal conditions affect competition; vertical integration is irrelevant.

In short, there is no single element by which monopoly power can be identified. Several elements may be important, and economists continue to debate their relative importance. In most cases, market share is the most important single element, as noted. But others can matter, and the judgments will sometimes affect the choice of the best policies.

V. CATEGORIES OF PARTIAL MONOPOLY

The six main types of markets are summarized in Table 2–5. They shade into one another, rather than being sharply separate, so that some industries are in the shaded areas. Moreover, each of the categories in Table 2–5 covers a range of conditions, rather than just one form.

Nevertheless, this set of categories shows the main features of monopoly power. Note how certain familiar markets fit into these groups. Local banks, for example, are usually a tight oligopoly, with two or three leaders. Clothing stores and restaurants are often loose oligopolies, while local electric and telephone service are pure monopolies. Table 2–3 presented examples of actual industries fitting almost all of the categories.

1. The Dominant Firm

A firm is said to be dominant when it has over half of the sales in the market and is more than twice the size of the next largest firm. Panel I of Figure 2–3 shows such a case. The higher the dominant firm's market share, the closer it comes to being a pure monopoly.

The dominant firm, therefore, acts like a pure monopoly, even though its power over the market is less than complete. There is some competition from the small competitors, but it is usually not severe. Mainly, the dominant firm just sets its profit-maximizing decisions unilaterally, given the degree of monopoly that its demand curve provides. The resulting profit rates are often high.

---

[14]See John Kenneth Galbraith, *American Capitalism: The Theory of Countervailing Power* (Boston: Houghton Mifflin, 1952).

[15]See McGee, *Industrial Organization;* and William F. Shughart II, *The Organization of Industry* (Homewood, Ill.: Richard D. Irwin, 1990), Chapter 13.

Table 2–5   **Types of Markets, Shading over from Pure Monopoly to Pure Competition**

Market Type	Main Condition	Familiar Instances
Pure monopoly	One firm has 100 percent of the market.	Electric, telephone, water, bus, and other utilities; patented drugs.
Dominant firm	One firm has 50–100 percent of the market and no close rival.	Soup (Campbell), razor blades (Gillette), newspapers (most local markets), film (Eastman Kodak), hospitals.
Tight oligopoly	The leading four firms, combined, have 60–100 percent of the market.	Copper, aluminum, local banking, TV broadcasting, light bulbs, soaps, textbook stores.
Loose oligopoly	The leading four firms, combined, have 40 percent or less of the market.	Lumber, furniture, small machinery, hardware, magazines.
Monopolistic competition	Many effective competitors, none with more than 10 percent of the market.	Retailing, clothing.
Pure competition	Over 50 competitors, all with negligible market shares.	Wheat, corn, cattle, hogs, poultry.

Entry barriers are also often so high that the dominant firm need not fear large new competitors. If entry is easy, then the dominant firm's choices may be restrained.

The competitors will usually follow the dominant firm's policies, since they fear retaliation if they try aggressive actions. These firms usually focus just on holding costs down and surviving. The dominant firm commonly adopts aggressive actions to limit and intimidate its small rivals. Its actions include selective "pinpoint" price discrimination among specific customers.

Alternatively, a "declining-dominant-firm" situation may occur, according to some theorists.[16] The dominant firm passively accommodates the little firms, letting them take away its market share as time passes. This narrow theory ignores the setting of differential prices and of dynamic interactions over time, and so it is not a reliable guide to actual cases. Dominant firms do not usually decline very rapidly in real markets.

---

[16]See Dean W. Worcester, Jr., "Why 'Dominant' Firms Decline," *Journal of Political Economy* 65 (August 1957), pp. 338–47; and Donald Hay and John Vickers, eds., *The Economics of Market Dominance* (Oxford: Basil Blackwell, 1987).

Schumpeter's Competitive Process. There is an alternative view about
dominant firms, often called the Schumpeterian process. Joseph A.
Schumpeter (rhymes with "zoom-greater") was a conservative theorist
who argued that big businesses, even ones that hold market dominance,
could give results even better than the neoclassical competitive outcome. His concept of "creative destruction" (published in 1944) dissents sharply from the mainstream view.[17]

It posits competition as a *disequilibrium process,* rather than a set of
equilibrium conditions. Competition and progress occur together, according to him, but in a series of temporary monopolies. The Schumpeterian process is the exact reverse, point by point, of the neoclassical
analysis. In each time period, each market may be dominated by one
firm, which raises prices and earns monopoly profits.

These profits attract other firms, one of which soon innovates a superior product and displaces the first dominant firm. The new dominant
firm then has its chance to set monopoly prices, causing the usual distortions and monopoly burdens. Soon, however, it is also pushed aside
by the next newcomer.

This cycle of "creative destruction" continues: Innovation creates
dominance, which gains monopoly profits, which stimulates new innovation, new dominance, and so on. As time passes, the average degree
of monopoly profits may be high. Indeed, the profits, disequilibrium,
distortions, and market dominance may all be large at each point of
time. Yet, the process of innovation is rapid, and it might soon generate
benefits of technical progress far exceeding any costs of misallocation
caused as market power is created and destroyed.

The Schumpeterian process is exciting, and some specialists regard
themselves as Schumpeterians because they favor rugged, progressive
processes, even if they involved some monopoly power. Moreover, the
concept is a refreshing contrast to austere neoclassical theory.

Schumpeter's theory requires certain doubtful assumptions. Dominant firms must be vulnerable and easily toppled. Entry barriers must
be low or weak enough to permit rapid entry, on a scale large enough
to displace the dominant firm with one blow. Few entrenched dominant
firms will let that happen. The newcomers must attack by innovation,
rather than through other less glamorous tactics.

Moreover, the contrast with neoclassical analysis is not really so
stark. Effective competition also envisions a process of adjustment. It
can also involve firms with some significant market shares, rather than
just swarms of atomistic firms. As for monopolies, they can set high
prices, which attract new competition. Therefore, there is a good deal

---

[17]See his *Capitalism, Socialism and Democracy* (New York: Harper & Row, 1944), pp.
85–106.

of common ground between the two concepts of competition and monopoly.

Yet the two approaches to competition do stress different features: The neoclassical theorists posit an efficient equilibrium among many firms, and Schumpeter sees a rugged, creative process involving a sequence of monopolies. They are both equally valid, as a matter of internal logic. The factual relevance of the Schumpeterian process to real markets (e.g., to Kodak in film, AT&T in long-distance telephone service) remains debatable.

Instances and Effects of Dominance. Dominant firms are unusual because a high market share is hard to capture and maintain. Yet the firms that do get market dominance often become household names. Notice the familiar company names in Tables 2–3 and 2–5. Their names and brands are well known precisely because the firms are dominant, producing a large share of the goods in their markets. Many local markets also contain dominant firms. Your local newspaper is probably one, and so perhaps is the biggest local bank, lumberyard, taxi company, and hospital.

2. Oligopoly[18]

The term *oligopoly* means "few sellers." Because they are few, oligopolists (1) can jointly influence the market and (2) must anticipate each other's strategies. The key element of oligopoly is the concentration of market sales in the largest few firms.

Concentration obviously can vary continuously from near zero for a purely competitive market all the way up to 100 percent when there are only four or fewer firms. In *tight oligopoly,* concentration is above 60 percent or so, while loose oligopoly has concentration in the range of about 20 to 40 percent.

The typical oligopoly has several leading firms plus a fringe of little competitors. Those leading firms normally taper down from the biggest one, with each firm substantially smaller than the next. It is often not exactly clear where the oligopoly firms end and the fringe firms begin. Nonetheless, the key economic feature of oligopoly is the presence of a group of leading firms.

These firms are *interdependent*. They must be constantly aware of one another's actions, planning their own moves carefully, and ready to

---

[18]Leading references on oligopoly include Edward H. Chamberlin, *The Theory of Monopolistic Competition,* 6th ed. (Cambridge, Mass.: Harvard Univ. Press, 1962); William J. Fellner, *Competition among the Few* (New York: Knopf, 1949); George J. Stigler, "The Theory of Oligopoly," *Journal of Political Economy* 72 (February 1964), pp. 44–61; and Jean Tirole, *The Theory of Industrial Organization* (Cambridge, Mass.: MIT Press, 1988).

react to one another's tactics. Therefore, oligopoly is permeated with *strategy*. Actions cannot be simple unilateral steps as they are in pure competition, pure monopoly, or dominance.

Tight oligopoly is often like a chess game or a war. Each firm's choices hinge on what it expects the others to do in response to its actions or in following their own strategies. An oligopolist needs to think three or four moves ahead to have a *strategy*.

Oligopoly thus differs from other market forms, where each firm merely finds and achieves its profit-maximizing levels of price and output and ignores possible responses by specific other firms. Oligopoly is also distinctive in its great variety. It embraces a remarkable diversity of conditions. *Concentration* may range from 20 percent on up. The leading firms may be about *equal* to one another in size or, instead, strongly *different*. The *products* may be "homogeneous" (like cement and lumber) or "differentiated" (like electrical generating plants and brands of cereal or beer). *Entry barriers* to the market may be high, medium, or low.

Conflicting Incentives Can Make Oligopoly Unstable. Each firm in an oligopoly has *mixed incentives* toward its several rivals. Depending on how the balance tips, a firm may fight, or cooperate, or reach some mix of actions toward its fellow oligopolists.

The rewards from cooperation and collusion depend largely on how concentrated the market is. The higher the concentration, the stronger are the firms' incentives and opportunities to cooperate successfully and thus to maximize their joint profits. But often they cannot suppress the urge to compete. Once the high, collusive price is set, each firm could gain by secretly cutting its own price just below the jointly agreed-upon price. Cooperation may well collapse, and a price war may break out.

Oligopolistic industries often veer between being restrictive and stagnant when cooperation holds and being aggressive and progressive when competition breaks out. There is always the tension between opposing choices.

Each oligopolistic setting provides a range of possible outcomes. The specific results of each one are usually *indeterminate*. The structures are too diverse, and the attitudes of the firm's managers are varied and unpredictable.

Despite this variation of specific cases, there are some predictable basic patterns. When the following three conditions occur, collusion is likely to stick:

1. Similarity of the Firms' Conditions. If the firms have similar demand conditions and/or similar cost conditions, they will be more able and more likely to cooperate.

2. *Familiarity over Time*. Each firm's managers get to know the other companies as time passes, and they learn to judge and predict one another's behavior more accurately.

3. *Concentration*. The likelihood of cooperation varies closely with the *degree of concentration*. Higher concentration breeds more collusion, for two main reasons. First, the few firms can organize, understand, and enforce their mutual agreements more thoroughly. Moreover, the leaders—having most of the market—face little pressure from those small fringe firms that are outside the price ring. Second, price cutting by any renegade oligopolist is easier to discover and penalize when there are only a few firms. If there are only three firms, the other two will quickly know that the third firm is the chiseler. In contrast, if there are 15 or 20 firms involved, any one of them or several—or all—will be more sorely tempted to chisel, since each one can expect to succeed for a longer time before being discovered.

Tight oligopoly crystallizes cooperation. When the few rivals control nearly all of the industry, collusion can often be nearly as compete as with a pure monopoly. Loose oligopoly, in contrast, is usually a scene of chronic strife, often degenerating into flexible, competitive pricing action.

The contrast is not absolute. Tight oligopolies often undergo bouts of fierce competition when collusion collapses, and loose oligopolies can sometimes be effectively collusive.

Types of Collusion. The kinds of collusion that may occur in oligopolies range from tight, explicit collusion to informal, loose arrangements.

Explicit Collusion. If price fixing is legal, the price fixing in tight oligopolies can be so complete that it approaches the level that a pure monopoly would achieve. *Cartels* may be formed. A cartel is a formal organization created by companies to manage their cooperation. It fixes prices and enforces penalties against members who violate the agreement. The cartel may also set output quotas, control investments, and pool profits.

Abroad, cartels, such as OPEC in the world oil market, have been widespread and powerful, especially during their heyday in 1900–1960. For example, Germany, Sweden, and Britain each had more than 2,000 cartels from 1935–55.

Price fixing has been against the law since about 1900 in most U.S. industries, under Section 1 of the Sherman Act and various state antitrust laws. The U.S. antitrust laws, therefore, shift the margin of choice away from collusion and toward competition in most U.S. oligopolies. However, there is nonetheless some hidden price fixing done through secret meetings, phone calls, and other covert ways.

Tacit Collusion. Price fixing can also occur in a milder form, called *tacit collusion*, or parallel pricing, or price signaling. The oligopolistic firms do not conspire directly or sign binding agreements, mainly because it is against the law to do so, but a firm can give indirect hints and signals of its preferred price levels. Then all the other firms simply go along with the same price changes. Often, a cooperative price is reached, just as if formal collusion had occurred.

One version of this tacit collusion is called *price leadership*. In it, one firm periodically judges the best new joint maximizing price for them all and then sets that price. The others simply follow the leader, quickly matching its price. The pattern then is: long periods of stable prices, punctuated by simultaneous price jumps, usually led by the same firm.

3. Monopolistic Competition[19]

Loose oligopoly shades into another market type, *monopolistic competition*. It has low levels of concentration, but each firm has a slight degree of monopoly. This market structure is a highly diluted form of monopoly, in which firms' demand curves have only a slight downward slope. The firm's market share is less than 10 percent.

The distinctive features of monopolistic competition are as follows:

1.   There is some *profit differentiation,* which means that consumers can develop preferences among the sellers. This slight degree of market power gives the firm's demand curve a slight downward slope. The product differentiation can occur either (1) because the products themselves *differ physically or in brand images* (like various brands of bread, jewelry, or shirts) or (2) because of the sellers' *locations* (as when a local grocery store, hotel, or restaurant is convenient to a neighborhood).

2.   There is *free entry into and exit from* the market. New firms enter whenever any excess profit (above the normal competitive rate) is being made in the industry.

3.   There is *no interdependence* among individual firms. No firms have large enough market shares to influence the rest of the market. Each firm merely feels the competitive pressure from all of the many other firms in the market.

These conditions are common among retail outlets and in other markets, as shown by the examples of monopolistic competition in Table 2–3. A typical case of monopolistic competition is a grocery or clothing store, with some loyal clientele in its neighborhood but steady competition from many other stores farther away. The firm's demand is

---

[19]See Chamberlin, *The Theory of Monopolistic Competition.*

highly, but not infinitely, elastic. Because the demand curve is nearly flat, the firm has only a little room for choice.

In the short run, the demand curve may lie above the average cost curve. That permits the firm to earn short-run excess profits. But then free entry takes its toll. New firms, seeing that excess profits are being made, enter the market, and that forces down this firm's demand curve until it is just tangent to the average cost curve.

The demand curve is nowhere above the cost curve, so that no excess profits are possible. The firm can just survive, barely earning the competitive rate of profit.

Yet, monopolistic competition does cause two deviations from the efficient results of pure competition. *First,* cost and price will both be slightly higher than under perfect competition. This added cost is not just a dead loss, for consumers benefit from the extra price they pay. For example, the local grocery store may charge higher prices, but to its neighborhood customers, the extra convenience can be worth the extra cost of shopping there.

The *second* deviation is idle capacity. Some of the firm's capacity stands idle most of the time. In practical terms, most retail shops have near-empty aisles for much or all of every day; most restaurants would like more customers than they have.

These two distinctive features—idle capacity and extra pricing "for convenience"—are evident in many stores. Monopolistic competition is a special analytical case, but a familiar phenomenon in many day-to-day businesses.

QUESTIONS FOR REVIEW

1. "Managers are supervised by their board of directors, by their bankers, and by the stock market generally." True?
2. "By maximizing long-run profits, managers maximize the firm's present value." True?
3. "The stock market helps to enforce efficient business management." True?
4. "Though market types differ, all forms of competition have similar effects: pressing prices down toward costs." True?
5. "Profitability is best measured as a rate of return on sales, not on assets." True?
6. "X-inefficiency is called the 'burden of misallocation,' as shown by the welfare triangle." True?
7. "In the crucial distinction between right oligopoly and loose oligopoly, the former usually gives higher collusion and profits." True?

8. "Entry barriers can matter, but potential competition is often weaker than actual competition." True?

9. Choose and explain two actual markets that illustrate the main categories of competition (e.g., loose oligopoly, dominant firm).

10. Why is the rate of erosion of market power important?

11. Why is competitive parity important in providing for effective competition? Explain why dominance may not provide effective competition and why Chicago-UCLA economists think that it does.

12. Explain how the Chicago-UCLA-school's superior efficiency hypothesis reverses the mainstream direction of causation between structure and performance. Show how it would make dominant firms beneficial rather than economically harmful.

13. Explain how the Schumpeterian process reverses many of the neoclassical features of competition.

C·H·A·P·T·E·R 3 Patterns and Effects of Actual Market Power

From concepts of competition and monopoly, we now turn to facts about real markets: the extent and effects of market power in the U.S. economy. How much is there, in what sectors, and how is it evolving? Does it fit the Chicago-UCLA view: rare, brief, and beneficial? Or is it extensive, powerful, and harmful? With the spread of global competition during recent decades, have the dimensions changed?

The evidence will suggest a middle picture in which market power is still important, though it was reduced in the United States after 1960. We study the causes and effects of market power. Do economies of scale and superior performance justify dominance in many or most industries? And are market power's negative effects very strong, on the whole? The facts will not strongly support the Chicago-UCLA view of weak, beneficial monopoly, though some cases do fit that view. In most cases, dominance has strong effects and defends itself tenaciously.

The chapter ends with two industries that have been at the forefront in recent policy debates: airlines and long-distance telephone service. They neatly illustrate the pricing, merger problems and complex policy choices that arise when there is market dominance.

There is room for varying interpretations of the evidence, but market power is still a serious problem in many markets. If public policies can prevent, reduce, or constrain market power, then antitrust may have high economic yields.

I. THE EXTENT AND TREND OF MARKET POWER

To understand the possible role of market power, it is best to begin by reviewing the whole business population.

1. The Business Population

Among 17 million private enterprises in the United States, the greater mass of activities occurs in small and medium-sized firms. *Small firms* number over 11 million, a vast population of tiny producers and local shops, each with less than $100,000 in yearly revenue. They embody the Jeffersonian ideal of hardy, independent enterprises.

About 5,000 *medium-sized firms* (with revenues between $10 million and $1 billion) conduct over half of the total production of the country. They are often substantial, well-established companies, often producing a variety of products and selling on a regional or national scale. In all sectors, except farming and services (where small firms are prevalent), these medium-sized firms are a major factor.

The *largest corporations* include about 300 manufacturing firms with sales above $1 billion, plus about another 125 in such other sectors as banking, retailing, transportation, and utilities. These firms operate on a national or global scale, often in many different industries. They have at least 15,000 workers each, with the largest seven of them employing over 300,000 workers apiece.

The largest corporations in the main sectors of the economy are shown in Table 3–1. Only their U.S. operations are shown, in order to focus on domestic conditions. General Motors is by far the largest U.S. firm. In manufacturing, DuPont, GE, Ford, and IBM are next. Most of these firms are long-established, familiar companies with large shares of their markets. Most of them continue to attain healthy profit rates despite the turbulence of the 1980s.

Portions of the manufacturing, utility, and financial sectors lend themselves to large-scale technology, which, in turn, requires large firms. That is why large corporations are prominent in these sectors.

From 1910 to 1960, the largest 100 or 200 firms in the manufacturing sector significantly increased their shares of total assets and value-added. But their shares appear first to have stabilized in the 1960s and then to have slightly declined in the late 1970s. Therefore, the 20th-century dominance of the economy by big business now appears to have tapered off.

Most of the large firms focus on just one or a few product lines, such as Exxon in oil, IBM in computers, and AT&T in telecommunications. Other firms, however, are highly diversified, with operations in many kinds of products.

Table 3-1 The Largest U.S. Firms, in Various Sectors

Name of Company	Main Products	Sales 1989	Assets 1989
		($ billions)	
Manufacturers			
General Motors	Cars, trucks	126.9	173.3
Ford	Cars, trucks	96.9	160.9
IBM	Computers and related	63.4	83.2
General Electric	Electrical equipment	55.3	128.3
Phillip Morris	Tobacco products	39.1	38.5
Chrysler	Cars, trucks	36.2	51.0
DuPont	Chemicals	35.2	34.7
Procter & Gamble	Personal products	21.7	16.4
Boeing	Aircraft	20.3	13.3
United Technologies	Diversified	19.8	14.6
Eastman Kodak	Photographic supplies	18.4	23.7
USX	Steel, diversified	17.8	23.7
Dow Chemical	Chemicals	17.7	22.2
Xerox	Copiers	17.6	30.1
Pepsico	Beverages and related	15.4	15.1
RJR Nabisco	Tobacco and foods	15.2	36.4
McDonnell-Douglas	Aircraft	15.0	13.4
Digital Equipment	Computers	12.9	10.7
Westinghouse	Electrical equipment	12.8	20.3
Rockwell International	Weapons and diversified	12.6	8.9
Oil Firms			
Exxon	Oil and products	96.9	83.2
Mobil	Oil and products	51.0	39.1
Texaco	Oil and products	32.4	25.6
Chevron	Oil and products	29.4	33.9
Amoco	Oil and products	24.2	30.4
Utility Firms			
AT&T	Telephone service	36.1	37.7
GTE	Telephone service	17.4	32.0
BellSouth	Telephone service	14.0	30.1
Nynex	Telephone service	13.2	25.9
Bell Atlantic	Telephone service	11.4	26.2
Retail Firms			
Sears, Roebuck	Household goods	53.8	87.0
K mart	Household goods	30.0	13.9
Wal-Mart	Household goods	25.8	8.2
American Stores	Groceries	22.0	7.3
Kroger	Groceries	19.1	4.1
Banks			
Citicorp	Banking services	38.0	230.6
Chase Manhattan	Banking services	13.9	107.4
Bank of America	Banking services	11.4	98.8
J.P. Morgan	Banking services	10.4	89.0
Security Pacific	Banking services	10.1	83.9

Source: *Fortune Directory of the 1,000 Largest U.S. Corporations,* 1990, and *The Business Week 1,000,* 1990.

2. Competition in Individual Markets

Because there are thousands of individual markets and the evidence about them is incomplete, economists cannot be precise about the degree of monopoly in the whole economy. Yet close study over several decades has clarified the main patterns.

According to the Census Bureau, there are about 440 manufacturing industries in the United States; it reports their four-firm concentration ratios about every fourth year. However, about half of these ratios are seriously inaccurate for two reasons: (1) The Census Bureau defines many industries too broadly (for example, it lumps together all drugs, including heart, kidney, contraceptive, and others, most of which do not substitute for one another); and (2) the ratios omit imports, which are a major factor in automobiles, steel, cameras, and many other markets.

These ratios do not permit precise measures of true concentration. Using them and other sources, a recent study has classified U.S. markets into four categories: pure monopoly, dominant firm, tight oligopoly, and all others.[1] The "all others" category includes loose oligopoly, monopolistic competition, and pure competition, which together can usually be regarded as very close to the fully competitive situation.

To set the trends over time, the study made estimates for three widely spaced years, 1939, 1958, and 1980. These estimates are summarized in Figure 3–1.

This study makes two main points: *First,* the economy contains a wide variety of market conditions; and *second,* there was a marked rise in competition in the economy. Pure monopolies were about 6 percent of national economic activity in 1939, but their share had shrunk to 2 percent by 1980. Dominant firms decreased almost as sharply, from 5 percent in 1939 to a 2 percent share of national income in 1980. Tight oligopolies had no less than 36 percent of national income in 1939 and 1958, but then shrank sharply to 19 percent in 1980.

These three categories of market power have decreased dramatically, from nearly half of national income in 1939 to less than one quarter in 1980. The 1980s have probably not changed the main pattern, even though some industries (such as the airlines) have changed.

3. Causes of Increased Competition

Why did competition increase so sharply and widely? Four causes were probably at work: (1) rising import competition and (2) antitrust actions reduced market power in many markets; (3) de-regulation unleashed

---

[1]This section is based on William G. Shepherd, "Causes of Increased Competition in the U.S. Economy, 1939–1980," *Review of Economics and Statistics* 64 (November 1982), pp. 613–26.

Figure 3–1 **The Trend of Competition in the U.S. Economy 1939 to 1980**

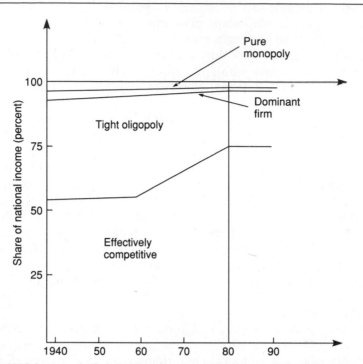

In 1939, just over half of all national income arose in markets that were effectively competitive (they were either loose oligopoly, monopolistic competition, or pure competition). The competitive share rose to 56 percent in 1958, and then to 76 percent in 1980. The main patterns have probably changed little during the 1980s.

competition in a few key sectors; and (4) the economies of scale shrunk in many markets (as will be shown in the next section). Table 3–2 shows the main markets that have probably been affected by these causes. There is some overlap among the causes, especially in numerous industries where antitrust actions were the stimulus for de-regulation.

1. Import Competition. The table includes industries which clearly had a substantial rise in import competition during the 1958–80 period, to above 15 percent of all U.S. sales in 1980.

In general, imports have risen strongly in importance since the middle 1960s, when they were over 10 percent of U.S. sales in relatively few industries. Now the import share exceeds 10 percent in scores of industries, with effects that are widely recognized.

Table 3–2   The Role of Imports, Antitrust, and De-regulation in Increasing Competition, 1958–1980

Industry (1980 Category)	Industry's National Income, 1978 ($ millions)	Industry (1980 Category)	Industry's National Income, 1978 ($ millions)
1. Antitrust		**2. Increasing Imports**	
Meatpacking	2,469	Steel and products (A)	16,269
Baked goods	3,310	Automobiles	15,844
Drugs	4,735	Aircraft	6,823
Aluminum and products	3,754	Tires and tubes	3,534
Metal cans	2,521	Shipbuilding	3,287
Heavy electrical equipment	6,422	Television tubes	3,156
		Artificial fibers	2,246
Telephone equipment (D)	3,416	Television sets	2,090
Cable T.V. equipment	(120)	Cameras	(1,000)
Photographic equipment & supplies	4,905	Copiers (A)	(3,900)
		Vacuum cleaners	361
Telephone service (long-distance) (D)	17,843	Motorcycles	284
		Sewing machines	181
Radio and television broadcasting	4,741	Total	57,975
		3. De-regulation	
Banking (D)	24,649	Telephone equipment (A)	3,416
Security, commodity brokers (D)	5,428	Railroad transportation (A)	14,217
Real estate agents	13,677	Trucking	25,917
Photofinishing labs	1,435	Air transportation (A)	12,054
Automotive rentals	2,807	Telephone service, long-distance (A)	17,843
Motion pictures and theaters	3,347		
		Banking (A)	24,649
Commercial sports	1,426	Security, commodity brokers (A)	5,428
Legal services	16,232		
Total	123,287	Total	103,524

(D) indicates de-regulation.
(A) indicates antitrust.
Source: William G. Shepherd, "Causes of Increased Competition in the U.S. Economy, 1939–1980," *Review of Economics and Statistics* 64 (November 1982), Table 4, p. 621.

The competition from imports has special force, beyond what their market shares alone would indicate. This is because these low-cost competitors are able to ignore the incentives for tacit agreement with U.S. producers in order to establish higher prices. By causing a shift toward cost-based pricing, the imports have introduced a marked change toward the competitive outcome. Steel and automobiles are prominent examples; electronics and cameras have also felt strong effects from imports.

2. Antitrust Actions. Evaluating the effects of antitrust actions is not straightforward, for two main reasons. *First,* formal antitrust cases that proceed to final court decisions are only a small fraction of all antitrust activity. Many other cases are brought formally but settled by compromise. Others achieve effects by threats and responses without reaching formal litigation at all. Others are started but dropped after the companies yield in order to avoid further litigation. In still other industries, there are indirect effects: Firms in industries A through X change their behavior because landmark cases in industries Y and Z set precedents that apply generally.

Also, the two antitrust agencies pursue many actions (both formally and informally) in other public agencies and forums. They intervene with many regulatory agencies (the ICC, FERC, FCC, and others) to prevent mergers, stop price fixing, and revoke monopoly franchises. These actions are often important and widely known in reliable detail, even though they do not take the form of an official antitrust decision.

In all these ways, antitrust's economic effects have gone well beyond the instances that the legal casebooks report. Moreover, *private* antitrust cases provide added antitrust effects. Increasing from several hundred cases yearly before 1960 to over 1,000 yearly during 1975–85, these actions have had many direct and indirect effects.

Second, antitrust's economic effects are hard to estimate accurately. No complete evaluation of individual cases has been done, beyond pioneering efforts to assess various leading cases that have led to structural changes.

An additional question is the duration of antitrust effects. Some actions have only brief impacts, as when price fixers are penalized with fines but soon resume their collusion. Other actions have effects that develop over the course of many years; examples are the dissolution of the Standard Oil trust in 1913 and the *Alcoa* case outcome in 1945–50.

Despite these complexities, reasonable estimates are that antitrust has had a substantial influence on the degree of competition in the economy. Yet Table 3–2 probably understates antitrust's *total* influence.

Antitrust restraints on price fixing and mergers maintain competition throughout the economy at a much higher level than would otherwise exist. If antitrust were suddenly to cease, then a large wave of new mergers and collusion would soon raise the degree of market power in a wide range of sectors. Indeed, the 1980s' merger boom reflected such a loosening of antitrust restraints. By continuing to prevent that increase, antitrust has made possible the overall trend toward a rise in competition.

3. De-regulation. Since 1975, much publicity has been gained by de-regulation as a source of new competition. Yet the real impetus behind de-regulation has often been the antitrust agencies, especially in the transportation, communications, stock market, and banking sectors.[2]

Therefore, most of the de-regulation cases in Table 3–2 also reflect a large element of antitrust activity. In any event, Table 3–2 shows that de-regulation has affected seven main sectors, accounting for 4 percent of national income in 1978 and about 20 percent of the 1958–80 rise in competition.

Taken altogether, de-regulation's part in the increase in competition has been limited and closely intertwined with antitrust.

II. FAVORABLE SOURCES OF MARKET POWER

The two possible positive sources of market power are (1) superior performance and (2) technical economies of scale. Each of them is present in some markets to some degree, but whether they are minor, moderate, or near universal (the Chicago-UCLA view) is a matter of debate.

1. Superior Performance

Dominant firms have resulted from three main types of causes: mergers, superior performance, and anticompetitive actions. Many of the actual cases have combined more than one of the factors, and superior performance has rarely been the sole cause. Superiority is not easy to judge, because it is usually complex and a matter of degree. The people in the firm itself usually try to exaggerate their brilliance and efficiency. Despite these complications, it is often possible to find a consensus about the performance of many leading individual firms.

Case Studies. The common pattern is: some early superiority, followed by little or no superiority. Many firms acquire dominance with the help of some degree of superiority at the outset, by new products or marketing arrangements. Then they use their strategic advantages to retain the dominance after their superiority fades.

For example, Eastman Kodak (film), Kellogg (cereals), IBM (computers), Gillette (razors), and General Motors (automobiles) had some important innovations during their early rise to dominance. But all of

---

[2]For example, railroad mergers and pricing were the target of vigorous antitrust interventions before the Interstate Commerce Commission (ICC). During 1968–75, it was Antitrust Division pressure that led the Securities and Exchange Commission to abolish the fixing of stockbrokers' fees in 1975. New competition in the telephone sector has partly been created by antitrust cases and pressure on the Federal Communication Commission. The de-regulation of banking entry and pricing has also been advanced by a variety of antitrust actions.

them soon adopted selective pricing and strategic actions in order to beat back rivals. All of them evolved down to ordinary levels of efficiency and innovation; yet they retained dominance and high profit rates for decades. Only with increased competitive pressures during the 1980s did they begin to lose significant market share. They were exposed as having been mediocre and bureaucratic.[3]

Therefore, the Chicago-UCLA view is possibly relevant to their early origins, not to the long intervals of their continuing dominance. The lesson applies generally to other dominant firms of all sizes. Also, many other dominant firms were formed by mergers, not internal excellence and growth. They lacked the performance justification, and some of them (such as U.S. Steel after it was formed in 1904) were notably inefficient. However, many such firms yielded their dominance very slowly.

Statistical Patterns. Chicago-UCLA proponents have not offered systematic research on case studies, but they have suggested that the statistical relationship between market shares and profitability proves their hypothesis. That relationship (presented in the next section) is strong: Higher market shares do yield higher profit rates. That suggests the traditional lesson: that dominance applies market power to reap high profits.

Supporters of the Chicago-UCLA school instead simply reinterpret the pattern as reflecting greater efficiency. That possibility exists, but the correlation itself does not distinguish between market power and efficiency. Other evidence is needed about actual efficiency and innovations, the use of strategic devices, and rates of decline when performance is inferior.

In short, the superior-performance hypothesis lacks factual support. The mainstream evidence still stands: Nonefficiency causes are often important, and the burden of proof is on those who have a naive faith in superior performance. Moreover, even when the performance of a

---

[3]For example, in the 1980s, IBM was described as "a giant, calcified institution in deep need of modernization. Even with its work force slashed, the colossus has been one of the world's most luxuriantly thick bureaucracies." After 1987, IBM went through major changes, "hacking away at bad habits and inefficient processes that have taken root over seven decades." See "Akers's Drive to Mend IBM Is Shaking Up Its Vaunted Traditions," *The Wall Street Journal,* November 11, 1988, pp. 1 and A9. Five of 19 plants were mothballed, 50,000 "indirect" jobs (planners, secretaries, etc.) were eliminated, and "an entire layer of management, some 9,000 people," was removed.

Eastman Kodak's monopolizing conditions are described in Don E. Waldman, *Antitrust Action and Market Structure* (Lexington, Mass.: Lexington Books, 1978), Chapter 7; James W. Brock, "Structural Monopoly, Technological Performance, and Predatory Innovation: Relevant Standards under Section 2 of the Sherman Act," *American Business Law Journal* 21 (1983), pp. 291–306; and Brock, "Persistent Monopoly and the Charade of Antitrust: The Durability of Kodak's Market Power," *University of Toledo Law Review* 14 (Spring 1983), pp. 653–83.

specific firm can be shown to be superior, those net benefits need to be weighed against the negative effects of the monopoly power.

2. Economies of Scale

If the average-cost curve slopes down over a large range, compared to the size of the market, then there may be room for only one or several firms. "The mandates of modern technology" may dictate dominance by making its products cheaper. The idea has been common since the 1880s, and there has been extensive research on scale economies.[4]

These economies set a "minimum efficient scale" for firms (often called 'MES for short). If there are diseconomies of scale, the average-cost curve may turn up at sizes greater than MES. "Optimal" or "efficient" size is the point or range where the average-cost curve is at a minimum. Such optimal size may determine market structure by fixing minimum and maximum market shares for firms. Figure 3–2 illustrates this. At one extreme (*Case* 1): With steep cost gradients and a single optimum size, all firms would be about identical in size (and market shares). At the other extreme (*Case* 2): With a small MES and gentle cost gradients, firms could be viable at nearly any size. If so, costs would not determine market structure. Actual structure would depend on the interplay between competitive activity and the gains from monopolizing. Or (*Case* 3): Economies could be large, extending beyond the market's total size. This would be a "natural monopoly."

The key concepts are (1) the gradients of average costs, both downward and upward sloping; and (2) the level of optimal scale, either a point or a range.

Technical versus Pecuniary Economies. Before analyzing *technical* economies of scale, we must distinguish between them and *pecuniary* gains to scale.

Technical economies of scale are those arising from the actual physical organization of production activities. They reduce the ratio of inputs to outputs, thereby achieving a genuine increase in economic efficiency. This is a true *social* gain, whether or not the gains are cap-

---

[4]The topic has been discussed in detail since the 1890s. Among the important treatments are Charles J. Bullock, "Trust Literature: A Survey and Criticism," *Quarterly Journal of Economics* 19 (February 1900–1901), pp. 167–217; J. M. Clark, *Studies in the Theory of Overhead Costs* (New York: Macmillan, 1922); E. A. G. Robinson, *The Structure of Competitive Industry*, rev. ed. (Chicago: University of Chicago Press, 1958); W. A. Lewis, *Overhead Costs* (London: Allen & Unwin, 1948); Joe S. Bain, *Barriers to New Competition* (Cambridge, Mass.: Harvard Univ. Press, 1956); and F. M. Scherer, Alan Beckenstein, Erick Kaufer, and R. Dennis Murphy, *The Economics of Multi-Plant Operation: An International Comparisons Study* (Cambridge, Mass.: Harvard Univ. Press, 1975).

For recent discussions, see F. M. Scherer and David Ross, *Industrial Market Structure and Economic Performance,* 3rd ed. (Boston: Houghton Mifflin, 1990), Chap. 4.

Figure 3–2   Several Alternative Forms of Average-Cost Curves

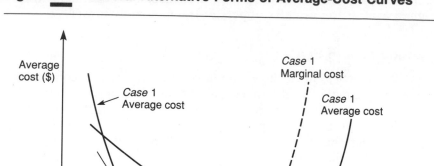

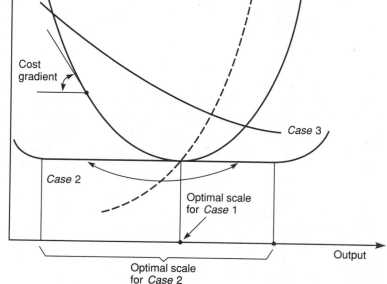

tured by the firm as profit or passed on to customers by means of lower prices.

Pecuniary gains stem mainly from lower input prices paid by the firm. Volume discounts are a common form of these price cuts. From these lower input prices, the larger firm is able to show lower costs, but *not* because its production technology is better organized. Therefore, pecuniary gains are not regarded as social gains.

Technical and pecuniary gains are often mingled together, so that separating them can be difficult. Yet the conceptual distinction is clear, and it should always be kept in mind. Always ask of any suggested economy of scale: Is it really technical, or pecuniary? If it is both, what are the proportions of the two parts? How can they be separated?

Both plants and whole firms are in question. At the plant level, physical factors tend to be most important. The layout of the factory, its equipment types, the training of specialized workers, and the engineering features of production all tend to govern costs. The cost curve is likely to have rather steep economies and diseconomies and to have a distinct minimum efficient scale.

At the firmwide level, where companies can simply add more plants to enlarge their production, the cost curves are likely to have lower gradients and possibly a range of constant average costs. Companywide conditions of management and research may be influential, and bureaucracy may gradually take effect at larger sizes.

Before reviewing the main research findings, we can consider the broad tends in the economy since the 1880s. They first favored large sizes until about the 1940s–50s, but since the 1960s have reversed in favor of small-scale operations and innovation in a wide range of industries. The age of industrial dinosaurs has given way to "small is beautiful" in many markets.

There are three main reasons for this reversal:

1. The *industrial mix* has changed. There has been a broad shift from "heavy," relatively crude industrial outputs to more complex, delicate products involving high technology. From such typical products as cast-iron bridges, bricks, and battleships around 1900–10, the economy's array of products has shifted toward computers, antibiotics, missiles, and stereo sets. The more refined products often require close controls and small-scale assembly, rather than crude mass production that could turn out simple industrial products. Therefore, the newer goods are often best produced in smaller factories and firms.

2. *Technology* has shifted broadly in favor of smaller-scale power sources and controls. The power to drive production comes nowadays not from large steam engines but from small electric motors, applied precisely. Small, powerful computers permit exact controls on production, even in small plants. Trucks traveling on the highway network can link numberless small factories much more efficiently than the earlier system of railroads and waterways. In earlier decades, the transport system typically involved a few big factories along the major railroad lines. That favored concentration, rather than a dispersal among many small plants and companies. The telephone system, too, has fostered small-scale efficiency by making close coordination possible even among many separate small firms.

3. *Workers' attitudes* are now more independent, less easy to regiment on a large scale than around 1880–1920, when immigrants were flooding into the labor force. Now, under the pressure of import competition, there is a trend toward more worker responsibility and more flexible work arrangements. These conditions also favor smaller-scale operations.

In retrospect, the 1880–1940 period is like an age of industrial dinosaurs. "Giantism" was widely praised by some business interests. The confidence in bigness has lingered in some quarters, and, of course, some industries do have large genuine economies of scale. But in most industries, we can no longer assume that bigger is better.

In contrast to this, the Chicago-UCLA views of the 1980s are in the opposite direction, toward favoring bigness and market dominance. The issue of whether bigness is better can only be resolved by considering the facts of real markets.

Patterns of Scale Economies. The best estimates of scale economies have come from "engineering estimates," gained by asking the opinions of engineers and managers in the industries themselves. From the consensus of those views, Scherer and others have estimated the cost curves for the capacity size that reflects the "best current practice": the newest facilities that are actually in use.

For *plants,* the cost conditions for 35 industries as of about 1967 are summarized in Table 3–3. The first column shows MES as a percentage of total U.S. demand. Thus, the 3.4 percent for "beer brewing" means that an efficient plant could be as small as just 3.4 percent of actual national production. In that case, there would be room for at least 30 efficient plants in the industry.

The second column shows how steep the gradients are. Thus for beer brewing, a plant only one third as big as MES would have average costs only 5 percent higher. That is a pretty small gradient, as you can see by sketching it on graph paper.

Though the measures are not precise, they show two clear general patterns. (1) MES is usually less than 5 percent of the market. Therefore, there is room for at least 20 plants in most of these industries. (2) Cost gradients are usually small rather than steep. Therefore, there is little case for large market shares based on the technology of factories.

For *firms,* the cost conditions are similar, as Table 3–4 indicates. The first column shows estimates of the cost gradients. They are mostly slight or moderate, rather than steep. The next column shows estimates of the MES for whole firms, as a percentage of total U.S. market in 1967. Most of these MES estimates are below 10 percent market shares.

Columns three and four compare the MES estimates with the actual market shares held by the largest three firms. Most of those market shares are substantially larger than the MES estimates, which suggests that there were significant amounts of excess market share. These figures underestimate the excess market shares of the largest single firm. For example, the leading beer company (Anheuser-Busch) had a market share closer to 25 percent than 13 percent. Therefore, its own excess market share would have been at least 10 percent of the market.

On the whole, scarcely any instances of high market shares appear to be fully justified by economies of scale as of the late 1960s. If MES

Table 3–3   Measures of Scale Economies, 1967

	MES as Percent of 1967 U.S. Demand	Percent by Which Cost Rises at ⅓ of MES
Scherer's estimates		
Leather shoes	0.2%	1.5%
Cotton and synthetic broad-woven fabrics	0.2	7.6
Paints	1.4	4.4
Antifriction bearings	1.4	8.0
Glass bottles	1.5	11.0
Portland cement	1.7	26.0
Automobile batteries	1.9	4.6
Petroleum refining	1.9	4.8
Beer brewing	3.4	5.0
Cigarettes	6.6	2.2
Refrigerators	14.1	6.5
Pratten's and Weiss's estimates		**At ½ MES**
Machine tools	0.3	5.0%
Bread baking	0.3	7.5
Iron foundries	0.3	10.0
Bricks	0.3	25.0
Flour mills	0.7	3.0
Tufted rugs	0.7	10.0
Bicycles	2.1	n.a.
Soybean mills	2.4	2.0
Detergents	2.4	2.5
Sulfuric acid	3.7	1.0
Passenger auto tires	3.8	5.0
Liner board	4.4	8.0
Printing paper	4.4	9.0
Synthetic rubber	4.7	15.0
Transformers	4.9	8.0
Nylon, acrylic, and polyester fibers	6.0	7–11
Commercial aircraft	10.0	20.0
Automobiles	11.0	6.0
Cellulosic synthetic fibers	11.1	5.0
Computers	15.0	8.0
Electric motors	15.0	15.0
Turbogenerators	23.0	n.a.
Diesel engines	21–30	4–28

n.a. = Not available.
Source: F. M. Scherer, *Industrial Market Structure and Economic Performance* (Chicago: Rand McNally, 1980), pp. 96–97; see also Leonard W. Weiss, "Optimal Plant Size and the Extent of Suboptimal Capacity," in *Essays on Industrial Organization in Honor of Joe S. Bain,* ed. Robert T. Masson and P. D. Qualls (Cambridge, Mass.: Ballinger, 1978), pp. 128–31; and C. F. Pratten, *Economies of Scale in Manufacturing Industry* (Cambridge, Eng.: Cambridge University Press, 1971).

Table 3–4   Multiplant Scale Economies in U.S. Markets, 1967–1970

	Multiplant Cost Gradient	MES as Percent of U.S. Market, 1967	U.S. Big-Three Firms, 1970	
			Average Market Share (percent)	Average Excess Market Share (percent)
Fabric weaving	Slight	1%	10%	9%
Shoes	Slight	1	6	5
Paints	Slight	1.4	9	7.6
Cement	Slight	2	7	5
Automobile batteries	Slight	2	18	16
Steel	Very slight	3	14	11
Petroleum refining	Slight	4–6	8	3
Glass bottles	Slight to moderate	4–6	22	17
Bearings	Slight to moderate	4–7	14	8
Cigarettes	Slight to moderate	6–12	23	14
Beer	Moderate	10–14	13	1
Refrigerators	Moderate	14–20	21	4

Source: Adapted from F. M. Scherer, *Industrial Market Structure and Economic Performance* (Chicago: Rand McNally, 1980), pp. 118–19.

levels have generally been falling, compared to growing total market sizes, then excess market shares might have risen. Much of the 1970s' rise in competition has probably come from a squeezing out of excess market shares.

Basic Cost Functions. Research has tended to fit the two basic cost diagrams shown in Figure 3–3. Figure 3–3A is close to the definition of *long-run* costs, while Figure 3–3B is often said to show *short-run costs*. The two figures also show, respectively, the cost curves for *industries* and individual *ongoing firms*.

The typical "industry" cost curve for the firm is dish shaped, with MES at 5 percent of the market or less. The constant-cost range may be wide, though presumably average cost rises eventually because of (1) bureaucracy, from absolute size, and/or (2) X-inefficiency caused by the firm's market power. If one filters out pecuniary economies, the typical cost curve may slope upward instead of being flat. For example, General Motors' shrinkage and low profits in the 80s seemed to reflect the higher costs of being "too big." In short, the typical cost conditions do not require high market shares or concentration. There are excep-

Figure 3–3   Typical Cost Curves for an Industry and an Ongoing Firm

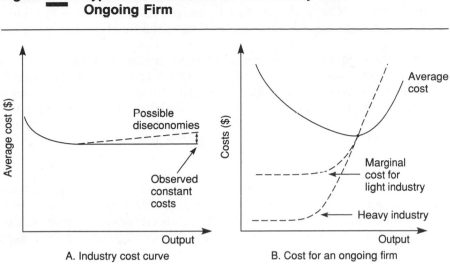

A. Industry cost curve

B. Cost for an ongoing firm

tions, of course, especially in smaller-sized markets. The cardinal question—how important the exceptions are—is still under debate.

Cost curves for an ongoing firm (Figure 3–3B) reflect the firm's capacity. Above that capacity, costs usually rise sharply.

Vertical Economies. Vertical economies occur when combining two stages of production (such as flour and baking, or weaving and clothing) reduces costs. Such a "vertical integration" of operations is widespread. Nearly all firms perform a series of operations that could, in principle, be done separately. Integration is also variable. Some firms do much of it, while their rivals do little or none of it.

Economies of integration are often large. Scheduling, coordination of the various stages of operations, saving heat or shipping costs, and many other technical benefits can apply. Most economists freely grant the importance of economies of vertical integration while remaining skeptical of most claims of horizontal economies of scale.

Yet these vertical economies are not always large, and they can often be achieved by long-term contracts, adjacent location, or other devices between separate companies, as well as by formal integration. Therefore, it is the *net* economies of integration—compared to the alternative ways of coordinating operations—that matter for policy choices.

Economies of Scope. Still narrower are the "economies of scope," a phrase referring to "network effects" that may occur among the products of a firm offering many related products.[5] For example, an airline flying between New York and San Francisco may be able to add New York–to–Chicago and Chicago–to–San Francisco flights at low marginal costs.

These economies can be large, but they are most often found in a few specialized cases, usually of the "public utility" type (telephone systems, air travel, and city bus lines). In this instance the case for a single monopoly system may be strong. Yet even in these cases, competition is often possible. Coordination among firms may be as efficient (as in airlines, railroads, and even telephone firms) as having them all in one big system.

In Summary. The general lesson is that several kinds of economies are possible and important. But their extent is often exaggerated, especially compared to alternative methods of coordination. Market power is probably much larger than true net economies require in many cases of dominance and tight oligopoly.

III. OTHER CAUSES

The other main causes of market power are (1) simple capture of the market, (2) random processes, and (3) various public policies.

1. Market Capture

Firms can capture a market share higher than MES in a great variety of ways. Various strategies can be used to drive competitors out, merge with them, or gain their acquiescence. Pricing, product design, and restrictive dealings offer many opportunities. Some of these methods are called unfair, destructive, or simply monopolizing; quite a few will be encountered in later chapters of this book.

2. Random Processes

"Random" includes all the historical, personal, accidental, and unpredictable events that flow together in shaping a firm's evolution. The effects of each event may be small or large or long lasting.

---

[5]For more detailed discussion of economies of scope, see Scherer and Ross, *Industrial Market Structure and Economic Performance,* Chap. 4; and William J. Baumol, John C. Panzar, and Robert D. Willig, *Contestable Markets and the Theory of Industry Structure* (San Diego: Harcourt Brace Jovanovich, 1982).

Perhaps the random element itself causes market power to evolve and then to fade away.[6] Williamson has pointed out that dominant firms can emerge by sheer luck and historical oddities, as well as by economies of scale and a direct effort at monopolizing.[7] Once established, they can persist even if there are no economies of scale.

3. Public Policies

In addition to economic forces, several kinds of public policies shape market structures. Some increase competition, others reduce or block it. Antitrust policies, for example, have reduced dominance in a number of markets. But utility regulation has tended to prevent competition in some sectors where competition would be possible. Examples include the airline industry during 1938–78 under the Civil Aeronautics Board, and banking.

Patents grant exclusive rights over inventions for 17 years. By conferring monopoly over the product, they can shape a new market toward dominance.[8] Tax laws have favored mergers by permitting the pooling of profits and losses. As a result, some industries have become more concentrated. Tariffs and other barriers on imports have reduced competitive pressures.

Public policies may, of course, create market power rather than reduce it. Chicago-UCLA analysts argue that the only lasting monopolies are those created by government actions. According to them, the state is easily exploited to create harmful monopolies, and those monopolies, once entrenched, are extremely hard to remove. That is one reason that Chicago-UCLA proponents favor minimal government action of all sorts.

4. The Rate of Erosion of Market Power

High market shares do tend to decay over time. In the Chicago-UCLA view, they decline rapidly (unless supported by state action), as is illustrated in Figure 3–4. According to Chicago-UCLA proponents, policy actions to reduce monopoly should be avoided unless they act even more rapidly than the market does.

Others are less optimistic, and some experts note that many dominant firms have retained high market shares for decades, as is illus-

---

[6]Scherer and Ross show that a plausible process of random growth could generate industrial concentration similar to what exists in the U.S. economy; see Scherer and Ross, *Industrial Market Structure and Economic Performance*, pp. 141–44.

[7]Oliver E. Williamson, *Markets and Hierarchies* (New York: Free Press, 1975), Chap. 11.

[8]Instances include pharmaceuticals, copiers, glass, photographic supplies, and electrical equipment.

Figure 3–4   How Fast Does Market Power Decline?

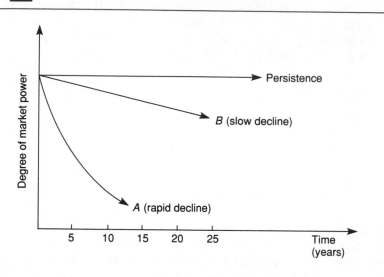

trated in Figure 3–4 by the horizontal arrow. That slowness makes it more advisable to rely on policy actions to reduce the dominance.

Generally, one's view about the rate of erosion is critical in forming one's judgments about policy choices. Consider it carefully as you observe actual firms in current markets and as you evaluate the past antitrust cases. The evidence suggests that erosion usually does occur, but only at an average of one-half to one percentage point per year.[9] For instance, a market share of 70 would normally take about 10–15 years to decline to 60 percent.

IV. THE EFFECTS OF MARKET POWER

Mainstream research has indicated that market power often has strong effects on price levels, price discrimination, profits, efficiency, innovation, fairness, and other values. The new IO theories suggest the opposite, and so there is a need to summarize briefly the research findings about actual markets.

There are two main kinds of evidence about prices and profits: (1) specific cases and (2) statistical cross-section patterns. Consider spe-

---

[9] For measures of the rate of decline of dominance, see W. G. Shepherd, *The Treatment of Market Power* (New York: Columbia University Press, 1975), Chap. 4; and Paul Geroski's chapter on "Do Dominant Firms Decline?" in *The Economics of Market Dominance*, ed. Donald Hay and John Vickers (Oxford: Basil Blackwell, 1987).

cific cases first: A number of them show dramatically that market power can have sharp effects.

1. Effects on Prices

Knowledgeable experts agree that various monopolies have raised prices to double, triple, or even much higher multiples of cost. The most massive example is the OPEC oil cartel, which sets oil-production quotas on its members (most of them located in the Middle East). In 1973–74, OPEC raised the price of oil from about $3 per barrel to about $14, and then in 1979 the price was pushed up again to over $30 per barrel.[10] This tenfold rise brought in over $100 billion yearly in extra profits to OPEC members.

In 1985, OPEC cut the price to the $13–18 range, reflecting both strategic pricing and a decline in OPEC's control. OPEC's colossal impact and gains are all the more striking because the "organization" is a heterogeneous and often divided cartel.

In the 1960s, Miles Laboratories set the price for a medical kit at 43 times the cost. The kits, for prediagnosing mental retardation in infants, were produced under an exclusive license for about $6 and priced at $262 each.

Soft contact lenses are a similar case.[11] From 1971 to 1975, Bausch & Lomb was virtually the only seller. The cost was under $5 per pair of lenses, while the price was set at over $60. Though its market power has been lower in recent years, its price is probably still a multiple of cost.

The DeBeers diamond monopoly has held control over world diamond prices for over five decades.[12] Its central selling organization can alter the price of diamonds over a wide range.

Eastman Kodak, with over 80 percent of film sales in the United States, has been able to price "largely without regard to cost" (in one of its own officials' words) for over 80 years.

---

[10]Among an outpouring of writings about OPEC, see James M. Griffin and David J. Teece, *OPEC Behavior and World Oil Prices* (London: Allen & Unwin, 1982); John M. Blair, *The Price of Oil* (New York: Pantheon Books, 1976); Albert L. Danielson, *The Evolution of Oil* (New York: Harcourt Brace Jovanovich, 1982); Steven A. Schneider, *The Oil Price Revolution* (Baltimore: The Johns Hopkins Press, 1983); and Paul W. MacAvoy, *Crude Oil Prices* (Cambridge, Mass.: Ballinger Press, 1982).

[11]See "Bausch and Lomb: Hardball Pricing Helps It Regain Its Grip in Contact Lenses," *Business Week,* July 16, 1984; and Roberta Reynes, "New Contact Lens Competition Focuses on Bausch and Lomb," *Barron's,* August 1, 1983.

[12]See David Koskoff, *The Diamond World* (New York: Harper & Row, 1981); Godehard Lenzen, *The History of Diamond Production and the Diamond Trade* (London: Barrie and Jenkins, 1981); and Steven Lohr, "Why a Diamond Cartel Is Forever," *The New York Times,* September 7, 1986.

The drug industry offers many instances in which patented drugs, protected against competition, were produced at 10 cents or less per pill and sold at over 50 cents per pill. When fixed brokers' fees were made competitive on the New York Stock Exchange in 1975 (under pressure from the Antitrust Division), the fees dropped by 43 to 64 percent.

Price Discrimination. Monopoly power also increases price discrimination; it sets a structure of differing price-cost ratios in line with differing demand elasticities (recall Chapter 2). Such demand-based pricing can generate large volumes of profits. Price discrimination is common in many markets, but the drug and airline industries will serve to illustrate it.

Drugs are sold to groups with sharply differing elasticities, especially individual patients (who merely buy what the doctor's prescription tells them to) and large hospital chains (which shop around and often extract rock-bottom prices). The price-cost ratios to these groups usually differ sharply.

Airline fare–cost ratios also vary steeply among customer groups and city routes, reflecting demand elasticities. The same plane often contains customers getting equal service (including scheduling convenience) but paying prices varying by multiples of three or four.

2. Profitability

These price effects—with higher levels and discriminatory structures—yield higher rates of profit. Monopoly profit rates are often in the range of 20 to 30 percent of invested capital. Compared to competitive rates of return that are commonly near 10 percent, monopoly profit rates may seem as if they are only a little higher. But the extra 10 to 20 percent returns translate into large capital gains for the owners.

In the strict Chicago-UCLA view, these are not monopoly profits but rather merely rents, earned by the firms' superior efficiency and innovations. Also, some dominant firms may be riskier, and so their higher profit rates may be regarded as a risk premium paid to shareholders for bearing more risk.

More probably, a substantial part of the high profits usually does reflect market power; the proportions vary from case to case. Evaluating this element has often been an important part of the leading antitrust cases to be covered in Chapter 7.

3. Effects on Efficiency

Market power may have three main effects on efficiency: X-inefficiency, allocative inefficiency, and functionless advertising.

X-Inefficiency. X-inefficiency occurs when average costs are higher than good management would yield. It reflects (1) inferior levels of efforts by employees and (2) the use of unnecessary amounts of inputs when cost controls are weak.

There are no general, precise methods for measuring X-inefficiency, but the business press provides a large flow of evaluations of managerial performance. Assessed realistically, these reports provide relatively reliable indications.

Important examples are also helpful. When General Motors, Ford, and Chrysler came under strong new competitive pressure from Japanese imports in 1979–81, they had to cut X-inefficiency sharply. They were able to cut employees, equipment, and inventories by 10 to 30 percent, often closing whole sections and layers of management.

By the 1980s, the IBM Corporation had become "a giant, calcified institution," with "bad habits and inefficient processes that had taken root over seven decades."[13] It was "one of the world's most luxuriantly thick bureaucracies." In 1989, it cut its staffing by some 10 percent and mothballed 20 percent of its factories.

There are abundant smaller examples, and altogether there are two main lessons. First, X-inefficiency is a common problem that often raises costs by more than 10 percent. Second, X-inefficiency is closely related to monopoly power. Some firms with high market power avoid X-inefficiency, but many do not.

Allocative Inefficiency. This is the welfare triangle, showing the loss of consumer surplus as price is raised from competitive to monopoly levels (recall Figure 2–2). Its size reflects (1) the size of the price rise, from case to case, and (2) the elasticities of demand. From a variety of research, a range of estimates of the triangle's size has emerged.

The estimates reflect the *remaining market power, after its reduction by antitrust since 1890*. If there were no antitrust, of course, the inefficiency would be much bigger, because there would be much more market power.

Most of the estimates range between 4 percent of national income down to negligibly small slivers. There is a rough consensus in the range of 1–2 percent of national income, which means roughly $50–$100 billion yearly.

Superior Efficiency by Dominant Firms. Against the notions of X-inefficiency and allocative inefficiency, Chicago-UCLA analysts urge that

---

[13]IBM's own Chairman, John Akers, was among those describing these conditions most candidly as he aimed to cut costs by at least 10 percent. See "Akers' Drive to Mend IBM Is Shaking Up Its Vaunted Traditions," *The Wall Street Journal*, November 11, 1988, pp. 1, A9.

dominance gives higher efficiency, not less of it. The few Chicago-UCLA studies offered to support the hypothesis have been faulty. In the absence of thorough empirical studies, some leading cases of dominant firms are suggestive.

IBM has dominated the mainframe computer market for some 35 years. It gained dominance partly because of nonefficiency advantages from its 90 percent share of the tabulating-machine market.[14] It fell behind its rivals in the early 1960s in rate and quality of innovation, and it retained its dominance by a series of actions widely regarded as being anticompetitive.[15] At least some of its dominance can therefore be attributed to conditions other than superior performance.

Eastman Kodak has held over 80 percent of the U.S. amateur film market for about 90 years. It has retained that share partly through its position in the related markets for cameras and film processing. Its innovativeness has been regarded at times, especially in the 1970s, as mixed, even mediocre.[16]

Campbell Soup's share of the canned soup market has been over 75 percent for at least six decades. Its management is frequently characterized as cautious, unimaginative, and unexceptional. Innovations have not been rapid, and there is little evidence that its efficiency is unusually high. In earning only about a 14 percent rate of return on equity, Campbell may be adopting an entry-limiting strategy. Or it may simply be relatively inefficient, in some significant degree.

Procter & Gamble has held about half of the detergent market for at least 40 years. Its record as an innovator is marked by extreme caution, and yet it has created a significant number of unsuccessful products. Its strength appears to be in heavy advertising of brand-name products, rather than in extreme cost-efficiency or rapid innovation.

Finally, *Kellogg's* extended its early monopoly on corn flakes into other breakfast cereals, holding at least an approximate 45 percent mar-

---

[14]See Shepherd, *Market Power and Economic Welfare* (New York: Random House, 1970); Gerald W. Brock, *The U.S. Computer Industry* (Cambridge, Mass.: Ballinger, 1975); and Richard Thomas DeLamarter, *Big Blue* (New York: Dodd, Mead, 1986).

[15]They include anticompetitive price discrimination, the use of money-losing "fighting ships" to drive out specific competitors, and unduly early announcements of new models in order to deter sales of superior computers by Control Data Corporation; see Brock, *The U.S. Computer Industry,* and DeLamarter, *Big Blue,* among others. That the U.S. antitrust case based on these actions was eventually withdrawn in 1982 does not indicate that the actions had no anticompetitive effects. The withdrawal was based on legal considerations and the fact that the case had been drawn out for many years. Among knowledgeable observers, IBM's actions were indeed in the range of probable anticompetitive methods.

[16]Thus, its disc camera and instant-picture cameras were failures during 1975–88, as was its "long-life" battery during 1985–90.

ket share for over five decades.[17] Despite a proliferation of brands and cereal variations, Kellogg's is not known as a highly innovative or cost-minimizing firm.

In these cases, marketing factors—particularly advertising—have been a powerful element. Brand loyalties have important effects in limiting new competition and permitting supranormal pricing.[18] Superior efficiency is not readily apparent.

Variance analysis has also been used to test for market-power effects.[19] But the findings have been inconclusive. Altogether, there is little systematic evidence for the Chicago-UCLA hypothesis, while the indications of market power's effects are widespread and strong.

Advertising. How much of advertising is wasteful?[20] Advertising comes in two main types: informative and persuasive. *Informative advertising* improves buyers' knowledge, so that they can apply their preferences more effectively in making choices which maximize their welfare. *Persuasive advertising,* instead, attempts to change those preferences. Therefore, it alters choices away from the efficient lines that "consumer sovereignty" would yield. Persuasive advertising, therefore, is largely economic waste. That applies both to the bulk of television advertising and much magazine advertising, and to some persuasive selling efforts by sales staffs.

Another category of advertising is "stand-off" advertising among oligopolists. It occurs when each firm would be willing to forgo the expenditure but all are afraid to stop for fear of losing ground to the others. Much oligopoly advertising is of this sort, with no economic gain.

---

[17]See F. M. Scherer, "The Breakfast Cereal Industry," in *The Structure of American Industry,* 6th ed., ed. Walter Adams (New York: Macmillan, 1982), pp. 191–217; and Richard Schmalensee, "Entry Deterrence in the Ready-to-Eat Cereal Industry," *Bell Journal of Economics* 9 (Autumn 1978), pp. 305–27.

[18]See William S. Comanor and Thomas A. Wilson, *Advertising and Market Power* (Cambridge, Mass.: Harvard Univ. Press, 1975); Comanor and Wilson, "The Effect of Advertising on Competition: A Survey," *Journal of Economic Literature* 17 (June 1979), pp. 453–76; and Scherer, *Industrial Market Structure,* Chap. 14.

[19]Richard Schmalensee, "Do Markets Differ Much?" *American Economic Review* 75 (June 1985), pp. 341–51; and Birger Wernerfelt and Cynthia A. Montgomery, "Tobin's q and the Importance of Focus in Firm Performance," *American Economic Review* 78, (March 1988), pp. 246–50.

[20]See also Comanor and Wilson, "Advertising and Competition"; Julian L. Simon, *Issues in the Economics of Advertising* (Urbana, Ill.: University of Illinois Press, 1970); Richard Schmalensee, *The Economics of Advertising,* Amsterdam: North Holland, 1972; and Robert E. McAuliffe, *Advertising, Competition, and Public Policy* (Lexington, Mass.: Lexington Books, 1987).

No precise measures of advertising waste have been made, but there is a rough consensus that perhaps half of advertising may be an economic waste, possibly $50 billion.

4. Retarding of Innovation

Monopoly is likely to retard the rate of innovation, for reasons to be presented shortly. However, in certain situations, monopoly power may speed it up. In order to grasp the analysis and judge the facts, one must first recognize several concepts about technological progress.[21]

Invention, Innovation, and Imitation. The procedure involved in bringing in new processes and products can be divided into three phases. *Invention* is the creation of the new idea. It can range from basic scientific concepts to strictly practical ideas (such as a new notch in a gear).[22]

Innovation brings the idea to practical use. The innovator establishes production facilities and brings the new product or process to the market.[23]

Imitation then follows as the innovation is copied by others. Such diffusion of the innovation across the market may be rapid or slow. It is usually an easier and safer action than innovating.

The three phases require different skills and resources, and the incentives are distinct for each. Invention is usually a lonely activity requiring intensive mental exploration.

Innovation is a business act, by contrast. Financing, arranging of complex engineering details, and risk taking must often be dealt with under difficult conditions. Though many innovations are small and safe, some are large.

Autonomous and Induced Changes. *Autonomous* changes arise naturally with the onflow of knowledge and technology. Discoveries in areas

---

[21]For an excellent survey and discussion of the empirical literature concerning this question, see Morton I. Kamien and Nancy L. Schwartz, *Market Structure and Innovation* (Cambridge, Eng.: Cambridge University Press, 1982). For a more theoretical discussion, see Partha Dasgupta and Joseph Stiglitz, "Industrial Structure and the Nature of Innovative Activity," *The Economic Journal* 90 (June 1980), pp. 266–93. A recent empirical study is William L. Baldwin and John T. Scott, *Market Structure and Technological Change* (Chur: Harwood, 1987).

[22]See, for example, Edwin Mansfield and others, *Research and Innovation in the Modern Corporation* (New York: W. W. Norton, 1971); John Jewkes and others, *The Sources of Invention,* 2nd ed. (New York: W. W. Norton, 1969); David Huettner, *Plant Size, Technological Change, and Investment Requirements* (New York: Praeger Publishers, 1979); and F. M. Scherer, *Innovation and Growth: Schumpeterian Perspectives* (Cambridge, Mass.: MIT Press, 1984).

[23]Bela Gold, "Technological Diffusion in Industry: Research Needs and Shortcomings," *Journal of Industrial Economics* 29 (March 1981), pp. 1247–69.

1 and 2 often make inevitable an advance in areas 3 and 4, which in turn causes progress in areas 5 and 6. Autonomous inventions occur also from the sheer curiosity of creative geniuses.

By contrast, *induced* inventions occur from the hope of making money. Without that stimulus, they would happen later or not at all. Much commercial R&D activity fits this type. Teams of scientists in company laboratories, working under carefully budgeted plans, are usually seeking inventions that will pay. No payoff, no inventive effort.

The distinction helps one appraise social policies toward technical change. A patent system, for example, has no social value if inventions are autonomous. Even if some inventions are induced, one needs to ask (1) what share these are of all inventions, (2) whether they are important or trivial inventions, and (3) how much they are accelerated by money rewards.

Technological opportunity varies among industries. Some industries bristle with chances for progress. In others, the state of the art is largely fixed. In computers and related electronics, for example, there has been great technological opportunity since 1950. By contrast, brickmaking, papermaking, and ball-point pens have had little chance for progress. Once one compares actual trends with opportunity, the faster changes often seem normal. Without such a comparison with opportunity, one simply cannot make intelligent, normative appraisals.

5. Competition Usually Promotes Technological Progress

The *inventive* effort will normally be optimized by competition. A monopolist is able to capture all the value of an invention in its industry. It will, therefore, apply a restrictive policy to inventions, seeking and using them less fully than would occur under competition. Competitors cannot apply such controls, and, therefore, they must undertake inventive activity up to the socially optimal level. Competitors will also *innovate* more fully than monopolists. A monopolist is able to be concerned about the fact that a new innovation will destroy some or all of the value of its existing technology. Consequently a monopolist will usually bring in new processes and products at slower than the socially optimal rate.

Some innovations may be too costly and risky for pure competitors to undertake. They may require the firm to have a sizable market share and financial resources. Schumpeter's process of "competition" via innovation by successive monopolists presumed that there were such requirements (recall Chapter 2).[24] Galbraith noted in the 1950s that

---

[24]See Joseph A. Schumpeter, *Capitalism, Socialism and Democracy* (New York: Harper, 1942); also John Kenneth Galbraith, *American Capitalism: The Theory of Countervailing Power* (Boston: Houghton Mifflin, 1956).

oligopoly might provide the ideal setting for innovation. The firms are large enough to undertake important innovations, but they are also small enough to feel great incentives to innovate, so as to increase their shares sharply.

Yet most innovations can be accomplished as rapidly by a series of competing firms as by a monopolist. Therefore, loose oligopoly is the first approximation to the optimal setting for innovation.

Effective competition—especially with a loose oligopoly structure—tends to optimize both invention and innovation. It also passes on their benefits to consumers. Monopolists tend, by contrast, to innovate below the optimal levels. They also retain much of the value of progress in their excess profits.

Research Results. A large and growing research literature broadly supports these predictions.[25] Inventions appear to come at least proportionally as much from small and independent firms as from the large laboratories run by leading firms. Patenting also seems to be done most actively by firms with market shares of 20 percent or less, rather than by dominant firms.

As for innovation, the research consensus is that high market shares and concentration retard innovation. Studies have covered scores of important industries. With few exceptions, it is firms with market shares below 20 percent that lead and those with shares above 30 percent that follow.

6. Inequality in Distribution: Wealth, Income, and Opportunity

Fairness has three economic dimensions: wealth, income, and opportunity. Market power increases inequality in all three dimensions, with especially sharp effects on wealth.

Wealth. Market power can cause excess profits, and these are capitalized into the market value of the enterprise. A sharp rise in market power can yield a large, immediate rise in the wealth of the owners. Wealth is moved away from the many customers and to the few owners of the firm.

Estimates of the actual impact of monopoly on wealth suggest that about one fourth to one half of the present highest family wealth was originally created by monopolizing.[26] This is affirmed by the prominence of such monopoly wealth as the Rockefellers, DuPonts, Dukes,

---

[25]Scherer and Ross, *Industrial Market Structure and Economic Performance,* Chap. 17.

[26]The leading study is William S. Comanor and Robert H. Smiley, "Monopoly and Wealth," *Quarterly Journal of Economics* 89 (May 1975), pp. 177–94.

Morgans, Stanfords, Mellons, and scores of other leading family fortunes. Fortunes also arose from market positions in steel, newspapers, cameras and film, aluminum, soap, razor blades, and scores of other markets, and, of course, banking.

Thousands of smaller such cases extend down to many local wealthy families, who typically drew their fortunes from a bank, hotel, department store, newspaper, lumber yard, or the like. Wealth arises from other sources, such as luck, effort, and innovation, but some kind of monopoly power has been a common source.

Income. Such flows and opportunity have also been made more unequal by monopoly power, but the effects are more complex and difficult to measure than in the case of wealth.

Opportunity. There is probably more equal opportunity in the U.S. economy than in any other Western country. Business opportunities— to set up a firm or to rise within existing firms—are relatively open. Yet these opportunities are abridged by market power in many ways, including racial and sexual discrimination. Dominant firms do reduce or prevent fair competition and entry in a series of national and local markets. Family connections and wealth provide head starts for many people in business and finance.[27]

V. TWO LEADING INDUSTRIES ILLUSTRATING MARKET CONCEPTS AND POLICY CHOICES: AIRLINES AND LONG-DISTANCE TELEPHONE SERVICE

Passenger-service airlines and long-distance telephone service provide unusually rich illustrations of the market concepts and how they related to policy choices. By reviewing the industries here, you can sharpen your ability to understand the specific policies that emerge in later chapters.

1. Airlines[28]

The airline industry is *the* most prominent and closely debated case of de-regulation, posing complex issues and a controversial, changing set of results.

---

[27]Discrimination in hiring also reflects monopoly power. Empirical research has shown that the more concentrated industries have largely excluded blacks from upper-level white-collar jobs; the more competitive industries have been much more open. A similar lesson holds for the hiring of blacks and women in large firms: Far fewer have been hired and/or promoted (until recently) compared with smaller firms.

[28]This section on airlines draws on my chapter on "The Airline Industry" in *The Structure of American Industry*, 8th ed., ed. Walter Adams (New York: Macmillan, 1990).

From 1938 to 1977, the airline industry was controlled by about eight major airlines, whose power was protected and lightly regulated by the Civil Aeronautics Board. During 1977–84, the CAB's controls were removed entirely and effective competition set in. But then U.S. policies went lax, permitting market power to be reasserted. By 1983, the airlines were beginning to quell price competition along rigid lines, and, after 1985, the largest airlines were permitted to merge, creating even higher concentration than existed before 1978.

Sharp debate continues. Some optimistic observers see strong competition, efficiency, and innovation.[29] Others see market power and anticompetitive pricing.[30]

In fact, the industry combines strong competition on some routes with high degrees of monopoly on many others. The hub-and-spoke system involves high dominance of many large-city markets. Price discrimination is anticompetitive on many routes and areas. And several ancillary conditions aggravate market power.

1. Brief History. During the 1920s and on to 1938, air travel grew from a group of hedge-hopping daredevils into a new industry dominated by about six trunk airlines.[31] By 1938, the biggest airlines sought friendly "regulation" as a way to minimize competition. Under the new Civil Aeronautics Board, virtually no entry was permitted into the scheduled-airlines part of the industry during 1938–75, while the number of airlines shrank from 16 to 11. Structure was monopolistic: in 90 percent of the city-pair routes (e.g., the route from Chicago to New York), with 59 percent of all passenger miles, there was a genuine monopoly. The airlines behaved largely as a market-rigging cartel, agreeing on fares and then getting CAB approval and enforcement. Maximum fares became minimum fares, in practice. Price cutting was largely prevented.

The airlines did compete indirectly by raising amenities (such as decor and meals) and scheduling more frequent flights, even though planes few half-empty on average. Pay rates for workers were also gen-

---

[29]See especially Alfred E. Kahn, "Surprises of Airline Deregulation," *American Economic Review* 78 (May 1988), pp. 316–22; and Elizabeth E. Bailey, David R. Graham, and Daniel P. Kaplan, *Deregulating the Airlines* (Cambridge, Mass.: MIT Press, 1985).

[30]See Melvin A. Brenner, "Airline Deregulation—A Case Study in Public Policy Failure," *Transportation Law Journal* 16, no. 2 (1988), pp. 179–228; and his "Rejoinder to Comments by Alfred Kahn," *ibid.*, pp. 253–62; and "The Big Trouble with Air Travel," *Consumer Reports,* June 1988, pp. 362–67.

[31]See Richard E. Caves, *Air Transport and Its Regulators* (Cambridge, Mass.: Harvard Univ. Press, 1962); William A. Jordan, *Airline Regulation in America: Effects and Imperfections* (Baltimore: The Johns Hopkins Press, 1970); and Bailey, Graham, and Kaplan, *Deregulating the Airlines,* which covers the de-regulation steps thoroughly.

erous. CAB regulation therefore tended to raise costs, possibly by 30 to 50 percent over efficient levels.[32]

Economic research uncovered these costs, and, by 1975, a loosening of barriers began as part of the de-regulation "movement" affecting telephones, railroads, and natural gas. Formal de-regulation began in 1977 and was virtually complete by 1981. Competition exploded as old airlines moved flexibly to change routes and fares and scores of new airlines entered thousands of city-pair routes. Hub-and-spoke patterns developed, with each airline routing most of its traffic through one or two airports. New maverick airlines such as People Express and World Airways entered rapidly, cutting fares steeply while offering "few-frills" service.

Fare discounts spread to over 75 percent of tickets by 1983. Competition became widely effective, especially on the high-volume routes such as New York–Chicago. De-regulation brought economic gains, as productivity increased and fares were cut. Choices were more diverse and flexible. Yet lower costs came partly from "union bashing," by cutting work forces and pay rates.

In 1984–86, a reversion to monopolistic patterns occurred. The leading airlines adopted rigid patterns for most ticket discounting, and they were permitted to make a series of mergers that raised their dominance over their hubs. National concentration increased. Table 3–5 suggests the changes in concentration and shows the main mergers. The dominance of hub traffic is indicated in Table 3–6.

At most of the largest airports, loading gates and the time slots are overcrowded, especially during the preferred travel times of the day. The congestion has spread in the 1980s, because traffic has doubled while airport capacity has stayed about the same.

The airlines in Table 3–5 are the survivors. The carnage among the new airlines has been severe, with some 50 airlines disappearing. Most of the scores of regional feeder lines have been absorbed into or subordinated to large airlines.

De-regulation's proponents estimate that fares have been reduced sharply below their likely levels under regulation: savings of $6–12 billion per year have been claimed. Figure 3–5 shows the basic trend of fares per passenger mile, adjusted for inflation. Fares have been declining since 1960, and there have been many factors besides de-regulation at work, including new aircraft types and changing fuel prices.

---

[32]See Caves, *Air Transport;* Jordan, *Airline Regulation in America;* and Theodore E. Keeler, "Airline Regulation and Market Performance," *Bell Journal of Economics* 3 (Autumn 1972), pp. 399–424.

Table 3–5   Structure of the Domestic Airline Industry

1978 Carrier	Percent of Revenue Passenger Miles	1983 Carrier	Percent of Revenue Passenger Miles	1987 Carrier	Percent of Revenue Passenger Miles
1. United	21.1%	1. United	18.7%	1. Texas Air*	20.3%
2. American	13.5	2. American	13.8	Continental	10.2
3. Delta	12.0	3. Eastern	11.1	Eastern	10.1
4. Eastern	11.1	4. Delta	11.1	2. United	17.3
5. TWA	9.4	5. TWA	7.1	3. American	15.4
6. Western	5.0	6. Republic	4.2	4. Delta†	13.0
7. Continental	4.5	7. Northwest	4.2	5. USAir	8.9
8. Braniff	3.8	8. Western	3.9	USAir	4.0
9. National	3.6	9. Continental	3.5	Piedmont	3.5
10. Northwest	2.6	10. Pan Am	3.3	PSA	1.4
11. USAir	2.2	11. Southwest	1.7	6. Northwest and Republic	7.9
12. Frontier	2.0	12. Frontier	1.7	7. TWA‡	6.4
				8. Southwest	2.5
				9. American West	1.8
				10. Pan Am	1.6
				11. Braniff (New)	1.0
				12. Alaska	0.9
Top four	57.7	Top four	54.7	Top four	66.0
Top eight	80.4	Top eight	74.1	Top eight	91.7
Top twelve	90.8	Top twelve	84.3	Top twelve	97.0

Note: Northwest's workers were on strike for part of 1978. Data for 1987 reflects mergers of American with Air California and USAir with Piedmont and PSA, even though operations were not affected for the entire year.
*Continental acquired People Express, Frontier, and New York Air, all discount airlines.
†Delta acquired Western.
‡TWA acquired Ozark.
Source: Congressional Budget Office, *Policies for the Deregulated Airline Industry* (Washington, D.C.: U.S. Government Printing Office, July 1988), p. 15.

Table 3–6   Dominance at Selected Airports, 1988

Airports	Airline Shares of Passengers
Atlanta	Delta 58%, Eastern 35%
Chicago	United 50%, American 30%
Denver	United 44%, Continental 41%
St. Louis	TWA 82%
Detroit	Northwest 60%
Pittsburgh	US Air 85%
Dallas–Ft. Worth	American 64%, Delta 26%
Minneapolis	Northwest 78%
Charlotte, N.C.	US Air 92%
Salt Lake City	Delta 80%

Source: U.S. General Accounting Office, *Report on Airline Competition*, June 1989.

**Figure 3–5   The Trend in Airline Fares per Mile,
in Constant 1967 Values**
(Cents per Mile)

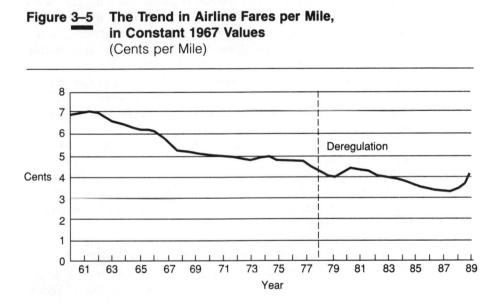

By 1986, there were rising complaints that de-regulation had been subverted, creating an unconstrained cartel. How competitive is the sector? Do its behavior and its performance fit monopoly patterns?

2. Defining the Markets. The airline sector poses especially sophisticated problems of market definition. Product features are relatively simple, while the geographic features are complex and debatable.

Product substitutability. Airline travel is highly distinct from its alternatives on virtually all routes over 200 miles. On some shorter routes, land travel may compete (e.g., driving or taking the Amtrak shuttle between New York and Washington, D.C., takes about as long as flying, in total).

Geographic substitutability. Geographic substitutability is a more complicated matter. For most observers, the whole of the United States is clearly not one big market. Other observers go to the other extreme, saying that *each* city-pair route is a separate market. Among hundreds of cities, there would be thousands of individual-route "markets." But that goes too far, because some city-pair routes overlap others quite closely; for example, New York–Denver can also be flown by New York–Chicago–Denver, New York–Detroit–Denver, New York–St. Louis–Denver, and so on, often at identical fares.

City pairs are often only parts of larger regional or multicity area travel markets. Yet there is no simple pattern to this. Many of the spokes on the airline hubs are true individual markets. In general, some of the main trunk routes have a degree of substitution by alternative routes, but most of the minor city-pair routes do not.

Major hub airports are also local markets of their own, because they control access along their spoke routes. Those hub markets, too, are not simple or rigid, because some of those spoke routes are paralleled by the spoke routes of *other* hubs.

Economic experts have therefore come to hold a complex view in defining markets within the industry. Many market edges are blurred, and for some parts of the sector no clear markets can be agreed on. Each case can be inspected on its merits, in terms of the availability of other flights that (1) take about as long, (2) are at similarly convenient times, and (3) involve similar ticket prices.

3. Structure and Degrees of Competition. *Shares of Traffic.* In this complex industry, the conditions are mixed. Some markets are dominated by one airline, as Table 3–6 shows for major hub cities. Trunk routes tend to have low concentration, especially if parallel routings are considered. Minor routes often have high concentration, and many spoke routes are virtual monopolies. As for the total concentration of U.S. air travel, it grossly understates the market power of the main airlines.

Conditions of Entry. Some experts and officials replaced mainstream concepts of competition with a fixation upon entry and contestability. During 1978–83, Kahn, Bailey, Baumol, and others urged that airplanes were "capital with wings." Airlines could expand instantly into any route where a dominant airline was making excess profit, making dominance irrelevant.

The obsession with contestability led officials to permit the new monopoly pricing and mergers.[33] But airline markets were never actually contestable, for several reasons. First, to enter the industry by creating a new airline company takes large funds and skills and a long time to build reputation and attract staff. The entrants of 1978–85 have been eliminated, and entry into the sector has been virtually closed since about 1984.

Second, entry into major airports is blocked, because boarding gates and time slots are already taken by the dominant airlines. Little airport expansion is planned, and dominant airlines will undoubtedly control most of any new capacity.

Also, new entry is met by sharp retaliation. It usually takes months to develop profitable repeat-business clientele for new routes, while rivals' fares can easily be cut in minutes, to levels below the entrant's prices.

Third, American and United Airlines own the most widely used computer reservations systems, which have helped them steer travel agents and passengers their way.[34] Combined with the dominance of major hub airports, the reservations systems add to the difficulty of small or new airlines.

In short, in 1978, officials replaced inefficient regulation with highly effective de-regulation, because the competition was strong and flexible. But during 1983–88, officials let the leading airlines take actions that have tended to suppress competition. Taken together, the industry's concentration, hubbing, entry barriers, and reservations systems have restricted competition. Large parts of the industry now appear to be ineffectively competitive. The policy choices to reduce the monopoly now are limited.

4. Pricing. Pricing has largely fitted tight-oligopoly patterns. The airlines tend to match each others' prices quickly, hold them for long intervals, and then change them quickly, with a minimum of continuous flexibility and uncertainty.

---

[33]See William J. Baumol, John C. Panzar, and Robert D. Willig, *Contestable Markets and the Theory of Industry Structure* (New York: Harcourt Brace Jovanovich, 1982); also Elizabeth E. Bailey and William J. Baumol, "Deregulation and the Theory of Contestable Markets," *Yale Journal on Regulation* 1 (1984), pp. 111–37, for admissions that airlines are not contestable after all.

[34]Bias is possible because the flight desirability hinges on departure times, the number of plane changes, the fare charged, the time interval between departure and arrival, and other features. It is easy to set the computer's priorities for listings so that they favor one airline over another. See the CAB's analysis of the problem in its *Report to Congress on Computer Reservations Systems* (Washington, D.C., 1983).

Since 1985, the leading airlines have adopted the same structure of fare discounts, the "supersavers" and "maxsavers," with similar restrictions on advance payments, Saturday night stayovers, and nonrefundability. No airline offers fare discounts on one-way flights. With all maverick airlines eliminated, aggressive price cutting has ended.

The pricing rules keep most business flyers from getting discounts, because they usually need last-minute reservations and don't stay over Saturdays. It is vacationers, who can plan ahead, who are best able to get large discounts. The pricing also leaves the airlines able to pinpoint any rival and cut deeply to hurt it. That helps to assure that no low-price airlines will be able to enter the industry.

Recently, *The New York Times* noted that "In general, the major airlines have decided to compete not by cutting fares but by increasing service. They now promote convenient departure times and frequency of service, as well as improvements in food and a better handling of baggage."[35] That precisely describes the indirect, ineffective competition that occurred under the CAB *before* 1977. But now there is no public regulation, and concentration is greater than it was then.

Fare discounts are common on over 80 percent of tickets, but the structure of the discounts now tightly segments the market, rather than giving free play for flexible price cutting. Each large airline has a large staff working on "yield management." They maximize the revenue from each flight by repeatedly adjusting the number of seats offered on discounts.[36] As the day of the flight approaches, the decisions may change hourly. This process approaches the extreme result of perfect price discrimination.

It tends to be anticompetitive for reasons explained in Chapter 10. It makes entry difficult, and it milks the customers for maximum revenue within a rigid pricing structure. The behavior is similar to that of a single monopolist. In addition, there have been anticompetitive pricing actions, directed against specific airlines. During 1980–85, large airlines eliminated some small rivals from the market by setting extremely low prices on key routes.[37]

---

[35]*New York Times,* "Air Fares Rise for Many Travelers as Big Carriers Dominate Market," March 15, 1988, pp. A1, D8.

[36]For example, American's yield managers "monitor and adjust the fare mixes on 1,600 daily flights as well as 538,000 future flights involving nearly 50 million passengers. Their work is hectic: A fare's average life span is two weeks, and, industrywide, about 200,000 fares change daily." *New York Times,* "The Art of Devising Air Fares," March 4, 1987, p. D1. The managers repeatedly adjust the number of seats on each plane that are available at the various discounts.

[37]For example, in June 1984, People Express entered the Newark–Minneapolis route, at fares of $99 on weekdays and $79 on evenings and weekends. Previously, the lowest fare had been $149, and the standard coach fare was $263. Northwest, the dominant firm, promptly cut its fares to $95 and $75, for service that was much better (in seating, meals, baggage handling, etc.). Therefore, Northwest was undercutting People's fare.

5. Performance. The effective competition of 1978–85 brought significant gains in airline load factors and relative ticket prices. The volume of air travel rose rapidly as more people could afford to fly. Yet the net benefits are debatable and rising market power since 1984 may have erased them.

Prices and Service Quality. Morrison and Winston attribute to de-regulation a 30 percent cut in ticket prices.[38] But Figure 3–5 suggests no such large impact. The downward price trend continued after 1978, but several factors were at work, and de-regulation's effect is not clear. Indeed, the severe fall in the price of oil during 1986–87 did not reduce ticket prices, and airline fares rose during 1988–90, reflecting the rising market power.

Moreover, the quality of service has fallen, perhaps even more than fares. Service quality includes several main elements.[39] All of these have deteriorated since 1978. Flying is now much like bus travel. Moreover, the cost reductions are partly from cutting pay rates, without reducing the real resources used.

Small-Airport Service. De-regulation always raises fears that small cities will lose service. It led to full-size jet aircraft being withdrawn from many smaller airports. However, new, small-craft commuter lines emerged to maintain or increase service in most cases, but their fares are higher; those on small-city routes have risen roughly 30 to 50 percent compared to those on the major routes.

6. In Summary. Airlines illustrate important aspects of antitrust, regulation, and de-regulation. Regulation unnecessarily blocked competition, causing predictable rises in costs. De-regulation proved successful at first, because the industry had small scale economies and entry was initially easy.

Desperately, People cut further, to $79 and $59; Northwest matched those cuts. People Express could not survive these deep cuts. Eventually, People disappeared, bought by Texas Air; Northwest merged with Republic and held over 80 percent of traffic into Minneapolis; and its fares rose sharply.

See Melvin A. Brenner, James O. Leet, and Elihu Schott, *Airline Deregulation* (Westport, Conn.: Eno Foundation for Transportation, Inc., 1985); Melvin A. Brenner, "Airline Deregulation—A Case Study in Public Policy Failure," *Transportation Law Journal* 16, no. 2 (1988), pp. 179–228; and Brenner, "Rejoinder to Comments by Alfred Kahn," *ibid.*, pp. 253–62; *Consumer Reports*, "The Big Trouble with Air Travel," June 1988, pp. 362–67; and F. Spencer and F. Cassell, *Eight Years of U.S. Airline Deregulation* (Evanston, Ill.: Transportation Center of Northwestern University, 1987).

[38]Morrison, Steven and Clifford Winston, *The Economic Effects of Airline Deregulation* (Washington, D.C.: Brookings Institution, 1986).

[39]They include the time interval taken by the flight (including time spent at the airport checking in), the risk of missing flights or connections, the risk of delay or loss of baggage, the crowding in lines and in the plane itself, and the general quality of the experience.

Leading airlines then reasserted control, and officials, under mistaken ideas of contestability, permitted dominance and rigid pricing structures to emerge. It seems that the problems cannot now be removed by antitrust, and re-regulation would scarcely be effective.

2. Long-Distance Telephone Service

Until it was divided up in the spectacular divestiture of the Bell System in January 1984, the American Telephone & Telegraph Company was the world's largest private enterprise.[40] It was also this century-old firm that had controlled nearly all of the telephone sector in the United States for over seven decades.

In that divestiture, forced by a successful antitrust action by the U.S. government, AT&T kept (1) its virtual monopoly of U.S. long-distance telephone traffic in the United States, (2) its research arm (Bell Laboratories), and (3) Western Electric Co., its wholly owned firm that had monopolized the supply of equipment to the Bell operating systems.

The long-distance telephone market is our topic here, because AT&T's continued dominance of it provides one of the leading U.S. examples of dominance in a large, rapidly growing market. It also poses a leading policy question: When is competition effective enough to permit a removal of all regulation?

AT&T's total (but regulated) monopoly in long-distance service was subjected to new competition in the 1970s, as MCI, GTE-Sprint (now US Sprint), and a few others forced their way in under new regulatory policies. But AT&T fiercely resisted these new competitors, and, as of 1990, AT&T still held over 70 percent of total traffic. As dominant firms do, AT&T claimed to be under severe pressure and risk from its little rivals, and, by 1986, it began to demand full de-regulation. The little rivals claimed to be small and vulnerable, in need of continued protection. By 1989, U.S. regulators had loosened most restraints and were considering removing all of them.

1. The Market. The extent of this market is open to debate. At its broadest, it would be a single market, embracing all long-distance traffic by residences and all sizes and types of businesses. Narrower market definitions are possible, by types of users, types of messages,

---

[40]Among numerous books on the AT&T divestiture, see Peter Temin, *The Fall of the Bell System* (Cambridge: Cambridge University Press, 1987); Alvin von Auw, *Heritage and Destiny: Reflections on the Bell System in Transition* (New York: Praeger Publishers, 1983); and David S. Evans, ed., *Breaking Up Bell* (New York Elsevier–North Holland, 1983). See also Paul W. MacAvoy and Kenneth Robinson, "Winning by Losing: The AT&T Settlement and Its Impact on Telecommunications," *Yale Journal on Regulation* 1 (1983), pp. 1–42.

and geographic regions. The market is segmented to some degree, because large-scale business traffic does have different characteristics than small-scale residential use. And 800-line service (free to those calling in) has still further differences.

All of the significant firms (mainly AT&T, MCI, and Sprint) compete across the range of customers, message types, and regions. Therefore, all of the parts of the market are linked by the firms' larger strategies, as they compete broadly. Moreover, all customers of each company share basically the same capacity as they use the local systems for access. Altogether, it is safest to proceed as if there is one broad market for long-distance service.

2. Structure. AT&T's share of all long-distance revenue has decreased from 100 percent before 1970 down to about 90 percent by 1980 to about 70–75 percent in 1990. MCI and US Sprint are "second-tier" firms, with about 12 and 8 percent, respectively. "Third-tier" firms are very small, with none above 2 percent. AT&T continues to hold clear dominance.

AT&T has been highly profitable, while the small rivals have been only marginally profitable in most recent years. The emerging structure is a dominant-firm/tight-oligopoly situation, with the two small rivals becoming more passive. The further decline of AT&T's market share is not at all assured.

3. Determinants. Long-distance service involves several components: (1) city-based systems connecting individual customers ("the local loop"), (2) intercity transmission, by wires, satellites, optical fibers, lasers, or other means, and (3) coordinated switching to complete and hold the connections. Until the 1970s, all of these elements were thought to be parts of a necessary natural monopoly, providing a single, coordinated national network in the Bell System. Bell System officials urged that view, and they sought to extend control to all related activities, such as the new transmission technologies, data transmission, burglar alarm systems, and the like.

However, by 1968, the Federal Communications Commission (FCC) recognized that most or all of the market was becoming naturally competitive. Other companies could develop intercity facilities and handle traffic at costs below AT&T's costs, but they needed access to local Bell systems so as to connect to individual customers. The Bell System simply prohibited this crucial "interconnection" until the FCC (ultimately backed up by the U.S. Supreme Court) forced it to give access in the 1970s.

In the 1980s, the small competitors demonstrated that they can establish their own intercity networks, in parallel with AT&T's capacity and often at lower costs. The market is naturally competitive, as long as city-based interconnection is open and fair. That crucial link was assisted by dividing the Bell System in 1984, which separated the local Bell monopolies from AT&T. Those newly independent local firms (the "baby Bells") no longer serve AT&T's old interest in blocking competition. In contrast, they have now sought to enter the lucrative long-distance market themselves, in competition with AT&T, but, so far, the judge supervising the divestiture has prevented that. The baby Bells would have incentives to control interconnection and block MCI, Sprint, etc., to their own advantage. Therefore, the baby Bells might exclude every other supplier, including even AT&T.

This risk might be worth taking, because the baby Bells would be a powerful source of new competition, able to compete strongly with AT&T's dominance. If MCI, Sprint, and others do not provide effective competition against AT&T, then the baby Bells may be needed. Policies would then be needed to prevent them from controlling the gateways to local interconnection.

4. Pricing. The small entrants have set prices below AT&T's rates, initially by 30 to 50 percent. Recently, the gap has narrowed so that now the prices are largely identical, except for special discounts. Until 1989, the FCC continued to regulate AT&T, keeping it from fully matching the specific price discounts given to get good customers. The price gaps permitted MCI, Sprint, and others to get started, and their rising quality of service enabled them to narrow the discounts while still growing. Therefore, the three main firms—AT&T, MCI, and Sprint—have increasingly behaved like a three-firm oligopoly, without severe price differences.

Whether AT&T will be permitted to give discounts freely is the critical question now pending. Such price discrimination would enable AT&T to pinpoint the most lucrative customers and try to obtain them, without cutting prices to others. In 1989, the FCC applied a new "price cap" method in place of the traditional rate-of-return regulation. It provides AT&T with virtually unlimited freedom to adjust prices to specific customers. Within months, AT&T established at least 30 major specific discount tariffs for large customers such as General Electric and Holiday Inns. This fits the classic behavior of dominant firms. It could enable AT&T to succeed in its aim of regaining market power and strengthening its dominance.

5. Performance. Because AT&T has been regulated since the 1930s (though mildly, on the whole), it is difficult to assess its performance. The Bell System's past innovation is widely recognized to have been slow, in line with its monopoly incentives. Bell Laboratories may have performed invention and patenting actively, but the practical use of those ideas in innovations were often restricted and delayed. Notable examples of slowness include rotary dialing (to replace live operators), microwave transmission, fiber optics, and the computerized electronic switching of calls. In the 1970s, AT&T was widely recognized to have narrow, obsolete technology in many of its products and service offerings.

6. In Summary. New competition has had the classic effects of reducing costs and prices, increasing innovation, and widening freedom of choice. A seeming natural monopoly has turned out to be naturally competitive, but dominance has remained, receding only gradually. In the early 1990s, the market is in a delicate phase, partly competitive but still subject to anticompetitive actions by AT&T if it is freed to apply them.

Normally, the dominant firm's market share would need to fall below 50 percent, with at least five strong rivals in place, before there could be confidence that competition is effective. The second tier of small firms will need to expand markedly in order to provide that balanced, competitive structure. Only if AT&T's customer base is vulnerable to rapid shifts will competition become fully effective. The next five years are likely to show whether that is true.

VI. LESSONS FOR POLICY

Altogether, the social costs of market power can be high. As a firm's market share goes above 20 percent, the social costs begin to accumulate. For monopolists, the costs are usually large. They may be offset in unusual cases, where technical scale economies, the conditions of innovation, or managerial skill depart from the norm. But the basic patterns hold.

One basic lesson for policy is that market shares above the 15–20 percent range—and concentration ratios above 60 percent—usually cause net social losses and may need policy treatment.

Another lesson is that the strictness of policy limits should be related directly to the firms' market shares. Dominant firms, in particular, need to meet tighter standards of competitive behavior, because they can so easily eliminate lesser firms that are otherwise comparably efficient.

A *third* lesson is that each case needs a weighing of costs and benefits, so the policy action can be carried just up to the right level (to be defined in the next chapter). The costs and benefits grow mainly out of the monopoly effects reviewed in this chapter.

Fourth, the costs of monopoly are usually especially high for pure monopolies and dominant firms. The correct policy effort, therefore, is to reduce the degree of monopoly in those cases—moving it down toward loose oligopoly. Practical debates are usually about marginal adjustments, not about radical changes.

Finally, most of the important problem industries have long existed and raised policy issues. Policy choices taken now are only one step in a long series of evolving actions. Few cases are ever "permanently" settled. Instead, policies are adjusted as conditions change, groping toward a reasonable balance in an uncertain world.

QUESTIONS FOR REVIEW

1. "Aggregate concentration rose before 1948 but has fallen since then." True?
2. "Changes in aggregate concentration tell little about the degree of competition in individual markets." True?
3. Are pecuniary economies of scale a major justification for actual concentration in most local markets?
4. "Competition rose during 1960–80 in the United States mainly because antitrust was cut back." True?
5. How could aggregate concentration increase after 1960 if individual market competition was rising strongly?
6. How might fading scale economies help explain the rise of competition after 1960?
7. In three markets of your choice, assess economies of scale and the degree of competition.
8. What trends in technology since 1900 may have tended to reduce minimum efficient scale (MES) in a wide range of industries?
9. Explain several ways in which governmental actions create positions of market power.
10. Discuss several instances in which market power has raised prices significantly.
11. Discuss two firms that fit the superior efficiency hypothesis and two firms that don't.
12. Which elements of the airline sector still contain significant market power?

C·H·A·P·T·E·R 4   Policy Choices and Biases

Before turning to actual policies, we need to know what defines good policy choices. Actual policies are quite fallible, because they are hammered out in a rugged political process, not in a pure setting of ideal choices. They are not applied unilaterally, the way a doctor selects and dictates a treatment for a patient. Policies may be inefficient or unfair, in varying degrees, as each interest group tries to bend political actions to suit their own interests.

Economists have some general rules for deriving good policies. The most familiar method is "cost-benefit analysis," which compares marginal costs and marginal benefits. The method has some defects, but it is a good starting point. Economists also have developed some specific theories that suggest when policies will systematically diverge from efficiency and fairness.

This chapter first presents the general cost-benefit conditions that help in defining efficient policy choices. Section I discusses the basic policy choice that is based on a comparison of the benefits and costs of reducing the effects of monopoly. Next, Section II presents a simple cost-benefit analysis. Section III explains several reasons that policies may be biased toward being too strict or too lenient. Section IV presents the basic economic features of the policy agencies and legal processes. Finally, an appendix at the end of the chapter gives students advice on designing and carrying out research for term papers on the topics covered in this book.

Figure 4–1   Simple Monopoly Effect on Efficiency

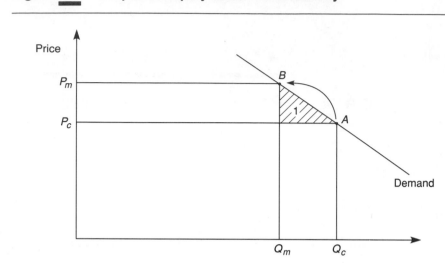

I. THE COSTS AND BENEFITS OF MONOPOLY

The basic policy choices are made by comparing: (1) the benefits gained by reducing monopoly's impacts with (2) the possible costs incurred in doing so. This comparison has always been recognized as the basic issue, although Williamson was the first to embody it in the form shown in Figure 4–1.[1] The comparison applies to the broad range of antitrust and regulatory policies, though in slightly different forms.

The demand conditions are shown by the demand curve, and supply conditions (not shown) involve constant average and marginal costs. The possible competitive price-output result is at point *A*, where supply (the sum of the individual firms' marginal cost curves) equals demand. As noted in Chapter 2, price equals marginal costs, and therefore allocation is efficient.

Point *B* illustrates a monopoly result, with price higher and output lower. Triangle 1 shows the misallocation burden caused by the loss of consumer surplus (recall this from Chapter 2). If antitrust or regulatory actions can get the price down to the competitive level, then they would deliver the benefit shown by Triangle 1. Estimates of triangles such as this one have usually turned out to be rather small: Mainstream estimates are in the range of 1 to 4 percent of sales revenue, while Chicago-UCLA estimates are usually closer to one-tenth of one percent.

---

[1]Oliver E. Williamson, "Economies as an Antitrust Defense: The Welfare Tradeoffs," *American Economic Review* 58 (March 1968), pp. 18–34, with a later correction, *American Economic Review* 59 (December 1969), pp. 954–59.

Figure 4–2   Additional Analysis of Monopoly's Effects

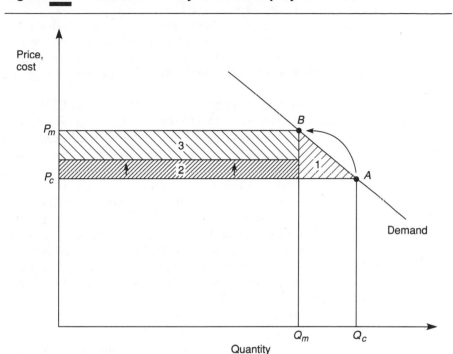

Because they regard this triangle as the only *economic* cost of monopoly, Chicago-UCLA supporters conclude their discussion at this point by saying that monopoly causes little harm. In their view, policies to reduce monopoly therefore cannot provide significant benefits.

However, monopoly may indeed have additional effects, even though Chicago-UCLA advocates disregard them. X-inefficiency may occur, shown by the upward shift of the supply curve in Figure 4–2. The shaded bar labeled 2 is a loss. Even if costs are raised only by several percentage points, that rise may easily exceed the triangle.

Innovation may be retarded by monopoly, which would also cause the supply curve to shift up higher than it would otherwise be. That would add to the loss represented by the shaded area 2. Also, advertising may be increased, if there is tight oligopoly that engages in mutually cancelling stand-off advertising. That would be a further waste of resources.

Inequity may also occur as the few monopolists gain wealth at the expense of the many consumers. That shift is shown by the shaded area 3. It is not a waste of resources comparable to those just noted, but it is a social cost if the disequalizing violates standards of fairness. And finally, the larger costs of monopoly include the reduction in freedom of choice and the loss of competition itself.

So overcoming the loss to consumers represented by Triangle 1 is merely the first part of a series of benefits that policies to reduce monopoly may deliver. Their relative and total size is a matter of continuing debate. But if they are larger, then extensive policies to obtain them may be justified.

However, there may be offsetting benefits, which Chicago-UCLA advocates have particularly stressed. First, there may be economies of scale or mergers may achieve economies by bringing mediocre firms under more efficient management. Second, the monopoly may reflect superior performance, as noted in Chapter 2. Those cost gains would be illustrated by down-shifts in the supply curves in Figures 4–1 and 4–2. Those down-shifts might offset the up-shifts from X-inefficiency, retarded innovation, and the rest.

Most economists doubt that these down-shifts are very large in most cases. Instead, the monopoly costs are likely to be substantial. Accordingly, mainstream economists generally support antitrust policies and the regulation of genuine natural monopolies. Chicago-UCLA supporters have the reverse perspective. They see large benefits from monopoly and small costs. Hence, they regularly advise accepting monopoly by easing antitrust and removing regulation.

In reaching your own judgments, the basic concepts are the same regardless of your evaluations of the facts. However, there are more complex features that involve the costs and benefits of the policy tools themselves.

II. DEFINING OPTIMAL POLICIES

1. Cost-Benefit Analysis

The general approach for defining efficient policy choices is called *cost-benefit analysis*.[2] It is merely a specialized version of all rational economic choices. Recall that each *private* economic action provides benefits, usually in the form of a good that people will pay money for. The same action will also incur costs: the effort and resources needed to produce the good. Efficient economic decisions will carry production up to the level where the marginal benefits just equal marginal costs, as we noted in Chapter 2. The marginal unit is just worth its cost.

---

[2]See E. J. Mishan, *Cost-Benefit Analysis* (New York: Praeger Publishers, 1976); and Dennis C. Mueller, *Public Choice* (Cambridge, Eng.: Cambridge University Press, 1979).

Figure 4–3   Simple Cost-Benefit Analysis

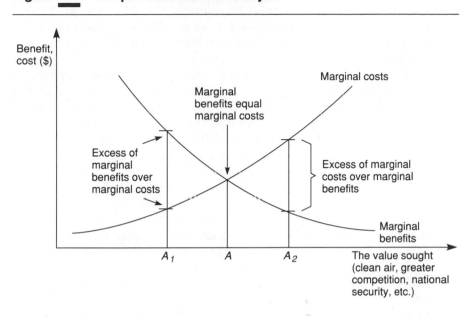

Public policy choices face exactly the same criterion of efficiency: Each action should be carried out up to the level where its marginal benefits just equal its marginal costs. Here the benefits are the public's benefits that arise when monopoly's effects are prevented: greater efficiency, lower prices, more rapid innovation, and other desirable goals. If the action is wise, then the public reaps these benefits through the improved performance of the economy.

There are also policy costs to consider. They are mainly incurred by the public in paying for the agency to take the action (other costs are discussed below). Agencies use resources (in staff members' salaries and other costs) in applying their policies. For example, the antitrust chief considers whether to prosecute five bakers in St. Louis for fixing the prices of their bread. It is a marginal case among 40 other small price-fixing cases. This case will cost $10,000 to carry out (in working time, travel, and so on), and it will only improve conditions in one small market. Ideally, the official weighs the benefits and costs, at least approximately, in such marginal cases and decides to take on those that have the larger yield. In practice, the judgments may be faulty or the agencies may be given either too many or too few resources.

The choice is illustrated in Figure 4–3. At point *A*, the marginal benefits of added degrees of competition will just equal their costs. Any level below *A* is too little; at *A₁*, for example, the marginal benefits of doing more are well above the marginal cost. Therefore, doing more is worth it at the margin. That holds for successive levels up to A. Beyond A, action is not worth it. At A_2, for instance, the marginal cost is far above the marginal benefits. Action, therefore, should be cut back, step by step, to level A.

Cost-benefit analysis has faults and limits. The people reaping the benefits are often different from those bearing the costs, and so the comparison is not direct. Should group A be required to pay for actions that give benefits only to group B? This problem is critical when environmental regulations impose costs on polluters in order to reduce harms to other citizens. The workers and owners of the polluting businesses fiercely resist the burdens, as when smoke-emitting midwestern businesses must incur costs to give cleaner air for New Englanders.

In antitrust and regulation, this problem is often not significant. The actions are generally paid for by the general taxpayers, and the benefits (in lower prices and better products) are also widely spread among the consuming public.

Another problem of cost-benefit analysis is that the actual measures of costs and benefits are often rough and uncertain. Therefore, as in Figure 4–2, the wide bands illustrate the range of estimates of the values. For example, the splitting up of the Bell System in 1984 still stimulates disputes over the sizes of the costs and benefits. And the Reagan shift in antitrust policies in the 1980s reflected the Chicago-UCLA school's radically lower estimates of the benefits of antitrust, compared to mainstream evaluations. Those debates continue. You will need to learn to make your own estimates and recognize the uncertainties and disputes.

2. Design and Amount

Policy choices have two main elements: *design* and *amount*. Each policy's *design* is to be as close to ideal as possible. An ideal design attains a maximum of benefits for a given amount of cost. That will involve applying the correct set of incentives to the firm and will minimize its efforts to resist and to induce its behavior to fit optimal lines. For example, an antitrust treatment of a monopolist might deftly negotiate compliance at little cost; or, instead, the officials might launch a vast, costly court battle that eventually achieves little.

The best-designed policy is then to be carried out to the efficient *amount*, just up to the efficient margin—or, in plainer terms, to be just strict enough. The efficient outcome, a balance between policy costs and benefits, is illustrated at A in Figure 4–3 for any public policy (it could be an antitrust or regulatory action, or funds for a public enterprise or for pollution control).

Figure 4–4   Cost-Benefit Choices Can Be Uncertain When the Amounts Are Uncertain

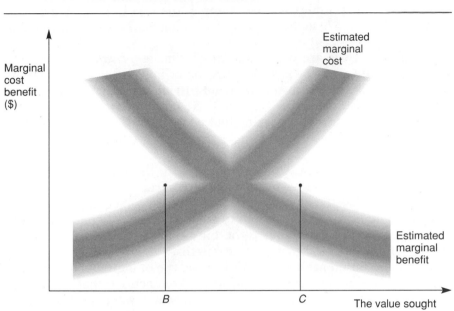

These concepts are rarely applied precisely in practice; data are often lacking, and the terms are not familiar to most officials. The choice often appears, as in Figure 4–4, with wide bands of estimated possible values for costs and benefits. A person who estimates benefits low and costs high will choose point *B,* with little policy effort. But one who rates benefits high and costs low will urge level *C,* which is far more ambitious. In general, Chicago-UCLA analysts lean toward point-*B* results, with minimum action, while others lean toward higher results. Both *B* and *C* can appear to be correct, and there may be intense debate concerning them. Intelligent decisions about policies proceed *as if* they were fitting these logical concepts, using the best evidence at hand. They informally weigh the main good effects against the likely costs and try to go as far as seems "reasonable." If done consistently, such rough judgments often will come close to the patterns given by complete analysis. They are an informal but often effective way of accomplishing cost-benefit analysis.

3. Costs of Policies

Now we need to consider the costs of policies in more detail. Certain elements of cost are common to all policies.

1. **Direct** costs are the dollar budgets spent for public agencies. They can be substantial. Yet some agencies have tiny budgets, compared to the interests they supervise; for example, the two U.S. antitrust agencies spend about $70 million yearly in treating markets totalling at least $3 trillion of gross national product.

2. **Indirect costs** are of several kinds. One is *private-firm response costs*. They are spent by firms in resisting or influencing public actions, or both. For example, a firm may spend $10 million in defending against an antitrust case that the FTC spends $1 million on. Or a utility may spend $2 million on a rate hearing that costs the regulatory commission $300,000 to hold. Such private costs are often a multiple of the direct public costs.

Another indirect cost is **public supervision:** the scarce ability of the political process to evaluate and to exert control in the public interest. Information is costly, and the ability of citizens to acquire it, weigh it, and act upon it has high opportunity costs. This social control process, such as it may be, is of course the only one we have. It needs to be used sparingly, in ways that fit its strengths.

Costs of interference are the third main type of indirect cost. Policies set limits, preventing some private firms from actions that they would prefer to take. Firms may also lose efficiency when profits are restrained. The result is often some loss of productivity among the constrained firms. Of course, a well-designed policy can also cause *increases* in the efficiency of firms.

These effects vary from case to case; often, too, they are hard to measure and predict. Therefore, they are often highly debatable.

III. CAUSES OF BIASES IN POLICIES

The fundamental fact is that policies evolve in a political process in which the targets of possible action are not passive. They participate, at all levels, in forming the policies. Business interests work hard in shaping the general laws of antitrust and regulation at the national and state levels. They also work to influence the officials appointed to run the agencies. And, in specific cases, the targets also act aggressively to argue their individual cases, to lobby in Congress or public debates, and to try other ways to achieve their goals.

Meanwhile, the groups benefiting from competition also seek to influence the laws, appointments, and specific case outcomes. Often these consumer and small-business interests are more diffuse than the target companies, so that consumer and small-business groups commonly mobilize more weakly than the larger companies do. Thus, IBM, a major newspaper chain, or a group of oil companies may often have more political effectiveness than masses of unorganized consumers or small businesses.

The possible biases can be clarified by (1) presenting several theories of regulation that explain defects in the way policies are applied, and (2) noting several specific economic elements that can distort the effects.

1. Theories of the Policy Process

In the ideal public agency, the officials would determine the optimal design and level of policies in each case and then apply them effectively. The agency would act unilaterally, applying legal powers— much as a local police department enforces "the law" or a doctor treats a patient.

However, real agencies depart from the ideal, often substantially. Several theories have been offered to explain the defects of "real" regulation.

1. Compromise. Agencies' policies are partly a form of compromise among the interests involved in each market: companies, consumers, workers, suppliers, and the like. These groups could thrash the matter out in Congress or in the courts by a pluralistic bargaining process. But an agency can often be more efficient by striking a balance. For example, an electric utility requests a regulatory commission to permit higher prices to raise its profit rate to 12 percent. The commission holds hearings at which consumer groups assert that 8 percent is enough. The commission chooses 10 percent as a fair balance. The matter could have been fought out in Congress, but it would have taken long, complex hearings and stirred great emotion and struggle. Hundreds of such hearings would clog Congress; the commission dispatches them more briskly and skillfully.

Many policy choices do appear to be compromises. Often the officials give other reasons for their choices, claiming that they have been determined by clear logical criteria, rather than by just striking a balance. But economists look for the real effects beneath the surface verbiage and often find a mere attempt to split the difference or to minimize political trouble.

Compromise need not be "wrong," either as an approach or a result. Most optimal decisions contain at least some element of compromise. And indeed, compromise is often optimal in reconciling conflicting claims. At any rate, compromise is a conceptual basis different from ideal, unilateral control by authorities.

2. Capture. Agencies can come under the control of the firms that they supposedly control.[3] The degree of capture can vary, but some observers believe that it is usually nearly complete. If so, the agency acts merely as a tool of the firms. Compared to compromise, this basis treats the agency as one-sided and passive, rather than responsive to many influences.

The capture concept is consistent with both right-wing and left-wing views: with Chicago-UCLA-school neoliberal opinions and with Marxian theories that the state is merely the arm of capitalist interests. A capture theory is also consistent with a third, more cynical, view: that many officials are simply corrupted by the firms. Such corruption, however, is not necessary for capture. Indeed, the managers of captured agencies often have high personal standards of integrity.

In practice, capture does occur frequently, in at least some degree. Several examples of this will appear later in this book. Flagrant capture often evokes corrective actions, via new appointees or policies. And there are clear cases where agencies' actions are opposite to captive behavior. Therefore, the capture theory is useful, but it is short of being a general explanation.

3. Inefficiency and Lags. Another theory is that agencies develop as much bureaucratic fat and slowness as is permitted. Officials seek to build empires, to minimize their own risk, and to prolong their careers. Accordingly, the agencies may make mistakes and operate poorly because of sheer ineptitude and bureaucracy.

This theory, too, has some validity. Nearly all large bureaucracies—private and public—develop some X-inefficiency. Economists, therefore, look skeptically at the larger policy departments (such as the U.S. Departments of Energy and Interior) and expect smaller, streamlined agencies to perform better. In practice, there are examples at both extremes, plus many cases in the middle range. Policies are often slow or wrong because of bureaucratic incompetence, rather than (or as well as) because of compromise or capture.

Altogether, the underlying realities influencing the policy agencies can lead to sharp distortions from ideal results. Yet these forces are often weak, absent, or mutually offsetting. Some agencies have performed very close to the ideal patterns during some periods, and so there is no reason to regard distortions as inevitable or universal.

---

[3]For theories of how policies may merely reflect interest-group influences, see George J. Stigler, "The Theory of Economic Regulation," *Bell Journal of Economics* 2 (Spring 1971), pp. 3–21; Sam Peltzman, "Toward a More General Theory of Regulation," *Journal of Law and Economics* 19 (August 1976), pp. 211–42; and William F. Shughart II, *Antitrust Policy and Interest-Group Politics* (Westport, Conn.: Quorum Books, 1990).

2. Specific Causes of Economic Distortions in Policies

On a more technical level, policies are subject to certain specific biases, which often cause predictable distortions. The main such biases are as follows.

1. Spending What Is at Stake. The firm being treated by a policy will naturally consider how much money it should spend on its own efforts to resist (that is, to bend the policy to its own interests). As a general rule: *The rational firm will ultimately be willing to spend as much as the profits at stake, in order to protect those profits*. The resulting spending may be large, where the profits at stake are large. For example, a firm making $20 million a year in monopoly profits would, as a sound, routine business decision, be willing to spend up to that $20 million amount in legal and other costs in defending them against antitrust policies that would remove the monopoly power. Usually, it is not necessary to spend the full amount, but the firm's incentives make it ready to do so. The same logic applies to actions toward other policies, such as regulation, subsidies, and exemptions.

Note, therefore, that the resulting spending can dissipate in advance the very benefits that the policy is intended to recapture for the sake of consumers and the public. Moreover, the firm can *threaten* to eliminate all of those benefits by overspending on its resistance.[4] If that threat deters the agency from acting, then it frustrates the policy action in advance! Even if the firm does not actually spend away the amount at stake, the incentives still encourage huge resistance efforts. That spending, or the threat of it, can effectively discourage the public agency from trying to enforce the policy.

2. Time Bias. Two biases related to time are frequently important. *First:* Often one side (the agency or the firm) can impose delay on the proceedings and gain benefits from doing so. The stalling then distorts the outcome. Such a bias from "having time on your side" can sharply affect both antitrust and regulation, as we will see. Often the bias is unnecessary; it could be prevented if specific rules or procedures could be so altered that time is on no one's side.

Second: The time bias is strengthened by the brevity of most policymakers' tenure. New policies often require at least 3 years to prepare and at least 10 years for benefits to be fully harvested. Yet most top antitrust and regulatory decision makers are in office less than four years. Their inexperience often neutralizes them for the first year or

---

[4]For example, "If you sue us to remove our dominance, we will spend whatever it takes to win."

two, when they are learning the ropes. They commonly apply a high rate of time preference in their eagerness to get results. This myopia favors quick, visible, and shallow steps, rather than basic ones. It also makes the firms' advantage of having time on their side particularly strong.

3. Information Bias. Public agencies need complete and timely information on sensitive variables (market shares, prices, costs, innovation choices, competitive tactics, and alternative treatments), both past and future, but they often lack it. Such information is known intimately by firms, and when it endangers their profits, it will naturally be secreted. Because firms also try to influence public fact-gathering policies, the data put out in the public realm are often scanty. This can cause a bias in specific policy choices, as well as in the general evaluation of policy needs and urgency.

4. In Summary. Taken altogether, these biases have three effects. First, industrial policies are less complete than they would otherwise be, because the problems and potential yields are underestimated. Second, whole problems, areas, and cases are probably slighted, because of ignorance. Third, more agency resources have to be spent on mere fact gathering than a neutral information state would require. These biases may cumulate to large distortions.

These possible distortions add up to an impressive array, and some analysts react by rejecting virtually all policy actions. Thus, the Chicago-UCLA view that markets generally give good results, except when the state interferes, reflects estimates that monopoly's net harms are small, compared to the costs imposed by government actions. There are many examples of mistaken policies, and so students need to be cautious and skeptical on all points.

Mainstream judgments, on the other hand, generally find the policy costs to be less severe and often very low. Moreover, the biases may generally tend to suppress procompetitive actions. Accordingly, there may be a sound general case for enlarging antimonopoly policies in order to overcome consistent biases against them.

At any rate, experts learn to approach all policies and claims skeptically, looking for their real economic content and effects. One will need to use mature judgment as well as objective indicators, because the conditions are often complex and not well measured.

IV. THE SETTING FOR POLICIES

Certain features of the laws, executive agencies, legislatures, and the courts have important effects on the policies toward business.

1. The Law

Laws are simply rules of the game. They (1) define certain actions, (2) attach rewards or penalties to them, and (3) specify the means for enforcement. The executive, legislative, and judicial branches often share in the origins of law, and all three are involved in applying every important law. The executive agencies choose how—and how extensively—to enforce laws (total enforcement is commonly impossible or absurd). Legislatures control the agencies' funds and modify the laws repeatedly. The courts interpret, and often reject, parts or all of a law.

Therefore, "the law" is often a core of legal phrases embedded in a tissue of informal customs and actions that really control what is done. The bigger the stakes, the more complex are the controversies about what the law "really is." The struggles often shift freely among the government units as the parties at interest seek their best chances one way and another, skirmish by skirmish.

So the formal divisions among the three branches of government often obscure the real interactions. Overlap and conflicts among official bodies occur frequently. Moreover, most agencies are managed by lawyers. They have been trained to *advocate* one side and win, rather than to weigh social interests and create balanced solutions. They may have economic advisers and staff economists, but these may be from an extremist school and their advice may be wrong and/or ignored.

2. Executive Agencies

These units apply the policies, using resources and powers voted by the legislatures. Their heads are usually political appointees, often with only modest technical experience. They hold office only briefly, usually less than three years.

The body of the agency is staffed by career experts, who provide continuity. Their salaries are modest, markedly lower than those of the private lawyers they contend with. On occasion, agency staff members are skilled, ample in numbers, and tenacious. But often, instead, career staff members are outnumbered and outmaneuvered.

Agency resources come from the legislature, which can exert control by the purse, by hearings, or by changing the law itself (perhaps even abolishing or reorganizing the agency). These resources are usually scarce, and so it is important to allocate them carefully. Much agency effort goes to persuading the legislature and higher executive officials, as well as to making formal presentations in the courts—and simply to the minutiae of keeping the agency in being.[5]

---

[5]Usually, small matters with deadlines force aside large issues that can be postponed. This situation, a Gresham's Law of Public Policy, appears to be universal and will recur throughout this book.

3. Legislatures

Legislators are politicians whose trade is compromise and whose aim is to get re-elected. They are part of an imperfect process. Legislators' formal actions (votes, bills, and so on) are always for public display, and their real intent and effect are often hidden. Bills or votes *to do X* are often done really *to prevent Y* (a bigger step) from being done. Moreover, action is piecemeal. Rarely are industrial policies appraised and revised broadly. Finally, legislative rules provide many points for applying influence: at the committee stage, in one house, in the other house, in joint committee, at final votes; *and* then in authorizing funds; *and then* appropriating funds in both houses. Legislatures, therefore, strongly *reflect* the established pattern of interests, especially in dealing with industrial policies. Once firms gain monopoly power, they have many opportunities to protect it by influencing the government.

4. Courts

The three tiers of the federal courts—district courts, appeals courts, and the Supreme Court—handle most of the important industrial policy cases. Judges have small resources (their few clerks do much of the research and drafting). Their chief resource—courtroom time—is usually overburdened.

An aggrieved party (the plaintiff) files suit in the appropriate district court. Major cases are usually tried in New York, Chicago, or Los Angeles, where the defendant's company headquarters usually are. Trial is held after all issues and facts needed in the case have been prepared. The basic rule is: There are to be no surprises at trial, only reasoned arguments and facts. All facts and arguments to be used by either side are disclosed *before* the trial itself begins. In such pretrial discovery, the two sides fire lengthy lists of questions ("interrogatories") at each other, both to get facts and often to confuse or delay. This pretrial activity often takes even more than the usual three-year delay on most federal court calendars. Either side can demand a trial by jury, rather than by the judge alone. Complex cases usually are tried and decided by judges; but in damage cases (for example, claims of unfair competition or monopoly damages), one side usually prefers appealing to a jury.

Trial may be lengthy, involving masses of documentation and ranks of expert witnesses on both sides. It is supposed to cover all issues of fact. Economists are frequently brought in to testify that the market is (or isn't) competitive or that scale economies are (or aren't) important. In major cases, decision by the judge often takes another several months.

Figure 4–5   The Basic Policy Sequence

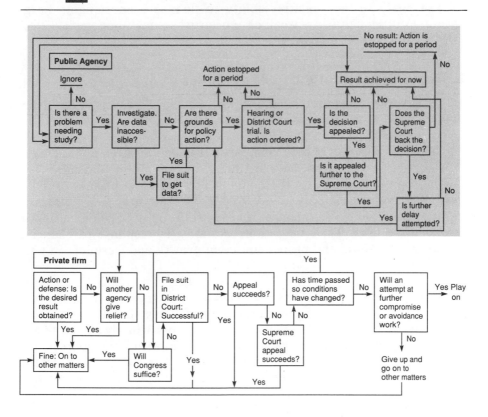

Either side may appeal. The appeals court hears only a brief discussion of legal points by both sides; the original trial record (often running to thousands of pages) contains the facts. Further appeal to the Supreme Court is also possible. The delay is often a year before each appeal hearing and half a year more before the decision is given out.

The upper courts can declare for either side—revise the issues or send the case back down to the district court, or both, for (1) retrial on some or all points or (2) a practical remedy. The whole sequence can take 10 or 15 years in complex cases, as each side exhausts its chances to win or delay; see Figure 4–5. At any point, a compromise may be reached or relief may be obtained from some other quarter (for example, getting Congress—or a city council—to change the law directly).

This slow process can be favorable for airing facts, probing issues, and resolving many disputes, but it can be abused. There are many ways of stalling for tactical advantage. The merits of the two sides often do not relate to their relative ability to finance a court fight: Large resources often can win a weak case or crush a small opponent.

5. Three Features of the Policy Process

In these various forums, the substance of policies evolves. Three special features of the process need to be stressed.

1.   The Law Grows. The economy evolves new business methods and new social interests. New ways are devised to get around old rules. The law must grow to deal with these and to reconcile new clashes of interests. This growth can occur by rewriting the laws or by new actions in enforcing the old ones. Agencies and courts usually have discretion in applying the laws. Their new interpretations, in response to changing issues, are a natural and proper source of growth and freshness in public policies.

2. Agency Power Is Less Than It Seems. Many laws set absolute prohibitions on activities, results, or stages of being, but the limits are usually diluted in practice. The agency's powers will always be tested if it challenges important private interests. Even with full resources, the agency will need support from above, and this often wavers. Therefore, the ultimate *power* to carry out a balanced and optimal economic policy is problematical.

3. Due Process. Due process is the phrase covering all those customs and explicit rules that try to give every side its say. But due process is not a magic wand. *First,* the hearing itself does not guarantee a fair result. A process that seems to air all interests may, instead, be simply a device for deflating social protest or for deceiving the parties into believing that they have been listened to. *Second,* due process takes time. There often are time biases, favoring one side or the other. Therefore, due process can inherently tip the outcome, or be deliberately abused.

Third, due process is not free. It takes resources, including legal talent, research efforts, and simply the time and attention absorbed in mounting and winning one's fight. One side or the other may be better able to bear these costs, or to use them to have its way. *Fourth,* due process proceeds within the setting provided by existing law. If the need is to go outside current law and develop new treatments, due process in itself does not bring it about.

6. Comparing Formal with Actual Policies

Given such biases and intricacies in the policy process, actual policies will often diverge from their formal roles. A genuine social need often causes a formal treatment to be put on the books. But enforcement is less than complete, and the true effect can be well short of the supposed effect. Though monopoly (or excess utility profits, or price fixing, or patent abuses, and such) is illegal, it is only partly likely to be detected, treated, and remedied. How likely? That is what you will learn to evaluate for yourself in the following chapters.

QUESTIONS FOR REVIEW

1. "An agency's ability to act depends on its legal powers as well as its resources." True?
2. "Monopoly is against the law, just as speeding and shoplifting are. Therefore, monopoly has been eliminated." True?
3. "If a policy offers social benefits, then it certainly should be carried out." True?
4. Which of the following cause biases in policies: (a) an uneven burden of proof, (b) having time on one side, (c) taxes on private profits, (d) lack of information about market conditions, and (e) intensive private lobbying?
5. " 'Optimal' policies generally have marginal social benefits in line with marginal social costs." True?
6. "Cost-benefit analysis usually provides officials with precise answers to policy questions." True?
7. "A precedent-setting case can have much larger ultimate benefits than its own payoff provides." True?
8. "Profit taxes encourage firms to resist public policies much less fiercely." True?
9. "All lobbying by business groups tends to distort public policies away from good patterns." True?
10. Is slowness in court processes always bad?
11. How might one judge if an agency's tasks were in line with its resources?
12. What main defects is cost-benefit analysis likely to have in guiding industrial policies?
13. Would a "perfect" democratic political process yield optimal policies, or at least reasonable approximations of them?

APPENDIX: METHODS AND SOURCES FOR TERM PAPERS

Approaches

Usually, the good term paper focuses on a specific topic that you are interested in and willing to explore. You define the issue, read the main sources in the literature, decide what you can add by new analysis or measures, and then write it up in 10 to 20 pages. The project is a smaller version of the professional research and writing that appear in the literature itself. Your aims are (1) to think for yourself, reaching your own conclusions and (2) to show your skill in using the concepts fluently.

There are three main kinds of topics: general issues, specific policy tools or cases, and specific industries or sectors. Every part of this text offers issues that need further thinking and debate. Part of your task is to pick out an issue which stirs or irritates you, where new points or facts are needed. General issues include such points as: Has antitrust reduced industrial concentration? How does one define a "public utility?" What concept of "predatory pricing" is valid for use in antitrust actions?

Specific tools or cases might be approached as follows: Was the Alcoa decision (or Standard Oil, Von's Grocery, or DuPont cellophane, or another leading case of your choice) economically sound? What economic effects did the AT&T divestiture have? Were they positive, on balance? How tightly should horizontal merger limits be drawn? Do patents promoted competition or monopoly, ultimately? Which parts of the telephone industry still have "natural monopoly?" What policy changes might be appropriate for the airline industry?

The purpose of doing a paper is to practice the same steps that professionals do in their research—frame an issue, try to "solve" it with new hypotheses or evidence, and then write up the results. If the student does a first draft about two thirds through the course, the teacher can then give suggestions for revision or new work. This process of comments and revision is exactly what most expert articles and books (including this text) go through. The paper lets you take a position on an issue and restate it your way. That, too, is what research papers and monographs do. In your paper, the specific conclusions you reach are secondary. What matters is that you treat the issues carefully, with a professional degree of skill.

Sources

The main research sources for your papers are precisely those references that are given in the notes. They, in turn, often cite other books, articles, and reports that would be helpful. Usually, it is better to focus on one or two main books and a few articles, rather than to try to read all possible references. Your teacher can often suggest which references are most valuable.

The core sources are professional journal articles and monographs. The leading journals include the *Antitrust Bulletin,* the *Journal of Law & Economics* (with, generally, a Chicago-UCLA-school viewpoint), the *Antitrust Law & Economics Review,* the *Yale Journal on Regulation,* and the *Journal of Regulation.* The National Regulatory Research Institute puts out frequent reports on utility matters, and *Regulation* offers Chicago-UCLA-oriented summaries of recent studies and actions. See the law journals of such ranking universities as Harvard, Yale, California at Berkeley, Chicago, Pennsylvania, Columbia, and Michigan, among many others.

There are many valuable books covering broad topics, as well as others dealing with specific industries and policies. Some of them are written from a strong point of view.

Broad coverage is found in:

Walter Adams, ed., *The Structure of American Industry,* 8th ed. (New York: Macmillan, 1990).

Walter Adams and James W. Brock, *The Bigness Complex* (New York: Pantheon Books, 1986).

Dominick T. Armentano, *Antitrust and Monopoly: Anatomy of a Policy Failure* (New York: John Wiley & Sons, 1982).

Robert H. Bork, *The Antitrust Paradox: A Policy at War with Itself* (New York: Basic Books, 1978).

Eleanor M. Fox and Lawrence A. Sullivan, *Cases and Materials on Antitrust* (St. Paul: West Publishing, 1989).

Walton Hamilton and Irene Till, *Antitrust in Action,* Monograph No. 16, Temporary National Economic Committee, Investigation of Economic Power (Washington, D.C.: U.S. Government Printing Office, 1940).

Alfred E. Kahn, *The Economics of Regulation,* 2 vols. (New York: John Wiley & Sons, 1971, reissued by the MIT Press, 1989).

Carl Kaysen and Donald F. Turner, *Antitrust Policy* (Cambridge, Mass.: Harvard University Press, 1959).

Arthur D. Neale and D. G. Goyder, *The Antitrust Laws of the United States,* 3d ed. (Cambridge: Cambridge University Press, 1980).

Leonard W. Weiss and Michael W. Klass, eds., *Regulatory Reform: What Really Happened* (Boston: Little, Brown, 1986).

Oliver E. Williamson, *Antitrust Economics* (Oxford: Basil Blackwell, 1987).

Books about more specific topics include:

Zoltan Acs, *The Changing Structure of the U.S. Economy: Lessons from the Steel Industry* (New York: Praeger, 1984).

Walter Adams and James W. Brock, *Dangerous Pursuits: Mergers and Acquisitions in the Age of Wall Street* (New York: Pantheon, 1989).

Elizabeth E. Bailey, David R. Graham, and Daniel P. Kaplan, *Deregulating the Airlines* (Cambridge, Mass.: MIT Press, 1985).

William Breit and Kenneth G. Elzinga, *The Antitrust Penalties* (New Haven: Yale University Press, 1976).

Kerry Cooper and Donald Fraser, *Banking Deregulation and the New Competition in Financial Services* (Cambridge, Mass.: Ballinger, 1984).

Andrew F. Daughety, ed., *Analytical Studies in Transport Economics* (Cambridge: Cambridge University Press, 1985).

Richard Thomas DeLamarter, *Big Blue: IBM's Use and Abuse of Power* (New York: Dodd, Mead, 1986).

David S. Evans, ed., *Breaking Up Bell* (New York: Elsevier-North Holland, 1983).

Paul J. Feldstein, *Health Care Economics,* 2d ed. (New York: John Wiley & Sons, 1983).

Franklin M. Fisher et al., *Folded, Spindled, and Mutilated: Economic Analysis and U.S. v. IBM* (Cambridge, Mass.: MIT Press 1983).

James M. Griffin and David J. Teece, *OPEC Behavior and World Oil Prices* (London: Allen & Unwin, 1982).

Paul M. Joskow and Richard Schmalensee, *Markets for Power* (Cambridge: MIT Press, 1986).

Gorham Kindem, *The American Movie Industry* (Carbondale, Ill.: Southern Illinois University Press, 1982).

John Moody, *The Truth about the Trusts,* (Moody Publishing, 1904).

Willard F. Mueller, *The Celler-Kefauver Act: The First 27 Years,* House Subcomittee on Monopolies and Commercial Law, 96th Congress, 1st Session, (Washington, D.C.: U.S. Government Printing Office, 1980).

David J. Ravenscraft and F. M. Scherer, *Mergers, Sell-Offs and Economic Efficiency* (Washington, D.C.: Brookings Institution, 1987).

Stephen A. Rhoades, *Power, Empire Building, and Mergers* (Lexington, Mass.: D.C. Heath Lexington Books, 1983).

Emmanuel N. Roussakis, *Commercial Banking in an Era of Deregulation* (New York: Praeger, 1984).

F. M. Scherer et al. *The Economics of Multiplant Operation* (Cambridge, Mass.: Harvard University Press, 1975).

J. Tunstall, *Disconnecting Parties* (New York: McGraw-Hill, 1985).

U.S. Bureau of the Census, *Concentration Ratios in Manufacturing, 1982,* MC82-S-7 (Washington, D.C.: U.S. Government Printing Office, 1985).

Lawrence J. White, ed., *Private Antitrust Litigation* (Cambridge, Mass.: MIT Press, 1988).

Simon N. Whitney, *Antitrust Policies,* 2 vols. (New York: Twentieth Century Fund, 1958).

To locate specific antitrust and regulatory cases, there are various legal reporting services, particularly West's *Supreme Court Reporter; Federal Reporter* (for appeals court decisions); *Federal Supplement* (for important district court opinions); and *American Law Reports*. Current cases and actions are presented in summary form in two private periodicals: *Trade Regulation Reports* and *Antitrust and Trade Regulation Reporter*.

Topics

Using such sources as these, one can treat a great many topics, involving a variety of cases, issues, and factual comparisons. The following list of suggestions is only a start.

1. Antitrust Cases. Review the economic content and effects of any of these: *Standard Oil* (1911), *U.S. Steel* (1920), the *Meatpackers* decree (1920), *Addyston Pipe* (1897), *Alcoa* (1945), *American Tobacco* (1946), *United Shoe Machinery* (1954), the electrical equipment price conspiracy cases (1960), *Brown Shoe* (1962), *Von's Grocery* (1966), *P&G-Clorox* (1967), *Utah Pie* (1967), *IBM* (filed 1969, dismissed 1982), *Telex* (1973), *Xerox* (1975), *DuPont* (titanium dioxide, 1980), *AT&T* (settled 1982), *Kellogg* (1982), *Aspen Skiing* (1985), *Matsushita* (1986).

2. Regulatory Decisions. Review the economic content and effects of any of these: *Hope Natural Gas* (1944), *Permian Basin* (1968), *Carterfone* (1968), *MCI* (1969), *Ingot Molds* (1968), *El Paso Natural Gas (1964)*, *Otter Tail Power* (1973), FCC price caps on AT&T (1989).

3. General Issues:
    What biases operate on actual antitrust polices?
    How could the courts improve their methods for defining markets in antitrust cases?
    Were antitrust policies too strict in the 1960s? If so, in which specific instances?
    Do most dominant firms reflect only "superior efficiency"? Discuss several leading instances.
    Which government actions have been strongest in creating unjustified monopoly?
    What conditions are needed for the de-regulation of former natural monopolies to be effective? How can premature de-regulation be avoided?
    Are all supposedly anticompetitive actions really just forms of healthy "hard" competition?
    Has "natural monopoly" ceased to exist in most former "utility" sectors?

How might regulation cause inefficiency in utility firms? Does it actually do so? Discuss several cases.

Show how marginal-cost pricing may lean against tendencies to overexpand capacity and output.

4. More Specific Questions:

Does the AT&T-case result indicate that major Section 2 actions can still be effective? Discuss whether the AT&T case has yielded high or low returns.

What actions toward airline competition were especially effective? Which actions were not effective?

Reassess U.S. merger policies during the 1980s, including both horizontal mergers and takeovers.

Is the per se prohibition on price fixing still an efficient rule?

Evaluate the U.S. Postal Service's performance, indicating where it may depart from efficiency. Are the problems internal to the firm or imposed from outside?

Should the leading soda pop and beer firms be permitted to set exclusive territorial limits on their local bottlers and distributors?

Are patents an efficient device to promote innovation? Is there good evidence that they do?

P·A·R·T T·W·O   **ANTITRUST**

C·H·A·P·T·E·R 5   Antitrust Tasks and Tools

We now turn to antitrust policies. There are many possible methods for promoting competition, but relatively few of them have been tried in practice. The U.S. method of procompetitive policies is called *antitrust,* because it was started with the Sherman Antitrust Act of 1890, when industrial "trusts" were the then-current form of dominant firms. The Sherman Act is regarded as "the magna carta of economic freedom" in the country, because it promotes open, free competition.

The name *antitrust* has something of an antique tone, and antitrust policy is often said to be a quaint relic of a past era. In fact, antitrust is extremely important as the bedrock of the U.S. policy of fostering efficiency and innovation. Antitrust policies permeate the economy, setting the rules of competition just as every sport has its own elaborate rules. Senator Sherman is a ghostly presence in executive offices of companies of all sizes as they consider taking actions that might harm competition. Though Reagan-Bush officials have greatly diminished antitrust's role since 1980, the main lines of the laws and policies remain clear.

The economic aim of antitrust is conceptually clear: to bring about the optimal degree of competition in individual markets. How and whether this occurs is the question before us in the next seven chapters.

This part of the book presents the policies applied by the two main-line U.S. antitrust agencies: the Antitrust Division and the Federal

116

Trade Commission.[1] We begin with the economic objectives and the laws, and then we analyze the economic patterns in which enforcement occurs.

I. THE ECONOMIC OBJECTIVES

An efficient policy to promote competition will be just strict enough, and it will be well designed. How much is enough is determined by the marginal cost and benefits (recall figures 4–3 and 4–4) that arise from increasing competition in real markets.

Perfect competition is *not* sought or expected. Rather, agencies operate in the middle range of markets where a somewhat higher degree of competition is often economically justified. The rationale for antitrust is firmly grounded on research and experience about effective competition in real markets.

The aim is for antitrust to have optimal *design,* applying the right set of incentives. And in each market, antitrust is to be applied just to the *extent* at which marginal social benefits equal marginal costs. The two basic classes of industrial pathology are:

1. Market dominance (a tight *structure,* plus certain types of strategic actions). This occurs when a firm gets and holds a large share of a market. The dominant firm can control production and pricing internally, whereas smaller firms could control them only by collaboration with each other. Mergers that would increase market power are also part of this structural problem.
2. Collusion among firms and other anticompetitive *behavior* or *conduct.* This takes many forms, including direct collusion among competitors to fix prices, informal ties, tacit collusion, price discrimination, and exclusion.

An effective procompetitive policy will try to treat these conditions in all markets, including finance, utilities, professions, and services, as well as in the standard sectors of industry and trade.

1. Broad versus Narrow Evaluations

A full policy evaluation will include all of the benefits of competition, from allocative efficiency to broader economic values. That broad basis

---

[1]Among basic sources on antitrust policies, see Hans Thorelli, *The Federal Antitrust Policy* (Stockholm: P. A. Norstedt and Sons, 1954); William Letwin, *Law and Economic Policy in America* (New York: Random House, 1965). For a review of case law, see Eleanor M. Fox and Lawrence A. Sullivan, *Cases and Materials on Antitrust* (St. Paul, Minn.: West Publishing, 1989).

is consistent with the original legislative setting of antitrust and with the policy decisions that have been taken during nine decades of enforcement.

On the other hand, there are more restrictive proposals that would limit antitrust solely to the static efficiency benefits of competition (to maximize consumer and producer surplus, as treated in Chapter 2). This approach would leave it to other policies to achieve the other economic benefits. Yet this basis is neither logical nor wise. The broader benefits follow directly from competition and are often important and inseparable. Moreover, other policies are frequently unable to attain those broader benefits as effectively as antitrust can.

2. The Focus on Market Share

Because market share is a central element of market power, market share is the natural focus for antitrust policies. Firms holding small shares of the market can be involved in many potentially anticompetitive practices without actually reducing competition. These firms are too small to harm other competitors, and by improving their own positions they can promote competition against larger firms. These same practices (including price discrimination, vertical restrictions, tie-ins, and other restrictions) will usually *suppress* competition when they are done by firms which hold high market shares. The correct policy, therefore, is broadly geared to the market shares of the firms involved in these practices.

II. THE ANTITRUST LAWS

The basic U.S. laws are firmly set, after a century of development. Their language is wide: They simply outlaw collusion and monopoly. Yet their enforcement has been held back in some directions to "reasonable" levels, and many sectors of the economy have been exempted from their reach. We consider first the laws, next their origins, and then their coverage. An appendix at the chapter's end presents the terms most commonly used in antitrust enforcement.

1. The Laws

In brief summary: The Sherman Act of 1890 is the first and basic law, outlawing collusion and monopoly in broad terms. In 1914, the Clayton Act was added to make certain specific acts illegal; it was amended in 1936 to deal with price discrimination and, in 1950, with mergers. A trickle of small amendments has continued in recent years. In practice, the laws have become a well-knit body of rules and precedent, with clear main lines but much change and debate at the margins.

The Sherman Act's two main sections are:

> **Section 1.** Every contract, combination in the form of a trust or otherwise, or conspiracy, in restraint of trade or commerce among the several states or with foreign nations, is hereby declared to be illegal. Every person who shall make any such contract or engage in any such combination or conspiracy, shall be deemed guilty of a misdemeanor. . . .
> **Section 2.** Every person who shall monopolize, or attempt to monopolize, or combine or conspire with any other person or persons, to monopolize any part of the trade or commerce among the several states, or with foreign nations, shall be deemed guilty of a misdemeanor.

The **Clayton Act** outlawed four specific practices, including discrimination in prices, exclusive and tying contracts, and interlocking directorates. A broader prohibition contained in Section 5 of the accompanying Federal Trade Commission Act provided, simply, "that unfair methods of competition in commerce are hereby declared unlawful."

In 1936, the **Robinson-Patman Act** amended Clayton Section 2 to limit price discrimination in more detail. In 1950, the Celler-Kefauver Act amended Clayton Section 7 to prevent anticompetitive mergers.

Certain other more specific laws cover procedural points and penalties. From 1903 to 1974, an expediting act provided for government appeals directly to the Supreme Court. The agencies can invoke either civil or criminal proceedings, seeking fines or jail terms, or both. The maximum fine has risen from $5,000 in 1890 to $50,000 in 1955, and then to $100,000 for individuals and $1 million for firms in 1974.[2] Maximum prison sentences were one year during 1890–1974, after which they were raised to three years. The FTC itself can only impose maximum fines of $5,000 (per day if the offense continues). An injured private party can sue to claim treble damages as long as it can show direct injury.

If a defendant is found guilty in a public-agency case, that becomes a prima facie basis for treble-damage claims by private parties. A consent decree does not provide that basis, and a nolo contendere plea is regarded as a consent, not a proof of guilt.

---

[2]To ensure that mergers do not happen so quickly that the antitrust agencies cannot consider them, the Hart-Scott-Rodino Act of 1976 provided for prenotification of all substantial mergers. It applies to mergers where one firm has over $100 million of net sales or total assets, while the other firm has over $10 million of net sales or total assets. The merging partners must file requested data, and then the agencies have 30 days to act, if they choose to.

The FTC and Antitrust Division largely share the application of the basic antitrust laws, invoking them freely as the case at hand may warrant.

2. History of the Laws

These laws derive from traditions and precedents deeply rooted in the country's history. In earlier centuries, economic power had been woven into the cultural fabric, especially where the economy was feudal and agrarian. The rise of mercantile trading eventually challenged this structure in the latter Middle Ages. The "industrial revolutions" in Britain (1780–1840) and then in the United States (1850–1900) created problems of industrial monopoly on a new order of magnitude. The policy treatments that emerged in the United States during 1890–1920 reflected a long competitive tradition.

Early Common Law. In England, during the 17th century, grants of monopoly by the Crown were held illegal under common law by the courts and were voided by Parliament in 1623.[3] The abolition did not extend to grants conferred by Parliament, to monopolies acquired through individual effort, or to those resulting from private agreement. In the 18th century, however, monopolistic agreements came usually to be condemned, unless they were merely ancillary to some innocent actions and were also thought to be of a "reasonable" scope. A single person could still monopolize, but not a group. The courts had also refused since the 15th century to enforce contracts that restrained trade. This refusal was narrow at first but gradually broadened.

During the 19th century, the doctrine of restraint of trade was extended to cover any arrangement whereby competitors sought to exclude outsiders from the market or otherwise to limit freedom to compete. In most jurisdictions, the courts came to reject all contracts that involved such practices as curtailment of output, division of territories, fixing of prices, and pooling of profits. Here no rule of reason was applied; these practices were held by their very nature to harm the public interest, and contracts that required them could not be enforced.

Supportive though it was, the common law was of limited effectiveness. If all conspirators stayed in line, and if no victim sued, then the action went scot-free. If competition were to be restored in such cases, public action was needed.

---

[3]On the extent of these monopolies, see W. H. Price, *The English Patents of Monopoly* (Cambridge, Mass.: Harvard Univ. Press, 1913). The leading court decision was *Darcy* v. *Allein,* 11 Coke 84, 77 Eng. Rep. 1260 (K.B. 1603), striking down a monopoly on playing cards.

The Antitrust Movement. In the turbulent post–Civil War boom of industry and railroads, many local markets broadened to national scope. In some industries, mergers created monopolies; price fixing emerged in many other industries. During the 1880s, there were mergers or price agreements in scores of industries, from meatpacking, coal, and whiskey to gunpowder and iron. Workers, farmers, consumers, and independent businessmen were harmed in varying degrees, and so they organized to resist exploitation. Because *trusts* was the common legal name for the new combinations, the opposition to them was called the *antitrust* movement. The trust as a legal device was soon abandoned, but the antitrust name has continued.

The grassroots antitrust movement achieved antitrust laws in many states during the 1880s. Finally, in 1890, the Sherman Antitrust Act was passed, amid moderately active debate that did *not* focus clearly on purposes or criteria.

The Sherman Act. The act contained little new doctrine. Its real effects were to turn restraint of trade and monopolization into offenses against the federal government, to require enforcement by federal officials, and to set specific penalties. The penalties were small, and during 1890–94 the act was used mainly as a weapon to break labor strikes. Then, in 1897, it was used to convict a price-fixing ring, and, in 1901, Theodore Roosevelt started "trust busting" with Section 2. That campaign culminated in landmark decisions in 1911. Since then, the Sherman Act has been the fulcrum of all U.S. competitive policy.

The Clayton and Federal Trade Commission Acts. There were soon demands for more exactitude in listing specific anticompetitive acts. Businesses wanted detailed guidance, and critics wanted action against abusive practices. Lengthy hearings were held after 1912, seeking to define anticompetitive actions clearly. But agreement could be reached only on four specific acts.[4] These were written into the Clayton Act, and a general clause against "unfair" competition was included in the Federal Trade Commission Act. Both were enacted in 1914. The new FTC's powers were slight: It could only tell violators not to repeat.[5] But as an independent agency, the FTC was supposed to be expert and independent of politics.

---

[4]The act was much diluted during its passage and was shorn of strict penalties. Few of the powers and resources needed to reduce monopoly were provided for. See Walton Hamilton and Irene Till, *Antitrust in Action,* TNEC Monograph no. 16 (Washington, D.C.: U.S. Government Printing Office, 1941), and the references in footnote 1 above.

[5]For an argument that the Clayton and FTC Acts were part of a conservative move, see Gabriel Kolko, *The Triumph of Conservatism* (Glencoe, Ill.: Free Press, 1963).

Robinson-Patman. By 1936, there arose a widespread reaction by small grocers against the new chain stores, enough to cause a protective amendment in the Clayton Act. The aims were (1) to eliminate any unfair advantage of the chain stores in buying their goods and (2) to restrain their ability to use "predatory" price cutting against their small rivals. The Robinson-Patman Act has had a checkered reputation (see Chapter 9), but, until the 1980s, it limited price discrimination in some degree.

Celler-Kefauver. The original Section 7 of the Clayton Act was construed by the courts to permit mergers even by direct competitors.[6] From 1920 to the 1950s, this detour around the law was heavily traveled. Concentration was both induced to rise (by the prohibition on price fixing) and permitted to rise (by the merger loophole). Absurd though it clearly was, competitors who could not legally cooperate on prices were free to merge and then fix prices within their new company. This loophole was finally closed in 1950 by amending the Clayton Act's Section 7 to cover all legal devices of merging. A merger could not "substantially . . . lessen competition or . . . tend to create a monopoly in any line of commerce in any section of the country."

3. The Coverage of Antitrust Policies

In principle, antitrust is the universal policy in the U.S. economy, applying to all markets except those with specific exemptions. It covers the broad run of industry, trade, construction, mining, and services. Although certain conditions in several utility and financial sectors are partly exempt by law, antitrust applies to other conditions in these sectors. The courts have consistently been liberal in defining the reach of the antitrust laws.

Yet coverage actually has many holes, like Swiss cheese. Because federal policy covers only *interstate* commerce, much local activity is untouched. Numerous explicit exemptions have been given by Congress, such as for railroads, ocean shipping, milk producers, insurance, and newspapers. Moreover, the enforcement agencies leave untouched (either by custom or by political choice) many markets that are legally covered.

Table 5–1 summarizes many of these legal and de facto exemptions. Certain large cases of exemptions are presented more fully in Chapter 16. It is difficult to estimate antitrust's coverage with precision, be-

---

[6]*Thatcher Manufacturing Co.* v. *FTC; Swift & Co.* v. *FTC*, 272 U.S. 554 (1926); and *Arrow-Hart & Hegeman Electric Co.* v. *FTC*, 291 U.S. 587 (1934). The decisions turned on a technicality, rather than substance.

Table 5–1
The Main Antitrust Exemptions

As a Matter of Law	Discussed in Chapters
Agriculture and fishing organizations	16
Milk and certain other farm products	16
Labor unions	16
Most public enterprises	15, 16
Regulated industries (in their main activities)	12–14
Baseball (partly)	9
Newspaper joint operating arrangements	8
Export cartels	16
As a Matter of Usage	
Many trades and services (intrastate and larger)	16
Urban services (transit, sewage, water)	15
Certain national defense suppliers	16
Certain patent-intensive industries (drugs, and so on)	16

cause many markets are only partly included and enforcement often lapses in others. Moreover, there are always ongoing legal contests in many markets over whether they *should* be under antitrust jurisdiction. Still the true coverage probably is not much above one half of the economy.

The 1970s brought a de-regulation of some sectors, a rise in imports, a decline in scale economics, and other conditions that favor natural competition. Therefore, the scope for effective antitrust policy has probably been rising.

The Rule of Reason. The wording of the Sherman Act is absolute, prohibiting "every" monopoly and trade restraint. At first, this seemed to go beyond the common law, which had allowed certain secondary (ancillary) restraints to stand. But in 1911, Chief Justice White read a "rule of reason" into both sections of the Sherman Act, finding Standard Oil and American Tobacco guilty for monopolizing "unreasonably": for being "bad" trusts, not just for having monopolized.[7] This criterion sharply limited antitrust, because it reversed the burden of proof. Agencies had to prove both (1) that a monopoly or restraint existed and (2) that it had "unreasonable" origins or effects. Further, the Court in the 1920 *U.S. Steel* case held that later good behavior could exculpate a monopolist.

---

[7] *Standard Oil Co. of N.J.* v. *U.S.*, 221 U.S. 1; *U.S.* v. *American Tobacco Co.*, 221 U.S. 106.

The rule of reason has continued to govern much of antitrust policy, guiding it to take only "sensible" actions. It requires a weighing of benefits and costs, as noted in Chapter 4, and those assessments are subject to biases and mistakes. In the 1980s, the Chicago-UCLA approach led officials to stretch the rule of reason into virtually every part of antitrust. A claim of "economies" could be used to deny almost any antitrust action, even those against price fixing (see Chapter 9).

The antitrust debate inevitably centers on these evaluations. The economy is full of degrees of monopoly and collusion, of probabilities of effect, and of trade-offs among competitive effects. Moreover, agency resources are scarce, and so only the more serious instances of market power can be treated. A balancing is needed.

In short, the U.S. antitrust laws have become a set of specialized tools that are applied in certain ways to certain sectors. Courts will usually apply them broadly, but Congress grants many legal exemptions, and large de facto exemptions also occur. The content of antitrust policy depends heavily on the agencies' specific actions in bringing effective cases and in requiring adequate remedies.

III. ENFORCEMENT

In this light, the record of U.S. antitrust enforcement is broadly as follows: Its jurisdiction is wide and its tasks are difficult, yet its powers and resources have been moderate. It has become strict in some directions (price fixing, mergers) but relatively lenient in others (especially toward dominance). There have been fluctuations in the severity of enforcement, but the reductions of the 1980s were more severe than ever before.

1. Pulses of Antitrust Activity

Antitrust activity has come in pulses, rather than at a steady pace. The first great wave was in 1901–20, starting with Theodore Roosevelt's "trust-busting" campaign. The second wave arose and crested during 1937–52. A third, smaller wave occurred during 1968–75. In each case, a merger boom stirred popular anxiety and political pressures to take action against big business.

The merger and antitrust waves can be seen in Figure 5–1 and, in different detail, in Tables 5–2 and 5–3. Three merger waves are visible, and a fourth probably began in the late 1970s. Antitrust activity is represented (if only roughly) by the number of significant cases. That measure is imperfect, for it mingles together (1) a few true landmark cases that have large effects, (2) many lesser (but not landmark) cases, and (3) some large, costly cases that have no precedent value. Yet the mea-

Figure 5–1
The Pulses of Merger and Antitrust Activity

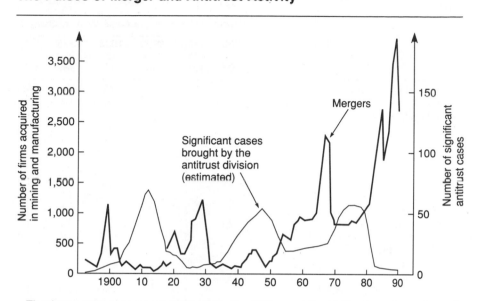

The three merger waves—of 1897–1901, the 1920s, and the 1960s—have been dramatic and turbulent. Antitrust actions have also come in three distinct waves, as shown by the number of cases (weighted for importance). To some extent, the actions have been a response to the mergers and other industrial events.

Source: Mergers: W. G. Shepherd, *The Economics of Industrial Organization* (Englewood Cliffs, N.J.: Prentice-Hall, 1979); Antitrust: adapted from Richard A. Posner, "A Statistical Study of Antitrust Enforcement," *Journal of Law and Economics* 13 (October 1970), pp. 374–81.

sure is at least broadly valid. In each period, the degree of effort and the degree of impact (which need not be closely related) reflect all manner of disparate causes, rather than a direct response to economic needs.

Before 1901, antitrust activity was minimal. Then Theodore Roosevelt seized the issue, becoming the "trust-buster." Yet Taft outpaced him. Roosevelt's officials started 44 suits in his two terms; Taft's started 90 in one. Wilson's appointees also started 90, but this beginning was interrupted by World War I. Then, under Harding, Coolidge, Hoover, and in Franklin Roosevelt's first term, the Antitrust Division went into hibernation. This lapse and the doctrines favoring big business were similar to the cutbacks of the 1980s.

Then, in 1938, Franklin Roosevelt mounted a highly publicized campaign against monopoly, managed by Thurman Arnold. This effort con-

Table 5–2
Types of Cases Brought: Antitrust Division

	Period in Which the Case Was Instituted					
	1890 to 1904	1905 to 1919	1920 to 1934	1935 to 1954	1955 to 1969	Total
Horizontal conspiracy	15	119	105	449	301	989
Monopolizing	4	37	24	201	104	370
Acquisitions short of monopoly	1	6	7	13	167	194
Boycott	1	6	35	115	68	245
Resale price maintenance		6	2	5	14	27
Vertical integration		5	4	30	14	53
Tying arrangements		5	2	47	11	65
Exclusive dealing	1	1	4	73	51	140
Territorial and customer limitations				14	65	74
Violence	4	2	21	14	6	47
Price discrimination	2	11	5	70	35	123
Other predatory or unfair conduct	1	8	4	6	19	88
Interlocking directorates			2	10	4	16
Clayton Act, sec. 10				1	2	3
Labor cases	3	8	29	72	13	125
Patent and copyright cases		7	13	106	39	165
Total cases in period	16	173	165	596	605	1551

The table shows the distribution of allegations, not of cases
Source: Computed from the *Bluebook,* as reported in Richard A. Posner, "A Statistical Study of Antitrust Enforcement," *The Journal of Law and Economics* 365 (1970).

tinued under Truman, with major cases coming along until 1952. The Eisenhower years of moderation brought a deliberate pullback in cases against dominant firms, especially cases in progress against IBM and AT&T. After several slow years, there was a modest revival after 1958.

The moderate pace continued in the 1960s, with some rise in economic consistency during 1965–68 and new actions toward regulated utilities. However, the problem of tight oligopoly, which seemed ripe for new, innovative cases, was not treated. The only major case was one filed against IBM in 1969; virtually no action was taken against the rising tide of conglomerate mergers in 1966–69. Enforcement in the 1960s was decidedly moderate, despite later Chicago-UCLA claims that it was extreme.

During 1969–75, the pace of enforcement rose amid the post-Vietnam era of dissent, with major cases against AT&T, Xerox, oil companies, and cereals firms. The agencies also promoted new competition in many regulated sectors, and penalties for price fixing were raised. But activity receded after 1976, and it was sharply cut back under Reagan's appointees at the Antitrust Division and at the FTC. During the Reagan

Table 5–3
Antitrust Cases Commenced, Fiscal Years 1960 through 1989

Fiscal Year	Total	Government Cases (Antitrust Division and FTC)		Private Cases
		Civil	Criminal	
1960	315	60	27	228
1965	521	38	11	472
1970	933	52	4	877
1971	1,515	60	10	1,445
1972	1,393	80	14	1,299
1973	1,224	54	18	1,152
1974	1,294	40	24	1,230
1975	1,467	56	36	1,375
1976	1,574	51	19	1,504
1977	1,689	47	31	1,611
1978	1,507	42	30	1,435
1979	1,312	50	28	1,234
1980	1,535	39	39	1,457
1981	1,434	60	82	1,292
1982	1,148	29	82	1,037
1983	1,287	21	74	1,192
1984	1,201	24	77	1,100
1985	1,142	30	60	1,052
1986	935	25	72	838
1987	858	21	79	758
1988	794	18	84	692
1989	745	15	91	639

Source: Administrative Office of the U.S. Courts, *Annual Report of the Director: 1980* (Washington, D.C., 1981), p. 63; and data from the agencies.

years, virtually no Section 2 actions were begun, and the IBM case was dropped (though the AT&T case was finished up during 1982–84). Merger restraints were largely withdrawn, and cases against price fixing were focused mainly on small instances of bid rigging on public contracts. Virtually all efforts against allegedly unfair tactics and against vertical restraints were stopped.

This self-proclaimed "revolution" reflected Chicago-UCLA doctrines, but it was like the Harding-Coolidge lapse of antitrust in the 1920s.[8]

---

[8]See the trenchantly critical review by Eleanor M. Fox and Lawrence A. Sullivan, "Antitrust—Retrospective and Prospective: Where Are We Coming from? Where Are We Going?" *New York University Law Review* 62 (November 1987), pp. 936–88; the sustained criticisms by Charles E. Mueller, ed., in successive issues of the *Antitrust Law & Economics Review;* and the candid defense of the "revolution" in John E. Kwoka, Jr., and Lawrence J. White, eds. *The Antitrust Revolution* (Glenview, Ill.: Scott, Foresman, 1989).

2. Resources

The agencies have been small in comparison to their tasks (see Table 5–4). The total budgets and expert staffs are slender, and much of them are taken up by secondary chores. They contend with private resources that often dwarf them.

The Division's yearly budget is less than the cost of an ordinary military aircraft. It is less than one month's profit at stake—and therefore available for the companies' efforts to resist the policies—for several large firms. Even if they were sharply raised, antitrust resources would be minor in a federal government budget of over $1 trillion and a GNP over $4 trillion. No precise economic appraisal guides the setting of these agencies' budgets, even though the marginal yields on antitrust resources may be high.

The internal budgeting of the resources has improved in recent years; recent Division budget reports are lengthy and contain some discussion of economic cost and yields. The allocation decisions may now consider costs and benefits somewhat more carefully than before. However, the total agency budgets are set by the political process, often under erratic influences.

The 1980s' cutbacks in antitrust resources are evident in Table 5–4. During 1980 to 1989, the budget of the Division decreased by 45 percent in real terms, and the number of lawyers fell 51 percent from 422 to 209. The FTC cuts were comparably severe. The number of economists also declined at both agencies, and many of those remaining were Chicago-UCLA-trained economists with interests in analyzing the limits and harms of antitrust.

Even before the 1980s, the resources were thinly spread. On average, there is only the equivalent of several full-time lawyers in each agency working on each of the five or so largest industries. For the rest—and especially for new industries—there is little or no continuous attention by lawyers assigned part-time to several industries. A single big case, such as the *AT&T* and *IBM* cases during 1975–84, can take a large portion of agency resources and attention.

Agency lawyers commonly face superior numbers of lawyers on the defendant's side, except when the firm is small or the case is minor. The average quality of antitrust staff also tends (with exceptions) to be lower than that of their private adversaries. This reflects their far lower pay and the relative youth and inexperience of much of the staff.

The imbalance shown in photographs of the two sides in the *Du Pont–General Motors* case is normal for large cases; a 20–1 ratio is common. The abundance of private lawyers reflects the underlying incentives for defendants to spend at least the full amount of the aftertax profits at stake in the case. More recent examples include claims by AT&T that it spent half a billion dollars against the Division's 1974–84

Table 5–4
Budgets and Staffs of the Antitrust Division and FTC, 1950–1990

	Antitrust Division			Federal Trade Commission			
	Total Budget ($ millions)	Attorneys	Economists	Total Budget ($ millions)	Competition Policy Actions	Staff	Economists
1950	$4	290	n.a.*	$4	n.a.	n.a.	n.a.
1960	4	241	n.a.	7	n.a.	n.a.	n.a.
1965	7	289	n.a.	14	n.a.	n.a.	n.a.
1970	10	291	25	21	n.a.	325	46
1975	18	343	36	39	n.a.	414	n.a.
1976	22	385	43	47	n.a.	500	n.a.
1977	28	421	40	55	n.a.	551	81
1978	42	383	44	62	13	542	83
1979	48	394	45	65	13	557	86
1980	48	422	45	66	13	580	89
1981	45	409	38	77	14	554	90
1982	44	338	41	69	13	491	90
1983	44	292	43	67	14	465	102
1984	44	275	43	64	13	421	96
1985	43	258	46	66	13	419	93
1986	43	256	44	63	13	397	92
1987	44	224	40	65	13	351	82
1988	45	219	39	66	12	326	73
1989	45	209	36	66	12	321	69
1990	43	254	40	74	13	320	70

*n.a. = Not available.
Source: Antitrust Division and FTC budget and staff records.

Francis Miller, *Time-Life* Agency

Officials of Du Pont (seated) and their senior attorneys in the *Du Pont–General Motors* case (shown November 1952). A larger number of younger lawyers (not included here) also assisted.

Resources Differ. In this large case, the Division lawyers were far outnumbered by their opponents. Such an imbalance is still common in antitrust cases involving large firms and large amounts of money at stake.

Francis Miller, *Time-Life* Agency

Antitrust Division attorneys on the *Du Pont-General Motors* case (shown November 1952).

Note that the Division's trio did win the case in the end, despite the disadvantages of numbers and resources. Yet superior resources do have at least some effect in the average case.

case and rumors that IBM spent comparable amounts against the Division's 1969–82 case. A large share of those resources were voluntarily deployed by the firms. Whether such vast resources were efficiently used is another question.

There are some offsets to the imbalance of resources. The agencies can invoke broad powers, impose expensive litigation, and call on some

Figure 5–2
The Setting of the U.S. Federal Antitrust Agencies

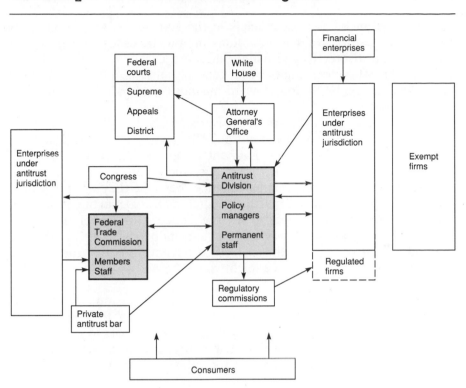

outside resources in many cases. On some matters, the heads of the agencies need to apply only a little willpower, rather than a large volume of new resources. But there are counteroffsets, too, such as the firms' better access to crucial data and their frequent recourse to other public agencies (Congress, the White House, the Defense Department, and so forth) for help.

3. The Setting

The resources and their uses are not decided in a vacuum. They are influenced by the setting of the agencies, as illustrated in Figure 5–2.

Congress. The agencies' budgets are set by Congress after yearly hearings. Congress also acts on exemptions from antitrust; there are usually a few in the mill. Members of Congress (on behalf of companies and others in their districts) supply a stream of inquiries and gentle persuasions, and sometimes a hard sell. From industry and the public come information, persuasion, and complaints by customers, competitors, takeover targets, and so on.

Executive Branch. Various officials in the Executive Branch often try to influence Antitrust Division actions in specific cases, though this is usually done discreetly and mainly in acute cases. The White House also sets broad implicit limits by its general policies in favor of large or small businesses, by its tone toward business, and by its appointments to both agencies.

Appointees to head the Antitrust Division are usually of good technical quality, thanks to long traditions. By contrast, the FTC has suffered from many mediocre appointments: political hacks and beginners, lawyers inexperienced in antitrust issues, and so on.

The agencies have much independence, because they are not within a large business-oriented department, such as the Department of Commerce. At the Justice Department, the concern of higher officials is mainly with legal consistency, rather than industrial politics. This independence also keeps antitrust free of adventurous or "radical" actions, which political guidance might cause on occasion.

Judiciary. The courts are the main arena for the Division's actions, and they can also reverse FTC actions (though recently they have rarely done so). They will usually enforce the agencies' efforts to get evidence and pursue "reasonable" actions. The courts are often slow, however, and they stress legal decisions by the adversary process rather than neutral economic evaluations.

The private Antitrust Bar is the approximately 10,000 lawyers—in law firms and on corporate and banking staffs—who specialize in antitrust matters. They range from famous older lawyers whose mere presence commands respect, down to small-town attorneys with small-scale clients. Some of them specialize in trial work in open court; others solely advise, prepare strategy, and negotiate. They are an influential and well-paid group, dedicated to the continuation of active antitrust. It is their livelihood, win or lose.

Large firms have their own legal staffs, some with score of attorneys working on antitrust and related matters. They advise and warn managers about risky courses of action, handle private and public suits, and negotiate with all parties. "Outside counsel" are often brought in to handle or help with delicate and critical matters and to manage cases at trial. Fees are high, often $150 per hour on up to over $400 per hour for leading lawyers. Fees for larger firms and cases cumulate into many millions of dollars. It is a fascinating world, blending diplomacy, a mandarin language and poker-playing strategies, plus plain scrambling and grit over stakes often reaching into billions of dollars.

The federal courts consider and decide only the minority of actions that become formal cases because they are not resolved by negotiation or pre-avoidance. And filtering into the agencies and courts are new research conclusions from economists about the elements of the problem: economies of scale, monopoly effects, trends, Chicago-UCLA views, and the like (as summarized in Chapters 2 and 3).

4. Inner Conditions

In short, antitrust is embedded in a setting of influences, traditions, budget limits, and mechanisms that define what it can do and is expected to do, at each point. What *is* done depends also, in part, on who is running the agencies.

The top decision positions are filled mainly by lawyers—always at the Antitrust Division, mainly so at the FTC. During their brief tenure, these appointees can set a new level of effort, start some new actions, and reach into the pipeline to pull ahead some pending cases.[9] But most basic policy actions take five years or more to prepare and carry through, and so the degree of strictness has tended to vary within a fairly narrow range.

The 1980s were a marked exception. Chicago-UCLA-oriented officials were appointed with clear missions to change antitrust policies, rather than merely to maintain and adjust the established patterns. They moved decisively, in most cases by reducing levels of case action and staffing. Such reductions are much easier to accomplish than the development of new cases, and so the effects were particularly sharp. These reductions have accentuated the technical conditions that restrict the reach of the agencies.

Since the agencies' resources are scarce, the choices among the policy directions are often critical. One result is that large areas of enforcement are routinely neglected; existing powers are not applied. Big cases that are brought are accused (often fairly) of being too episodic and unexpected, of singling out a few victims, rather than treating all offenders evenly.

The agencies' ability to learn key facts is limited. Because the Census Bureau secretes all data on individual companies, the agencies lack direct and timely information. They do *not* have access to secret infor-

---

[9]They are also often amateurs in three key respects: (1) They often know little about managing an agency. (2) They are not expert in economic analysis. (3) They often are not skilled in handling the political pressures that surround them.

For analysis of the agencies, see Suzanne Weaver, *Decision to Prosecute: Organization and Public Policy in the Antitrust Division* (Cambridge, Mass.: MIT Press, 1977); and Robert A. Katzmann, *Regulatory Bureaucracy: The Federal Trade Commission and Antitrust Policy* (Cambridge, Mass.: MIT Press, 1980).

mation in other agencies. They must conduct their own research, such as it is, from scattered sources including the opposing firms themselves. There is little chance of mounting thorough, complex research on major industries, on the large scale that the Bureau of Corporations reached during 1906–14.

Therefore, the agencies' reach has been turned toward simpler cases. They must usually rely on court trials to bring out information. This means that, for a broad range of major industries, antitrust choices have to be made without adequate information. And the courts often lack means or procedures to carry out well-informed remedies, even when the need for change has been established.

5. Allocation

In the grip of these pressures, the heads of the agencies divide their resources mainly among:

1. *Policing conduct,* to stop cooperation among firms that are attempting to fix prices or restrain trade in other ways (Sherman Act, Section 1, and Clayton Act, various sections).
2. *Restoring competitive conditions in established near monopolies and tight oligopolies* (Sherman Act, Section 2).
3. *Preventing new structural monopoly* via mergers (Clayton Act, Section 7).

The two agencies have to discover these violations, proceed against them, and get convictions in the courts, and then make sure the remedies are adequate. Table 5–2 shows the broad earlier trends in litigation activity among these directions.

Some of these tasks are hard, others quite easy. Restorative cases against existing monopoly are hard; the agencies usually must prove—against severe resistance by the firms—that sharp changes are needed in the dominant firm's market position. Price-fixing cases are much easier, for the agency lawyers need prove only that an attempt to fix prices was made, not that it was successful or that the industry's conditions need changing.

The bulk of antitrust resources go to *policing* conduct: price fixing, patent restrictions, predatory pricing agreements, and so forth. Table 5–5 shows the changing patterns in the cases filed by the Antitrust Division during 1970–89. Cases against dominance stayed low after 1977. Merger cases declined very sharply compared to the huge volume of mergers in the 1980s. The true scope of cases against price fixing declined substantially because most of them in the 1980s were merely against small-scale bid rigging on public construction projects. Data on

Table 5–5
Antitrust Division Cases Filed, 1970–1989

	Number of Cases Filed in Each Year				
	Total Civil Cases	Total Criminal Cases	Monopoly and Oligopoly	Mergers	Restraints of Trade
1970	54	5	11	15	19
1971	52	12	17	24	23
1972	72	15	14	19	45
1973	42	20	6	16	38
1974	33	34	9	13	31
1975	37	35	4	3	58
1976	45	20	7	7	34
1977	34	37	3	4	53
1978	27	31	0	7	47
1979	31	27	0	11	39
1980	28	50	1	10	69
1981	26	70	1	4	88
1982	18	94	0	8	100
1983	10	98	1	4	97
1984	14	100	0	5	103
1985	11	47	0	7	45
1986	6	53	0	6	47
1987	15	92	0	6	88
1988	11	87	0	6	74
1989	6	86	0	5	80

Source: Internal agency summaries.

the numbers of people assigned show much the same patterns, at both the Division and the FTC.

Before 1980, there were shifts among these main categories but they were not this sharp, as Table 5–5 shows. Moreover, resources were not simply cut back toward zero in major categories.

Preventive actions are mainly toward mergers. These absorbed a rising share of resources in the 1960s and then again in the late 1970s, as the merger waves rose. Only several score mergers at the most, among thousands each year, were intensively studied, and even fewer were eventually opposed. These set precedent in marginal areas. These cases tend also to be quickly dispatched, except for the more subtle issues raised by conglomerate mergers. Also, the Antitrust Division is often involved in treating mergers by regulated firms, such as airlines, electric utilities, banks, and railroads. This often requires lengthy efforts to convince the regulatory commissions to disallow or modify merger proposals.

The steep drop in merger cases after 1980 unleashed much of the merger boom of the 1980s, thus reflecting the power of merger policies to influence merger activity.

Restorative activities toward existing market power deal with both regulated and unregulated sectors. Antitrust attempts to reduce monopoly and open up entry into regulated markets grew strongly after 1965, in such sectors as communications, transportation, and stock exchanges.

In the other sectors, by contrast, restorative policies were reduced during 1952–68. In a revival after 1968, large changes were sought in the computer, copying equipment, cereals, oil, and telecommunications industries. The results were mixed, as Chapter 7 will show. Such cases are complex and face severe resistance by the defendants. They face burdens of time and proof, which are heavier than in the other policy directions. Since 1980, no new restorative cases have been brought.

6. Sanctions and Levers

Certain Costs Can Be Inflicted. The agencies' tools are narrow, but they pack various kinds of power. They can penalize past actions, but they can do little to change basic conditions in industry.

1. *Investigation.* The study process can be large, long, and costly to the firm, by choice either of the agencies *or* of the firms themselves.
2. *Suit.* A case inflicts:
    a. Direct costs of litigation. These can run very high, as we have seen, and cases usually involve far more legal activity than lay observers realize.
    b. Diversion of executive attention. This indirect burden on management can be extensive.
    c. Bad publicity. This can affect a company's image and goodwill, though it usually has little direct effect on its market position and long-run yields.
3. *Stoppage of company action.* The contested action is often stopped as soon as it is challenged, even if it is eventually exonerated. In merger cases, a stay or preliminary injunction is often obtained to prevent the merger until the case is argued and decided.
4. *Conviction.* This is only a decision on the legal outcome. Its power lies solely in leading to these penalties:
    a. Fines and other civil or criminal penalties, including jail terms.
    b. Remedies, which are of two main sorts: (1) constraints on behavior ("injunctive relief"), (2) changes in company structure, primarily via divestiture (the selling of assets).

   c. Private damage suits. (But note that a consent decree or a nolo contendere plea, if accepted by the court and agency, does not give a basis for private damages.)

It is widely believed that the probability of getting caught is more important than the severity of the resulting penalty. Presently, the chances of getting caught are regarded as low, except for flagrant offenses. The litigation and adverse publicity are themselves often the main penalty.

Fines have been unimportant for most large defendants, even though the ceilings have recently been raised. The $5,000 limit set in the Sherman Act was raised to $50,000 in 1955, but this was a flyspeck for the largest several hundred firms. In December 1974, the ceiling was raised to $100,000 for individuals and $1 million for firms;[10] in the 1980s, the limits were raised to $250,000 for individuals and $10 million for firms. However, most judges' actual fines are well below the limits.

Lawyers incessantly figure the odds and values of their clients' alternatives and advise them accordingly. The yield to be gotten *now* from taking a potentially illegal action often well exceeds the discounted present value of a small, distant—and perhaps avoidable—fine. The average fine in price-fixing cases has risen above $100,000 in recent years. Though the impact can be great for small firms, it is small for large companies. Thus, the average fine during 1960–69 was only 0.2 percent of the sales of the conspiring firms. Violations can pay handsomely even after deducting the fine.

Criminal penalties were rarely used; before 1959, no significant industrialist had spent a day in jail for violating the Sherman Act. Then two cases brought some change. Four officers of hand-tool companies were sentenced to 90 days in jail. And the electrical equipment price-fixing case of 1960 put seven officials in jail for 30 days (see Chapter 9). Criminal penalties were stiffened in 1974 for Section 1 offenses, but they are still usually applied sparingly. Violators are often assigned to community service rather than jail.

Private damages can be levied at triple the amount of harm shown to have been caused to an injured party. Therefore, a clear agency victory can trigger scores of private suits by overcharged customers, excluded competitors, and so forth. This impact often dwarfs all the other penalties, and fear of it often induces defendants to resist more fiercely.

---

[10]For a major analysis of the optimum types and levels of fines, see Kenneth G. Elzinga and William Breit, *The Antitrust Penalties* (New Haven, Conn.: Yale University Press, 1975).

Certain Market Conditions Can Be Changed. *Injunctive reliefs* can stop specific actions, but without penalizing what has been done earlier. They are specific to the firm and action in question: Other firms and tactics are not touched. They have recently become effective against certain mergers.

Restorative actions can change existing structure, but they have been sparingly used since 1913. District court judges have to settle on the remedies in the end. These judges have been easily persuaded that "breaking" up companies is hazardous. In any event, they have scant resources or expertise to carry out the changes. The courts only decide; the agencies and firms have to agree on remedies. The old maxim is: "The agencies win the decisions but lose the remedies."[11] Though it is normal in private affairs, altering business structure has come to be treated by the courts as an exotic act, used only as a last resort. Judge Greene in the AT&T case of 1974–84 provides a dramatic exception to this rule.

Consent decrees are a compromise reached in a civil suit; in fact, about nine tenths of the suits are settled in this way. Settlements are possible to arrange at any point, as each side reckons its prospects, comparing one bird in the hand with two in the bush. The agreement is then filed with the court, subject to the judge's approval. It is a flexible, cheap, and often sophisticated method, especially attractive to hard-pressed agencies. Often it achieves creative results, as in the break-up of AT&T in 1984.

Yet there are drawbacks. The settlements are reached in private, with no records of the issues and facts at stake. Soft bargains are often reached, or simple surrenders by the agency. Settlements prevent a clear legal answer. This eliminates any precedential multiplier. It also leaves no basis for damage claims by injured private parties. Economic aspects are regularly neglected as the lawyers bargain. Finally, many decrees are quickly forgotten and unenforced.

To correct these problems, the Tunney Act of 1974 (also known as the Antitrust Procedures and Penalties Act) requires consent decrees to be explained in open hearings, at which intervenors and the judge can raise objections.[12] Judges can refuse to accept settlements until they are changed to be acceptable.

---

[11]See Walter Adams, "Dissolution, Divorcement, and Divestiture: The Pyrrhic Victories of Antitrust," *Indiana Law Journal* 27 (Fall 1951), pp. 1–37; and Kenneth G. Elzinga, "The Antimerger Law: Pyrrhic Victories?" *Journal of Law and Economics* 12 (April 1969), pp. 43–78.

[12]For an evaluation of the effects of the Tunney Act, see Eric J. Branfman, "Antitrust Consent Decrees—A Review and Evaluation of the First Seven Years under the Antitrust Procedures and Penalties Act," *Antitrust Bulletin* 27 (Summer 1982), pp. 303–54.

7. Legal versus Economic Criteria

Although economists often have some role in preparing cases, the process and the decisions are mainly legal, set by legal criteria. Lawyers advocate one side and oppose the other. Their arguments are all reducible to two assertions: "My client fits those precedents," or "My client does not fit those precedents." The defendant is to be labeled either guilty or innocent. By trying to fit complex economic cases into such simple legal boxes, the process often ignores the fundamental economic conditions at issue. Those conditions usually involve *gradations* in the degrees of monopoly, of price fixing, of scale economies, and of efficiency.

Moreover, the matter at stake in a trial is the behavior of an industry in the future. The matter discussed is the evidence of its wrongdoing in the past. Whatever the issues, the prosecution must seek a conviction, the defense an acquittal. And the process often becomes a ritualized struggle, in which economic issues are neglected. The issues are often complex, even though the typical district court judge has little training in economics or antitrust.[13] An appeal from the decision of a lower court is taken on the basis of error in the application of the law, not on the basis of economic considerations.

Therefore, the legal process often mistreats the economic issues at stake, ignoring true values or forcing them into ill-fitting categories. As a result, economists inspect every case critically, since economic errors can be large. Yet the problem is not hopeless. Judges often try to make allowances for economic factors. The basic issues in a case are often straightforward. Therefore, some economic issues can be accurately treated in the adversary process.

8. The Economic Meaning of Wins

Agencies seek to win the cases they bring, and so a high batting average in cases that reach the Supreme Court is often taken as a sign of strict policy. Yet it can show just the opposite.

In the agencies, the staff members seek to bring cases that they might win in court. The policy managers then select from the evolving portfolio of possible suits those cases that look best in legal and, perhaps, economic terms. The courts then further select and give convictions in those cases that have merit, with the judicial procedure leaning toward conservative results. The Supreme Court, at the end, can also

---

[13]Since 1975, nearly half of all judges have had a short course in "legal economics" at a program staffed mainly by Chicago-UCLA economists and funded by large corporations.

select the correct margins of policy treatment. In short, a rule of reason can be applied at all levels. But only if the agencies lean on balance toward strictness, by bringing a wide variety of cases, will the courts have a range for selection.

Therefore, a high "batting average" in the Supreme Court is ambiguous. It might show that the Court is a "rubber stamp" for the antitrust agencies, even in dubious cases. That is a common view encouraged by defendants. But instead, it can suggest the opposite: that the agencies are timid or lax, sending up only the minimum set of acute cases that they can inevitably win. This deprives the Court of a range of choice. It reflects weak enforcement, not strictness.

IV. THE AGENCIES

1. The Antitrust Division

We now look at the two agencies separately. The Antitrust Division is centered in the third floor of the gray Justice Department building at 10th and Constitution Avenues in Washington, D.C. The head offices there are elegant, the lesser offices and halls rather bleak. Here one finds both lofty power over industry and mind-numbing drudgery; a certain messianic spirit and plodding details.

In the Antitrust Division, there are a variety of functional sections, all staffed by career lawyers. Above these sections are the current antitrust chief and his small appointed staff, who (during their tenure of two or three years) make the decisions and policies. The staff lawyers develop possible cases that, if eventually approved by the appointed top officials, are signed, filed, and litigated in court. Or instead, the suit may be sent back down for further action or delay.

The Process. The process by which antitrust decisions are posed and made is fascinating and important to understand.[14] The main steps are illustrated in Figure 5–3. The basic actor is the staff lawyer, specializing in one or several industries. He or she is like a small entrepreneur, seeking to maximize his or her record of successful cases—and to be promoted to section chief or higher. Each lawyer is usually assigned to a specific industry or sector. The lawyer has latitude to ferret out possible violations, either on his or her own, or on an assigned investigation, or solely in response to a private complaint or tip.

---

[14]This is essential to evaluating the results and the alternative approaches. See Hamilton's and Till's description of it in their *Antitrust in Action*, pp. 23–100. See also Weaver, *Decision to Prosecute*.

Figure 5–3
The Process of Antitrust Decisions and Litigation

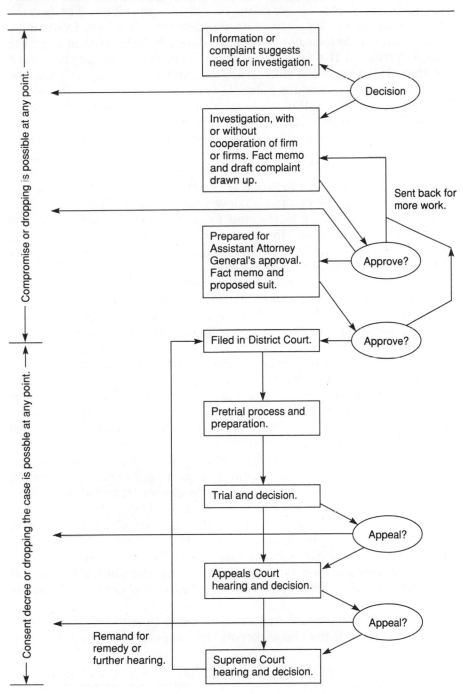

A case or investigation is usually triggered by a complaint or an important change reported in the press. Investigation may also involve staff economists and, on occasion, an outside consultant. The investigation looks mainly for *documents* and also for witnesses. Documents are of all sorts (letters, notes, reports, data), and the critical ones are usually buried in the target company's own files. The agencies must somehow learn or guess where they are and ask for them. Then the firm's lawyers may produce them (1) voluntarily, if the firm is cooperating (to show it has nothing to hide), or (2) under a court order (a civil investigative demand: CID), if the firm is fighting the action.

The antitrust investigator or group eventually does a research report (a "fact memo") on whether a violation of antitrust law has occurred and whether a suit against the offender might be justified. The criterion is, of course, legal: Can a violation of the law be proven? If the attorney recommends suing, he or she also draws up a draft complaint. This pair of drafts then passes up in the mill for discussion, further work, and decision at higher levels.[15] In the Antitrust Division, the Assistant Attorney General for Antitrust decides, usually after more study, whether to approve suit. Then the case is filed.

One to three years of pretrial preparation may occur before the trial itself begins. The trial creates the "record" in the case, in which all points of law, economics, and facts are to be covered. Antitrust trials often last between a week and a month, but some run several months. In a jury trial, the verdict is immediate; in a nonjury trial, the judge may take many months to prepare and issue the decision and supporting opinion. Either side (or both) can appeal the decision, but the appeals court holds only a brief hearing on the points of law (no facts or issues can be added to the trial record). Any appeal to the Supreme Court is even more focused and brisk, but the delays at each appeal stage often take more than a year.

Delay. Most Division actions require at least a year to run their course, but the variation in times is extreme. Some matters take but a few days (for example, a merger folds when the Division announces it will investigate or when price fixers immediately offer to plead guilty when caught). But other cases can take years (for example, about 1953 to 1975 for the *El Paso Natural Gas* case, and 1974 to 1983 for the *AT&T* case). The average time for completing a litigated antitrust case has been about 5 years. This period has stayed relatively constant down the decades.

The delays are partly inherent, since it takes time to investigate, prepare suit, carry out pretrial jockeying, try, appeal, and win a suit, and

---

[15]The firm under study is usually able to keep well informed of matters as they progress, and commonly its lawyers come in to make frequent efforts to persuade against action.

then apply remedy. Also, time is often needed to let the issues ripen so that a clear basis for settlement can be agreed upon.

Where the stakes are high, private parties have managed to stall for years (and reap further monopoly gains) by astute procedural tactics. All manner of requests, demands, and objections can be filed, and all rulings can be appealed. In major cases, it requires great skill for the judge to keep the case moving. More commonly, judges take a passive role, permitting cases to become lengthy and top-heavy with details.

Delays have suggested to some observers that big cases are too complex for the legal process (and particularly for juries) to handle. However, the basic issues are often simple and clear, and juries are often fully capable of seeing through legal smoke screens. A firm judge can move even the biggest case quickly, as occurred in the *AT&T* case during 1978–84 (see Chapter 6). The alternative methods, such as congressional actions or special commissions, might be even more cumbersome.

2. The Federal Trade Commission

The FTC's headquarters are in a charming triangular building about halfway between the White House and the Capitol. The main hearing chamber is suitably impressive, but there is also a bureaucratic ambience. The FTC is an independent agency, with its own power to frame, process, and decide cases. Ideally, five commissioners apply expert judgment in managing the staff and in briskly settling issues along sound economic lines.

The FTC overlaps with the Division's tasks and tools. It could avoid the Division's problems in the courts and provide better enforcement, but, in practice, these ideals have scarcely been realized. The FTC has two tasks: antitrust and "consumer protection." The latter takes about half the FTC's resources and effort, most of it in small-scale, case-by-case activity.[16] The antitrust resources have frequently been diverted to small, even trivial, cases.

As with most commissions, the FTC's appointees have mainly been of mediocre quality. Many of them have scarcely understood the FTC's economic tasks. There has usually been no clear leadership by the

---

[16]In addition to its duties under the Clayton and Trade Commission acts, the Commission administers the antitrust exemption granted to export trade associations under the Webb-Pomerene Act of 1918; polices the advertising of goods, drugs, and cosmetics under the Wheeler-Lea Act of 1938; and enforces the Wool Products Labeling Act of 1939, the Fur Products Labeling Act of 1951, the Flammable Fabrics Act of 1953, the Textile Fiber Products Identification Act of 1958, the Fair Packaging and Labeling Act of 1966, the Truth-in-Lending Act of 1969, the Fair Credit Reporting Act of 1970, the Fair Credit Billing Act of 1975, and the Equal Credit Opportunity Act of 1975. It has also tested cigarettes for tar and nicotine since 1967.

Figure 5–4
Steps in FTC Actions

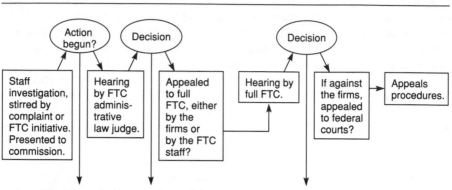

Resolutions of matter by stopping action, compromise, or compliance.

chairman, nor a set of economic priorities. Moreover, some of the big cases are appealed to the courts. Though the courts will now reverse the FTC only on issues of law (not of fact), the shadow of appeal leads the agency to be as meticulous and slow about procedures as most district court judges.

The FTC's procedures are summed up in Figure 5–4. The three main parts of the Commission are the bureaus of Competition, Consumer Protection, and Economics. Investigations begin with private complaints, which come in by the thousands, or—in the more important cases—by FTC staff initiative. If a formal complaint is lodged, the respondent can reply and settle (as most do), or the issue goes to an FTC "administrative law judge" (ALJ). After judicial-like hearings, the judge either acquits or finds guilt to some degree. Until recently, only a "cease and desist" order could be applied, with no real penalty. The firm or FTC staff can appeal the decision of the ALJ to the whole Commission, which handles the issues and trial record like an appeals court. The FTC's decision is final, unless the firm can persuade the Supreme Court that the FTC erred on the law or in procedure.

The FTC also has developed rule-making powers. It issues rules governing all members of an industry, rather than trying to establish precedents only by individual cases. In 1975, Congress formally backed this practice. In 1982, Congress backstepped (under pressure from several trade associations) and gave itself the power to reject individual industrywide rules. In other matters of structure and behavior, the remedy is often weak. There is much procedure but often little tight remedy or control.

The FTC's economic yield has been much less than its potential. The Commission comes under intense political pressure when it ventures to be active. Its independent status also leaves it exposed to attack. Congress controls its funds tightly and has reached out to forbid specific actions. The FTC, therefore, has often bent with political winds and avoided difficult actions, despite its formally independent status.

Swings in FTC zeal have been even wider than those of the Antitrust Division. The high point was roughly 1945 to 1951, when the FTC attacked basing-point pricing, horizontal mergers, and several major oligopolies, all on a shoestring budget. During the 1920s and 1930s, the agency probably did more to promote collusion than resist it. It decayed in the 1960s so far that abolition was seriously suggested.[17] A revival occurred during 1969–80, featuring a crackdown on deceptive advertising. This seemed severe; yet, in fact, it skirted the core problems of market power.

Important FTC actions toward cereals firms, Xerox Corporation, major oil companies, the professions, and retail industries began during 1971–72, reaching mixed results to be seen in Chapter 6. This moderate shift toward strictness encountered a sharp reversal under new appointees after 1981, as noted earlier.

Dual Enforcement. The two agencies have come to overlap widely in their coverage and basic actions. Mergers, restructuring, collusive and possible predatory devices, and others are treated by both agencies over nearly the whole range of industries. This could cause strife and error, and it does mean that there is no single agency that bears full responsibility. Accordingly, there occasionally are proposals to replace them with one agency in order to coordinate and fortify the treatments.

Yet most experts favor the duality for enabling variety, experimentation, and—yes—competition in carrying out policy. There are few serious disputes over jurisdiction. One agency can add its own treatment if it regards the other as too weak; this has happened in several important cases. And a passive—or hyperactive—spell in one agency may be offset by the other. To force the Division and the FTC into one agency would invite a degree of monopoly. In any event, the dual-agency method is an unique experiment, and the ultimate wisdom of it is debatable.

---

[17]American Bar Association, *Report on the Federal Trade Commission,* 1969. The special ABA study committee concluded "if change does not occur, there will be no substantial purpose to be served by its continued existence." See also E. F. Cox, R. C. Fellmeth, and J. E. Schultz, *The Nader Report on the Federal Trade Commission* (New York: R. W. Baron, 1969).

V. PRIVATE ACTIONS AND ANTITRUST ABROAD

1. Private Suits

Private parties also use and, indirectly, enforce the antitrust laws. Such cases have mushroomed in recent years from about 300 per year in the 1950s to over 1,200 per year in the 1970s. They declined sharply in the 1980s, to about 600 per year, as Reagan policies leaned against them in numerous ways.

Private actions can be important in compensating for declines in public enforcement. The 1960s, in particular, showed that private cases can fill in for moderately weak public enforcement. Yet the Reagan years showed that determined public officials can undercut private cases by rejecting the precedents that would favor plaintiffs or by actually intervening in cases on behalf of the defendants.

The stakes are often high, when a plaintiff (a customer, competitor, or other) can assert large losses from an anticompetitive act and claim triple that amount in damages. Frequently, the plaintiff has been persuaded to sue by an outside law firm, which handles the case on a "contingency basis" (collecting a fee only if the suit wins). Damages of $100 or $200 million are typically claimed, often in the expectation of reaching a settlement of only $10 or $20 million. Dominant firms normally face a steady drumfire of private cases (IBM had 20 in the 1970s and AT&T had 35).

Treble damages have become controversial.[18] They were added to the Sherman Act to give it teeth (because the fines were not heavy) and to encourage spontaneous private enforcement. After 1960, the teeth became sharp, as private cases against large firms multiplied, often seeking large damages. Trebling such sums can yield immense financial rewards for the plaintiffs.

It is possible that the trebling has overstimulated private antitrust suits, as some critics have charged. They argue that small firms file meritless nuisance suits claiming large damages, expecting to win (or settle for) "only" a few million dollars.

The prospect of trebled damages undoubtedly does stimulate private suits. Moreover, it is true that treble damages can be excessive, penalizing an offender far above the amount of its monopoly profits or the

---

[18]For a recent review of damages and their relation to private cases, see Lawrence J. White, ed., *Private Antitrust Litigation: New Evidence, New Learning* (Cambridge, Mass.: MIT Press, 1988), especially pp. 1–103. Reagan officials endeavored to "detreble" damages down to simple damages for most offenses, as part of their efforts to reduce "needless" private litigation. The White book was part of the effort to supply evidence for such a change. But the evidence turned out to be ambivalent, and the drive for "detrebling" receded by 1990.

economic damage to society. But there are opposing influences that discourage private cases. There are the risks of losing the case, either at trial or on appeal. Cases are costly and prolonged, and defendants often hit back, countersuing with claims of some kind against the original plaintiff. Therefore, private cases may not be overstimulated, on balance. Treble damages may provide an appropriate degree of stimulus, or even too *little* encouragement. The issue has had very little hard research, and it is therefore open to debate.

Private cases might affect public action in two ways. They might *preempt* policy, taking matters out of the agencies' hands, as when landmark issues are decided in private cases. The private cases may have framed the issues in ways that the agencies do not agree with, and so the precedents are distorted or obscured. Or, instead, private cases might *add* to public efforts, by leading the way into new problems, filling in gaps or reinforcing the agencies' suits. The whole effect is not yet clear, but it is evident that private cases often fail to crop up where they are most needed and most expected (for example, against dominant firms and price fixers).[19] The agencies still bear the burden of setting mainstream policy.

2. Foreign Experiments

Abroad, there has been a growth of antitrust in Britain and Australia since 1948 and—more mildly—in Canada, France, Germany, and other Common Market countries. Of course, all countries take actions affecting competition, often abridging or excluding it, rather than promoting it. But the more formal policy ventures favoring competition deserve a brief mention here, for comparison with U.S. treatments.[20] (There will be more detail in Chapters 6 through 10.)

Much of the activity is merely formal—studying but not deciding or enforcing. Since foreign trade usually plays a strong role in these economies, antitrust policies are often heavily diluted to allow for the effects of import and export competition. Foreign products, it is said, already apply stiff pressures against any tendencies toward domestic

---

[19]For one view, that "much of private enforcement has little to do with improving resource allocation and deterring market power," see Kenneth G. Elzinga and William C. Wood, "The Costs of the Legal System in Private Antitrust Enforcement," a chapter in White, *Private Antitrust Litigation;* the quote is from page 143.

[20]See Ingo Schmidt, "Different Approaches and Problems in Dealing with Control of Market Power: A Comparison of German, European, and U.S. Policy Towards Market-Dominating Enterprises," *Antitrust Bulletin* 28 (Summer 1983), pp. 417–60; Barry E. Hawk, *United States, Common Market and International Antitrust: A Comparative Guide* (New York: Law & Business, Inc./Harcourt Brace Jovanovich, 1979); and Henry W. de Jong, "Competition Policy in Europe: Stimulus, Nuisance, or Drawback?" in K. Groenveld, J.A.H. Maks, and J. Muysken, eds., *Economic Policy and the Market Process: Austrian and Mainstream Economics* (Amsterdam: North-Holland, 1990).

monopoly. And rather than stopping mergers, governments often apply pressure to encourage firms to merge or cooperate in order to overcome the foreign "giants." Although similar arguments about supposed foreign giants are heard frequently in the U.S., urging a softening of antitrust, the arguments are more common and influential abroad.

Britain has had the leading antitrust experiments outside the U.S.[21] During 1956–61, it put a stop to nearly all formal price fixing, and resale price maintenance was stopped in 1965. The U.K. Monopolies and Mergers Commission has deflected some mergers and required certain changes. It has scarcely affected most dominant firms, though it has studied many of them thoroughly. British procedures for treating price fixing and market dominance are much more brisk than those in the United States, mainly because lawyers are not given a crucial role in the hearing process. But after 1980, antitrust policies were eased under the conservative Thatcher government, in parallel with U.S. changes.

West Germany has applied mild limits against horizontal mergers, and since the 1960s it has also attacked industrial price fixing. But, like all other foreign countries, it has not moved against existing dominant firms. The Common Market has moderately enforced several rules against dominance and price fixing.[22] French policies are dominated by a penchant for informal action between government and industries.[23]

Since 1950, Japan has had a Fair Trade Agency, with formal powers to promote competition, but action has been largely negligible. Instead, the most important Japanese policy initiatives (much as in France) generally involve informal links between the government (especially MITI, the Ministry of International Trade and Industry) and industries, often encouraging mergers or temporary cartels.

Canada has agencies with formal powers to stop price fixing and anticompetitive mergers, but action has generally been minimal.[24]

In short, the United States has had by far the strongest antitrust policies, although in the 1950s Britain also developed important poli-

---

[21]See J. Denys Gribbin, "The Origins of Competition Policy," a chapter in Peter de Wolfe, ed., *Competition in Europe: Essays in Honour of Henk W. de Jong* (Dordrecht: Kluwer Academic Publishers, 1990).

[22]See Dennis Swann, *Competition and Industrial Policy in the European Community* (London: Methuen, 1983); and C.J. van der Weijden, "European Competition Policy," in de Wolfe, *Competition in Europe*.

[23]See William J. Adams and Christian Stoffaes, eds., *French Industrial Policy* (Washington, D.C.: Brookings Institution, 1986), and William J. Adams, *Restructuring the French Economy* (Washington, D.C.: Brookings Institution, 1989).

[24]See Christopher Green, *Canadian Industrial Organization and Policy,* 2nd ed. (Toronto: McGraw-Hill Ryerson, 1985); Bruce Dunlop, David McQueen, and Michael Trebilcock, *Canadian Competition Policy: A Legal and Economic Analysis* (Toronto: Canada Law Book, 1987); and Christopher Green, "Mergers in Canada and Canada's New Merger Law," *Antitrust Bulletin* 32 (Spring 1989), pp. 253–73.

cies to deal with price fixing. But the 1980s reduction in U.S. antitrust made it similar to the mild experiments in a number of other countries, particularly in western Europe.

VI. SUMMARY

The economic tasks of antitrust are to stop cooperation and exclusive actions and to limit dominant positions to the margin where the benefits of competition are balanced by possible economies of scale. The basic laws, the Sherman and Clayton acts, appear to fit these tasks well in concept. They reflect long traditions but a checkered legislative history. There are many exemptions to them, and "reasonable" enforcement of them leaves further gaps.

The two antitrust agencies are small compared to their responsibilities. They are influenced by a variety of public and private groups. They are run by lawyers, who are concerned to apply rules and win cases. Access to the critical data is often limited. Recently, most effort has gone toward collusive conduct and mergers, rather than to remedial actions against dominant firms. The agencies frequently penalize the offending firms by onerous proceedings and by reinforcing private damage claims, more than by formal convictions and fines.

Activity has fluctuated sharply, but the long trend is to bear down on medium firms while letting the largest dominant firms stand. The FTC has mostly had a mediocre record. Dual enforcement probably promotes balance and variety, though it avoids direct responsibility. Private suits are numerous, but they are not a full substitute for public action. Antitrust abroad is often mere ritual, even more than in the United States.

The U.S. experiments in antitrust have had their own specific forms, coverage, and incidence. The economic effects are likely to be complex, perhaps with unknown side effects as well. It seems obvious that price fixing is reduced and structure is less tight than if antitrust had not existed. Chapter 11 will consider the effects, after the detailed coverage of Chapters 6 through 10.

QUESTIONS FOR REVIEW

1. "The Sherman Act contains an explicit 'rule of reason.' " True?
2. "The Sherman and Clayton acts merely codified the common-law precedent." True?
3. "The Sherman Act did not have a clear legislative intent, either in hearings or floor debate." True?

4. Effective exemption from the antitrust laws includes (*a*) labor unions, (*b*) export cartels, (*c*) intrastate commerce, (*d*) most public enterprises, (*e*) patent-intensive industries. Which?

5. "Because the agencies' lawyers are always outnumbered by the other side, they rarely win." True?

6. "The courts' slowness always makes antitrust actions too slow." True?

7. "Restructuring has been the main line of antitrust since the trust-busting days of Roosevelt and Taft." True?

8. "Since fines are small, the agencies have little leverage on firms." True?

9. The recent cut in antitrust budgets definitely makes them (*a*) about right, (*b*) still too small, (*c*) too large, (*d*) we cannot know. Which?

10. "The average antitrust case takes about 5 months, but there is much variation." True?

11. "Legal processes cannot possibly yield good economic solutions for antitrust matters." True?

12. "Overlap between the Antitrust Division and the FTC means that neither—indeed nobody—assumes ultimate responsibility for antitrust policy." True?

13. Has the increased numbers of staff economists at the agencies ensured that policies have sound economic content?

14. In the 1980s, virtually all of the agencies' enforcement efforts shifted toward price-fixing violations. Make the case that this shift (*a*) was too severe and (*b*) actually did not provide strict enforcement against price fixing. Then make the opposite case.

APPENDIX: Legal Terms Often Used in Antitrust

Appeal: request for a reversal of a lower court decision.

Citation: in the title of a case the plaintiff is named first; for example, *Victim v. Offender*. On appeal, the final decisions may be cited with the defendant named first.

Consent Decree: a formal compromise of a lawsuit, filed with a court. The court may require changes in it before accepting it.

Conspiracy: a joint action among two or more parties.

Damages: a dollar measure of harm suffered by a party.

Defendant: the alleged offender. In antitrust, usually a firm that holds, or has tried to gain, market power, either by itself or by colluding with others.

Deposition: a method for taking testimony outside the court. The witness is sworn in and "deposed." Strict legal standards apply, but the court's own time is saved. Used extensively to prepare for large cases.

Discovery: the pretrial process of investigation by both sides, to discover (1) the arguments to be used by the other side, and (2) whatever facts may be thought to be relevant. Discovery is often carried to excess.

Divestiture: separation of part of a firm so as to create more competition. It can be done by selling the part to another firm or by setting the part up as a new enterprise.

Estoppel: prevents retrying of a matter that has already been tried. Once a case is brought and settled, further action is estopped until conditions have changed markedly.

Expert Witness: engaged by one side to present a skilled opinion that strengthens that side's claim. In antitrust and regulation, often an accountant, engineer, economist, or financial specialist.

Guidelines: a public listing by an agency of the conditions or actions that will cause it to sue; often couched in vague terms.

Injunction: a court order stopping a specified act, under possible penalty of contempt of court.

Interrogatories: questions exchanged by parties before trial on matters of fact or anything else germane to the trial. May be brief or extensive.

Nolo Contendere: ("no contest"), a hybrid plea that does not formally admit guilt but does not attempt to disprove the alleged offense. It cannot be used by other parties as a proof of guilt on which to base their damage claims.

Per Se: "as such," without further evidence; for example, price fixing is a per se violation if a mere showing that price fixing existed will always bring a conviction.

Plaintiff: the party bringing the suit (filing the complaint). Commonly a consumer or small competitor.

Precedent: a line drawn in one case that governs decisions in later similar cases. What the line *is* is often intensely debated.

Prosecutorial Discretion: the latitude that agency managers have to choose specific cases and to interpret the law.

Record: the printed account of all materials presented at trial and all proceedings of the trial. Appellate decisions cannot go beyond it.

Remedy (or relief): the corrective changes required after decision, in order to stop further violations.

Snow: legal vernacular for overwhelming an opponent's investigation with a mass of useless, undigested materials. Routinely successful in buying time.

Treble Damages: successful private antitrust actions can claim triple ("treble") the amount of damage suffered.

C·H·A·P·T·E·R 6   Actions toward Dominant
Firms: Concepts

Actions brought under Section 2 of the Antitrust Act against dominant firms have been the most decisive and dramatic element of the U.S. antitrust experience. In the first wave of "trust busting" during 1904–20, the U.S. government challenged nearly all of the largest 10 enterprises in the country. And seven decades later, in 1984, it achieved the astonishing divestiture of the Bell Telephone System, then the world's largest corporation.

Since 1980, no significant new Section 2 cases have been started and there are currently no prospects for action, even toward firms with market shares of 80 percent and higher. Chicago-UCLA doctrine has taken over the antitrust agencies, but their policies may shift again. Therefore, a review of the leading Section 2 actions will highlight spectacular cases and prove to be instructive.

The wording of Section 2 is not precise; it prohibits monopoly, and yet "monopoly" is a matter of degree, not a simple, distinct category. Ideally, the degree of strictness in the enforcement of Section 2 would be based upon the firm's degree of monopoly, but, instead, the law has been applied more crudely. In some periods, the actions have been aggressive; in other periods, they have been hesitant.

Section 2 policies have also displayed, with particular clarity, some of the biases noted in Chapter 4. Some obvious candidates for action (such as Eastman Kodak and Campbell Soup) have been untouched for decades. A few, including the Bell System in 1984, have undergone severe changes even though they had seemed untouchable.

The success of a Section 2 action depended on meeting two criteria. First, there must be proof that monopoly exists (from 1945 to 1975, that usually meant a market share of over 60 percent). Second, the firm must be shown to have sought monopoly deliberately or in an abusive way, as shown by its actions of various kinds. These points have been difficult to prove in the courts, and most judges have imposed other criteria as well. Before 1980, the Section 2 route had looked increasingly long and uncertain, even impossible, but the AT&T case defied all the usual lessons.

Despite the inconsistencies and difficulties, the long series of Section 2 actions has dealt with many of the leading candidates, and there remain only a handful of prominent dominant firms. How the criteria have been developed and applied is among the most complex and important aspects of U.S. antitrust policy. It shows with special clarity how policy evolves as an interaction between agencies and firms, rather than simply being applied unilaterally.

The first section of this chapter covers criteria for assessing market power. Included in this is a discussion of defining the market. Section II focuses on actual market definitions by presenting examples of Section 2 cases. The third section deals with measuring market power according to specific criteria, including market share, barriers to entry, and abuses. Section IV rounds out with the more general hurdles that Section 2 must meet in practice. This sets the stage for the presentation of actual Section 2 cases in Chapter 7.

I. CRITERIA FOR APPRAISING MARKET POWER

Ideally, a Section 2 case would cover the structural, behavioral, and performance conditions that were shown in Figure 1–1 in Chapter 1. The court would consider the structure and behavior of the dominant firm in judging whether monopoly power was large. It would assess possible scale economies and past superior performance to see how much of the monopoly power was necessary or deserved. It would assess the monopoly harms that had occurred, and then it would reach a balanced judgment about what cure, if any, is appropriate.

In practice, however, certain steps are taken to estimate and apply some of the conditions. First, the firm's market power is assessed. If it is found to be large, then the firm's actions are reviewed to see if they have been abusive or improper. If they have, then a verdict of monopolizing is possible. But a more general assessment of economic impacts and the chances for effective remedies must also be made. Finally, if all signs indicate that monopoly has been excessive and abusive, and can be remedied, the firm may be convicted of monopolizing and some changes may be required.

We consider these steps one by one.

1. Defining the Market

Defining the market is a critical topic in appraising market power.[1] In order to assess the internal structure of any market, one must first determine its boundaries. Defining the market involves drawing those boundaries as accurately as possible, including all products that belong *in* the market, and excluding all others that are *outside* the market.

The exercise can be controversial, because the size of the market affects the apparent degree of monopoly that exists inside it. Firms said to have monopoly power (such as IBM or Eastman Kodak) usually assert that the market of their products is very large; accordingly their own share of it seems small. The other side in the debate (such as a little firm suing a dominant firm) makes the opposite claim: The market is small and the defendant has a high share of it.

In research, too, the debates can be sharp, and there is always a possibility of bias. Researchers often have general beliefs about the extent of monopoly power, and that can shape their views of individual markets. For example, a Chicago-UCLA analyst may write or testify in an antitrust case that a market is big and monopoly power in it is small, while other economists may say that the market is small and the monopoly power in it is high.

A *market* is a group of buyers and sellers exchanging goods that are highly substitutable for each other. Markets are defined by demand conditions; they embody *the zone of consumer choice* for the good.

Markets exist in two main dimensions: (1) *product type* and (2) *geographic area*. In the pure case, there is one distinct product, sold in a distinct geographic area, such as fresh whole milk in an isolated town. That market's extent is determined by the true zone of consumer choice for that good, as illustrated in Figure 6–1A. In this illustration,

---

[1]Among the vast literature on the topic, many leading papers are collected in Kenneth G. Elzinga and Robert A. Rogowsky, eds., "Relevant Markets in Antitrust," *Journal of Reprints for Antitrust Law and Economics* 14 (1984).

A classic source is the early paper by Robert L. Bishop, "Elasticities, Cross-Elasticities, and Market Relationships," *American Economic Review* 42 (December 1952), pp. 779–803; see also Philip Areeda and Donald F. Turner, *Antitrust Law* (Boston: Little, Brown, 1978), pp. 346–88; and Kenneth G. Elzinga and Thomas F. Hogarty, "The Problem of Geographic Market Delineation in Antimerger Suits," *Antitrust Bulletin* 18 (1983), pp. 45–81.

For further variety in viewpoints, see Terry Calvani and John J. Siegfried, eds., *Economic Analysis and Antitrust Law* (Boston: Little, Brown, 1979); Kenneth D. Boyer, "Is There a Principle for Defining Industries?" *Southern Economic Journal* 50 (January 1984), pp. 761–70; William W. Landes and Richard A. Posner, "Market Power in Antitrust Cases," *Harvard Law Review* 94 (March 1981), pp. 937–96; and George J. Stigler and Robert A. Sherwin, "The Extent of the Market," *Journal of Law and Economics* 28 (October 1985), pp. 555–85.

Figure 6–1
Illustrations of Market Definition

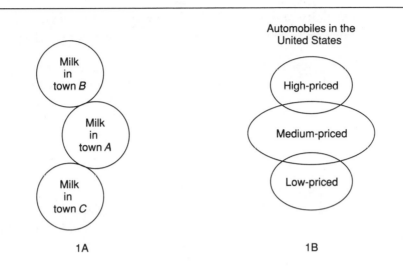

the market boundaries are sharply defined, both by product types and by geographic area.

There may also be adjacent markets for other drinks such as soft drinks, fruit juices, beer, wine, and liquor. If buyers never choose among these drinks, then each market is sharply distinct. However, if the drinks are regarded by many or most buyers as close substitutes for one another, then there may be one larger market embracing all drinks.

Consider the same condition in reverse: A market can contain *sub-markets*. For example, Figure 6–1B illustrates the U.S. market for new automobiles. Within it are submarkets for low-, medium-, and high-priced automobiles. The larger market is meaningful in assessing broad patterns of choice, as all car buyers make purchases and there is substantial substitution among these groups, not just within them. The submarkets also are relevant in defining the main range of choices made by many consumers, who usually focus within one of the groups of cars.

Substitutability. *Substitutability* is the key criterion for defining market boundaries. Close substitutes are in the same market; other goods are outside it. The economy can be seen as a honeycomb of these individual markets.

1. Cross-Elasticity of Demand. The technical definition of substitutability begins with *cross-elasticity of demand,* which shows how much a price change for one good will cause the quantity sold of another product to change. The formula is:

$$\frac{\text{Cross-elasticity of demand}}{\text{between goods 1 and 2}} = \frac{\text{\% Change in quantity of good 2}}{\text{\% Change in price of good 1}}$$

For example, let good 1 be red apples and good 2 be green apples. A 20 percent rise in the price of red apples could cause a 40 percent rise in the quantity of green apples sold, as buyers switch. The two goods are therefore close substitutes with a *high positive cross-elasticity of demand,* and so they are in the same market. Comparable pairs would be Coke and Pepsi, Fords and Chevrolets, and different brands of gasoline. By contrast, shoes and ice cream are clearly in different markets; so are houses, pencils, tractors, and popcorn. Their sales quantities do not respond to one another's prices.

Cross-elasticities of demand are also valid for defining geographic market areas. Goods 1 and 2 are the same physical good, but sold in different locations. If beer prices in Illinois closely affect beer sales in Wisconsin, then the two states are in the same geographic market. Otherwise, they are separate markets. On this basis, stock markets and gold markets are international in geographic scope, whereas the markets for bricks, bread, and ready-mix concrete are local ones, because shipping costs are high relative to the value of the products.

Though they are clear and logical in concept, cross-elasticities have rarely been available in practice. They are virtually impossible to measure accurately: Markets are not laboratories in which neat price-quantity experiments can be performed. Moreover, the critical variables do not exist in categorical boxes, but along the following continuums:

1. *Time Periods.* Responsiveness exists in a time dimension, with infinite variability in the length of time for response between goods. The shorter the period chosen, the less the responsiveness will be. The choice of the time period to examine is arbitrary in some degree: Is it short run, long run, in-between? Moreover, the practical length of "short-run" and "long-run" differs from industry to industry.
2. *Gradations of Product Characteristics.* There are usually a range of attributes of goods, varying by degrees. This causes gradations of cross-elasticities, rather than a distinct break between close mutual substitutes and all other goods.

Therefore, even if cross-elasticity values could be estimated, they would reflect at least two continuums (time and product features); thus, they will vary continuously. There are seldom clear jumps or gaps in cross-elasticities that show definitely where the market's edges are.

Even if gaps do occur, there are no fundamental criteria for deciding which level of cross-elasticity (.6, .93, or 1.77) is the "correct" threshold level for setting the market edges. The choice of the threshold value is not entirely arbitrary, but it does not rest on a clear conceptual benchmark.

Finally, cross-elasticities of demand contain two other logical problems, which make it necessary to use them cautiously. First, they are not helpful in testing two goods that each have small market shares in highly competitive markets. Because so many other goods are also highly substitutable, a price rise in good A will not cause a significant rise in the quantity sold of good B.[2] This problem is not fatal, because it arises only where goods are obviously highly substitutable (which can be seen from other evidence), but it warns against the blind use of cross-elasticities alone in trying to define market boundaries.

Second, the evaluation of substitutability needs to be made at *competitive* prices, while the actual prices may be far apart.[3] A leading example of this has been the cellophane case.[4] Cellophane is a transparent film used to wrap cigarette packages and other products. To defend itself in an antitrust case alleging that the Du Pont company held monopoly power from its dominant share of sales of cellophane, Du Pont asserted that the market really included all flexible wrapping materials.

What matters here is that cellophane's price was far above the prices of wax paper and the other supposed substitutes and that the Supreme Court evaluated the matter on that basis. In fact, this price differential was a valid indicator of Du Pont's monopoly power. If the materials were substitutable, the prices would all have been in line; but, at equal prices, cellophane would have been at far higher sales levels.

---

[2]For example, suppose that firm A and firm B each sell 2 percent of the eggs sold in a region, and that all eggs (including theirs) are close substitutes. If A raises its price by 10 percent and loses all its sales, those sales will shift to all other sellers. But they are only 2 percent of the total, and so B itself will gain only a small addition (namely, 2 percent) to its quantity sold.

$$\text{Cross-elasticity} = \frac{\% \text{ Quantity rise for } B}{\% \text{ Price rise for } A}$$
$$= \frac{2\%}{10\%}$$
$$= 0.2$$

This is a low cross-elasticity, which clashes with the fact that everybody's eggs are in fact extremely close substitutes.

[3]See Richard A. Posner, *Antitrust Law: An Economic Perspective* (Chicago: University of Chicago Press, 1976), pp. 127–28; and Areeda and Turner, *Antitrust Law.*

[4]The case was *U.S. v. Du Pont,* 351 U.S. 377 (1956).

Hence the lesson: Substitutability must be judged at competitive prices, which usually means reasonably equal prices. Price differences reflect the monopoly power that is in question. Economists usually resort to a variety of evidence besides cross-elasticities of demand in defining actual markets. The main types are summarized in Table 6–1.

2. The General Character of the Goods, as Tested against Experience. Can and will they be interchanged easily by most buyers? Tuxedos and blue jeans can conceivably be used in place of each other for a few uses, but not by most users under normal conditions. The same is true for bicycles and running shoes, and for newspapers and bath towels. In contrast, many brands of small cars are close substitutes for each other.

3. The Judgment of Participants in the Market, Especially the Sellers. They know on the basis of daily experience exactly which firms and goods compete in the market. They study the matter continuously because their success depends precisely on knowing the interactions among the firms and goods. Their view will often be a solid consensus, especially when, as in antitrust cases, they testify under oath.

Caution: Learn to handle "uniform" products cautiously. Usually they are less uniform than they seem. (An example is electricity. Though kilowatt hours are technically uniform, their cost and demand conditions differ sharply by time of day, time of week, and time of year as well as by the type of user—residence, factory, etc.) Be careful to identify groups within the market who can be charged different prices;

**Table 6–1
Specific Conditions Defining "the" Market**

The general criterion is substitutability, as it may be shown by
  Cross-elasticity of demand
  The general character and uses of the goods
  Judgments of knowledgeable participants
Product dimensions
  Distinct groups of buyers and sellers
  Price gaps among buyers
  Independence of the good's price moves over time
Geographic Area (local, regional, national, international):
  The area within which buyers choose
    Actual buying patterns
  The area within which sellers ship
    Actual shipping costs relative to production costs
    Actual distances that products are normally shipped
    Ratios of goods shipped into and out of actual areas

---

they may form a distinct market of their own. Also define any clear cost differences among groups; these too can create distinct markets and different prices.

Product Dimensions. Now we turn to the more specific kinds of evidence that can show the product dimensions of markets. First is groupings of buyers and sellers. If a product is sold to distinct groups of buyers, that can indicate distinct markets. For example, many pharmaceuticals are sold to druggists for resale to individuals, and to huge-volume-buying hospital chains. Those two markets are distinct. The sellers may also be distinct; thus lumber is sold by lumber companies to lumber yards, which then resell it to final users. The lumber companies, which are selling at wholesale, are in a different market from the lumber yards, which are selling at the retail level.

Second is an evaluation of whether the *goods' prices* are close together and whether they move in parallel or independently. Equal prices can often indicate close substitutability, because the competition among the goods naturally forces their prices into line. Sharply divergent prices suggest that the goods are sold to different buyers for different purposes. A $25 motel room at the edge of San Francisco, for example, and a $220 room at the Fairmont Hotel on Nob Hill may both be the same size, but the price gap indicates that they are in separate markets.

If the two goods' prices move independently of each other, that also indicates that they are not easily substitutable. The converse is not necessarily true. Prices may move in parallel if one good is an important input to the other (such as copper ore and copper) but *not* substitutable for it.

Geographic Extent. The geographic extent of markets can be indicated by other kinds of evidence. One is the *size of transport costs* compared to the value of the good. For example, bricks are a high-weight item, with high shipping costs compared to their value. That alone suggests that market size is limited. Another kind of evidence is the *actual miles shipped*. Cement in bags, for example, is rarely shipped over 150 miles, so that is a good indicator of the maximum radius of most cement markets. A third kind of evidence is the *amount shipped into and out of a given region*. Ten percent is a common rule of thumb. For example, in testing if Missouri is a geographic beer market, one asks if more than 10 percent of its local production is shipped out of the state and more than 10 percent of its consumption is shipped in. If both figures were 50 or 70 percent, then Missouri would be merely part of a multistate regional beer market.

The criteria in Table 6–1 are the most commonly used ones, but others have been employed from time to time. All require care and judgment in their use, and none gives simple, definitive answers. Market definition is complex because most markets are complex.

The reason most markets have shaded edges is that the close substitutes are surrounded by a range of partial substitutes. In extreme cases, the shaded edge is very wide, but most markets can be defined at least well enough to permit some judgment about the degree of competition.

Levels of Markets. Within many industries, there are a number of true markets. The drug industry sells at least eight distinct types of drugs, and each type contains specialized subtypes. The chemicals industry includes hundreds of distinct product markets, from sulfuric acid to plastics. Moreover, an industry may have several tiers of product and geographic markets (from local to international), with the same firms operating at *all* levels. For example, banks in large cities usually compete for business clients in local, regional, and national markets. They also compete in local "retail banking" for small depositors. Such banks are operating in several levels of markets at the same time.

2. An Alternative Method for Estimating Markets

In 1982, Reagan administration officials at the Antitrust Division of the Justice Department announced a new technique for defining markets in antitrust cases.[5] Although it was offered as more scientific than previously used methods, it is actually based on speculation and arbitrary criteria. It is interesting enough to deserve space here, even though it is probably less practical and less reliable than the conventional approach.

To use it, one begins by selecting the narrowest plausible version of the market in question. (An example might be wool skirts.) Then one hypothesizes a "significant" price rise (usually assumed to be 10 percent) for this good and asks whether within a "reasonable" time period (usually taken to be one year) there occurs a "significant" shift of buyers (usually taken to be 5 percent) to specific substitute goods. If so, then the market is redefined to include these substitutes. (Thus, if buyers shifted to polyester and cotton skirts, these goods would

---

[5]The most recent version is U.S. Department of Justice, "Merger Guidelines Issued by Justice Department, June 14, 1984, and Accompany Policy Statement," no. 1169, *Antitrust and Trade Regulation Report* (BNA), June 14, 1984, S-1 to S-16. For one appraisal of the approach, see Eleanor M. Fox, "The New Merger Guidelines—A Blueprint for Microeconomic Analysis," *Antitrust Bulletin* 27 (Fall 1982), pp. 519–91.

For a defense of the method by staff members who helped develop it, see David T. Scheffman and Pablo T. Spiller, "Geographic Market Definition under the U.S. Department of Justice Merger Guidelines," *Journal of Law and Economics* 29 (April 1987), pp. 123–48; and Gregory J. Werden, "Market Definition and the Justice Department's Merger Guidelines," *Duke Law Journal,* October 1983, pp. 524–79.

be included in "the" market.) The speculation is continued, product by product (perhaps to dresses and slacks), until there is no further "significant" substitution, as defined. The market is then defined.

If the data were accurate and complete, this method might rival or surpass the conventional methods. However, the new technique has several defects. The estimates are speculative, not genuinely scientific. Meaningful tests, using objective data, can rarely be done.[6] All three of the new method's benchmarks (for price changes, time periods, and quantity shifts) are arbitrary and debatable; they have no special justification either in theory or in practice. And adjusting them to plausible other values can make the "defined" markets much larger or smaller.

In any event, the assumed benchmark values would need to be different for each different industry case (e.g., fresh lettuce versus oil-refining equipment), but there is no scientific basis for guiding the selection of "correct" benchmark values. Moreover, the responses may show no sharp break or gap among the products in question that could be used for drawing the market boundary.

As has frequently been the case with the new industrial organization ideas since 1970, this new "scientific" technique is far less valuable than its authors have claimed. It is largely a formalistic restatement of concepts that have long been applied, with more practical value, in other ways. Where really reliable estimates of responses can be made by using the Department of Justice approach, they can, of course, be helpful, but that will be infrequent. In the meantime, markets must continue to be defined somehow, and the standard criteria, used with cautious judgment, are still the most effective way.

3. Supply Conditions

While markets are defined by the zone of choice that *consumers* have, certain conditions of *supply* can also be relevant. Some analysts suggest relying heavily on the cross-elasticity of supply. That reflects the ability of producers now outside the market for good 1 to switch their productive capacity from other goods to good 1. If they are hovering at the edges of the market, then their quick entry when prices rise can affect the degree of monopoly. Obviously, the quicker and bigger the entry, the less will be the market power in this market.

---

[6]In one case involving banks in adjacent small towns in northwest Michigan, customers were asked if they would shift deposits under certain assumed differences in interest rates, etc. Their answers were usually vague and showed no clear pattern. Being hypothetical, they revealed very little about actual depositor choices.

See also Richard J. Wertheimer, "DOJ Tries Out Its 5-percent Geographic Market Test," *Legal Times,* August 30, 1982, reprinted in Elzinga and Rogowsky, eds., "Relevant Markets in Antitrust," pp. 1079–86, for an example involving Virginia banking.

The cross-elasticity of supply relates goods *adjacent to* the market for good 1 to the prices of goods *in* this market:

$$\begin{array}{l}\text{Cross-elasticity of supply} \\ \text{between good 1 inside the} \\ \text{market and adjacent goods} \end{array} = \dfrac{\begin{array}{c}\% \text{ Change in quantity} \\ \text{of adjacent goods}\end{array}}{\begin{array}{c}\% \text{ Change in price} \\ \text{of good 1}\end{array}}$$

Some analysts have gone so far as to give these supply conditions the major role, but that is an error.

Supply conditions deal with entry *into the market*. It is nonsense to mix the definition of the market with the *possible* entry of firms into the market. Instead, it is logical to define the market first, on the basis of demand conditions of consumer choice. After that is done, then any relevant entry conditions can be clarified.

Of course, factories and equipment can often be shifted quickly and costlessly from one product to another, such as from quilts to sleeping bags. Firms not currently making the product may be poised to shift into the market in response even to small price changes; but these are *potential* entrants, and it is erroneous to treat them as if they are in the market already. They are not.

The "supply-side" method is frequently used by antitrust defendants trying to draw wide market boundaries, but it poses practical problems as well as logical error. The degree of transferability of capacity is often hard to assess objectively. Transferability of capacity is frequently slower and more costly than is claimed. If capacity is fully engaged in other, more profitable uses, as it often is, no transfer into this product will actually occur, even for sizable price shifts.

It is correct and prudent to ignore such potential entrants when defining the market. Once the market is defined, these outside firms can be considered in judging the importance of potential entry, in light of all possible barriers. Potential entry may indeed neutralize market power, in minor or major degrees, but that can only be assessed after markets have been correctly defined.

II. ACTUAL MARKET DEFINITIONS IN SECTION 2 CASES

The main legal tests have been the "line of commerce" (that is, the product dimension of the market) and the "geographic market." The choice usually comes down in the end, as it must, to a reasonable but arbitrary guess. Some leading recent court choices are shown in Table 6–2; note how strictness has waxed and waned.

Table 6–2
Evolving Ways of Defining the Relevant Market

| Case (year decided) | Relevant Market and the Resulting Share According to the | | | Decision |
	1. Defense (percent)	2. Agency or Other Plaintiff (percent)	3. Court in Final Action (percent)	
Alcoa (1945)	All ingot and scrap (33).	Ingot sold (90).	Ingot sold (90).	Violation
Times-Pica-yune (1953)	All local advertising.	Advertising in morning newspapers (100).	All newspaper advertising.	Acquitted
Du Pont "Cel-lophane" (1956)	Flexible pack-aging (18).	Cellophane (75–100).	Flexible pack-aging mate-rials (18).	Acquitted
Du Pont–Gen-eral Motors (1957)	Automotive fin-ishes and fabrics (1–3).	GM purchases of these items (60–100).	GM purchases (60–100).	Violation
Bethlehem-Youngstown merger (1958)	Structural met-als and plas-tics (1–3).	Regional steel markets (25 plus).	Regional steel markets (25 plus).	Merger enjoined
Brown Shoe (1962)	All shoes (5).	Various types of shoes, in various cities (up to 50).	Specific mar-kets (up to 50).	Merger enjoined
Philadelphia National Bank (1963)	National bank-ing (trivial).	Philadelphia banking (36).	Philadelphia banking (36).	Merger enjoined
Continental Can and Ha-zel-Atlas (1964)	Glass and metal con-tainers are separate markets.	Containers (25).	Containers (25).	Merger enjoined
Von's Grocery (1966)	Los Angeles retail gro-cery (7.5).	Los Angeles retail gro-cery (7.5).	Los Angeles retail gro-cery (7.5).	Merger enjoined
Grinnell (1966)	All protective services ("low").	Accredited central sta-tion protec-tive services (87).	Accredited central sta-tion protec-tive services (87).	Convicted
Aspen Skiing (1985)	All western skiing (low).	Skiing in Aspen (70 plus).	Skiing in Aspen.	Violation of Section 2

Sources: Opinions of the courts in these various cases, as discussed in the text and in-dexed at the end of the book.

1. Product Types

Since the 1940s, the courts have often mentioned the cross-elasticity of demand in defining products. But good measures of cross-elasticities have been lacking, and so the courts have relied on the items summarized in Table 6–1. Early decisions often drew the market too narrowly. Thus, sea green slate, linen rugs, red-cedar shingles produced in the state of Washington, parchment paper, and hydraulic oil-well pumps were held to occupy distinct markets, though in each case substitutes were readily available.

Alcoa. The *Alcoa* case (1945) poses with special clarity the problem of defining the product and the market.[7] The Aluminum Company of America (Alcoa) produced about 90 percent of all new ingots in the U.S. market during 1929–38. If one also includes scrap aluminum as an independent source in the market, then Alcoa's share of new ingots plus scrap would have been about 60 percent. If one went further, to exclude the new ingots that Alcoa made and then used internally in its own fabrication of aluminum end products, then Alcoa's share of that market (ingots that it sold, plus scrap) would have been only about 33 percent.

In Judge Learned Hand's final decision, all three categories of aluminum were considered substitutable (new ingots for sale or internal use, plus scrap). Judge Hand also noted that Alcoa had controlled the past production of virtually all aluminum that later returned as scrap. Therefore, Alcoa's effective control extended to a 90 percent share of the market. With a market share that high (rather than 60 or 33 percent), Alcoa was held to have substantial monopoly power.

Times-Picayune. In the *Times-Picayune* case, the Court leaned the other way, toward a broad version of the market. The question concerned a company publishing a morning newspaper (the *Times-Picayune* of New Orleans; 1950 circulation of 188,402) that competed with an afternoon paper (the *Item;* circulation 114,660). The Court decided on a market including all three papers' advertising lineage, with morning and afternoon papers all competing together. The Court also treated the *Times-Picayune* as separate from its sister paper, the *States*. Hence the *Times-Picayune*'s market share was below 50 percent, and it was held to lack market power.[8] Alternatively, the market share could

---

[7]The case is *U.S.* v. *Aluminum Company of America,* 148 F.2d 416, 424 (1945). Though criticized at the time, Judge Learned Hand's market definition is strongly supported in Darius Gaskins, "Alcoa Revisited: The Welfare Implications of a Secondhand Market," *Journal of Economic Theory* 7 (March 1974), pp. 254–71; and Peter L. Swan, "Alcoa: The Influence of Recycling on Monopoly Power," *Journal of Political Economy* 88 (January–February 1980), pp. 76–99.

[8]*Times-Picayune Publishing Co.* v. *U.S.,* 345 U.S. 594. See Chapter 8 for more on this case.

have been 100 percent (morning papers only) or 72 percent (the two sister papers treated as under unified control).

Du Pont Cellophane. The *Du Pont* cellophane case quickly became a landmark case in defining the market. Du Pont was charged with monopolizing cellophane during 1924–50. If the market in question were that for cellophane alone, it was clear that the company had a monopoly, since it accounted for 75 percent of the output of the product and, together with its licensee Sylvania, for all of it. If the market were, instead, all flexible packaging materials, including glassine, parchment papers, waxed papers, pliofilm, and aluminum foil, then Du Pont's share was only 18 percent. The first definition was urged by the government; the second by Du Pont. Judge Leahy, in the district court, found for the defense, but cited Du Pont's "creative" behavior as much as the definition of the market. The Supreme Court sustained the verdict by 4 to 3, viewing cellophane as "reasonably interchangeable by consumers for the same purposes." The relevant market, therefore, was that for flexible packaging materials, and Du Pont was acquitted.[9]

Yet the minority had a telling argument. Cellophane's price had been from two to seven times that of the other materials during 1924 to 1950. And when the price had been cut sharply, the price of others held steady or even rose. The minority cited this: "We cannot believe that . . . practical businessmen would have bought cellophane in increasing amounts over a quarter of a century if close substitutes were available at from one seventh to one half cellophane's price. That they did so is testimony to cellophane's distinctiveness."

Du Pont–General Motors. The line was drawn back the following year.[10] The defense had urged that Du Pont's sales of automobile finishes to GM were only 3.5 percent of all its sales of industrial finishes and its sales of fabrics to GM only 1.6 percent of all its sales of fabrics. However, the Court held that the characteristics of automotive finishes and fabrics were sufficiently peculiar to make them distinct and that GM in itself constituted a substantial market for these products.

Brown Shoe. In the *Brown Shoe* case in 1962, the Supreme Court recognized three markets: those for men's, women's, and children's shoes. The defense sought recognition for infants' and babies' shoes, misses' and children's shoe, and youths' and boys' shoes and, within the sex and age groups, for medium-priced and low-priced shoes. The Court refused:

> The outer boundaries of a product are determined by the reasonable interchangeability of use or the cross-elasticity of demand between the

---

[9]*U.S.* v. *Du Pont*, 351 U.S. 377 (1956).

[10]*U.S.* v. *Du Pont*, 353 U.S. 586 (1957).

product itself and substitutes for it. However, within this broad market, well-defined submarkets may exist which, in themselves, constitute product markets for antitrust purposes. The boundaries of such a submarket may be determined by examining such practical indicia as industry or public recognition of the submarket as a separate economic entry, the product's peculiar characteristics and uses, unique production facilities, distinct customers, distinct prices, sensitivity to price changes, and specialized vendors.[11]

Grinnell. In 1966, the Court decided that "accredited central station protective services" were a market, which Grinnell Corporation had monopolized.[12] This market reflected distinct characteristics, compared to watchmen, local alarm systems, proprietary systems, and unaccredited central systems.

Market definitions can be clear. In the *Du Pont* titanium dioxide case in 1979, for example, both sides agreed that the relevant market was sales of titanium dioxide in the lower 48 states. No close substitutes for the chemical exist, and shipments in and out of the United States are small.[13]

In the *IBM* case, however, the Division defined a "mainframe computer market," while IBM claimed that all computer-related products were included.[14] IBM relied on supply substitutability to include firms that might shift capacity to computer-related products.

2. Geographic Market Areas

The basic criteria of Table 6–1 apply to geographic market limits, in spatial terms. Are products in two areas substitutable? Courts look mainly at transportation costs and actual shipping patterns. If transport costs are high and shipments between two areas are small, they are usually defined as separate markets. The courts have also been willing to regard small geographic areas as markets (or submarkets), even where much larger areas could be accepted. This leaning to the narrower definition became marked in the 1960s.

In the *Paramount* case in 1948, where the lower court had found that the five major producers of motion pictures did not have a monopoly of the business of exhibiting pictures, the Supreme Court held that they did have a monopoly of exhibition at the first-run theaters in the 92 largest cities of the country.[15]

---

[11]*Brown Shoe Co.* v. *U.S.*, 370 U.S. 294, 324.

[12]*U.S.* v. *Grinnell Corp.*, 384 U.S. 563 (1966).

[13]FTC Docket No. 9108.

[14]*U.S.* v. *IBM*, 69 CIV 200, So. Dist. of N.Y.

[15]*U.S.* v. *Paramount Pictures*, 334 U.S. 141.

In the *Brown Shoe* case, the Supreme Court found different markets to be relevant in considering the probable effects of horizontal combination and vertical integration. The combination of retail outlets, it held, would affect competition in "every city with a population exceeding 10,000 and its immediate contiguous surrounding territory" in which both Brown and Kinney sold shoes at retail through stores they either owned or controlled.[16] The integration of manufacturing and distribution would affect competition in the United States as a whole.

In the *Philadelphia National Bank* case, the defendants argued that the combined bank would be in a stronger position to compete for business with banks in New York City and asked that the market be defined to include New York. The Court refused:

> The proper question to be asked . . . is not where the parties to the merger do business or even where they compete, but where, within the area of competitive overlap, the effect of the merger on competition will be direct and immediate. . . . In banking . . . convenience of location is essential to effective competition. Individuals and corporations typically confer the bulk of their patronage on banks in their local community; they find it impractical to conduct their banking business at a distance.[17]

On this basis, the Court found the relevant market to consist of the four-county area of metropolitan Philadelphia.

These landmark cases illustrate the criteria in practice. After 1975, there was increasing interest in redefining markets to allow for the influx of imports. At the extreme, the markets could be said to be "worldwide," including all production everywhere. If that were applied to automobiles and steel, then General Motors and U.S. Steel would have very small shares.[18]

This scenario was tested in 1983–84, when Republic Steel, the fourth-ranked steel firm, proposed to merge with third-ranked Jones & Laughlin (owned by LTV Corp.). Their combined share of U.S. sales of certain specific steel products, particularly stainless steel, ranged as high as 50 percent, after allowing for imports. However, if the markets were redefined as global, their combined share would be much smaller.

---

[16]*Brown Shoe* v. *U.S.*, 370 U.S. 294, 336.

[17]*U.S.* v. *Philadelphia National Bank*, 374 U.S. 321, 409–10.

[18]Some go further, saying that when imports into a market are significant, then *all* foreign production should be included in assessing the market. Such production could easily be switched into the local market, they say. This is an extreme version of the view that *supply* substitutability is important in defining the market. That, in turn, is another way of saying that all potential entrants should be regarded as equally powerful as existing actual competitors. That view is clearly extreme, and so potential entry should be assessed after the market is defined according to *demand* substitutability.

See Jeffrey J. Leitzinger and Kenneth L. Tamor, "Foreign Competition in Antitrust Law," *Journal of Law & Economics* 26 (April 1983), pp. 87–102.

The Antitrust Division decided that the relevant market was not global, because an international cartel existed to restrict imports into the United States. If no restrictions had existed, it is not clear what the decision would have been.

During the rest of the 1980s, antitrust officials adopted very broad definitions of the markets, including global markets for many products. In assessing mergers among department stores, for example, they regarded markets as regional or national, because of the ease (they claimed) of establishing new stores in any area. They relied on *supply-side* substitutability to define markets. In fact, it is a hallmark of Chicago-UCLA doctrine to emphasize the importance of supply elasticity.

III. MARKET POWER

Once markets are defined, attention shifts to the degree of monopoly inside the market. Two main *structural* features are usually important: the leading firm's market share, and possible barriers to entry. In addition, the courts look to see if there have been abusive or monopolizing *actions*. We consider them in turn.

1. The Market Share

Because it is inelasticity of demand that sets the range for controlling price, the ideal measure is inelasticity itself. This is rarely measurable, however, so courts have relied on market shares and entry barriers. As market share rises above the 10–15 percent range, market power is usually substantial, and at 50 percent it is almost always very high.

But Section 2 covers "monopoly," not "degrees of market power," and courts have tried to set a specific threshold level that is sufficient to indicate high monopoly power, deserving of conviction.

The court has been willing at times to convict "abusive" combinations with as little as 20 percent and yet to absolve "good" monopolists with as much as 90 percent. The consensus before 1980 was that an established market share below 60 percent was quite safe from challenge, and even 75 or 80 percent might exist untouched for decades. After 1980, the Reagan officials simply raised the level further, effectively to about 90 percent.

2. Barriers to Entry

In recent cases, defendants have argued that a low barrier to new entry should be considered in evaluating the degree of monopoly. If free entry nullifies market power, then even a 100 percent share might be "competitive" and escape treatment. Policy could turn on the height of entry barriers and "contestability" as well as (or even perhaps instead of) market shares.

Formally, policy has not yet included barriers in the evaluation. This is sensible, for barrier "height" is hard to estimate reliably, much less to measure precisely. Also, the relative weighting between barriers and market share is controversial. Yet, informally, policy probably does allow for barriers, to a degree. The agencies consider barriers to entry in deciding whether to bring suit, and the courts often note the entry conditions in their opinions. In practice, a low entry barrier can offset many points of market share.

Conversely, the absolute size of the firm or market has come to be treated in some cases as a source of entry barriers. Other than that, the courts have not usually accepted bigness, per se, as a source of monopoly power.

3. Abuses and Monopolizing Actions

If monopoly power is found to exist, then the court looks to see if the dominant firm has engaged in abusive or monopolizing actions. If so, then its dominance may not reflect superior performance, and it may have violated Section 2.

Several kinds of tactics that have been common in Section 2 decisions are discussed below. (Note that Chicago-UCLA economists deny that these actions reduce competition, and so they exclude them from Section 2 evaluations.)

Exclusion and Discrimination in Buying. A dominant firm often is able to exclude others from access to facilities, credit, equipment, and materials. It may make preemptive purchases, hoarding crucial supplies. It may force suppliers into exclusive contracts by refusing to buy from those who sell to its competitors. It may also pressure suppliers to give price cuts beyond what costs justify.

Such practices were pervasive in forming the early trusts, and they are still common. Thus, several of the trusts persuaded the railroads to grant them substantial rebates. Standard Oil not only recovered 40–50 percent of the sums that it paid the railroads for carrying its own products but also collected a similar share of the rates paid by its rivals. The Aluminum Company of America, enjoying a patent monopoly in its early years, made preemptive purchases of deposits of bauxite and sites for the generation of hydroelectric power, and it bought power elsewhere under contracts that forbade suppliers to sell to other producers of aluminum. In the 1930s, producers of the leading brands of cigarettes bought up the stocks of tobacco required for the production of 10-cent brands. And exhibitors of motion pictures prevented other houses from obtaining films by renting more features than they had time to display in their own theaters.

Exclusive Selling. Dominant firms may also impose contracts upon their distributors that forbid them from handling goods produced by other firms. Contracts of this sort have been employed, in the past, in the sale of biscuits and crackers, cameras, dress patterns, canned syrups, petroleum products, and many other goods.

Firms also "tie in" their products, requiring the buyer to take A if it wishes to buy B.[19] Shoe machinery, cans, computers, mimeograph machines, and many others have been sold under tying arrangements. Tie-ins by dominant firms can reduce competition, although others are usually harmless (see Chapter 10).

There has been "full-line forcing," requiring dealers to carry a whole line of products, thus keeping specialized producers off the markets. Farm equipment and movies have been among those involved, and it is present, to a degree, in many markets.

Discriminatory and Predatory Pricing. Systematic price discrimination by dominant firms is both (1) anticompetitive and (2) a main source of monopoly profits (see Chapter 10 for a full treatment of discrimination). It may arise impersonally, or it may be a series of incidents aimed at specific rivals. Sharp versions of it helped to build up and maintain the early trusts. Nowadays, one finds mainly the impersonal types, with complex systems of discrimination persisting for years, even decades. It is defended as "rational," as "meeting competition," and as "necessary to build up the market" and to "get funds for innovation." But it is anticompetitive even if—or, perhaps, especially because—it is inherent in the monopoly situation.

These monopolizing actions have surrounded many dominant positions, helping to create, maintain, and exploit them. They often provide the second leg of Section 2 cases—monopoly *plus* monopolizing behavior—in the United States. Yet they are often hard to discover and interpret, for their intent can often be made out as merely good "vigorous" or "hard" competition.

---

[19]William James Adams and Janet L. Yellen, "Commodity Bundling and the Burden of Monopoly," *Quarterly Journal of Economics* 90 (August 1976), pp. 475–98. See also M. L. Burstein, "A Theory of Full-Line Forcing," *Northwestern University Law Review* 55 (March–April 1960), pp. 62–95; and John S. McGee, "Compound Pricing," *Economic Inquiry* 25 (April 1987), pp. 315–39.

IV. CRITERIA FOR BRINGING AND DECIDING CASES

1. Formal and Practical Tests

The basic law is clear: Every monopoly or attempt to monopolize any part of trade or commerce is illegal. Yet decades of sinuous legal arguments have put large loopholes into Section 2. The tests for conviction are in three classes: formal, informal, and unspoken.

There are two *formal criteria*. Courts will now normally require proof (1) that monopoly exists (shown mainly by the firm's market share being at least 60 percent, or higher, since 1980), *plus* (2) that it was gained intentionally or abusively. These are the two prime points that the agencies and firms dispute at trial.

Two *informal criteria* also are invoked by the defendant. If it can show that its high market share arises from (1) "superior skill, foresight, or industry" (the Chicago-UCLA phrase is "superior performance") or (2) economies of scale, then acquittal usually will follow. Conviction would be criticized either as punitive against good performance or as irrational since no efficient remedy could be devised.

This good performance has become decisive in many recent cases. Firms now assert that their behavior has been good and that any conviction or penalty will stifle their (and other firms') incentives to do good in the future. Often the good performance is negligible or debatable, while the monopoly power is large. The effect of a decision for the defendant is to give the firm an unlimited right to pursue monopoly gains, even when its contribution has been modest. Moreover, the stifling effect of conviction itself has not been shown to exist, even though it is frequently alleged.

At least four *unspoken* criteria are also commonly applied: (1) The firm and its products must be relatively simple and standard, otherwise the courts are usually afraid to tamper with complex technology (such as computers or photographic supplies); (2) the firm must be shown to be innovative, otherwise the courts will fear discouraging or destroying a progressive enterprise; (3) the firm must be shown to be earning high excess profits, otherwise it will claim that it has no monopoly power; and (4) there must be no major threat to the price of the company's stock, otherwise the courts will fear that they will impoverish thousands of small investors.

These eight substantive criteria reflect the courts' conservatism and the slenderness of their expertise. Dominant firms can usually find one or more of these escape hatches. Even if they can't, the criteria provide fertile ground for litigation and stalling. In practice, the straightforward study of monopoly is often detoured at the trial into other complex issues. Anticipating this, the agencies often avoid cases where the four unspoken criteria will cause trouble.

At trial, the debate often proceeds in a strange limbo. The really decisive conditions are not addressed directly, while there is pretense that the formal criteria control the decision. The problems of remedy and penalties are allowed to preempt the basic question of whether monopoly power does in fact exist.

The upshot is often that the true conditions are not investigated in depth, neither by the agencies nor by a process of exposure in a court trial. If Section 2 were applied as it reads, no such paralysis would occur. Monopolists would be simply defined as such. The proper remedies would still pose intricate problems, but the law would apply as it is written.

2. Candidates for Treatment

The main firms eligible for study and treatment are in two categories: dominant firms and oligopolies. The two groups shade into each other, but they do present distinct problems. Actions have mainly focused on dominant firms, though Chapter 7 will also note several oligopoly cases.

Dominant firms are those with about 50 percent or more of the market. Their evolution is clarified in Table 6–3 and 6–4.

In 1910, there was indeed a large core of dominant firms in major industries, including U.S. Steel, Standard Oil, and American Tobacco. Most of these were created by the trust movement of 1890–1901. By 1948, as Table 6–4 shows, the cast of characters changed considerably. Automobile, electric, and other companies led the list, but they are scattered further down among the ranks of all firms than the leaders were in 1910. By 1973, there had been still further changes, as many of the dominant firms encountered new competition. Only IBM, Procter & Gamble, Eastman Kodak, Campbell Soup, Gillette, and various newspapers remain as major dominant firms in 1990.

Past antitrust actions, as well as imports and natural competitive processes, strongly reduced the list of cases needing action. The lessons for future policy will be reviewed at the end of Chapter 7.

3. Costs of Action

Section 2 cases are often long and costly. The burden of proof is against the agency, and the firm has time on its side. The firm usually is willing and able to use all tactics in order to escape or at least postpone conviction, incurring costs up to the monopoly profits that are at stake (recall Chapter 4). Even small firms can hold out through long and expensive cases. Large dominant firms make for fearsomely big cases, involving hundreds of lawyers, many tons of documents, scores of mil-

Table 6–3
Changes in Market Position, Leading Dominant Firms, 1910–1935

Asset Rank among All Industrial Firms in 1910		Estimated Assets, 1909–10 ($ millions)	Estimates for 1910		Estimates for 1935	
			Market Share (percent)	Entry Barriers	Market Share (percent)	Entry Barriers
1	United States Steel	$1,804	60%	Medium	40%	Medium
2	Standard Oil (New Jersey)	800	80	Medium	35	Medium
3	American Tobacco	286	80	Medium	25	Medium
6	International Harvester	166	70	High	33	Medium
7	Central Leather	138	60	Low	—	—
8	Pullman	131	85	High	80	Medium
10	American Sugar	124	60	Low	35	Low
13	Singer Manufacturing	113	75	Medium	55	Low
16	General Electric	102	60	High	55	High
19	Corn Products	97	60	Low	45	Low
21	American Can	90	60	Medium	51	Medium
25	Westinghouse Electric	84	50	High	45	High
30	Du Pont	75	90	Medium	30	Low
34	International Paper	71	50	Low	20	Low
37	National Biscuit	65	50	Low	20	Low
55	Western Electric	43	100	High	100	High
59	United Fruit	41	80	Medium	80	Medium
61	United Shoe Machinery	40	95	High	90	High
72	Eastman Kodak	35	90	Medium	90	Medium
*	Alcoa	35	99	High	90	Medium

*Not available.
Based on W. G. Shepherd, *The Treatment of Market Power* (New York: Columbia University Press, 1975).

lions of dollars in expense, and usually up to 20 years. A medium-sized case might cost the Antitrust Division at least 10 lawyers and $1 million per year; the defendant normally would multiply those resources by 5 to 10 times. A recent Antitrust Division chief estimated that the Division could handle only two important Section 2 cases at a time, given current budget levels. The recent cutbacks in funds have reduced that ability further.

4. Benefits and Costs of Actions

Each case aims to restore full competition more quickly than natural market forces would. As Figure 6–2 illustrates, the gain is the shaded area, where competition is greater than it otherwise would be. If the natural decline of market power is slow and the case progresses rapidly,

Table 6–4
Changes in Market Position, Leading Dominant Firms, 1948–1973

Asset Rank among All Industrial Firms in 1948	Estimated Assets, 1948 ($ millions)	Estimates for 1948		Estimates for 1973	
		Market Share (percent)	Entry Barriers	Market Share (percent)	Entry Barriers
2 General Motors	$2,958	60%	Medium	55%	High
9 General Electric	1,177	50	High	50	High
20 Western Electric	650	100	High	98	High
29 Alcoa	504	80	High	40	Medium
33 Eastman Kodak	412	80	Medium	80	Medium
38 Procter & Gamble	356	50	Medium	50	Medium
47 United Fruit	320	80	Medium	60	Medium
60 American Can	276	52	Medium	35	Low
69 IBM	242	90	Medium	70	High
76 Coca-Cola	222	60	Medium	50	Medium
* Campbell Soup	149	85	Medium	85	Medium
* Caterpillar Tractor	147	50	Medium	50	Medium
* Kellogg	41	50	Medium	45	Medium
* Gillette	78	70	Medium	70	Medium
* Babcock and Wilcox	79	60	Medium	50	Medium
* Hershey	62	75	Medium	70	Low
* Du Pont (cellophane)	(65)	90	High	60	Medium
* United Shoe Machinery	(104)	85	High	50	Low

*Not available.
Based on W. G. Shepherd, *The Treatment of Market Power* (New York: Columbia University Press, 1975).

then the gain may be large, but if the natural decline is fast, then the case may not speed it up much at all, and so its benefits would be small.

The time sequencing of costs and benefits is also important. The costs of litigation and transition occur first. The resulting flow of benefits then, it is hoped, is large enough to justify the costs. Discounting the values for time will usually shrink the benefit-cost ratio, because the benefits come later, often after many years.

The benefit-cost results of these cases are usually debatable. Chicago-UCLA economists expect monopoly power to decline rapidly and cases to be so slow that little net gain in competition occurs. Moreover, because they regard monopoly as weak and beneficial, they regard the flow of benefits as small or negative. Therefore, Chicago-UCLA proponents favor little or no Section 2 cases.

Figure 6–2
The Net Effect of an Antitrust Case in Raising Competition

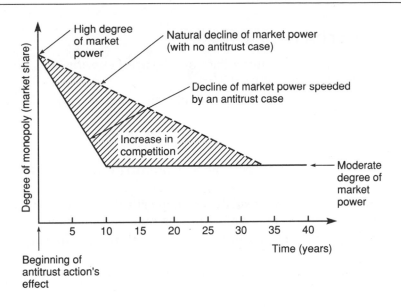

Some other experts expect natural declines in market power to be so slow that the cases can make large net gains in competition. Also, they think that the benefit flows will be large, and so they favor extensive Section 2 actions for some industries.

V. SUMMARY

The treatment of established market power had come to be slow and often ineffective, even before 1980.

There have been two main series of Section 2 cases, in 1906–20 and 1938–52. A series of several cases in the 1970s led only to the AT&T divestiture. These cases have often been unwieldy, and they have occurred long after the original monopoly was formed.

Conviction now requires (1) a monopoly market share, plus (2) monopolizing acts of some kind, plus also (3) high profitability, and (4) clear prospects for remedy that will not imperil innovativeness or harm shareholders. The burdens of proof and time are both set against Section 2 treatment, and court processes can usually be used to get long delays. The agencies must establish that a change will be superior enough to the existing structure to justify conviction and the costs of transition.

QUESTIONS FOR REVIEW

1. "Each Section 2 case turns only on abusive behavior plus superior skill, foresight, and industry." True?
2. "Cross-elasticities of demand, if available, would sharply define most markets." True?
3. "The courts have steadily gotten stricter in their judgments about market definitions." True?
4. "A market share of 50 percent will ordinarily trigger a Section 2 case." True?
5. "Entry barriers are not usually a formal criterion in Section 2 cases, but they often enter informally into the outcomes." True?
6. "Where monopoly exists, antitrust action will remove it even if scale economies justify it." True?
7. "A high market share is necessary but not sufficient for conviction under Section 2." True?
8. Choose three actual markets and try to define their extent precisely.
9. How would one make practical estimates of the benefits and costs of Section 2 cases?

C·H·A·P·T·E·R 7   Actions toward Dominant
                     Firms: Cases

The sequence of actual cases against dominance has occurred in three waves, each one smaller than the one before. The first wave of action during 1904–20 was extremely ambitious, and it achieved substantial results. After this peak, the trend has been toward moderacy, with fewer and milder actions. After 1980, action was virtually halted, as officials adopted the doctrine that dominant firms deserve their dominance.

Against this downward trend, the immense restructuring of AT&T in 1984 stands out sharply. It shows that large Section 2 actions can still deal with complex firms. Yet the case dealt with a monopoly that was created by government franchises rather than by activity in the marketplace. "Ordinary" dominant firms will apparently be largely exempt from Section 2 for the time being. Also, since all firms intend to achieve dominance if they can, the existence of an intent to monopolize will not be grounds for violation.

Discussed below are the leading cases, which illustrate the main issues.

I. PAST TREATMENTS, 1900–1953

The two big waves of Section 2 action were in 1904–20 and in 1938–52. The main cases are summarized in Table 7–1.

Table 7–1   Major Section 2 Cases, 1905 to 1986

Cases	Time between Monopolization and Remedy	
	Years	Interval (years)
1904 to 1920		
American Tobacco	1890–1916	26
Standard Oil	1875–1918+	43+
Du Pont (gunpowder)	1902–13	11
Corn Products	1897–1920	23
American Can	1901–	—
U.S. Steel	1901–	—
AT&T	1881–	—
Meatpackers (Armour, Swift, Wilson, Cudahy)	1885	—
American Sugar	1890–	—
United Shoe Machinery	1899–	—
International Harvester	1902	—
1938 to 1952		
Alcoa	1903–(1953)	(50)
National Broadcasting Company	1926–43	17
Pullman	1899–1947	(65)
Paramount Pictures	1914–48	34
American Can	1901–(1955)	(54)
Du Pont (GM holdings)	1918–61	43
United Shoe Machinery	1899–1970	71
United Fruit	1899–1970	71
American Tobacco	(1920)–	—
Du Pont (cellophane)	1925–	—
Western Electric	1881–	—
IBM	(1925)–	—
Since 1968		
IBM (1969 case)	(1925)–	—
Cereals (1972 case)	(1950)–	—
Xerox (1973 case)	1961–1975	14
AT&T (1974 case)	1881–1984	103
Berkey v. *Eastman Kodak*†	1890s–	—
Aspen Skiing†	1978–86	8

Parentheses indicate estimates.
*Based on evidence of the start of official investigation and the end of official action.
† Private case.
Sources: S.N. Whitney, *Antitrust Policies* (New York: Twentieth Century Fund, 1958); and case records and decisions.

Time between Beginning and End of Action*		Outcome
Years	Interval (years)	
1906–12	6	Divestiture of some assets.
1905–12	7	Dissolution into about a dozen regionally dominant firms.
1906–12	6	Mild dissolution; reversed quickly by effects of World War I.
(1910)–19	(9)	Slight changes from a consent decree.
(1909)–20	(11)	No change.
(1907)–20	(13)	Acquittal, informal limits on further mergers.
(1909)–13	(4)	Compromise. AT&T retained its position; agreed to interconnect and avoid further mergers.
(1909)–20	(15)	Compromise. Packers agreed to stay out of adjacent markets and to cease coordination.
1908–14	6	No action. American Sugar's position had slipped already.
(1908)–18	10	USM leasing restrictions were modified.
1906–18	12	Compromise. Trivial divestiture.
1934–50	16	War plants sold to new entrants.
1938–43	5	"Blue Network" divested (became American Broadcasting Corp.)
(1937)–47	(10)	Divestiture of sleeping car operation. Manufacturing monopoly was not directly changed.
(1935)–48	(13)	Vertical integration removed.
(1945)–50	(5)	Compromise: Certain restrictive practices stopped to foster entry.
(1945)–61	(16)	Divestiture.
(1945)–69	(61)	Share reduced to 50 percent.
1948–70	22	Moderate divestiture.
1938–46	8	Conviction but no significant remedy.
(1945)–56	(11)	Acquittal.
1946–56	10	Case effectively abandoned.
1947–56	9	Case effectively abandoned.
1965–82	17	Dropped.
1970–82	12	Acquittal.
1970–75	6	Compromise. Some opening of access to patents.
1965–84	19	Substantial divestiture.
1972–80	8	Kodak exonerated.
1979–86	7	Aspen Skiing held in violation, fined, and required to resume shared ticketing.

The first set of cases started with Theodore Roosevelt's trust busting and flowered under Taft.[1] Then action was stalled and stopped by World War I and its aftermath. Its coverage was remarkably complete, reaching most of the very largest corporations of the time. A few of the cases had sharp effects, but many cases ended with little or no impact.

The second wave during 1938–52 was confined to firms ranking much lower down in the national lists, but these firms still included nearly all of the major firms with market shares over 50 percent. Several of these cases were successful legally, but others were inconclusive, and the two most important ones—IBM and Western Electric—were abandoned in the 1950s.

After 1968, a modest revival occurred, with several sizable actions against IBM, cereals firms, Xerox, and AT&T. After 1980, however, all Section 2 actions (except for finishing the AT&T case) were stopped by the Reagan administration.

1. The First Wave, 1904–1920

After a slow beginning during the 1890s, antitrust burst upon the scene after 1903 in a wave of cases challenging many of the largest businesses of the time. These cases tested the reach of the law in reducing market dominance. The result was a form of compromise: Certain actual dominant firms were convicted and moderately changed, but legal precedents were set that limited the law only to "bad" trusts. Henceforth, the burden of proof favored dominant firms.

The new Sherman Act was first tested in a suit against the recently formed American Sugar Company, which then held a 95 percent market share. The court reached a frivolous decision, holding that manufacturing was not interstate commerce and was therefore exempt from the Sherman Act.[2] This narrow view would have nullified the law, but it was soon ignored.

In 1904, Theodore Roosevelt's first trust-busting venture, a challenge to J. P. Morgan, resulted in the Northern Securities decision.[3] The Supreme Court dissolved the holding company that controlled the Great

---

[1]See Simon N. Whitney, *Antitrust Policies,* 2 vols. (New York: Twentieth Century Fund, 1958), for narrative of the main cases.

Roosevelt's actions were moderate, despite his reputation as a trust buster. Thurman Arnold later described him as the man "with his big stick that never hit anybody." Taft's actions during 1909–12 were much more thorough and effective.

[2]*U.S.* v. *E. C. Knight Co.,* 156 U.S. 1. Also read Alfred Eichner, *The Origins of Oligopoly* (New York: Columbia University Press, 1971) for an exhaustive account of the trust and its fate.

[3]*Northern Securities Co.* v. *U.S.,* 193 U.S. 197 (1904).

Northern and Northern Pacific railroads, which were parallel competing systems that also competed against other transcontinental lines. Other railroad cases during 1904–22 established that mergers to achieve great market power were illegal, even if the power were not clearly abused.

More important, the 1904 case opened the way to spectacular investigations, trials, and changes in a series of leading industrial firms. The oil, tobacco, sugar, telephone equipment, steel, gunpowder, meatpacking, farm machinery, shoe machinery, and aluminum industries were among those touched. Six of the 10 largest industrial firms were treated. The Bureau of Corporations was formed to do large studies during 1904–15, and the whole series of cases was thorough and neatly handled. Several sharp changes in structure resulted, but the majority of the treatments had only modest effect.

"Bad" Trusts. 1911 was the landmark year, with decisions in the *Standard Oil* and *American Tobacco* cases. Each had approximately a 90 percent market share, had been ruthless, and had not been especially innovative nor realized large economies of scale. Each produced a simple product, had earned excess profits, and was closely held by a small group of owners. Both put up inept defenses and were the target of a wide groundswell of attacks by citizens, other businesses, and officials in many states.

Strict though they seemed, the decisions actually clipped Section 2's wings. In a tortuously worded opinion, Chief Justice White inserted a "rule of reason" as the precedent for future cases. The two firms were convicted because of their abuses, he said, *not* their monopolies per se. This rule of reason added the "plus" criterion to Section 2, and it placed the burden of proof on the Antitrust Division to prove the abuses.

Standard Oil had committed a number of abusive acts. It had gained control of all of the important pipelines and 90 percent of refining capacity. it had done so by exacting rebates from the railroads on its own shipments as well as those of its rivals, by selective local price cutting, and by other practices, which filled some 57 pages of the trial record. The Court ordered the Standard combine dissolved, and this was quickly done, by 1913.[4] Yet the treatment was scarcely timely or drastic. Standard Oil's market position was already slipping, and the monopoly had existed for nearly 40 years. The holding company was merely removed, leaving the previous series of regional monopolies still largely under shared ownership. The shareholders realized a 47 percent

---

[4]*Standard Oil Co. of N.J. v. U.S.*, 221 U.S. 1.

capital gain during the year after the dissolution. It took some 10 to 20 years for genuine competition to spread in the industry.[5]

American Tobacco, formed around 1890, had also used predatory practices; excluding rivals from sources of supply, buying plants to shut them down, using selective predatory pricing, and selling "fighting brands" at a loss to destroy competitors. This firm was required to sell some capacity.[6]

The virtual monopoly of Du Pont in gunpowder since the 1890s was also ended in 1913.[7] The firm had been less abusive, but its intent to monopolize was clear, its defense was inept, and spinning off some lesser parts was relatively easy. Yet Du Pont retained the better parts, and World War I immediately nullified the effects and vastly enriched the firm. The Du Pont family then took major holdings in General Motors, U.S. Rubber, and other firms.

The government also threatened action against AT&T for attempting to monopolize both telephone and telegraph services and for its internal monopoly with its equipment supplier, Western Electric. Moderate concessions were gained from AT&T in 1913, but it retained its monopoly in telephone operation in most cities and all long-distance traffic.

Major cases against International Harvester, U.S. Steel, American Sugar, American Can, the four major meatpackers, and Corn Products Company advanced in the courts, and by 1915 a broad restructuring of industry—reversing much of the trust movement—was in prospect. But then World War I intervened, the mood changed, the rule of reason began to tell, and the effort collapsed.

"Good" Trusts. In 1916, a lower court refused to convict the American Can Company, which controlled nine tenths of the output of tin cans, because the defendant "had done nothing of which any competitor or consumer of cans complains or anything which strikes a disinterested outsider as unfair or unethical."[8] In 1920, the Court acquitted U.S. Steel.[9] The doctrine contained in this decision granted virtual immunity to monopoly in manufacturing for the next 25 years.

---

[5]This lag is evaluated in George W. Stocking, *The Oil Industry and the Competitive System* (Boston: Houghton Mifflin, 1925).

[6]*U.S.* v. *American Tobacco Co.,* 221 U.S. 106.

[7]See Alfred Chandler and Stephen Salsbury, *Pierre S. Du Pont and the Making of the Modern Corporation* (New York: Harper & Row, 1971).

[8]*U.S.* v. *American Can Co.,* 230 F. 859, 861 (1961).

[9]*U.S.* v. *U.S. Steel Corp.,* 251 U.S. 417 (1920). For an excellent recent critique of this decision, see Donald O. Parsons and Edward J. Ray, "the United States Steel Consolidation: The Creation of Market Control," *Journal of Law and Economics* 18 (April 1975), pp. 181–220.

U.S. Steel, created in 1901, combined 12 firms, which had merged some 180 separate companies with over 300 plants. It was the largest merger in the nation's history, extending vertically from mining to fabrication and horizontally to all the types of steel-mill products, and controlling around two thirds of the output of the industry. In 1920, the company's market share was still 50 percent.

In absolving U.S. Steel by a 4–3 vote, the Court focused on two features. First, the firm's market share was continuing to slip, and so monopoly was not being sustained. Second, U.S. Steel had not been abusive toward competitors, as had Standard Oil and American Tobacco. Instead, it had cooperated with them in avoiding price cuts, thereby yielding some of its market share. Though formed by mergers that did create monopoly, the firm was exculpated by its "good" (if inefficient) actions.

When this decision was announced, the government withdrew its appeals in several pending cases, including the one against American Can. The Court had turned about, and treatment largely ceased. The courts were evidently determined now not to touch dominant firms except in the most extreme cases. Market shares were safe virtually up to 100 percent. The other cases ended in defeat or peripheral consent decrees.[10]

2. The Second Wave, 1937–1953

Treatment ceased until 1938 when Alcoa was brought to trial for the monopoly it had held since before 1900. Other cases followed under Thurman Arnold and on until 1952. The decisions on Alcoa in 1945 and United Shoe Machinery in 1953 revived Section 2 to a degree; in doctrine, shares of 60 percent could be treated, but in practice, large gaps remained even in this moderate coverage. After 1952, treatment lapsed once again.

Alcoa. The *Alcoa* case challenged one of the foremost monopolies in the economy, which had been briefly subject to a suit back in 1912. Alcoa first gained dominance after 1890 by controlling the key Hall and Bradley patents and then extended its dominance seemingly on a perpetual basis.

Alcoa claimed to be efficient and not abusive, but the government sued it in 1938 for monopolizing, as part of Roosevelt's revival of anti-

---

[10]The meatpackers decree of 1920 did prevent integration into adjacent markets. Though mild at the time, it came to be challenged vigorously by the firms in 1929 and the 1950s. Denied both times in the courts, the firms finally obtained a revision of the decree in 1976. It permitted the packers, now no longer dominant, to enter a number of concentrated industries that had been off limits.

trust policy. The Division sought to show that monopoly could be reduced by antitrust even if the firm had committed no single abusive action. The suit charged that Alcoa had monopolized the manufacture of virgin aluminum and the sale of various aluminum products, and sought to divide the firm into several parts. A prime charge was vertical price squeezes by Alcoa, involving the price charged for crude aluminum and the prices offered customers for finished goods. After a trial that ran for more than two years, the district court found Alcoa not guilty and the government appealed. The final decision was written by Judge Learned Hand in 1945.[11]

The court found that Alcoa manufactured more than nine tenths of the virgin aluminum ingot used in the United States, the rest coming in from abroad, and concluded that this was "enough to constitute a monopoly."[12] It then considered the argument that the power conferred by this monopoly, though it existed, had not been exercised. This distinction, said the Court,

> is . . . purely formal; it would be valid only so long as the monopoly remained wholly inert; it would disappear as soon as the monopoly began to operate; for, when it did—that is, as soon as it began to sell at all—it must sell at some price and the only price at which it could sell is a price which it itself fixed. Thereafter the power and its exercise must needs coalesce.

The doctrine of the *Steel* and *Harvester* cases, that the mere existence of unexerted power is no offense, was reversed. Price fixing was found to be inherent in monopoly.

The Court also considered acts that might show intent or abuse (the "plus" factor). It found many, showing that monopoly had not been "thrust upon" Alcoa.

> It was not inevitable that it should always anticipate increases in the demand for ingots and be prepared to supply them. Nothing compelled it to keep doubling and redoubling its capacity before others entered the field. It insists that it has never excluded competitors; but we can think of no more effective exclusion than progressively to embrace each new opportunity as it opened, and to face every newcomer with new capacity already geared into a great organization, having the advantage of experience, trade connections, and the elite of personnel.

The Court condemned the use of squeeze tactics in the past and enjoined their repetition in the future, but made clear that it was holding Alcoa guilty of monopolization "regardless of such practices."

---

[11]*U.S.* v. *Aluminum Co. of America,* 148 F.2d 416. When the justices who had previously been connected with the prosecution disqualified themselves, the Supreme Court could not muster a quorum of six to hear the case. It was then arranged to have a three-judge court hear the case with Judge Hand presiding.

[12]Ibid., p. 424. Recall the discussion of this market in Chapter 6.

The decision made a clean break with the *Steel* and *Harvester* precedents. It required dominant firms to meet a stricter code of competitive fairness than lesser firms must meet. But the sharp reversal in doctrine resulted in very modest economic changes. Alcoa's structure was not touched. Instead, government aluminum plants built during World War II (and operated by Alcoa) were sold off to new competitors, which turned out to be Reynolds and Kaiser. Alcoa still dominated the new tight oligopoly, being required only to license its patents and cut its ties with Aluminium, Ltd., of Canada.[13] The tight oligopoly has continued with little change into the 1990s.

The *Alcoa* doctrine was soon extended to the leading three cigarette firms and movie theaters.[14] By 1948, the Court was saying:

> It is not always necessary to find a specific intent to restrain trade or build a monopoly. . . . It is sufficient that a restraint of trade or monopoly results as the consequence of a defendant's conduct or business arrangements. . . . Monopoly power, whether lawfully or unlawfully acquired, may itself constitute an evil and stand condemned under Section 2 even though it remains unexercised.[15]

Several other cases during the 1940s resulted in modest structural changes, in nonmanufacturing industries. The National Broadcasting Company (NBC) was forced to divest its "Blue" network in 1943; this became the basis for the American Broadcasting Company (ABC). The Pullman Company was required to separate its production and leasing of railway sleeping cars, keeping the part it preferred.[16] In the *A&P* case, the company was found in 1946 to have gained discriminatory advantages through its wholesale produce subsidiary, the Atlantic Commission Company. A consent decree in 1954 dissolved ACCO.[17] The *Paramount* decision in 1948 cut the links between movie producers and theater chains.[18] It also stopped the "block booking" of movies, which had tied the best films to inferior ones (see Chapter 10).

American Can. This suit against the two leading can companies— American and Continental—resulted in a consent decree in 1950.[19] The

---

[13]See M. J. Peck, *Competition in the Aluminum Industry* (Cambridge: Harvard Univ. Press, 1961).

[14]*American Tobacco Co.* v. *U.S.*, 328 U.S. 781, 811; and *U.S.* v. *Griffith*, 334 U.S. 100, 105–7.

[15]*U.S.* v. *Griffith*, 334 U.S. 100, 105–7.

[16]*U.S.* v. *Pullman Co.*, 50 F. Supp. 123 (1943).

[17]*U.S.* v. *Great A.&P. Tea Co.*, 67 F. Supp. 626 (1946); affirmed 173 F.2d 79 (1949); Civil Action 52–139, District Court of the Southern District of N.Y., Consent Decree, January 19, 1954.

[18]*U.S.* v. *Paramount Pictures*, 334 U.S. 131 (1948).

[19]*U.S.* v. *American Can Co.*, Civil Action 26345-H, District Court, Northern District of California. Final Judgment, June 22, 1950.

firms agreed to stop various exclusionary actions, such as refusals to sell can-closing machinery, the tying of can and machinery contracts, and price discrimination of various sorts. The decree required no divestiture or other structural change. Concentration did decrease by 1955, but the industry long remained a tight oligopoly.[20]

United Shoe Machinery. In 1954, the second *United Shoe Machinery* case resulted in a landmark conviction but little economic change. The firm had held a virtual monopoly for some 50 years in a rather small market. Judge Wyzanski followed the precedent established in the aluminum case, but he also went further.[21] Monopoly, he said, is lawful if it is "thrust upon" the monopolist. Yet a concern's monopoly power is unlawful if that power is the result of barriers erected by its own business methods (even though not predatory, immoral, or restraining trade in violation of Section 1 of the Sherman Act). The firm can still escape if it shows that the barriers are exclusively the result of superior skill, superior products, natural advantages, technological or economic efficiency, scientific research, low margins of profit maintained permanently and without discrimination, legal licenses, or the like.

Systematic price discrimination was the main behavior pattern that, taken with the high market share, violated Section 2 (see Chapter 10 for more detail). United's business practices—such as price discrimination, leasing rather than selling its machines, and making long-term contracts on exclusive terms—were not per se illegal, but the company had not achieved and maintained its overwhelming strength solely by virtue of its "ability, economies of scale, research, and adaptation to inevitable economic laws." Instead, given its dominant position, its business practices excluded competitors from the field. Judge Wyzanski imposed on the monopolist a stricter standard of conduct than that applying to competitive concerns. This reaffirmed the tighter standards of behavior set by *Alcoa*.

Yet the decision set an important new standard by conceding that monopoly was acceptable if won by "superior skill, foresight and industry." Later, in the 1980s, this criterion became the test that validated the Chicago-UCLA policy of absolving all dominant firms. The firms were assumed to represent *only* superior skill, foresight, and industry.

Du Pont Cellophane. Du Pont had monopolized cellophane in the U.S. market from 1923 on, earning high rates of return but preventing the entry of new competitors. The Court chose instead to define the market

---

[20]For a defense of the decree, see James W. McKie, *Tin Cans and Tin Plate* (Cambridge, Mass.: Harvard Univ. Press, 1959).

[21]*U.S.* v. *United Shoe Machinery Corp.*, 110 F. Supp. 295.

as all flexible packaging materials (as noted in Chapter 6). Since Du Pont's share of that "market" was only 18 percent, the case stopped there, without reaching the other criteria.

After 1948, major cases were filed against AT&T and IBM. AT&T's vertical integration with Western Electric, its sole internal supplier of equipment to all the Bell operating companies, was challenged (see the later case, covered below). The IBM suit attacked IBM's monopoly of tabulating equipment and cards. The cases were ambitious, and action against IBM might have averted IBM's later dominance of the computer industry. Both cases were settled by the Eisenhower administration during 1955–1956 under murky circumstances and with little gain.[22] Section 2 treatment largely ceased until 1969.

II. SINCE 1969: A THIRD WAVE AND THE 1980s' FREEZE

During 1953–68, structural treatment of the main dominant firms slowed. Eastman Kodak agreed to end its tying of film sales and processing, but there was little change in its position in film by the 1970s.[23] United Fruit Company consented in 1958 to end its old, pre-1900 banana monopoly, agreeing to create from its assets a firm capable of handling 35 percent of the market by 1970. Castle & Cook and Del Monte entered the market strongly after 1964. By 1973, United Fruit (now United Brands) no longer led, and it had shifted mainly into other lines.

The Division started suits against GM's bus and locomotive monopolies (over 85 percent each), but the cases were dropped by 1966 for lack of foreseeable relief. With only one plant in each case, it was pointless to proceed. Grinnell Corporation was convicted in 1966 for monopolizing the market in "accredited central station protective systems," but the market was small and the doctrine was not new.[24] The 1960s brought much study but few cases. Tight oligopoly was not touched.

---

[22]On the improprieties in reaching the settlement, see Mark J. Green and others, *The Closed Enterprise System* (New York: Grossman Publishers, 1972), chap. 2.

[23]The Division chose rapid negotiation rather than full trial as a "more efficient" method. But this avoided disclosure of the facts, actions by injured third parties, and, in the event, effective changes (see Don Waldman, *Antitrust Action and Market Structure* (Lexington, Mass.: D. C. Heath, 1978). For a defense of the handling see Theodore P. Kovaleff, "The Antitrust Record of the Eisenhower Administration," *Antitrust Bulletin* 21 (Winter 1976), pp. 589–610.

[24]The relief given in 1967 was easy to arrange and remarkably effective. Grinnell Corporation divested American District Telegraph Company and the restrictive terms were stopped. Firms increased from 40 to 190 by 1969. ADT grew rapidly, became much more efficient, and was soon thriving. The economics of competition under Section 2 operated with high fidelity.

During 1969–78, five major cases were started: IBM, cereals, Xerox, AT&T, and Du Pont titanium dioxide. Private cases against IBM and AT&T also proliferated, but this wave ebbed by 1982, with effects only on AT&T, and, after 1980, no further Section 2 case has been planned or mounted. After reviewing these cases, we can consider the current state of policy and future alternatives.

1. IBM

This case challenged one of the two leading dominant firms in U.S. industry (the other, AT&T, is discussed below). It was almost an obligatory case if Section 2 were to be relevant to the numerous lesser dominant firms found in other industries. IBM clearly had substantial monopoly power, and its actions had been quite aggressive, seeking to remove specific important competitors. When the case was given up in the end, the range of permissible "hard competition" by all dominant firms increased greatly.

The firm has held between 60 and 85 percent of the mainframe computer market since 1955. It has not refrained from a wide variety of aggressive actions.[25] The Division sued IBM under Section 2 in 1969.[26] The filing was prompted by private suits against IBM, by the failure of several competitors, and by data showing IBM to have a market share of 70 percent and a thorough pattern of price discrimination. The suit charged that IBM held monopoly power, that the discrimination prevented effective competition by smaller specialized producers, and that the introduction of the major 360 line of computers in 1965 was done in ways that eliminated competition.

Discrimination has been both (1) vertical (among machine types, with higher profit rates on smaller systems, where competition was weaker) and (2) horizontal (among the various users of each computer model.) Vertical patterns were known from IBM pricing memos about the 360 line of computers about to be introduced in 1964. Further, IBM had used several "fighting ship" computer models (the 360/44 and the 360/67, which lost money) in order to defeat rivals' systems. Horizontal discrimination also occurred, as IBM salespeople promised free programming and other help to secure contracts. Discrimination is systematic and inherent in IBM's position.

---

[25]This is shown in Gerald Brock, *The U.S. Computer Industry* (Cambridge, Mass.: Ballinger Press, 1975). See also Richard T. DeLamarter, *Big Blue: IBM's Use and Abuse of Power* (New York: Dodd, Mead, 1986); and William G. Shepherd, *Market Power and Economic Welfare* (New York: Random House, 1970), chap. 15, for detailed accounts of IBM's strategic pricing and related actions. For defense of IBM, see Franklin M. Fisher, John J. McGowan, and Joen E. Greenwood, *Folded, Spindled and Mutilated: Economic Analysis and U.S. v. IBM* (Cambridge, Mass.: MIT Press, 1983).

[26]*U.S.* v. *International Business Machines Corp.*, 69 CIV 200, So. Dist. of N.Y.

After six years of poorly handled pretrial preparation, the trial began in 1975 and ran until 1982.[27] IBM's defense was primarily that: (1) its share of the business-equipment market was below 40 percent and falling; (2) its pricing was competitive, not predatory; (3) its market position reflected good performance and economies of scale; (4) its products were highly complex; (5) it had been innovative; and (6) its profit rate had not really been high. Moreover, its shares were widely held by small and large investors, who feared capital losses. IBM's relentless resistance was stiffened by the prospect of billions of dollars in private damage claims should the firm be convicted. Also, IBM gained from delay, probably at least $1 million per day.[28]

A number of private suits also sought damages or restructuring of IBM. Control Data Corporation filed a massive suit in 1968 but settled it in 1973, gaining benefits worth $101 million (including IBM's Service Bureau Corporation).[29] Over 20 other cases included suits by Greyhound Corporation, Western Union, Transamerica, and several firms making equipment compatible with IBM products. There were two core issues. First was market definition, where IBM's broad market version was not accepted by the courts. Second was the charge of predatory actions: that IBM had gone too far in cutting prices selectively and redesigning equipment to eliminate smaller rivals. Here IBM prevailed, relying mainly on arguments that its prices had not been cut below marginal or variable costs (see Chapter 10). The courts were persuaded that IBM's competition was merely vigorous and its success reflected superior innovation and efficiency.

In 1982, the Reagan appointee in charge of the Antitrust Division withdrew the *IBM* case shortly before the trial judge was expected to convict IBM. IBM's actions were said to be competitive, not excessive, and appeals would drag out the case too long. In part, IBM's delaying tactics had prevailed—by lasting until conservative officials came into office.

Altogether, IBM won nearly every case and point of law. The whole process was costly, involving hundreds of lawyers and witnesses, many

---

[27]The economic core of the case was highly compact and complete by mid-1968. The delay in bringing the case to trial reflected extreme efforts and clever strategy by IBM counsel and, during 1969–72, a lapse in Antitrust Division handling and passive behavior by the court. The Division staff permitted such tactics as extensive tangential interrogatories and snowing by masses of irrelevant documents. After 1972, the case was given far greater resources and was handled more aggressively. Incidentally, Thomas J. Watson, Jr., IBM's chairman in the 1960s, describes the case in his memoirs as valid and appropriate.

[28]Suppose that about one fourth of IBM's profits (then running around $1.7 billion yearly) were at stake under Section 2. This was equivalent to $1 million per day.

[29]Control Data also agreed to destroy, in the presence of IBM lawyers, a large computerized filing system for trial documents that it had been preparing for use by itself and the Antitrust Division. This destruction added at least a year's delay to the Division's case. Though cited as contempt of court, the action was evidently worth its cost to IBM.

millions of dollars, millions of pages of documents, and years of court time. It illustrated the weaknesses of the method. IBM is the leading industrial dominant firm, with great profitability and a nearly steady market position. Yet a full treatment of it was possible, using the traditional approach. Instead, *IBM* shifted back the margin of treatment, to let dominant firms commit with impunity a wide range of aggressive actions. This was a direct reversal of the *Alcoa* and *United Shoe Machinery* standards of behavior.

2. Breakfast Cereals: An Experimental Tight-Oligopoly Case

The burst of research on tight oligopoly from the 1930s to the 1950s had posed the difficult question: Could antitrust deal with tight oligopoly and its tendencies to tacit collusion? The treatment of tight oligopoly fell between Sections 1 and 2, because it involved neither explicit collusion nor single-firm dominance. Finally, in 1972, a case was brought against major cereals companies to test the reach of policy.[30]

In 1972, the FTC charged the major cereal producers—Kellogg, General Mills, General Foods, and Quaker Oats—with a shared monopoly. Lengthy preparations followed before a hearing examiner, and the formal hearings ran from 1976 to 1979.

The case tried to break new ground by covering tacit collusion in a tight oligopoly.[31] The firms were accused of (1) "packing the product space" by proliferating brands and, thus, heading off any new competitors, and (2) jointly taking steps to avoid price competition and package premiums.

The case had a firm economic basis, the firms were highly profitable, the products were simple, and there were no important economies of scale. Yet resistance was fierce, and, in the new conservative setting after 1980, the FTC decided the case in the firms' favor.

3. Xerox

This case challenged the spectacular-growth firm of the 1960s, which had been propelled by its patent-based monopoly of plain-paper copi-

---

[30]The case was largely originated by Charles E. Mueller of the FTC staff, later the founder of the *Antitrust Law & Economics Review*. It was an apt case for the purpose. The tight oligopoly had existed for decades with little change, its profits were high, and its familiarity to all consumers provided for public understanding and support for the case.

[31]See F. M. Scherer, "The Breakfast Cereal Industry," in Walter Adams, ed. *The Structure of American Industry,* 7th ed. (New York: Macmillan, 1986); and Richard L. Schmalensee, "Entry Deterrence in the Ready-to-Eat Breakfast Cereal Industry," *Bell Journal of Economics* 9 (Autumn 1978), pp. 305–27.

ers. Though Xerox had largely originated the industry in 1961, it had soon developed extremely complex strategic price discrimination to exploit and protect its monopoly.

The FTC started action against Xerox in early 1973, alleging a market share of 95 percent in plain-paper copiers and 86 percent in the whole office-copier market. A series of Xerox's pricing, leasing, and patent acts were said to exclude competition. Many of the conditions and charges closely paralleled *IBM* and *United Shoe Machinery*. Xerox had developed a thorough system of price discrimination, based on numbers of runs, numbers of copies per run, special large-user discounts, and still other complicated conditions. By leasing, rather than selling, its machines, Xerox was able to apply the discrimination fully. Xerox's sales network was a major factor in its dominance. Xerox's nearly 2,000 patents also provided protection against new competition. These acts and conditions were not clearly inherent or necessary. They reflected careful choices and could be enjoined.

Xerox's price discrimination showed that it had the intent to eliminate competition by making sharp discriminatory price cuts on products where it faced competition. On products where its market power was higher, Xerox set much higher price-cost ratios. The FTC further claimed that Xerox realized few scale economies, was not an innovative leader after 1965, and made high monopoly rates of return, averaging above 27 percent during the 1960s.

In its defense, Xerox defined the market as *all* copying during the 1960s, which would have given it a market share of only 65 percent, and all copying *and reproducing* (mimeographing and the like) in the 1970s. On that basis, Xerox's market share would have been well below 50 percent by 1973. Xerox also pointed out that the crucial patents it held were legal and binding. Therefore, it said, its large market share, pricing, and high profits were justified. Xerox also claimed that those profits, which dwindled below a 20 percent return on capital by 1973, merely reflected Xerox's scale economies and fruitful innovations.

The FTC complaint did not ask for restructuring or other drastic changes. Instead, patent licensing, the selling of machines, less price discrimination, and severing ties with Rank Xerox (the British affiliate) were sought. Xerox responded by negotiating for a quick settlement, which was accepted in 1975. Certain patents were opened up, and some discriminatory pricing was dropped (but soon replaced by even more complex pricing).[32] Xerox's position was scarcely affected. When new

---

[32]Xerox agreed to license patents at no more than 1.5 percent of sales or rental income and to supply its technical specifications and know-how. The prohibition of its "fleet" pricing plan was quickly nullified by an even more complex pricing system. Xerox agreed to put sale prices on all machines, but these were set high enough to induce most users to continue leasing.

competition arose in 1977 from Savin and Canon (selling Japanese machines), it was not because of the FTC action.

4. FTC: In re *Du Pont* (the Titanium Dioxide Case)

This case sought to intercept a monopoly during its formation, rather than afterward. Du Pont was implementing an explicit strategy to attain at least 65 percent of the market by exploiting a cost advantage from a new technology. The case was clear, compact, and a sharp test of the reach of policy.[33]

Titanium dioxide (TiO_2) is the best whitening pigment that exists. It is used in all kinds of paints, plastics, paper, clothing, wallboard— nearly everything that has a white color. Its sales during the 1970s were $600 to $900 million annually. During 1940–60, Du Point developed a better, complex method of producing TiO_2. Suddenly in 1968–72, this method became at least 15 percent cheaper than the other techniques, because the ore it used became relatively cheaper.

Seizing this opportunity, Du Pont launched a plan in 1972 to use that advantage to raise its market share from 30 to at least 65 percent by carefully excluding any other firm from building any new TiO_2 capacity. Under its plan, Du Pont set the TiO_2 price just low enough to make it unprofitable for rivals to build new plants and thereby learn the superior method. The price was also set high enough to generate funds for Du Pont to build its own new capacity. Therefore, Du Pont would capture all growth in the industry, and its market share would rise from 30 percent to 65 percent or higher.

Du Pont refused to license its method to others, seeking instead to gain a high market share and then reap high profits. The strategy aimed to convert a specific advantage into a virtually permanent dominance of the market.

In 1978, the FTC staff started an action charging Du Pont with monopolizing the market.[34] Du Pont could have licensed its technology at lucrative rates, the FTC staff said, and thereby profited fully from its innovation *without* creating market dominance in the TiO_2 industry.

---

[33]For a summary of the economic conditions of the case, see William G. Shepherd, "Anatomy of a Monopoly," *Antitrust Law & Economics Review* 11 (December 1979), pp. 93–104, 12 (March 1980), pp. 76–93, and 12 (June 1980), pp. 93–106. The author testified on behalf of the FTC staff in the case.

[34]FTC Docket No. 9108.

Du Pont responded that it had created an innovation and should be permitted to exploit it fully. To forbid it to do so would be to penalize innovation and success. Also, Du Pont noted that if it had held prices low to discourage rivals from growing, those very low prices had benefited consumers. Firms should not be penalized, it urged, for setting their prices low.

There was little dispute about the facts. Du Pont's actions could be interpreted in two contrasting ways: as illegal "monopolizing," or as merely the laudable outcome of innovation and self-restraint in pricing. The case was compact, clear, and quickly tried. In late 1980, the FTC acquitted Du Pont on all points. Its opinion turned on one point: Du Pont's beneficial role in innovating the new method. That good action immunized its monopolizing actions from attack. Otherwise, the FTC said, the fear of antitrust penalties would discourage future innovation by such firms as Du Pont.

The case thus ended by affirming the new Chicago-UCLA pro-dominant policy of the 1980s. Only if Du Pont had set clearly "predatory" prices would the FTC have been willing to see a violation. It had not, and so dominance was permitted.

5. AT&T

One epic exception to the new freeze on Section 2 came to a head during 1980–84: the *AT&T* case. This brought about by far the largest Section 2 divestiture of all, and it showed that even the world's largest private enterprise, with all its technological complexity, public esteem, investor reliance, and political influence, could still be forced to make major structural changes. The aftereffects are still occurring in the 1990s, as the sections of the old Bell Telephone System jockey over access to each other's markets. The case proved that big cases can still succeed, particularly in formerly regulated monopolies where vertical leverage is probably being applied.

After the 1913 agreement and the 1949–55 case, the issue of Western Electric was reopened in 1974 with a new suit by the Division. As a 50-person FCC task force report (of 1,500 pages) had recently recommended, the Division sought to separate Western Electric and possibly divide it into several competing firms within the whole market for telecommunications equipment. The new suit also contemplated separating out the Long Lines Department, "some or all" of the Bell operating companies, and Bell Laboratories. True natural monopoly could remain intact, but the Bell System would be prevented from using that advantage in order to capture other, naturally competitive markets. Because this case succeeded in 1982 in securing the most extensive

Table 7–2   Events in the AT&T Policy Sequence

1881	Western Electric added as supplier.
1890s	AT&T grows, adds most cities and states.
1910–13	Antitrust case prepared. AT&T agrees to divest Western Union and to stop acquiring phone companies.
1920–40	AT&T enters radio, movie, and sound and copper-recycling markets. Vertical integration with Western Electric is investigated by FCC.
1949–55	Antitrust Division sues to separate Western Electric. The case is largely dropped in 1955.
1962	Arguments grow against market capture by Bell.
1968–75	FCC decisions open possible competition in equipment *(Carterfone)* and long-distance service (MCI). AT&T yields slowly.
1969	Widespread service failures undercut Bell's reputation for quality, permit challenges to its monopoly.
1970s	Bell moves into numerous markets for electronic equipment.
1974	Antitrust Division case against AT&T is filed.
1975–78	Bell seeks congressional approval of monopoly throughout the sector.
1977	FCC orders competition in buying of equipment.
1979	Supreme Court requires FCC to permit competition in long-distance service.
1981	MCI wins $1.8 billion verdict against AT&T for preventing competition.
1981–84	Antitrust Division case tried; compromise announced January 1982; modified after hearings during 1982–83; divestiture occurs at beginning of 1984.
1986–	AT&T and regional Bell companies repeatedly petition Judge Greene and seek legislators' support for expanding into related markets, such as equipment, long-distance, and yellow pages.

(even astounding) divestiture ever attained, it requires a detailed discussion.[35]

It carried forward changes that had been developing for several decades—in new technology, in FCC actions, and in private antitrust suits. Table 7–2 shows the main events. Bell had frequently reached out to enter adjacent markets, ranging from telephone equipment, movies, and microwave transmission to copper-scrap recycling. However, it had come under increasing pressure to let competition into its own domain, especially by FCC actions in 1968–69 and 1977, and by the Supreme

---

[35]Among many sources on the topic, see David S. Evans, ed., *Breaking up Bell: Essays on Industrial Organization and Regulation* (New York: Elsevier-North Holland, 1983) for lucid analysis supporting the Antitrust Division's case. On the other side, see William W. Sharkey, *The Theory of Natural Monopoly* (Cambridge: Cambridge University Press, 1982).

On the rationale for the divestiture, see Timothy J. Brennan, "Why Regulated Firms Should be Kept Out of Regulated Markets: Understanding the Divestiture in *United States* v. *AT&T*," *Antitrust Bulletin* 32 (Fall 1987), pp. 741–91. Other books include Peter Temin, *The Fall of the Bell System* (New York: Cambridge University Press, 1987); and Alvin von Auw, *Heritage and Destiny: Reflections on the Bell System in Transition* (New York: Praeger Publishers, 1983).

Figure 7–1   The AT&T Structure before 1984

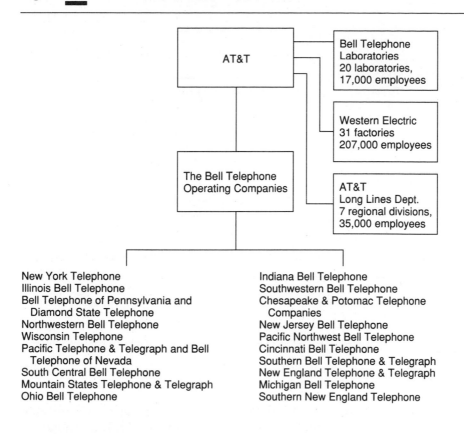

New York Telephone
Illinois Bell Telephone
Bell Telephone of Pennsylvania and
   Diamond State Telephone
Northwestern Bell Telephone
Wisconsin Telephone
Pacific Telephone & Telegraph and Bell
   Telephone of Nevada
South Central Bell Telephone
Mountain States Telephone & Telegraph
Ohio Bell Telephone

Indiana Bell Telephone
Southwestern Bell Telephone
Chesapeake & Potomac Telephone
   Companies
New Jersey Bell Telephone
Pacific Northwest Bell Telephone
Cincinnati Bell Telephone
Southern Bell Telephone & Telegraph
New England Telephone & Telegraph
Michigan Bell Telephone
Southern New England Telephone

Court in 1979. Technology now permitted competition in all but the local telephone calling market, where one set of wires and switches was still most efficient. The case simply forced AT&T into a new structure reflecting that reality.

Figure 7–1 shows the Bell System as challenged in 1974–81. The case lay largely dormant for three years, but then a new judge (Harold Greene) sped it forward. The two sides were forced to agree on simple points and, thus, identify the main issues for trial. Delay and excessive discovery were prevented, and Judge Greene forced the trial ahead briskly. After the Division's side was presented, he announced that AT&T had probably committed violations. When the rebuttal case went poorly, AT&T realized that settlement was preferable to conviction (and the resulting flood of treble-damage claims). A settlement was reached and announced (together with the *IBM* case withdrawal) in January 1982. After full hearings and some modifications by Judge Green, divestiture occurred on January 1, 1984.

Figure 7–2   AT&T after the 1984 Divestiture

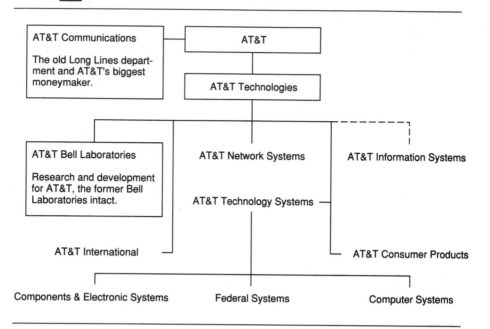

Note that Western Electric is absent, its plants now scattered among the various lines of business.

Source: AT&T.

The main change was to detach the Bell Operating Companies (BOCs), like Ohio Bell and Pacific Tel & Tel, from AT&T, as shown in Figure 7–1. Other changes in the remaining AT&T are given in Figure 7–2, which can be compared with Figure 7–1. The basic concept of the settlement identified two parts of the Bell System that needed to be separated: (1) *natural monopolies* (the local operations); and (2) the rest, which were regarded as *naturally competitive* or likely to become so. Dividing them would prevent the abuses of the past, in which the monopolies were the base for capturing and controlling other markets.

The 21 BOCs were grouped into seven regional firms (Nynex, US West, Bell South, Ameritech, etc.). They operate in the 164 LATAs ("local access and transport areas"), which cover all metropolitan areas. These BOCs were also permitted to sell (but not produce) new equipment to customers, in competition with AT&T and others, thus maximizing competition in equipment sales. To avoid letting the BOCs use their monopoly position to get advantages in equipment sales, the BOCs had to sell through separate subsidiaries.

AT&T has two main parts: regulated long-distance service (by AT&T Communication), and unregulated activities, including equipment production and marketing, and foreign activities (by AT&T Technologies). The old Western Electric is dissolved and merged into four new units under AT&T Technologies. Long-distance service by AT&T covers all transmission among LATAs, and so the coverage now extends to a lot of *intra*state calling. AT&T faces competition from MCI, Sprint, and others on long-distance service, but AT&T still has 70 percent of sales as of 1990.

There are two main competitive issues. First, on long-distance service, is competition effective? Not yet, because the newcomers are still small and vulnerable, as Chapter 3 noted. Only when AT&T's market share recedes to 50 percent or less will competition be fully robust and effective. Even then, there will be a need to supervise the key pricing patterns so as to prevent unfair treatment of the independents.

Second, is competition in equipment effective? Has vertical monopoly (between Western Electric and the BOCs and Long Lines) ended? Yes. The seven new BOCs have taken independent stances toward AT&T and are buying equipment from a variety of sources, on competitive terms.

In both areas (long-distance service and equipment buying), the case only added to changes already in process. The difference, however, is large, and the changes are now irreversible. The antitrust effort has worked, yielding classical benefits of increased competition. Old defenses of the Bell monopolies are now recognized to have been mistaken, such as the exaggerated claims of vertical economies and "systemic integrity." The new patterns fit well the true emerging technology and scope for competition. The case itself involved substantial costs, but much of AT&T's own costs were avoidable by a more limited and effective defense. The costs of divestiture have also been sizable, but the flow of greater innovation, efficiency, and choice are widely agreed to have offset them.

The case also dispelled fears that Section 2 actions had grown too large and complex to manage. Instead, a brisk judge proved that perhaps the most complicated sector of all could be assessed clearly at trial and reorganized efficiently by means of massive divestiture. Section 2 and the divestiture remedy have both been restored as effective tools. Most of the tacit obstacles to Section 2 action (such as technical complexity, fear of stockholders' losses, and an innovative reputation) turned out to be minor, even in this monumental case. They should be easily resolved in lesser cases.

6. Lessons

The series of antitrust-agency cases has not developed clear lines of treatment; the *AT&T* result was far stricter than the dropping of the *IBM* case. Two points have emerged.

Leveraging. First, *the leveraging of market power from one market to another will usually be resisted, even by Chicago-UCLA officials.* This point can apply most strongly in utility sectors, such as electricity and telephones. Firms often can use their franchised monopoly of utility services to gain control of an adjacent market.

A leading case in the electricity industry helped to set this precedent. Otter Tail Power Company is a private utility which provides power in Minnesota. When the town of Elbow Lake formed a city electricity system, Otter Tail refused to provide power to the town. Otter Tail's control over wholesale power enabled it to prevent competition at the retail level. This leveraging of power was held illegal by the Court in 1973, and a series of later cases has applied it to similar situations in other localities.[36] Private electric systems cannot use their control over bulk power to eliminate city-owned retail systems in their areas. They are not, however, required to give special advantages to the cities.

Similarly, *telephone* companies used their control over local systems to reduce competition in selling telephone equipment (see the *GTE* case, below). Both AT&T and GTE prevented outside firms from selling equipment to their own operating companies. The franchised monopoly made this leveraging possible.

Leveraging can also happen in ordinary manufacturing industries. Eastman Kodak used its dominance in the U.S. film market to hurt competitors in the film-*processing* market. It introduced the Instamatic II camera with a new film and format in 1972 so abruptly that Berkey Photo and other film processors were nearly put out of business. Berkey sued and won $90 million at trial. The appeals court reversed on most counts, but it did accept that Eastman Kodak had used leverage to transfer market power.[37] Only because, the court held, Kodak's film dominance was honestly earned by past innovation were its leveraging actions here not illegal. Even so, it must not "smother competition" in adjacent markets.

Dominant-Firm Restraint. Thus, leveraging was usually illegal, and secondly, until the 1970s, *dominant firms were under some degree of restraint in taking actions against their small rivals.* Dominant firms have always claimed unlimited rights to exploit their positions, while smaller competitors have resisted excesses and "unfair" competition. Economic logic calls for some restraint; otherwise, dominance can become perpetual and competition will be ineffective because competitive parity is lacking.

---

[36]*Otter Tail Power Co. v. U.S.,* 410 U.S. 366 (1973).

[37]*Berkey Photo, Inc. v. Eastman Kodak Co.,* 603 F.2d 263 (2d Cir. 1979).

However, IBM's victories in a series of cases since 1970 have illustrated the opposite lesson. IBM's actions were "hard competition," often removing competitors from market, but IBM claimed that such unrestrained actions were legal and efficient. IBM's wins, mostly gained in conservative appeals courts and by a conservative antitrust chief's dropping of the case in 1982, markedly increased the scope for bruising actions by dominant firms against small rivals. This change in antitrust policy was made complete after 1980 at both agencies.

Private suits have peppered a number of the larger dominant firms. IBM attracted over 20 during 1965–78, Xerox about 10, and AT&T over 30.

In 1972, ITT persuaded a district judge in Hawaii to order GTE to divest all of its operating and manufacturing firms acquired since 1950 (some $3.7 billion at GTE's $9.0 billion in assets). Though the verdict was reversed on appeal in 1975, ITT won a retrial in 1978 on the grounds that GTE's in-house purchasing policy for equipment had excluded competition.

Hundreds of lesser cases have gone through the mill, often yielding sizable damages to the plaintiff. Many are trivial, but most are a natural result of the existence of market dominance. The routine strategy of the defendant (pioneered by IBM) has been to file a countersuit on any possible basis, such as the stealing of trade secrets or patent abuse. The countersuit is then used as a weapon to force a neutral settlement.[38]

7. *Aspen Skiing* v. *Aspen Highlands Skiing*[39]

Against the official stoppage of Section 2 actions, the Supreme Court affirmed in a private case in 1985 that a dominant firm still must avoid deliberate actions to harm its smaller rivals. *Aspen Skiing* is the most recent case on dominant-firm actions, and it dilutes somewhat the Chicago-UCLA line adopted by Reagan-Bush officials.

Aspen Skiing has been the dominant skiing company in the Aspen, Colorado, area since the 1950s. It controls three mountains (Ajax, Buttermilk, and Snowmass), while its small rival, Aspen Highlands Skiing, controls only one (Aspen Highlands). In the 1970s, the two companies cooperated in developing a joint multiarea ticketing arrangement in which one ticket gave skiers access to all slopes. Highlands' share of revenues ranged from 13 to 18 percent, while Aspen Skiing took over 80 percent.

---

[38]Brock analyzes such tactics in *The U.S. Computer Industry*. The method worked in the *Telex* case, for example, by turning the tables and making the risk of appeal intolerable.

[39]The case is *Aspen Skiing Co.* v. *Aspen Highlands Skiing Corp.*, 472 U.S. 585 (1985).

In the late 1970s, Aspen Skiing refused to continue the multiarea ticket, effectively freezing Highlands out from most of the skiers coming to the Aspen area. Highlands suffered large financial losses, despite its attempts to devise other ticketing arrangements. Aspen Skiing gave no persuasive reason that the change was necessary or based on efficiency. It simply sought to increase its dominance and profits, at Highlands' expense.

A jury, affirmed by an appeals court and the Supreme Court, held that Aspens' action violated Section 2. Aspen Skiing had abused its dominant position, without offering any saving grace of efficiency or necessity for its action. Given its dominant control over the Aspen-area skiing market, Aspen had a duty to avoid gratuitous actions to defeat its small rival.

This decision in a private case could only lead to damages (trebled to $7.5 million), not structural remedies. It ran counter to the precedents set by the IBM decisions in the 1970s, in which appeals courts gave IBM virtual carte blanche to inflict "hard competition," with no restraints. Therefore, the Aspen case provides some softening of the Chicago-UCLA laissez-faire policy toward dominant firms.

III. EVALUATION OF SECTION 2 ACTIONS

Viewed broadly, Section 2 cases have had significant effects. No comprehensive studies of those effects, and of the net benefits, have been made, but the main lines seem fairly clear.

1. Coverage and Effects

Candidates. The cases have dealt with most of the prominent candidates, moving broadly from leading firms in 1906–14 to lesser ones in 1938–52 and 1968–82. The acute cases have mostly been treated by now, with some exceptions. The suits themselves, or threats of them, have abated many situations of dominance. Also, the rate of erosion of market dominance has risen since 1960, reducing the positions of such firms as Xerox, General Motors, and Polaroid.

To round out the treatment of dominance under Section 2, consider now the candidates that remain untreated. As noted in Table 2–3, they include Eastman Kodak, Campbell Soup, IBM, Gillette, and a large number of newspapers that dominate their local markets. Each is debatable, but the stoppage of Section 2 actions after 1980 has blocked an objective evaluation of the need for action. For example, Eastman Kodak's domination is now over 80 years old, and it continues despite apparent mediocrity in the quality of management and innovation. A cautious policy would at least review the conditions in these industries regularly.

The newspaper industry seemingly poses the most difficult problems of all. The degree of dominance is very high in scores of cities. Moreover, in about 20 cities the two major local newspapers have come to be jointly operated, and most of the economic competition between them has actually ceased. Advertising rates, for example, closely approximate the pure-monopoly levels in many of these cities.

On top of that degree of monopoly, large newspaper chains own many of the newspapers in the middle-sized and smaller cities, probably adding to the degree of monopoly power. The matter is more urgent than if this were the cabbage or rug industry. Newspapers are among the most powerful media, able to influence both the democratic process and the quality of social knowledge and activity. Monopoly here is likely to have unusually significant consequences.

Policy has yet to address these issues and explore actions to solve them. The antitrust treatment has been based on an acceptance of the newspapers' claims that the dominance merely reflects large technical economies of scale. Hence, the Newspaper Preservation Act of 1970 permits the newspapers to merge under joint-operating agreements rather than requiring them to maintain competition.

The underlying "economies" may actually be much smaller, arising partly from advertising factors rather than genuine economies. A number of smaller cities, in fact, such as Little Rock, Arkansas, manage to retain vigorous newspaper competition, even though much larger newspapers in big cities have claimed that giantism is inevitable.

The newspaper industry is ripe for objective study and possibly a reversal of the 1970 policy that permits mergers that eliminate virtually all competition. Yet there is little official interest in doing thorough research, and the larger newspapers seemingly have enough political influence to block any effective study and reversal of policy.

Benefits and Costs. The benefit-cost results have largely reflected the progression from acute to lesser cases, as well as the increasing cost of these big cases. The benefit-cost ratios of the early cases were very high.[40] Market power was sharply reduced, at relatively small costs of

---

[40]A recent estimate of the benefit-cost ratio for major cases gives a rough idea of the probable yields:

Standard Oil	67	Alcoa	19
American Tobacco	21	American Can	7
International Harvester	22	United Shoe Machinery	5
Corn Products	8		

For estimating procedures, see W. G. Shepherd, *The Treatment of Market Power* (New York: Columbia University Press, 1975), chap. 7 and Appendix 3. In these and other cases, more thorough and timely treatments could have given larger yields.

litigation and (because restructuring was simple or minor) of adjustment. The yields for more recent cases have been smaller, though
the benefits have easily exceeded the costs. (And the *AT&T* case of
1974–84 probably will provide a very high benefit-cost ratio.) The best-
yielding cases have (1) treated large near monopolies, (2) moved quickly
after the initial monopolization, and (3) required major structural
changes.

Severity of Remedies. The severity of remedies was moderate even in
the big 1911 cases; it abated sharply after 1911; and it has dwindled
further in most cases since the 1920s. Relief in the 1911 cases merely
undid earlier mergers. Since 1913, there has been little direct restructuring in industry (except for AT&T in 1984), and the conduct remedies
have been moderate. Some weak-performing firms in basic industry
were defendants that escaped treatment in the 1913–35 period: Examples are U.S. Steel (now USX), meatpacking, and glass. Major wars
have played a role in forestalling treatment. World Wars I and II and
the Korean War all interrupted the thrust of enforcement waves and
softened judicial attitudes toward major firms.

The *AT&T* case is a major exception, but it is also a specialized
instance. The anticompetitive features were well known and attacked
since 1910. However, AT&T saw how it could gain from divestiture by
focusing on growth segments, and the changes that resulted from divestiture were done mainly by separating distinct firms, not by splitting
existing firms. For these reasons, action was less abrupt and severe
than it might seem.

Duration. The duration of cases—from initial study to remedy—has
lengthened, from about 6 years to about 10 to 15 years. The average
interval from the original monopolization to remedy, which was already
over 20 years in 1911 (35 to 40 years for Standard Oil), has now grown
even longer. In the two major 1911 cases, *Standard Oil* and *American
Tobacco,* remedy was applied two or more decades after the monopoly
was created, and only after the firm's market position was already
weakening. And the 1984 AT&T changes occurred many decades after
the problems arose.

*Indeed, restructuring has always lagged at least 20 years behind mo-
nopolizing, and the lag is rising.* In no case has treatment been applied
quickly enough to intercept a rising position of market power. The 1951
IBM case could have turned out to have that effect on the embryonic
computer industry. The FTC action toward Xerox in 1973 also was
early, by traditional standards, and so was the *Du Pont* TiO$_2$ case. However, all three cases had little result.

Monopoly Gains. In no case has the action removed much or most of the capitalized monopoly gain from the original monopolizers. Rockefeller, Du Pont, Duke, and other major family wealth was virtually untouched by the early antitrust actions. The second set of actions was even more remote from the original gains. In effect, a full amnesty for monopolizers has applied. Only the later shareholders have been exposed to antitrust risk.

2. Conditions for Success

The two preconditions for bringing suit were (1) a high market share, and (2) a high degree of profitability. There were virtually no suits against oligopolists or against firms with average or depressed rates of return. Convictions and remedy occurred mainly when the firm's actions were clearly abusive. The elements of a legal victory were, in the main: (1) a well-conceived and thorough economic case for action, based on extensive research on the critical points; (2) grassroots support, both political and in the form of private and state suits against the target company; (3) brilliant antitrust strategy, particularly to prevent delay; (4) the private side's being caught by surprise, complacency, or ineptness, and its display of abusive actions and its markedly excess profits; and (5) an availability of a specific, feasible basis for remedy, lest the absence of a remedy chill the case from the start.

An effective remedy might be ordered, *if*: (1) there were a technical basis for splitting, such as decentralization and an origin in recent mergers; (2) the products were relatively simple and standardized, so that innovation or national military involvement were not major questions; (3) a moderate weakening in the monopolists' total position was already in progress, so that potential competitors were active and expectations were not sharply reversed by divestiture (but not so severe a weakening as to make action superfluous); and (4) the stock were closely held, so that the expected or actual impact was not widespread.

3. Foreign Experiments

Other countries face smaller problems, and several have been more inventive. Dominance is usually less extensive and durable abroad. It tends to attract imports or new foreign subsidiaries, when profitability is high. U.S. firms, especially, have added competitive elements in soaps, oil, automobiles, drugs, and tin cans, among many others, in Western European countries.

Antitrust strategies are being tried in interesting ways.[41] In Britain, in the 1960s, the Monopolies Commission issued thorough studies on some important dominant positions in industry.[42] Usually, proposed changes were mild and the Board of Trade would not apply them in full.[43] During 1975–79, the Price Commission restrained price increases by a number of dominant firms. This moved toward competitive conditions, with little loss of efficiency. The commission was abolished in 1979 by the new conservative government.

The British Prices and Income Board assessed profits and, on occasion, management performance, while reducing price increases and stopping restrictive practices, during its brief 1966–71 life. Public holding companies own part or all of certain leading firms in Italy and several other European countries. Public ownership—partial or complete—gives a degree of public influence in many industries, including coal in Britain and automobiles and aircraft in France (see Chapter 15). Large-scale privatizing has reduced the scope of public enterprise in Britain since 1980, as Chapter 15 discusses.

The European Community has given some force to Article 86 of the original 1957 Treaty of Rome, which forbade abuses of "dominant positions." Actions have involved intense diplomatic struggles, including companies and countries, and few of the actions have had much impact. But in 1984, IBM agreed to stop certain kinds of price discrimination and the bundling of software and hardware.[44] And Hoffman-LaRoche agreed to stop certain variants of price discrimination in selling drugs and vitamins.

The only important restructuring abroad occurred after World War II, when the victorious allies sought permanent preventives against fascism in Germany and Japan.

---

[41]See various reports of the U.K. Monopolies Commission; and C. K. Rowley, *The British Monopolies Commission* (London: Allen & Unwin, 1966); and W. Pengilley, "Australian Experience of Antitrust Regulation," *Antitrust Bulletin,* Summer 1973, pp. 355–74. In 1973, long efforts to reduce drug prices in Britain finally resulted in a government order to Hoffman-LaRoche to cut prices on its Librium and Valium tranquilizers steeply. Roche's British unit was paying its Swiss parent $925 a kilogram for Librium ingredients and $2,300 a kilogram for the Valium ones, when these materials could be bought from Italy at $23 and $50.

[42]These included light bulbs (1951), wires and cables (1952), tires (1955), gases (1957), electrical machinery (1957), fertilizers (1958), cigarettes (1961), gasoline (1965), color film (1966), flat glass (1968), beer (1969), tin cans (1970), cereals (1973), and shoe machinery (1973), among others. It also screened mergers (see chap. 8).

[43]Yet Kodak, Ltd., was required to cut the price of color film by 25 percent, and Hoffman-LaRoche was made to reduce the price of Librium by 60 percent and Valium by 70 percent in 1974.

[44]See Henry W. de Jong, "Competition Policy in Europe: Stimulus, Nuisance, or Drawback?" in K. Groenveld, J.A.H. Maks, and J. Muysken, eds., *Economic Policy and the Market Process: Austrian and Mainstream Economics* (Amsterdam: North-Holland, 1990), pp. 112–45.

Parallel programs were started in both Germany and Japan in 1945–46 to take apart the combines in heavy industry and finance. This restructuring contained mainly two elements.[45] The first was directed toward the industrial combines themselves. It sought to dissolve the central control of these systems, to create variety and independence out of what had been tightly knit systems. The second dealt with the links between banks and producing enterprises.

The programs were stopped in midcourse by political resistance from the United States, where industrial interests believed that these strict steps might eventually come to be tried also in the United States if they worked well abroad. As a result, both programs were incomplete. Within 10 years, in fact, both countries had seen most of the original industrial patterns restored. In Japan, coordination within the combines has been looser than it was before 1945.

4. Alternative Treatments

What alternatives are there to supplement Section 2 or take its place? There are several conventional alternatives. Useful as they may be, they are specialized and have a narrower reach than is often thought, and they are difficult to apply.

Reductions in Trade Barriers. This has been a staple and attractive proposal since Adam Smith's time. Tariffs were integral to the trust issue between 1870 and 1900 in the United States. In small, trade-oriented economies, these levers already are powerful. Since 1960, new import competition has reduced market power in many U.S. industries.

There are at least two limits to the effectiveness of reductions in trade barriers. First, it seems impossible to get deliberate, specific cuts in trade barriers in order to apply new competitive forces. The resistance to cuts is focused and effective; either the protected firms are profitable and have a large stake, or they are stagnant and so imports will cause extensive structural changes. There is also a natural unwillingness of any nation to reduce its own trade barriers unilaterally. Indeed, new import competition has been met by strong new controls, as in the cases of automobiles and steel.[46]

---

[45]T. A. Bisson, *Zaibatsu Dissolution in Japan* (Berkeley: University of California Press, 1954). See also Eleanor T. Hadley, *Antitrust in Japan* (Princeton, N.J.: Princeton University Press, 1971), for a favorable evaluation of the program and for other references.

On part of the German program, see Joseph Borkin, *The Crime and Punishment of I. G. Farben* (New York: Free Press, 1978).

[46]An informal international cartel arrangement to limit imports to the United States was created in 1968, with strong State Department efforts. These limits have not stopped

Second, the possible scope of tariff cuts would be selective, covering a limited range of industries and missing many of the main problem cases. In some instances, the leading U.S. firms are also leading actual or potential importers, and so the effects of tariff cutting would be diluted. Among examples of these instances are computers, film, oil, soaps, drugs, and toiletries.

Import competition has been powerful in many cases, particularly in steel and automobiles. Yet others, such as computers, soaps, film, soups, and glass, appear to be virtually immune. The causes of immunity vary, ranging from high transport costs for glass, soap, and many other products, to specific conventions or rules against buying imports (as in some telephone equipment, aircraft, drugs, and electrical equipment).

Applying Monopsony Power. Public agencies and firms purchase from many industries. Where they have monopsony power, it could be exercised to constrain market power and to induce a more competitive structure.

One candidate is the drug industry, which sells to retail druggists at prices far above those to bulk buyers (public agencies, nonprofit hospitals, and regulated buyers). Unified monopsony purchasing may be an important way to abate this market power. It works under some health programs in Western Europe. The present U.S. system of medical insurance—with passive, regulated paying groups, such as Blue Cross, fragmented among the states—operates almost as if it were designed to minimize the effectiveness of such monopsony behavior.

Other sectors are weapons supply and utility equipment, but past purchasing actions have been erratic and often perverse. The tendencies toward passivity and mutual interests in these cases may be inherent in their structure.

IV. SUMMARY

Over time, Section 2 has grown more moderate and narrower in its scope. The threshold market share has risen above 70 percent, and "ordinary" dominant firms will usually be exempt. The 1984 AT&T divestiture indicates that the technical management of even the largest cases can be handled. The real limit on action now is the Chicago-UCLA belief that dominant firms usually reflect superior efficiency.

---

import competition, but they have reduced it. In 1978, a set of "reference prices" to force imports to be priced up to near U.S. prices was applied by the government.

In automobiles, Japan has yielded to U.S. pressure and limited exports to the United States to 1.6 million cars during 1979–84 and 2 million since then (see Chapter 16).

The stoppage of Section 2 cases since 1980 reflects a specific interpretation of the costs and benefits of Section 2 actions. Only if that interpretation changes, on the basis of research or industrial events, will policies be further adjusted. The change would have to come from declining confidence in Chicago-UCLA doctrines, both in the agencies and among federal judges.

QUESTIONS FOR REVIEW

1. "The first wave of Section 2 actions stopped monopolies less than 15 years after they were formed." True?
2. "The AT&T precedent indicates that complex, innovative firms always escape Section 2 action." True?
3. "The *United Shoe Machinery* precedent suggests that enterprising firms can keep their monopolies." True?
4. "Private suits have occasionally stirred the public agencies to file their suits too." True?
5. "Private suits have become an important method for getting divestiture." True?
6. "IBM's victories have made the treatment of monopoly more severe by simplifying the criteria." True?
7. "The FTC–*Xerox* action apparently did not cause the subsequent rise in competition." True?
8. "The *AT&T* settlement is a large antitrust accomplishment, which contrasts with other recent futile actions." True?
9. Why have most Section 2 actions become long and ineffective?
10. Would you have designed a different result for the *AT&T* case? Explain.
11. Do the agencies act more slowly than market shares decline?
12. If treble damages were not allowed, might Section 2 work better?
13. Is the current moratorium on Section 2 cases economically wise?
14. What can be done about newspaper monopolies in many cities? Which conditions (such as economies of scale) should be studied to reach answers?
15. Would you have decided *Aspen Skiing* the same way as the Court?

C·H·A·P·T·E·R 8   Mergers

In the United States, merger policies took form during the 1958–66 period, with Supreme Court decisions reaching quite strict limits on horizontal and vertical mergers by 1966. The restraints then loosened gradually during the 1970s, and after 1981 the policies abruptly became extremely lenient. The policies have had strong effects on actual mergers. For example, the merger boom of the 1980s was unleashed in part by the permissive Reagan policies. By 1990, merger policies had only slightly re-tightened.

This chapter reviews the longer trend of landmark merger cases, so as to put the current policies in perspective. The merger phenomenon and its problems are often spectacular. The market for corporate control—for buying and selling whole companies—routinely bubbles with thousands of possible deals. Most of them are never concluded, but many of them are, in some cases involving over $10 billion. The 1980s' U.S. merger boom eased after 1989, but there are still over 1,000 substantial mergers per year. Most of these mergers promote efficiency in some degree, without harming competition, but some of them would reduce competition without adding to efficiency.

It is antitrust's task to sift out those negative cases and try to prevent them. The evaluations are controversial, because they invoke the same concepts of market power and efficiency that underlie all antitrust choices. Indeed, Chicago-UCLA doctrines have had particularly sharp effects on merger trends since 1980.

Moreover, the antitrust decisions must be made under the heavy pressures of high finance and short deadlines. Not only are the partners in each merger eager to finish the merger without delay, but there are

Figure 8–1   The Three Main Types of Mergers

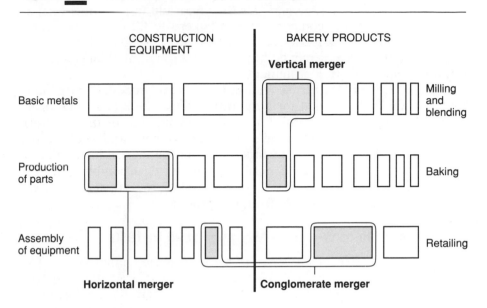

also legions of investors and arbitragers eager to cash in on the capital gains that monopoly-increasing mergers create.

The analysis in this chapter begins with the reasons why mergers are tried, the effects they have, the benefit-cost conditions they pose, and the waves of actual merger activity in the past.[1] Next we review the general features of U.S. merger policies. Then we turn to the specific U.S. policies toward horizontal, vertical, and conglomerate mergers. Policies abroad are also compared.

I. CONCEPTS

1. Types of Mergers

A *horizontal* merger unites side-by-side competitors (see Figure 8–1). A *vertical* merger links suppliers and users at different levels in the chain of production. A *conglomerate* merge is, in the pure case, anything with no horizontal or vertical element. Conglomerate mergers may link geo-

---

[1] Among the leading sources on the economics of mergers are F. M. Scherer and David J. Ravenscraft, *Mergers, Sell-Offs and Economic Efficiency* (Washington, D.C.: Brookings Institution, 1987); and Dennis C. Mueller, *The Determinants and Effects of Mergers* (Cambridge, Mass.: Oelgeschlager, Gunn, and Hain, 1980).

graphic areas (for example, bakeries in two distant towns); these are called *market-extension* mergers. Or they may add to a product line, as when a food-products company buys a bakery to fill out its offerings; these are called *product-extension* mergers. Most mergers of any significance mix the three elements, horizontal, vertical, and conglomerate, but one element is often prominent.

Mergers are only the visible fruit of the endless process of bargaining that goes on in the market for corporate assets. There is a small army of merger promoters at work in investment banking firms in New York and elsewhere. They profile candidates, seek partners, and work out the terms of possible mergers. This functioning of the market for corporate control helps to enforce good performance and to accomplish needed change. Some mergers, however, merely reflect the efforts of merger promoters who gain large fees from the process.

2. The Four Major Waves of Mergers, 1890 to 1990

There have been four major waves of mergers in the United States. **The first great wave** occurred in 1897–1904, a period of dramatic industrial turbulence and change.[2] The mergers primarily were horizontal, forming new dominant firms with 60 to 90 percent in scores of large and small industries. Much of the activity was strictly promotional, by Morgan, the Rockefellers, and other financiers. It was widely believed that these groups would combine their interests on a new plane of financial superpower.[3] This merger wave climaxed in 1901 with the blockbuster U.S. Steel merger. The wave was stopped primarily by adverse stock market and economic conditions, plus some effect of Theodore Roosevelt's new use of antitrust in 1902.[4] Many of these mergers were overblown and ill-fated, with the firms declining almost as soon as they were formed, but others created dominant firms that remain to this day.

The second merger wave, in the 1920s, involved both industrial firms and utilities. Mainly, they formed oligopolies rather than dominant firms. The industrial mergers tended to form second- and third-ranking firms, nearly as large as the existing dominant firms (for example, steel and tin cans). This occurred partly because many dominant firms had been put on notice not to make further mergers (recall Chapter 5). In

---

[2]See Ralph L. Nelson, *Merger Movements in American Industry, 1890–1956* (Princeton, N.J.: Princeton University Press, 1962); John Moody, *The Truth about the Trusts* (New York: John Moody, 1904); and Naomi Lamoreaux, *The Great Merger Movement in American Business* (Cambridge: The Cambridge University Press, 1985).

[3]See Moody, *The Truth about the Trusts;* F. L. Allen, *The Lords of Creation* (New York: Harper & Row, 1935); and F. L. Allen, *The Great Pierpont Morgan* (New York: Harper & Row, 1949).

[4]For a detailed narrative and analysis, see William Letwin, *Law and Economic Policy in America* (New York: Random House, 1965).

any case, by 1929, the main outlines of many leading industries were firmly set.

The third merger wave in the 1960s—the great "go-go years"—mainly involved conglomerate mergers. Yet there were also many horizontal and vertical mergers, and many conglomerate mergers had strong horizontal or vertical features. New conglomerates made a series of highly publicized mergers, some of them takeovers. A wide range of older firms—both unified and diversified—made conglomerate mergers, too.

Despite some fears that the whole of industry was being transformed, actually, structure and global concentration were only slightly altered. The merger boom was punctured by the 1969–70 bear-market drop of 40 percent in stock prices, by the antitrust attack on conglomerate mergers during 1969–71 (see below), and by growing disenchantment with the 1960s claims that mergers created "synergy." After 1970, many hundreds of the 1960s' mergers unravelled. Voluntary divestitures became as numerous as new mergers, as firms sifted out their losing operations.

After 1975, takeovers revived, focused mainly on leading firms in a number of industries. The acquirers now were established firms with large cash reserves, rather than new outsiders with shaky financial backing. A few sectors had many mergers (beer firms, agricultural cooperatives, and, after 1975, stock brokerage firms), but the lagging stock market and the antitrust limits kept merger activity down during the 1970s.

The fourth and greatest merger wave came during 1981–89, when rising stock prices and more lenient Reagan policies toward mergers stirred a vast, frenzied merger boom.

The 1980s' boom is shown in more detail in Table 8–1. Its scope far exceeded the three earlier waves, both in numbers of sizable mergers and in the total value. There were many major mergers of all kinds, horizontal, vertical, and conglomerate. Many of the horizontal mergers involved combined market shares well over 30 percent, much higher than the ceiling of about 10 percent during the 1960s and 1970s. Vertical mergers occurred without challenge during the 1980s, often involving very large market shares. Conglomerate mergers also were not challenged at all.

Because there were major effects on the structures of hundreds of markets, the merger wave was regarded as an unprecedented restructuring of U.S. history.

Table 8–2 lists the 20 largest mergers or buyouts, all of them occurring in the 1980s. They spread over a wide range of activity, even though they are only the peak of the 30,000 mergers during the decade. Some of them (e.g., Campeau-Federated, Kodak-Sterling) have worked out poorly.

Table 8-1   Corporate Mergers and Acquisitions 1980–1988

Year	Number of Mergers and Acquisitions	Value ($ billions)	Number Valued in Excess of $1 billion
1980	1,565	$33.0	3
1981	2,326	67.3	8
1982	2,296	60.4	9
1983	2,387	52.8	7
1984	3,158	126.0	19
1985	3,428	145.4	26
1986	4,323	204.4	34
1987	3,701	167.5	30
1988	3,487	226.6	42
TOTAL	26,671	$1,083.4	178

Source: Walter Adams and James W. Brock, *Dangerous Pursuits* (New York: Pantheon Books, 1989), p. 12.

Table 8–3 indicates the level of merger case activity by the two antitrust agencies during the 1980s. Evidently, enforcement activity virtually ceased.

3. Reasons for Mergers

Gains from Mergers. There are three main categories of gains to the firm: market power, technical economies, and pecuniary economies.

1. Straight Market Power. By stopping competition between the merging firms, mergers can raise market power well above the power held separately by the two merger partners. This, in turn, usually provides higher profitability, the basic goal of the firm. The increase in market share is the main indicator of the rise in market power.

2. Technical Economies. A merger may achieve economies of scale if the two firms were previously smaller than minimum efficient scale. Or the firm may be able to lower the average-cost curve itself by new innovation. Vertical mergers may gain vertical economies (for example, from avoiding extra handling, uncertainty, and reprocessing). More general economies may arise from reducing risks by pooling diverse operations.

Table 8–2   Twenty Largest Corporate Deals in U.S. History

Rank and Firms	Type of Deal	Value ($ billions)	Year
1. RJR–Nabisco	Leveraged buyout	$25.0	1989
2. Philip Morris–Kraft	Merger	13.4	1988
3. Chevron-Gulf	Merger	13.3	1984
4. Texaco-Getty	Merger	10.1	1984
5. Du Pont–Conoco	Merger	8.0	1981
6. British Petroleum–Standard Oil	Acquired half-interest not already owned	8.0	1987
7. Campeau–Federated Department Stores	Merger	7.4	1988
8. U.S. Steel–Marathon Oil	Merger	6.6	1982
9. General Electric–RCA	Merger	6.4	1986
10. Beatrice Foods	Leveraged buyout	6.2	1986
11. Royal Dutch Shell–Shell Oil	Acquired one-third interest not already owned	5.7	1985
12. Mobil Oil–Superior	Merger	5.7	1984
13. Philip Morris–General Foods	Merger	5.6	1985
14. Grand Metropolitan–Pillsbury	Merger	5.5	1988
15. Sante Fe–Southern Pacific	Merger	5.1	1983
16. Kodak–Sterling Drug	Merger	5.1	1988
17. Allied–Signal Companies	Merger	4.9	1985
18. R.J. Reynolds–Nabisco	Merger	4.9	1985
19. Burroughs-Sperry	Merger	4.8	1986
20. General Motors–Hughes Aircraft	Merger	4.7	1985

Source: Walter Adams and James W. Brock, *Dangerous Pursuits* (New York: Pantheon Books, 1989), p. 14.

3. *Pecuniary Economies.* All three kinds of mergers may make it possible for the firm to buy its inputs more cheaply. These *pecuniary* gains may affect any input used by the firm. Raw materials, advertising space, managerial talent, capital, and others may be bought more cheaply by the merged firms. Also, mergers often achieve tax benefits, in the pooling of loss-making and profit-making units. These gains are only pecuniary; they do not provide technical gains in the efficiency of production.

Technical economies provide *social benefits* by reducing the real resources needed for production. Market power and pecuniary gains give strictly *private benefits* (in greater profits) without providing real, social benefits.

Table 8–3   Merger Policy under the Reagan Administration

	Justice Department		Federal Trade Commission	
Year	Premerger Notifications Received	Cases Filed	Premerger Notifications Received	Administrative Complaints Filed
1981	993	3	996	6
1982	1,204	3	1,203	2
1983	1,101	2	1,093	1
1984	1,339	5	1,340	3
1985	1,604	5	1,603	2
1986	1,949	4	1,949	3
1987	2,533	4	1,346	0
TOTAL	10,723	26	9,530	17

Source: Walter Adams and James W. Brock, *Dangerous Pursuits* (New York: Pantheon Books, 1989), p. 28.

There are also more tactical reasons for mergers.

Tactical Reasons for Mergers.   *1. Entry to a New Market.* Entry is usually easier by merger than by creating new capacity. Conglomerate mergers always involve entry of a new outside firm into the market. Such entry does not add new capacity, and so its net competitive benefits are always less than from entry by internal growth. Moreover, the new entrant often had already applied some influence on the market as a potential entrant.

2. Exit: The "Failing Firm" Case. Many mergers involve the absorption of a firm that is in straits or even, in the extreme, failing. Failure means bankruptcy, which need not cause actual closure and dissipation of the company's activities. The difficult policy question often is: How much failure is required for failure? Often companies wanting a merger will don sackcloth and ashes, claiming that failure is imminent even though the firm is still strong. Note, too, that other methods of salvage are often possible, such as getting new managers.

3. Divestiture. Mergers often involve selling off parts of a firm to new owners, and so the reasons for disposing of assets also matter. Many firms carry marginal or even heavily losing branches for decades, either from inertia or as part of larger strategies (for example, to offer a full line of products). Disposal of them may reflect new financial stress or a change in managerial strategy. Divestiture is a common action. About half of all mergers during the 1970s involved divestitures of assets from one firm to another.

4. Takeover. Among the many merger types, takeover is the most colorful and, perhaps, socially important. It involves a move by one firm to take over, or seize, another firm against its management's will. In the byzantine world of business, one often has difficulty telling who is taking over whom and whether the takeover is amicable, hostile, or a mixture of the two.

The key element of a takeover is that management in the target firm comes immediately under different control. The would-be new owners typically make a "tender offer" to buy a controlling amount of the stock at a price above the current market price (usually 20–40 percent higher). This premium reflects their belief that they can manage the company so much better that profits will rise sharply and the stock value will rise substantially beyond the takeover price. Takeovers are often done by corporate outsiders, aiming primarily at sluggish firms with substantial market positions.

Mergers are frequently dramatic and enigmatic, and they often touch raw nerves of corporate and financial power.

4. Effects of Mergers

The direct effects of mergers fit three main categories: (1) affecting competition, (2) affecting performance, and (3) increasing global aggregate concentration.

Competition. *Horizontal mergers* obviously reduce competition. Part of the market process is enclosed under direct internal control. The power to raise price is increased. The larger the increase in combined share, the bigger will be the loss of competition. Though small firms often claim that by merging they can compete better against dominant firms, this point has little merit unless scale economies are present. Even if scale economies are present, the firm should be able to grow internally, rather than by merger, so as to reap those economies.

Vertical mergers need not alter competition at either level if market conditions are perfect.[5] Yet they will reduce competition if (1) the

---

[5]For a range of views and conditions about the effects of vertical mergers, see F. M. Scherer and David Ross, *Industrial Market Structure and Economic Performance,* 3rd ed. (Boston: Houghton, Mifflin, 1990), chap. 14; Walter Adams and Joel B. Dirlam, "Steel Imports and Vertical Oligopoly Power," *American Economic Review* 54 (September 1964), pp. 626–55; Richard A. Posner, *Antitrust Law: An Economic Perspective* (Chicago: University of Chicago Press, 1976), pp. 196–201; and Robert H. Bork, *The Antitrust Paradox* (New York: Basic Books, 1978), chap. 11.

merger raises entry barriers (by making new entrants set up new factories on both levels at once, thereby raising the level of capital that must be raised in imperfect capital markets) and (2) the merger triggers a wave of similar mergers that sharply reduce the scope of open-market sales. And if the possibility of price squeezes is increased by a vertical merger, the mere threat of this may induce independent firms to behave more passively. How much competition is reduced depends on these conditions.

Conglomerate mergers are usually neutral to competition. They don't change market shares or barriers directly. However, in certain conditions, they may reduce or increase competition.[6] The new parent company may have better access to capital, advertising, or other resources for competitive strategies. If these are made available to a dominant firm, the effect may be to entrench it further. Also, competition will probably be *increased* if the merger takes in a firm with a small share of its market. The new advantages will enlarge its opportunities to take market share away from the leading firms, thereby raising competition.

In the extreme, a web of conglomerate ties may induce behavior among conglomerates to become delicately diplomatic. Each can retaliate elsewhere against moves in any one market. So competition in the whole range of markets may subside.

One further angle: If the acquirer had been a known, important potential entrant, then the merger may reduce competition by subtracting one firm from the total of all actual plus potential competitors. The net effect on competition will often be slight, but still real.

Performance. Taken altogether, mergers may reduce competition in a number of ways. That, in turn, will usually reduce economic performance by impairing efficiency and slowing innovation. However, the level of performance may, on balance, be *raised* by any given merger.[7] (1) Economies of scale may be realized by horizontal merger. (2) Economies of integration may arise from a vertical merger. (3) A failing firm may be restored more fully than this could be done by other means (such as by drawing on new outside loans).

---

[6]Ronald W. Cotterill and Willard F. Mueller, "The Impact of Firm Conglomeration on Market Structure: Evidence for the U.S. Food Retailing Industry," *Antitrust Bulletin* 25 (Fall 1980), pp. 557–82; Ralph M. Bradburd, "Conglomerate Power without Market Power: The Effects of Conglomeration on a Risk-Averse Quantity-Adjusting Firm," *American Economic Review* 70 (June 1980), pp. 483–87; and Roger D. Blair and Robert F. Lanzillotti, eds., *The Conglomerate Corporation: An Antitrust Law and Economics Symposium* (Cambridge, Mass.: Oelgeschlager, Gunn, and Hain, 1981).

[7]For one concise analysis of merger effects, see Oliver E. Williamson, "Economies as an Antitrust Defense," *American Economic Review* 58 (March 1968), pp. 18–36, and "Correction and Reply," (December 1968), pp. 1372–76.

Also, takeovers may directly improve the degree of efficiency, by replacing inefficient managers or forcing them to perform more effectively. This direct effect is often strong, and it explains the tenacity with which most managers resist an attempt to take over their own firms.

Attempted takeovers also have an indirect effect on performance. Many managers will intensify their efforts precisely in order to raise their profitability and stock price so as to cease being a takeover target. For every actual takeover, perhaps scores of firms are indirectly prodded to perform better.

Chicago-UCLA economists praise takeovers strongly as a mechanism for enforcing efficiency by these effects on competition and performance. Any restraint on takeovers, they say, will impair this process and reduce efficiency.

All mergers do not, however, turn out ideally. Many may instead be mistaken or mishandled. Prime examples emerged during the 1980s' merger boom: "Leveraged buyouts" (LBOs) were used to take over hundreds of firms, using risky bonds to obtain funds. Some of the buyouts involved immense firms. Many of these LBOs were decidedly unwise and soon went into bankruptcy under the load of the interest payments on the debt. Others survived but continue to stagger under the burdens of large volumes of debt, at high rates of interest.

Even among ordinary mergers, some fail markedly, and the average degree of success is modest.[8] Mergers during the 1950–77 period generally were not profitable, and "operating efficiency fell on average following merger."[9] Many acquired firms were already well managed, and so the mergers were more likely to burden them than to improve them. Many mergers appear to reflect "empire-building" urges. The business press criticized scores of dubious and failed mergers during the 1980s.

Global Concentration. A series of large-firm mergers can increase the aggregate concentration of the economy. This can injure local community interests, as absentee managements ignore local conditions and use their power to extract advantages. It can also weaken the political and social fabric, at the expense of individual freedoms and self-determination. Marked rises in global concentration have occurred in the United States and abroad, with a range of negative effects. Even national sovereignty can be reduced by large international mergers that give firms more leverage on small countries; this may, on balance, cause social loss.

---

[8]See the scathing review in Walter Adams and James W. Brock, *Dangerous Pursuits* (New York: Pantheon Books, 1989).

[9]Scherer and Ravenscraft, *Mergers, Sell-Offs and Economic Efficiency*, pp. 195–215.

5. Special Cost-Benefit Issues for Policy Choices

Traditional Methods. To evaluate a merger, one first defines the market (recall Chapter 6) and then measures the increase in market share from the merger. From these structural facts, one can then roughly estimate the net social benefits and costs of the merger. This is the heart of sound evaluation: simple in concept, but possible to do only roughly in practice.

Net Gains. The crucial comparison is between (1) the gains from the merger and (2) those that can be obtained by internal growth or by long-term contracts. *Only the net gains that mergers give, compared to alternative approaches, are relevant for policy.* Accordingly, the direct social benefits from all three kinds of mergers will usually be quite small and of low probability. Economies from vertical mergers will often be larger than those from horizontal mergers. Yet these too can usually be gotten by building new plants or making long-term contracts for supplies.

Social costs from the loss of competition will usually be relatively large for horizontal mergers. By comparison, the costs of stopping the merger are relatively small. Time can also be on the agencies' side, because the merger needs to go through on the agreed terms, before conditions change. In contrast to policy dealing with existing structure (recall Chapters 6 and 7), merger policy can operate quickly and strictly.

Lessons. In short, traditional cost-benefit analysis usually favors stopping a wide range of horizontal mergers. Current antitrust arrangements make that relatively easy and cheap to do, but they also make it easy to stop conglomerate mergers, some of which are harmless or offer net social benefits. Therefore, the optimum social treatment of mergers would probably involve a relatively strict line on horizontal mergers, *and* a relatively open policy on vertical and conglomerate mergers.

There is an additional difficulty in markets that have dominant firms. In those markets, a strict line against horizontal mergers, even by small firms, may indirectly tend to defend the dominant firms, by keeping their competitors smaller and more passive.

Chicago-UCLA Evaluation of Mergers. Antitrust decisions in the 1980s followed somewhat different lines, explicitly rejecting the mainstream concepts of market share and monopoly effects. Mergers were to be questioned only if they would "facilitate collusion"; higher market shares themselves were held to be largely blameless. Moreover, Chicago-UCLA economists expect collusion to collapse rather than to persist. Therefore, the harms from collusion were regarded as small.

The likelihood of potential entry was regarded as strong and important. Therefore, any monopoly impacts were expected to be weak under the threat of entry. In contrast, gains in efficiency were usually expected to be significant, reflecting the general correctness of managerial decisions. Structure itself was to be measured only by the Hirschman-Herfindahl index (the H index), which is an abstract number.[10]

Moreover, the possible larger effects of mergers were ignored, as being unproven or "not economic." Global concentration was strictly ignored, and local effects were considered to be mere adjustments that markets perform well.

These ideas tipped the evaluation toward presuming net benefits from all mergers, unless large monopoly harms could be proven to exceed the expected efficiency benefits. Dominance was irrelevant; only "facilitating collusion" mattered, and its effects would be small.

From this reasoning, there was little reason to oppose any but the largest increases in market shares. Costs and benefits were to be compared, in some ultimate sense, but the evaluation was tipped strongly in favor of mergers, even horizontal mergers involving up to half of the market.

II. GENERAL FEATURES OF U.S. MERGER POLICIES

The Laws

The amended Section 7 of the Clayton Act is the main merger law. Sherman Section 2's "monopolizing" prohibition was used in early cases to stop railroad mergers, but the original Clayton Section 7 of 1914 was soon nullified by court interpretations.

The Celler-Kefauver Act amended it in 1950 to preclude mergers that would "substantially . . . lessen competition or . . . tend to create a monopoly in any line of commerce in any section of the county." After 1976, the Hart-Scott-Rodino Amendment required firms to give the agencies advance notice of mergers, so that any policy action could be prepared in time.

Development of Policies. Even well before 1950, some mergers were constrained by antitrust agencies, on an informal basis.[11] Although

---

[10]Eleanor M. Fox, "The New Merger Guidelines—A Blueprint for Economic Analysis," *Antitrust Bulletin* 27 (Fall 1982), pp. 519–91.

[11]Simon N. Whitney, *Antitrust Policies: American Experience in Twenty Industries* (New York: Twentieth Century Fund, 1958).

events aborted the first series of Section 2 actions after 1916, an implicit limit on some mergers remained. Dominant firms in major markets (such as U.S. Steel) were aware that substantial merger activity on their part would be opposed. Well before 1920, dominant firms were established in many industries, and, by 1950, many of the largest firms were also conglomerates (such as General Electric, Westinghouse, chemicals firms, RCA). In the financial sector, the Banking Act of 1933 had neatly fenced off banking from investment banking and other sectors. As one side effect of this, banks were free from takeover by firms outside their own sector, as were utilities.

Accordingly, the strict merger treatments after 1950 came upon a scene containing well-established industrial and financial positions of market power. Rather than prevent the growth of incipient monopoly in industry or finance, merger policies could only try to avert further rises in market power, in the hope that the dominant positions would be eroded.

The 1950 amendment to Clayton Act Section 7 made possible, for the first time, a meaningful treatment of mergers. After a pause, the 1950 act was tested by the Bethlehem-Youngstown merger in 1958 and applied strictly. Successive cases then quickly tightened the law by 1966 to strictly limit horizontal and vertical mergers. Treatment of conglomerate mergers evolved inconclusively after 1966 as the merger wave peaked. Then, the Supreme Court loosened the limits on all mergers somewhat in 1974. After 1980, Reagan officials radically reduced the restraints on all three types of mergers.

Coverage. Virtually all sectors are covered, even the numerous "regulated" utilities. Often, the antitrust agencies have to assert their role vigorously against the regulated firms and even, on occasion, the regulators themselves.

Procedure. Much policy is applied under the surface. Firms often come in ahead of time to urge officials not to oppose a planned merger. Negotiations may grow quite complex, and many times the agencies' threat or decision to sue will cause a proposed merger to fold. Mergers are often modified to fit antitrust criteria. Takeover targets often rush in to demand that the agencies stop the merger "to protect competition" (as well as their own jobs). Actual court cases often merely signal that informal bargaining has broken down or that a new policy line is being set.

Time and the burden of proof commonly favor the agencies. Mergers can often be delayed or stopped with minimal effort. Alternatively, judges can let the mergers occur, instructing the firm to keep the merged parts separate.

Table 8–4   Merger Guidelines: Mergers which Will Probably Be Challenged

---

I. 1968 Guidelines
1. **Horizontal Mergers.**   Criteria are mainly market structure.
    a.   In highly concentrated markets (over 75% in the four largest firms), these shares will normally not be challenged:

Acquiring Firm	*Acquired Firm*
4%	4%
10%	2%

   b.   In medium concentrated markets, the limits are looser:

Acquiring Firm	*Acquired Firm*
5%	5%
10%	4%

   c.   Also, *any* acquisition of a competitor that is unusually competitive or has unusual competitive advantages.
2. **Vertical Mergers.**   Mergers that foreclose competition and raise entry barriers are to be challenged. Normally, a merger will be challenged if one of the following conditions holds:
    a.   If a firm that is a customer for a product makes 6% of the purchases and a firm supplying the product makes 10% of the sales, unless their merger raises no signficant barrier to entry.
    b.   If a firm that is a customer for a product has 10% of its own market, if the product is essential to its business, and if a firm supplying the product makes 20% of the sales.
    c.   If a customer or a supplier is acquired by a major firm in an industry with a significant trend toward vertical integration, if such a combination would raise barriers to entry, and if it does not promise to cut the costs of production.
    d.   If a customer or a supplier is acquired for the purpose of barring competitors from the market or otherwise putting them at a disadvantage.
3. **Conglomerate Mergers.** Since policy is still formative, at least these categories of merger will normally be challenged:
    a.   If a firm that has a large share of a market seeks to acquire a firm that is one of the main potential entrants to the market.
    b.   If a merger creates the danger of substantial reciprocal buying.
    c.   If a merger creates severe disparity in size between the acquired firm and its competitors, or gives advertising advantages, or otherwise gives leverage to the acquired firm.

Criteria. The lines of policy are set by the Supreme Court, by precedents from their decisions. Table 8–4 codifies these precedents, showing the criteria that the Antitrust Division and the FTC normally use in deciding whether to challenge mergers. Part I gives guidelines set in 1968, mainly using market shares. New guidelines issued in 1982 and modified in 1984 are shown in Part II. They were issued in terms of

Table 8-4   Merger Guidelines: Mergers which Will Probably Be Challenged (continued)

II.   1984 Guidelines

Type of Merger	Challenge Is Very Likely, If:	Challenge Is Possible, If:
Horizontal	Firm *A* has dominance (a market share above 35 percent and more than twice the share of the next firm); and Firm *B* has more than 2 percent; and/or The H Index exceeds 2,000 (tight oligopoly), and merger will raise the H Index by 100 or more (7 percent plus 7 percent).	The H Index is 1,000–1,800 (medium concentration), the merger raises the H Index by more than 50 (5 percent plus 5 percent), and: Entry is difficult, or The market has been collusive, or Firm *B* is a maverick.
Vertical	The H Index in either market exceeds 2,000 (tight oligopoly), and the merger will: Make entry much more difficult, or Increase collusion, or if One firm is a franchised, regulated firm.	Similar but lesser conditions hold.
Conglomerate	The H Index exceeds 2,000 (tight oligopoly) in both markets, Firm *A* is a leading firm, and: Firm *A* is a leading one among few potential entrants, and Firm *B*'s market share exceeds 10 percent.	The H Index is 1,000–1,800 in both markets (medium concentration), both *A* and *B* are leading firms, and Firm *A* is a potential entrant.

Hirschman-Herfindahl indexes, but their rough market share equivalents are shown for comparison.

Before 1980, the agencies were likely to challenge any substantial horizontal merger, especially if the market's concentration was high or rising. Vertical mergers were much less strictly limited. Conglomerate mergers were largely free of limits, unless they sharply reduced potential competition. The agencies were usually not deterred by claims that the mergers would achieve economies. Rather, they required hard evidence that would stand up in court that there were net economies that could only be achieved by a merger.

After 1984, actual decisions were much more permissive even than the new guidelines (e.g., virtually no vertical or conglomerate mergers were challenged).

Table 8–4   Merger Guidelines: Mergers which Will Probably Be Challenged (concluded)

The Division will weigh economics in deciding if the merger tends to reduce efficiency.

The H Index is the sum of the squared market shares. For example, the H Index for four 25 percent oligopolists is $625 + 625 + 625 + 625 = 2,500$; for ten 10 percent firms it is $100 \times 10 = 1,000$. Rough equivalents with four-firm concentration ratios are:

Firms' Market Shares	Four-Firm Concentration	H Index
Ten 10 percent firms	40	1,000
Six 16 percent firms	64	1,660
Five 20 percent firms	80	2,000
Four 25 percent firms	100	2,500
Three 33 percent firms	100	3,300

Roughly, an H Index below 1,000 is loose oligopoly, while an H Index above 1,800 is tight oligopoly.

To measure the rise in the H Index, multiply the two market shares together and then double that number. Examples:

Firm A	Firm B	Multiplied		Rise in H Index	
5 percent	5 percent	25	$\times 2$	$=$	50
7 percent	7 percent	49	$\times 2$	$=$	98
10 percent	10 percent	100	$\times 2$	$=$	200
8 percent	4 percent	32	$\times 2$	$=$	64
15 percent	4 percent	60	$\times 2$	$=$	120

III. POLICIES TOWARD SPECIFIC KINDS OF MERGERS

1. Horizontal Mergers

Though mergers often mix horizontal and other elements, the policy lines have developed separately. Treatment of horizontal mergers began with the *Bethlehem-Youngstown* case of 1958, and tightened with *Brown Shoe* in 1962 and *Von's Grocery* in 1966. *General Dynamics* in 1974 eased the restraints, and Reagan officials removed most limits after 1980.

Bethlehem-Youngstown. The first case under the new law involved a proposed merger between Bethlehem Steel and Youngstown Sheet & Tube. Bethlehem, the nation's second largest steel producer, planned in 1956 to acquire Youngstown, the sixth largest, thus raising its own share of the nation's output from 15 percent to 20 percent, and the share of U.S. Steel and Bethlehem together from 45 percent to 50 percent. The Justice Department sued to enjoin the merger, and the case was tried in 1958.

The defense argued that the merger would make the industry more competitive, since it would enable Bethlehem to compete more effectively with U.S. Steel. It cited, in particular, the market near Chicago. Here, Bethlehem had no plant and shipped in less than 1 percent of its output. By acquiring and expanding Youngstown's Chicago facilities, it would provide more vigorous competition for U.S. Steel in this area. Bethlehem declared that it would not otherwise enter this market.

The judge was skeptical, however. Also, there were numerous specific products and regions (especially in Pennsylvania and Ohio) where Bethlehem and Youngstown did compete. The merger would end that competition. The judge set aside the possibility that the merged firms could compete more strongly against U.S. Steel. He said that Congress "made no distinction between good mergers and bad mergers. It condemned all which came within the reach of the prohibition of Section 7." The merger was enjoined.[12] In three years, Bethlehem *did* enter the Chicago market by building a large plant at Burns Ditch.

Brown Shoe. The Supreme Court's first, and strict, decision under the Celler-Kefauver Act was in the *Brown Shoe* case in 1962.[13] The Brown Shoe Company, which manufactured 4.0 percent of the nation's output of shoes, had acquired the Kinney Company, which manufactured 0.5 percent. Brown was the third largest distributor of shoes, with 1,230 retail stores; Kinney was eighth, with 350 stores. In certain local markets for particular types of shoes, the combined share of the two concerns amounted to 20 percent or more (the shares ranged from 5.0 to 57.7 percent).

The unanimous Court put less emphasis on the existing structure of the market than on the historical trend toward increasing concentration in the shoe industry. "We cannot avoid the mandate of Congress," it said, "that tendencies toward concentration in industry are to be curbed in their incipiency, particularly when these tendencies are being accelerated through giant steps striding across a hundred cities at a time. In the light of the trends in this industry, we agree . . . that this is an appropriate place at which to call a halt."[14]

---

[12]*U.S.* v. *Bethlehem Steel Corp.*, 168F. Supp. 756.

[13]*Brown Shoe Co.* v. *U.S.*, 370 U.S. 294.

[14]Ibid., p. 345. For approval of the decision, see David D. Martin, "The Brown Shoe Case and the New Anti-Merger Policy," *American Economic Review* 53 (June 1963), pp. 340–58. For an attack on the decision, see John L. Peterman, "The Brown Shoe Case," *Journal of Law and Economics* 18 (April 1975), pp. 81–146, and "FTC v. Brown Shoe Co.," *Journal of Law and Economics* 18 (October 1975), pp. 361–420.

Philadelphia National Bank.[15] In this important case, the Court set two precedents. First, it used a simple, clear rule—the market share of the merged firms—as the decisive criterion. The earlier decisions had, by contrast, cited many features of the market (for example, number of firms, concentration, and growth rates) in assessing the effect on competition. Second, this decision extended merger policy to the banking industry.

Von's Grocery. This case set the seal on horizontal limits in 1966. It involved the merger of two retail food chains in Los Angeles. Von's Grocery, the third largest food chain in the area, had acquired Shopping Bag, the sixth largest, thereby moving into second place. However, Von's share of the market, after the merger, was only 8 percent. The share of all the market leaders was declining, and there was no barrier to the entry of new concerns. The Court, however, noted that the number of stores operated by individual owners had fallen, and it found the merger to be unlawful on the grounds that it was the purpose of the law "to prevent concentration in the American economy by keeping a large number of small competitors in business."[16]

General Dynamics. Here, a merger among firms producing coal in Illinois and the vicinity raised the concentration of production in that region (in the top four firms) from 43 to 63 percent during 1957–67. The Supreme Court's decision in 1973 acquitted General Dynamics on two grounds.[17] First, the relevant market was held to be much broader than the Division alleged. This loosened the precedent that "any" significant market would show a violation. Second, the Court held that other facts about the industry must also be considered in judging the competitive effect. The clear simplicity of the 1960s' precedents was now diluted with flexibility, and the standard of proof for conviction was raised. The shift in policy was not sharp, since the changes were of degree, not kind.

The strict treatment of horizontal mergers was perforated by various exceptional cases.[18] Some "failing-firm" mergers were also permitted.

---

[15]*U.S.* v. *Philadelphia National Bank,* 374 U.S. 321 (1963). The case is discussed in Chapter 5.

[16]*U.S.* v. *Von's Grocery Co.,* 384 U.S. 280 (1966). There were sharp minority dissents in both *Brown Shoe* and *Von's Grocery,* arguing that the effect of the mergers would be trivial or procompetitive. The minorities were basically setting a higher burden of proof on the government.

[17]*U.S.* v. *General Dynamics Corp.,* 341 F. Supp. 534 (N. D. Ill. 1972), *affirmed,* 415 U.S. 486 (1973).

[18]These include the merger between the McDonnell and Douglas aircraft firms in 1967 and the Penn-Central merger in 1968.

RCA and General Electric sold their large computer operations to competitors in 1970–72 without official opposition. In 1975–78, many sizable mergers took place among brokerage firms, directly raising concentration. This reflected the new competition unleashed by the ending of brokerage-fee fixing (see Chapter 9). In 1978, a merger between LTV Corporation (which owned Jones & Laughlin Steel Corporation) and Lykes Corporation (which owned Youngstown Sheet & Tube Company) was permitted by the Attorney General, overriding the Division's decision. The merger created the third largest U.S. steel firm, with about 15 to 25 percent shares of various markets. Neither was running losses, but both were in difficulties.

The Reagan Era. During 1981–83, the rules were eased, in effect, from 4-plus-4 percent to roughly 7-plus-7 percent, but the change was accompanied by new "merger guidelines" that established a different method for defining markets and calculating concentration. Therefore, the true shifting of the limits was not clear. By 1983, the constraints had been loosened much further, and where the margins of policy lie has not been clear since then. Although some actions by the Division seemed to suggest that combined shares over 40 percent would be challenged, that was not a consistent policy; some larger shares were permitted, and some lower ones were challenged.

In any event, the dropping of merger constraints was the most dramatic and deliberate indicator that the Chicago-UCLA approach was at work. It continued into the Bush administration, despite some statements in 1989 about adopting a more cautious policy.

Early Cases. The new 7-plus-7 percent rules would themselves have prevented most of the previous leading cases (*Brown Shoe, Von's, General Dynamics*) from being brought, even though the policy limit was still nearly as tight.[19] A number of mergers quickly tested their policies. Stroh's acquired Schlitz, which was a declining, formerly major brewer. The combined market shares were above the old limits but still moderate, and Schlitz was perhaps on the brink of failure. The merger was not challenged.

In 1983, General Motors and Toyota proposed a joint venture to produce cars in California.[20] Though the link was far short of a full merger, it was likely to affect competition. The two firms could be regarded as the two largest competitors in the combined Japanese-American mar-

---

[19]Eleanor M. Fox, "The New Merger Guidelines—A Blueprint for Microeconomic Analysis," *Antitrust Bulletin* 27 (Fall 1982), pp. 519–91.

[20]See the thorough discussion by John E. Kwoka, Jr., "International Joint Venture: General Motors and Toyota," in *The Antitrust Revolution,* ed. John E. Kwoka, Jr., and Lawrence J. White, Jr. (Glenview, Ill.: Scott, Foresman, 1989), pp. 46–79.

ket, or, for that matter, in a worldwide market; or Toyota was the largest importer *and* potential entrant in the U.S. market. In any case, a significant reduction of direct competition was likely. Ford and Chrysler both opposed the joint venture vigorously. Yet, amid heavy debate, the FTC permitted the link, on grounds that it would create added capacity and strengthen GM's abilities to compete. Later benefits were actually "slight," at best.[21]

Then in 1983–84, a steel merger tested the limits further. Fourth-ranked Republic Steel proposed merging with third-ranked Jones & Laughlin, owned by LTV. Their combined share of total U.S. production would be 15.8 percent, in 1983, just under U.S. Steel's 16.7 percent. Their shares would be as high as 50 percent in specific steel products and regional markets.

The steel industry had long been ailing, and so a failing-firm basis might exempt them. Also, one could broaden the market to include all world steel, because imports had become substantial. In such a large market, the merged firms would have small market shares.

The industry's ills reflected past inefficiencies and mistakes encouraged by market power, and so the merger was likely to continue the problems, rather than cure them. The world market was not free, since restrictions on sales to the United States had been in place since the 1960s. The Republic–J&L merger was permitted nevertheless, and claims of economies were henceforth officially permitted in the revised 1984 Guidelines. This merger conspicuously failed to deliver its promised efficiencies. There was confusion and strife among the combined managements, and LTV went bankrupt within three years.

Coca-Cola and Dr Pepper. In 1986, Coca-Cola announced plans to buy the Dr Pepper company (primarily to cause trouble for a previously announced merger between PepsiCo and Seven-Up). The FTC resisted the merger, and it was eventually enjoined in federal court.

The firms' shares of the soft-drink market were 37 and 5 percent, respectively, for a new total of 42 percent. The FTC offered detailed studies of possible price effects and difficult entry, but its resistance hinged mainly on the traditional market shares. The judge agreed, and he rejected any serious attention to claims of economies. Therefore, this case marked a return to mainstream criteria, but at very high market-share levels.

Airline Mergers. During 1985–88, a series of mergers by leading airline companies markedly increased dominance at important hub airports, as well as concentration in the entire industry (recall Chapter 3). The

---

[21]See Kwoka's critical evaluation, ibid., pp. 75–76.

mergers were permitted by officials at the Department of Transportation, under the sway of "contestability" theory. Though Bailey and Baumol had by 1984 admitted that the markets were not contestable, and though the Antitrust Division opposed two of the mergers, incorrect doctrine led to unwise permissions for the mergers. Alfred E. Kahn, the prime mover for de-regulation, described the decisions as "abominable derelictions," and later studies showed that prices were raised in line with higher hub dominance.[22] The mergers and their effects are irreversible, and they illustrate the outcomes when Chicago-UCLA and free-entry doctrines are crudely applied.

Monfort v. Cargill. In 1983, Cargill sought to merge its beef-packing operations (named Excel) with Spencer Beef, to obtain 20 percent of the national market. That would have made it second only to IBP, which had 24 percent. Monfort, ranking fifth with 5 percent, filed a private suit to stop the merger, claiming that the monopoly-increasing effect would impair Monfort's ability to compete.

The case illustrated how far Chicago-UCLA doctrines could be stretched. The Supreme Court's final decision for Cargill did not deny that market power would rise. Instead, it simply questioned whether Monfort had shown a threat that it would suffer injury from the merger. The Court held that no unfair competition could occur in this competitive market, because "predatory pricing" was unlikely (see Chapter 10 for coverage of predatory pricing). Therefore, any harms suffered by Monfort would only reflect its own lesser competence. The precedent of this case effectively blocks any suits by firms seeking to stop mergers by their competitors.

After 1988, new Bush administration officials sought to project a stricter image, and they spoke of pressuring prospective merger partners to modify their combinations. But the changes by 1990 appear to have been minor, and those occurred mainly in an effort to repair some of the earlier setbacks in the airline industry.

The 1980s policies had assigned entry a major role; if entry appeared easy, then high market shares did not matter. In the new 1990 approach: "Ease of entry will rebut an inference of anticompetitive effect drawn from market concentration if, and only if, entry in reaction to an hypothesized price increase is *timely*, that is, if it would occur within two years; if it is *sufficient* to render the hypothesized price increase

---

[22]Thus, flights from the 15 airports with one or two dominant airlines had 27 percent higher fares, according to a General Accounting Office study. A Transportation Department study of eight cities found fares to be 19 percent higher. See "One Sure Result of Airline Deregulation: Controversy about Its Impact on Fares," *The Wall Street Journal,* April 19, 1990, p. B1.

unprofitable; and if it is *likely* given the risks and sunk cost associated with entry."[23]

Note the moderacy. Two years is a long time, particularly in fast-moving, flexible industries. Sufficiency and likelihood are both vague and difficult to assess.

Actions have been mild.[24] In 1989, Eastern Airlines had agreed to sell its rights to 10 gates at Philadelphia airport to USAir, which would raise concentration. The Division objected, and Eastern sold the gate rights to Midway Airlines instead. Also in 1989, the Division opposed a joint venture between American Airlines' "Sabre" and Delta's "Datas II" reservation systems. The venture would have increased concentration and the likelihood of biased listings of flights. The joint venture was dropped.

There are press accounts of proposed mergers that have been adjusted or withdrawn in the face of antitrust-agency pressure. But there is little hard evidence to show a tightening. As of 1990, the rules on horizontal mergers are unclear. Within a market-share zone roughly from 25 to 40 percent, the agencies may challenge mergers, but each case appears to be unpredictable.

2. Vertical Mergers

From 1940 to 1960, the restraints on vertical mergers developed to relatively tight levels. Enforcement tapered off after 1968 despite the rather strict criteria in the 1968 Guidelines. Since 1980, no significant cases have been brought, even though the 1984 Guidelines give the impression that the policy is still rather tight.

The earlier cases reflected the belief that vertical mergers can foreclose competition. When a major firm buys a substantial supplier (upstream) or customer (downstream), the flow of goods generally is diverted from outside market sales. Internal, "in-house" supply generally occurs, even if prices are somewhat higher than they would be in arm's-length market transactions.

Moreover, if the integrated firm is a major seller to one-level firms, it may apply a "squeeze" to them, by raising its price for the input but not the price for the output at the next level. Also, if new entrants must

[23]From a speech by the chief of the Antitrust Division, James F. Rill, "Merger Enforcement at the Department of Justice," American Bar Association, Washington, D.C., March 23, 1990. Italics are in the original.

[24]James F. Rill, "Competition in the Airline Industry," statement before the Subcommittee on Aviation, Committee on Commerce, Science, and Transportation, Washington, D.C., September 20, 1989.

now enter by creating capacity at both levels to compete against the integrated firm, then the merger may raise barriers to entry.

How serious these dangers are is debatable, and research has indicated only that they may occur in some degree. Chicago-UCLA analysts offer a blunt opposite view: Vertical integration never reduces competition.[25] The reasoning is that market processes are frictionless, with perfect knowledge, as in the ideal Chicago-UCLA world. They maintain that foreclosure, squeezes, and barriers are innocuous, because worthy competitors can always obtain ample capital.

A review of a few earlier cases will be instructive. The *Yellow Cab* decision in 1947, *Paramount* in 1948, and *A&P* in 1949 had established that vertical integration could not be used to foreclose competition at either level. However, specific practices had been adduced in these cases: No general rule against vertical integration, per se, was applied.

Du Pont–General Motors. The case was filed in 1949, alleging that Du Pont's holding of GM stock gave it preference in the market for automobile fabrics and finishes (recall the discussion in Chapter 7).

GM's purchases were over half of the fabrics and finishes markets; Du Pont's sales to GM were about 30 percent of the market, a "substantial share." The vertical tie had clearly affected GM's purchases, limiting Du Pont's competitor's ability to compete. The district court acquitted Du Pont in 1954, saying that a loss of competition had not been proven. On appeal, the Supreme Court reversed the decision by 4 to 2, citing the original Clayton Section 7.[26] The shares were divested, in 1961.

Vertical integration had only been partial, and the decision set a moderate limit on the market shares held by the firms. However, it did show that markets could be defined narrowly in vertical merger cases.

Brown Shoe. The *Brown Shoe* case had vertical aspects too. Brown made shoes and Kinney sold shoes. The Court looked less at the small market shares than at Brown's likely policy of requiring Kinney to carry Brown Shoes. This would foreclose competition in a market that already had rising concentration. Before the merger, Kinney bought no

---

[25]Among the leading treatments of this topic, see Morris A. Adelman's chapter on "Vertical Integration" in *Business Concentration and Price Policy,* ed. George J. Stigler (Princeton, N.J.: Princeton University Press, 1955); Michael Gort, *Integration and Diversification in American Industry* (Princeton, N.J.: Princeton University Press, 1962); Frederick R. Warren-Boulton, *Vertical Control of Markets: Business and Labor Practice* (Cambridge, Mass.: Ballinger Publishing, 1978); and Robert D. Blair and David L. Kaserman, *Antitrust Economics* (Homewood, Ill.: Richard D. Irwin, 1985).

[26]*U.S. v. Du Pont,* 353, U.S. 586 (1957).

shoes from Brown. Soon after, Brown had become Kinney's largest outside supplier, with 8 percent of Kinney's purchases. An incipiency test was applied.

Since 1980, no significant vertical merger cases have been brought.

3. Conglomerate Mergers

In perspective, the conglomerate merger problem posed several of the broader but softer risks as noted in the discussion of effects of mergers in Section I above: large firms would shift resources among their parts so as to gain unfair advantage in specific markets; spheres of influence would inhibit competition; and absentee owners would neglect local interests. Other costs include the impact on fearful managements as they fight off takeovers and the tying up of large volumes of capital. These possibilities have been real, but, in many cases, they are small and difficult to show.

Conglomerate mergers during the 1980s were likened to the mere repackaging of existing assets, in contrast to the creation of new assets and innovations. Moreover, large conglomerate owners often ignore local impacts and values when they abruptly close down branches.

Against these costs, there are possible benefits from the direct and indirect pressure to improve management. These gains are stressed by Chicago-UCLA analysts, who regard them as overwhelmingly large compared to the possible costs.

The conglomerate merger movement of the 1960s stirred initial fears that were probably overstated, but they did lead to a number of significant cases. Because Chicago-UCLA analysis accepts all conglomerate mergers as innocuous or positive for efficiency, the Reagan administration deliberately stopped all actions against conglomerates. In so doing, it opened the way for serious excesses in unmanageable and unwise mergers, especially those involving "junk bonds," including leveraged buyouts. Consequently, the early conglomerate cases are mainly of historical interest, while the aftershocks of the lenient 1980s' policies may continue for many years.

4. Policy Criteria

There were sharp turns in policy as the wave of conglomerate mergers mounted in the 1960s. One doctrine after another was tried by the Division and the FTC, all of them speculative. In 1969, the Division made a broad-scale attack on conglomerate mergers, with LTV and ITT the main targets. This helped to stop the merger wave, but the attack was compromised by interference from the Nixon White House, before reaching the Supreme Court for a clear decision on the merits.

There are several possible grounds upon which a conglomerate merger might be challenged. The agencies focused on the danger of reciprocity, on potential entry, on size disparity and the unfair advantages that a branch might acquire, and on the "toe-hold" issue. All have been ignored since 1980 under Chicago-UCLA doctrines.

Reciprocity. An early case, decided in 1965, cited reciprocal buying. The Consolidated Foods Corporation, operating a nationwide chain of groceries and buying large quantities of processed food, had acquired Gentry, Inc., a small wholesaler making a third of the nation's sales of dehydrated onions and garlic. Consolidated was thus enabled to require the food processors who sold to it to buy their onions and garlic from Gentry, thereby excluding Gentry's competitors from its market for these commodities. The Court held that the reciprocity made possible by the merger was anticompetitive enough to bar the merger.[27]

Some later cases also alleged reciprocity, but the point has largely been abandoned. Reciprocity actually has only shallow roots and effects in most cases (see Chapter 10).

Loss of a Potential Competitor. Recall that if a potential entrant X comes in by merger, a net loss of competition may result. Practical cases become complex: Was firm X *really* a potential entrant? Was competition reduced by enough to offset other gains?

P&G–Clorox. When Procter & Gamble Company bought Clorox Chemical Company in 1958, P&G was the largest household-products firm and was likely to enter the bleach business in any event. Some of its products were related to bleach, and P&G management had considered direct entry before undertaking to enter by acquiring Clorox. Clorox was the dominant bleach firm, with a long-established 55 percent market share (71 percent in the Mid-Atlantic region), compared to less than 15 percent for Purex, the next largest.

The merger clearly subtracted a leading potential entrant. Yet the FTC (later affirmed by the Supreme Court) cited P&G's advertising advantages as the main grounds for preventing the merger.

"Toe-Hold" Mergers and Entrenchment. Suppose that a merger provides financial, technical, and marketing advantages to the acquired firm. If that firm is dominant in its market, the merger will entrench it further. If the merger were instead with a smaller firm in that market—

---

[27]*FTC* v. *Consolidated Foods Corporation,* 380 U.S. 592.

giving the large acquiring firm only a "toe-hold"—then it could heat up competition against the leading firms.

The point is based on valid economics.[28] The importance of the entrenchment and toe-hold features depend on the strength of (1) the dominant market positions and (2) the advantages (from finances, advertising, and so forth). During 1967–78, the FTC adopted a 10 percent market share of the acquired firm as a rough dividing line in assessing the effect on competition: below 10 percent is toe-hold; above it is entrenchment. The Division and the courts also applied entrenchment and toe-hold doctrine where the effects were clearly strong.

In *P&G–Clorox,* the Court stressed that P&G would give Clorox overwhelming advantages and distribution.[29] P&G was the nation's largest advertiser (spending over $175 million in 1967), and its discounts and market power were likely to entrench Clorox further. A toe-hold acquisition would have met this problem. The same reasoning applied in the *General Foods* case.[30] S.O.S., the leading maker of kitchen steel-wool scouring pads, had been acquired by General Foods. To prevent entrenchment, the FTC required divestiture, and, in 1968, it was affirmed by the Supreme Court. The *Bendix-Fram* decision in 1970 went further, stating that toe-hold mergers were definitely superior to others.[31] A 17 percent market share (Fram's) could not be bought; a 9.5 percent market share would have been acceptable.

5. Other Countries

Distinct merger waves occurred in Britain and Western Europe in the 1960s and 1980s. In the 1960s, many of the mergers were actively promoted by government actions, under the claim that they would make

---

[28]It was advanced by a Presidential Commission on Antitrust in 1968, and in J. S. Campbell and W. G. Shepherd, "Leading-Firm Conglomerate Mergers," *Antitrust Bulletin,* 1968, pp. 1361–82.

[29]*FTC* v. *Procter & Gamble,* 386 U.S. 568 (1967). This effect was affirmed by an episode in Pennsylvania, where P&G had helped Clorox defeat an attempt by Purex to enter the market significantly. For severe criticism of the P&G–Clorox decision, see John L. Peterman, "The *Clorox* Case and the Television Rate Structures," *Journal of Law and Economics* 11 (October 1968), pp. 321–422.

[30]*FTC* v. *General Foods Corp.,* 386 F.2d 836; 391 U.S. 919, *certiorari denied.*

[31]"The threat of a toe-hold merger by a powerful firm may often serve as a much greater incentive to competitive performance in the affected market than the prospect of more costly and slower internal, *de novo* expansion." "In the Matter of the Bendix Corporation," Docket No. 8739, 1970.

Fram made automobile filters (oil, fuel, and air), with about 17 percent of the various submarkets, Bendix was a large diversified firm and producer of automotive parts. Bendix bought Fram in 1967 but was required to divest Fram after the FTC's decision was affirmed on appeal in 1971.

the combined firms stronger in meeting international competition. Though it was soon discredited, this claim has lingered into the 1990s in the United States as well as abroad.[32]

Outside the United States, merger policies have been most active in the United Kingdom.[33] After 1965, the Monopolies and Mergers Commission was assigned authority to screen mergers referred to it by the Board of Trade. Only about 2 percent of all actual mergers are referred, and the Commission has usually made only moderate recommendations to stop or modify the mergers. As in the United States, the 1980s brought special confidence that the pressures from foreign trade would nullify any serious pockets of monopoly.

The Commission's criteria for judging mergers were broad at first, covering many ways in which mergers might affect the public interest (labor relations, foreign control, etc.). In the 1980s, as in the United States, the criteria narrowed to a concern with monopoly effects on prices.

West Germany has also had active merger investigations. During 1974–85, 69 mergers were judged by the Federal Cartel Office. Some 26 of them were enforced, 20 were reversed by other agencies or courts, and 8 were withdrawn or modified. As many as 113 others were withdrawn after discussions with the agency.[34]

In Western Europe since 1971, the European Community has applied mild policies to mergers that would create large market shares. For the most part, the actions have been informal, encouraging firms to alter their planned mergers, but by 1989, the Community had developed a more formal program of screening sizable mergers.

France and Italy have held to the belief that large firms are superior, and so they have never sought to restrain mergers. Canada finally began a formal merger-screening policy in 1986. It permits economies defenses and gives weight to foreign competition.

In Japan, there are few restraints beyond strict prohibitions on foreign takeovers of Japanese firms. Horizontal mergers above about 30 to 35 percent may be blocked by the Japanese Fair Trade Commission. A 1972 merger, creating Nippon Steel with a 36 percent market share and second rank among all steel firms in the world, was permitted under pressure, and still larger market shares have been created in recent mergers.

As Eastern European countries emerged from Communist rule during 1989–90, there were immediate moves by Western European firms

---

[32]For a critique, see Keith Cowling et al., *Mergers and Economic Performance* (Cambridge: Cambridge University Press, 1980).

[33]See John Agnew, *Competition Law* (London: Allen & Unwin, 1985).

[34]See Scherer and Ross, *Industrial Market Structure and Economic Performance,* p. 196.

to merge with the state monopolies in the Eastern countries. The resulting monopoly effects were very large, and they may block the evolution of these economies toward effective competition.

These developments illustrate the common fact that fast-moving private interests often take action before even the rudiments of policy agencies are in place to assess them. Whether such mergers should be constrained depends, of course, on the facts of each case, including market definition, international competition, and possible entrenchment in domestic markets. However, these mergers are occurring before any evaluations can be done at all.

QUESTIONS FOR REVIEW

1. "The gains from mergers are strictly pecuniary, except for vertical mergers." True?
2. "For sound policy choices, one weighs the possible costs from reducing competition against the possible increases in genuine efficiency (including economies of scale and integration)." True?
3. "In assessing mergers, it is the net gains (compared to internal growth or long-term contracts) that count." True?
4. "Conglomerate mergers have virtually ceased since 1968." True?
5. "Before 1958, there were no effective formal limits on mergers, and so dominant firms could merge with impunity." True?
6. "Merger policies cover all sectors except utilities and banking, which are exempt under regulation." True?
7. "Clear rules toward mergers were set in the *Philadelphia National Bank* case, while *General Dynamics* made the evaluation more complicated." True?
8. "The criteria for a failing-firm exemption from merger policy are not clear or simple." True?
9. What are the main costs and benefits of takeovers? Be sure to include the direct effects on target firms' efficiency and the indirect effects on other firms.
10. Is the H Index a superior basis for making merger policy decisions?
11. In most mergers, the partners make claims that substantial efficiencies will result. Should the antitrust agencies consider those efficiencies in deciding whether to challenge the merger?
12. Explain how Chicago-UCLA doctrines led directly to the lenient merger policies of the 1980s.
13. Should there be any restraints on conglomerate mergers?

C·H·A·P·T·E·R 9   Restrictive Practices:
Collusion

The third part of U.S. antitrust policy deals with actions, rather than structure. Firms take all manner of actions toward each other, and most of them are merely parts of an effective competitive process. Some of their actions, instead, tend to restrict or exclude competition. The task of antitrust is to identify the harmful, restrictive actions and to devise ways to prevent them.

There are two main classes of restrictive practices: (1) Two or more competitors *cooperate,* such as by price fixing; (2) One firm *unilaterally* imposes exclusionary actions on other firms that unfairly reduce their ability to compete. Generally, cooperation raises the *level* of prices, while exclusionary actions tend to change the *structure* of prices toward price discrimination.

This chapter covers collusion, which is U.S. antitrust's most successful and consistent policy area. The precedents against price fixing have been strict and clear since 1899. Reagan officials nevertheless attempted to weaken some of them after 1980.

The economic analysis of collusion is summarized in Section I. Price fixing—the classic restrictive act—is the subject matter of Section II. One variant of it, "resale price maintenance," stirred debate in the 1980s as Reagan officials sought to make it acceptable. Next, Section III changes the focus away from direct price fixing to the softer versions of informal collusion often done by oligopolists.[1] There are also

---

[1]It also goes by a variety of other names, including *tacit collusion, indirect collusion, parallel pricing,* and *price signalling.*

several indirect types of cooperation: overlapping directors, joint ventures, and trade associations. These are reviewed in Section IV. Section V looks abroad, to U.S. policies toward international collusion.

Chapter 10 covers the unilateral actions that may reduce competition. Antitrust policies toward them have been less consistent and less effective, and far more controversial.

I. WHY COLLUSION OCCURS

Collusion is endemic in markets ranging from loose oligopoly up to virtual monopoly, roughly from four-firm concentration of 40 percent up to 100 percent.[2] Each firm's incentives are mixed. The firm can gain by colluding with its fellow oligopolists, but it may do even better by cheating them and defeating them. Its own best choices will often include a mix of cooperation on some matters and fighting on others. This mix can be unstable and changing, as conditions shift and the rivals try new tactics.

The resulting degree of cooperation is a form of partial monopoly. The colluders get part or perhaps even all of the gains that a direct merger would yield them. Done secretly, the collusion provides market power, and its fruits of higher prices and profits, beneath a surface illusion of competition. In the upper ranges of tight oligopoly, collusion can often be tacit, as if the cooperating firms were a "shared monopoly." In the lower range of medium and loose oligopoly, the collusion normally must be explicit, detailed, and mutually binding upon the firms, if it is to have much effect. The looser the oligopoly, the greater the likelihood that collusion will fail.

---

[2]Important references on oligopoly behavior include the following: Edward H. Chamberlin, *The Theory of Monopolistic Competition,* 6th ed. (Cambridge, Mass.: Harvard Univ. Press, 1962); John von Neumann and Oskar Morgenstern, *Theory of Games and Economic Behavior* (Princeton, N.J.: Princeton University Press, 1944); William J. Fellner, *Competition Among the Few* (New York: Alfred A. Knopf, 1949); Joe S. Bain, *Barriers to New Competition* (Cambridge, Mass.: Harvard Univ. Press, 1956); A. D. H. Kaplan, Joel B. Dirlam, and Robert F. Lanzillotti, *Pricing in Big Business* (Washington, D.C.: Brookings Institution, 1958); Carl Kaysen and Donald F. Turner, Jr., *Antitrust Policy* (Cambridge, Mass.: Harvard Univ. Press, 1959); Paolo Sylos-Labini, *Oligopoly and Technical Progress* (Cambridge, Mass.: Harvard Univ. Press, 1962); Lawrence E. Fouraker and Sidney Siegel, *Bargaining Behavior* (New York: McGraw-Hill, 1963); and George J. Stigler, "The Theory of Oligopoly," *Journal of Political Economy* 72 (February 1964), pp. 44–61.

Useful summaries of recent oligopoly theory can be found in Jean Tirole, *The Theory of Industrial Organization* (Cambridge, Mass.: MIT Press, 1988); Michael Waterson, *Economic Theory of Industry* (Cambridge: Cambridge University Press, 1984); Lester Telser, *Theories of Competition* (Amsterdam: North Holland, 1988); Joseph E. Stiglitz and C. Frank Mathewson, *New Developments in the Analysis of Market Structure* (Cambridge, Mass.: MIT Press, 1986); and Alexis Jacquemin, *The New Industrial Organization* (Cambridge, Mass.: MIT Press, 1987).

Figure 9–1   The Incentive to Cheat on Collusive Price Fixing

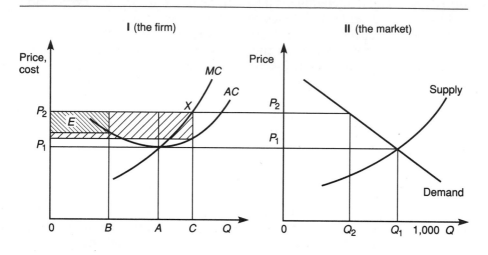

1. Cooperation versus Cheating

The basic question about cooperation is: Can it succeed? If it does, the group of colluders raises prices and gains excess profits. But then, paradoxically, it automatically rewards each member for cheating on the group. The dream situation is to be in an industry where collusion is keeping price high but you are holding your price just a little lower, getting large profits.

To Chicago-UCLA economists, price fixing is self-destructive, likely to collapse quickly amid mutual cheating. At the other extreme, some experts regard price fixing as inherently stable and powerful, even in unfavorable circumstances. The realistic view is in the middle: success will vary with the conditions.

Figure 9–1 neatly shows how incentives to cheat rise as price fixing succeeds. Supply and demand for the entire market are shown on the right-hand side in panel II; a typical firm in that market is shown in panel I, on the left. Under competition, supply and demand set the price at P_1 and total market output is Q_1, as shown in panel II. That forces the typical firm to choose output A in panel I, where it makes no excess profit.

Now suppose that the firms collude to increase the price, to price P_2. This price will continue only if total output can be held to the level Q_2, as shown in panel II. In cutting total output, this firm will be assigned an output quota limited to level B, in panel I. If all firms stay at B, then the collusion works and they each make profits shown by the shaded rectangle E.

This situation also gives the firm powerful incentives to set its own output at *C*, where marginal cost equals the fixed price (which is, therefore, its marginal revenue). At output *C*, the firm's profits are the larger striped area, much bigger than at the quota output *B*. Even if it doesn't go all the way to *C*, the firm gains strongly from every extra unit of output over its quota. The payoff from cheating is high.

Chicago-UCLA economists therefore argue that price fixing rarely lasts. Indeed, the OPEC oil cartel suffers chronically from overproduction by its members, and virtually all price fixing has broken down eventually.

2. Conditions Favoring Collusion

Some conditions do favor collusion, helping it to last. These include (1) high concentration, (2) uniform costs among the firms, (3) an entry barrier, (4) no powerful buyers able to exert monopsony power, (5) similar attitudes among the oligopolists, and (6) availability of information about price cutting.

1. When *concentration* is high, the few leading sellers can coordinate more easily. The balance of their interests shifts from competition toward cooperation. Fewness means simplicity of control, and it also means that price cutting can be found and penalized quickly. Usually, *tight oligopoly crystallizes collusion by making it more effective, while loose oligopoly permits little effective collusion.* There is no exact standard for tight oligopoly, though a four-firm concentration ratio of 60 percent of the market is a common rule of thumb.[3]

2. When *costs* are similar, agreement on the collusive price is easier. Cost differences undermine collusion. A firm with low costs will naturally prefer a lower price than will its high-cost rivals.

3. A *barrier to entry* will raise the price at which collusion will be effective. The added security also gives the cartel members a stronger net incentive to stay up at the cartel price level.

4. *Buyers* can neutralize collusion. Powerful buyers can isolate and pressure the sellers into offering special deals. This directly breaks up the cartel's pricing unity. Indirectly, it reduces the mutual trust among the sellers, and so the collusion is less stable when it does occur. When buyers passively accept collusion, there is usually some abnormal reason.[4]

---

[3]Joe S. Bain has emphasized this threshold (see his *Barriers to New Competition*).

[4]One cause of passivity is utility regulation. Utility firms under rate-base regulation in the United States may lack strong incentives to buy equipment at the lowest possible price. The equipment goes into the firm's rate base, and a higher rate base can give the firm higher profits. See the electrical equipment conspiracy in Section II below for one such instance. See also Chapter 14's analysis of the rate-base effect.

5. *Similar attitudes* can cause the firms' interests and expectations to converge. The managers may be from the same background and be long familiar with each other. With practice, they can fine-tune their signals and responses about pricing. The shared expectations can then become self-fulfilling, even without direct, thorough collusion.

6. If there is *full information about price cutting,* price cuts will be quickly known and there can be swift retaliation by the rest of the price fixers. Therefore, high concentration helps reveal price cutting and discourage it; the few sellers can quickly discover who is "cheating." Public bids are especially prone to this problem. The sealed bids are opened, and the lowest one is chosen, *but* the bids are fully revealed. This tends to discourage price cutters, and so public purchases are chronically subject to bid rigging.

For lasting success, collusion needs to cover all of the industry. Collusion may be tight and explicit, or loose and fluid. A formal cartel will bind its members by various tangible controls. These can include pricing formulas, output quotas, a set of penalties for specific violations, a staff for detecting and punishing the violators, and—in the very tightest of cartels—a direct pooling of profits.

Oligopoly is an arena for recurring strife, where the balance sways between collusion and independence. As concentration increases, higher prices are more likely. But the other conditions are also at work, and there may be a sequence of collusion and collapses.

3. Varieties of Collusion

There is an endless variety of processes and outcomes with strategies of all kinds, including bluffing, deceptions, and complex sequences.

Price leadership often occurs. In the extreme version, the largest firm will select the price that maximizes the joint profits of the group and then impose that price. The other firms then follow this leader. In these markets, long periods of rigged prices are punctuated by brief episodes of collusive, or dominant-firm, price-leadership. (They have also been called *administered prices.*) In softer versions, the leadership may rotate a bit, or, occasionally, not be followed rigidly. At the other extreme, this leadership may only be "barometric."[5] The leader merely *finds* the new price level that costs will require; it does not *impose* a higher price. A lock-step pattern of price leadership does not prove that collusion has occurred, though it strongly suggests that it has.

---

[5]See Jesse W. Markham, "The Nature and Significance of Price Leadership," *American Economic Review* 41 (December 1951), pp. 891–905. See also the extensive discussion in F. M. Scherer and David Ross, *Industrial Market Structure and Economic Performance,* 3rd ed. (Boston: Houghton Mifflin, 1990), pp. 248–61.

Explicit collusion is known to occur in various loose oligopolies where there must be tight controls in order to keep mavericks in line. It was long thought that tight oligopolies can rely, instead, just on tacit collusion. The facts suggest the opposite; many tight oligopolies do in fact engage deeply in explicit price-fixing schemes.[6] There is often concrete evidence of these schemes, including signed memoranda, notes, and charts.

The actual amount of collusive practices that do exist in the United States is not known, but the research literature and the business press suggest that it is not trivial. Standardized-product industries (such as metals and minerals) tend to be especially prone to it, as are sellers who enter sealed bids for public construction contracts.

Cartels have been common in other countries since 1900, especially in Germany, Sweden, and—during 1930–56—Britain.[7] Some cartels amount virtually to a merger of the members, for their production, pricing, marketing, and profit shares are all centrally handled. Looser cartels take endless varieties of these parts, reflecting both the range of market conditions and the sheer ingenuity of the human mind.

Under U.S. antitrust law, this kind of tangible collusion is illegal, and so the attempts at it must be secret. There are many looser forms of cooperation that, being on the margin of the law, are able to proceed in public; patent pooling and joint ventures are examples. All these versions of cooperation occur with much variety throughout most of the economy.

4. The Costs and Possible Benefits of Collusion

As a form of monopoly, collusion usually causes social harm, as Chapter 2 noted: inefficiency, lost innovation, inequity, and so on. Colluders often say that there are offsetting benefits from "orderly marketing," but the claims are always doubtful and often false. The main possible real benefit—economies of scale—is absent, for the firms remain separate as producers. Therefore, a clear policy line against price fixing is sound, as virtually all analysts agree. There might be certain valid defenses for certain situations. A discussion of the three most popular defenses follows.

Avoiding "Destructive" ("Ruinous" or "Cut-Throat") Competition. The claim is that fluctuations in demand cause price cutting to go too

---

[6]This is shown by George A. Hay and Daniel Kelley, "An Empirical Survey of Price Fixing Conspiracies," *Journal of Law and Economics* 17 (April 1974), pp. 13–38.

[7]George W. Stocking and Myron W. Watkins, *Cartels in Action* (New York: Twentieth Century Fund, 1946), is a massive study of cartels in world markets.

deep, down toward short-run marginal cost. Meanwhile, since industry demand is inelastic, the physical volume of sales stays nearly the same. The cut in profits causes firms to fail, even through they are able to produce at normal, long-run, average-cost levels. If price fixing could avoid these deep slashes, it is said, the capacity and efficiency of the industry would be greater. "Destructive" competition is most likely to occur when overhead costs are large, so that short-run marginal costs are low. So the research questions are: *Is* industry demand highly inelastic, *are* overhead costs large, *are* price cuts "too deep," and *are* capacity and efficiency reduced?

Research has rarely borne out claims that competition is destructive. Demand is often not very inelastic, marginal costs are often higher than the firms claim, and the causal effects on capacity and efficiency usually cannot be measured, much less proven. Short-run pricing shifts are not likely to affect long-run performance. Even if they were, price fixing is usually an inferior way to avoid the damage.

Long-term declines in "sick industries" are a separate matter. They induce chronic price cutting below profitable levels. That is the efficient economic process, in order to shrink the excess capacity. Competition may seem to do this too rapidly and cruelly. Yet if a genuine social harm occurs, it usually can be mitigated in better ways than by price fixing.

Reducing Risk. Price fixing often stabilizes prices and output, even down to the shares of individual firms. This reduces risk; yet it may not be a social gain. Some degree of risk is a spur for efficiency and innovation. Collusion has often induced slackness and slowness among its participants. For that matter, price fixing might *not* reduce risk. Prices may have sharper fluctuations, as collusion first works, then collapses, then holds again, then collapses, and so on. Such breaks are a common result of attempts to collude. Altogether, reducing risk is not a good justification for price fixing.

Making Other Valuable Actions Possible. The excess profits from collusion might be devoted to better service or innovation, it is said. The prime instance may be "resale price maintenance." If dealers earn extra profits because producers prevent price discounting, they may provide high-quality service and advice to their customers. Otherwise, discounters would reward customers for being "free riders," getting the advice from dealers and then buying from the discounters. The issue is addressed below. Colluders might also pool increased resources for large-scale projects (such as mining ventures or development of new technology).

Yet competition is at least as likely to bring about the optimal levels of these good things. Also, the excess profits might well be siphoned off for dividends or other uses, instead, rather than be used for the new projects. Few of these claimed needs have held up under objective study. Altogether, there is a compelling social case against explicit collusion and a strong presumption against most other forms of cooperation. A few marginal categories of cooperation may deserve a more selective treatment; some, but not all, of them will have minor social effects either way.

II. POLICY TOWARD PRICE FIXING

Recall the basic criterion of good policy: The optimum treatment will draw the line at the efficient margin, in light of benefits and costs. The costs include the costs of the practice *plus* the costs of the treatment, such as agency costs, court costs, and possibly the firms' costs of litigating. These costs of the treatment can grow large. A simple rule can save large volumes of policy costs by avoiding lengthy hearings and claims about the evidence. Generally, a clear, definite policy line is better than a complex, uncertain one, as long as it fits the efficient policy margin reasonably well.

1. Simple Price Fixing: The Per Se Rule

Simple price fixing is under such a clear rule. It has been illegal per se since 1899, without any further proof of intent or effect. The prohibition applies also to controls on output, to market-sharing agreements, and to cooperative exclusions of competitors by boycotts or other coercive practices. All that an Antitrust Division attorney (or private plaintiff) needs to show at a trial is that competitors actually tried to fix prices or rig the market in some other way. Any solid evidence of a conspiracy—a scribbled memorandum, an annotated price list, a tape recording of the discussions—can be enough to convict and invoke penalties. No evidence that prices actually rose, or rose up to some "unreasonable" level, is essential, though that sort of evidence will usually result in stiffer penalties and larger awards for damages.

There are certain marginal issues around this core of clear policy. They will be discussed shortly. First, we will review the mainstream cases that initially formed the per se rule in 1899, reaffirmed it in 1927, and set the seal on it in 1940.

Mainstream Cases. The earliest cases involving restrictive agreements among competitors were those of the Trans-Missouri Freight Association in 1897,[8] the Joint Traffic Association in 1898,[9] and the Addyston Pipe and Steel Company in 1899.[10] In *Trans-Missouri* and *Joint Traffic,* groups of railroads had fixed and enforced freight rates. In *Addyston,* six producers of cast-iron pipe (with less than half of the market) had assigned certain sales to each of their number and determined the allocation of contracts elsewhere by operating a bidding ring. In all three cases, the defendants argued that their restrictions were required to prevent ruinous competition and that the resulting rates and prices were reasonable. In each case, the Court rejected this defense, holding the arrangements to be illegal in themselves. After the *Addyston* decision, there was a merger among the former price-fixing firms.

The per se rule held for three decades, decisions being rendered against collusive bidding by purchasers of livestock, exclusion of competing railways from a terminal, the use of patent licenses to fix the price of bathtubs, and the operation of a boycott by retail lumber dealers.[11]

Trenton Potteries renewed the precedent in 1927.[12] Firms producing four fifths of the domestic output of vitreous enamel bathroom fixtures had agreed to fix prices and to sell exclusively through jobbers. The Court was emphatic in its refusal to accept the reasonableness of the fixed prices as a defense.

Doubts regarding all price fixing as negative were raised by the Court's decision in the *Appalachian Coals* case in 1933,[13] but in the *Socony–Vacuum* case[14] in 1940, the Court reaffirmed the rule of *Trenton Potteries*. This case involved an agreement under which the major oil companies in 10 midwestern states raised and maintained the price of gasoline by purchasing marginal supplies from independent refineries.

---

[8]*U.S.* v. *Trans-Missouri Freight Assn.*, 166 U.S. 290.

[9]*U.S.* v. *Joint Traffic Assn.*, 171 U.S. 505.

[10]*Addyston Pipe & Steel Co.* v. *U.S.*, 175 U.S. 211.

[11]*U.S.* v. *Swift & Co.*, 196 U.S. 375 (1906). *U.S.* v. *Terminal R. R. Assn.*, 224 U.S. 383 (1912). *U.S.* v. *Standard Sanitary Mfg. Co.*, 226 U.S. 20 (1912). *U.S.* v. *Eastern States Retail Lumber Assn.*, 234 U.S. 600 (1914).

[12]*U.S.* v. *Trenton Potteries Co.*, 273 U.S. 392.

[13]*Appalachian Coals, Inc.* v. *U.S.*, 288 U.S. 344. In this case, 137 companies, producing a tenth of the bituminous coal mined east of the Mississippi River and around two thirds of that mined in the Appalachian territory, had set up a joint agency to handle all their sales. The Court recognized that this arrangement established common prices for the firms involved, but it went on to find that the industry was seriously depressed, that competition in the sale of coal had been subject to various abuses, and that the selling agency did not control enough of the supply to enable it to fix the market price. On this basis, the arrangement was allowed to stand.

[14]*U.S.* v. *Socony–Vacuum Oil. Co.*, 310 U.S. 150.

The Court again rejected the defense that the price established was no more than fair. Said Justice Douglas:

> Any combination which tampers with price structures is engaged in an unlawful activity. Even though the members of the price-fixing group were in no position to control the market, to the extent that they raised, lowered, or stabilized prices they would be directly interfering with the free play of market forces. The Act places such schemes beyond the pale.

Any such agreement, even though affecting a minor portion of the market, was forbidden; any manipulation of prices, whatever its purpose, was against the law.

The Electrical Equipment Case. Bidding rings are one form of conspiracy. Many public purchases and construction projects are conducted by competitive bidding. Specifications are published, bids are invited and received by a fixed date, the sealed bids are then opened, and the lowest bidder wins. Nevertheless, the bids are often rigged beforehand, with the chosen winner low and the others high; the winners rotate among the group, and competition is avoided. Often, the nonwinners randomize their bids, so as to avoid all evidence of fixing.

These rings too are illegal per se. The biggest one yet caught was the conspiracy among the makers of *heavy electrical equipment,* who were caught and penalized in 1960. For decades, collusion had been a way of life in seven markets, including transformers, switchgear, and generators. Sometimes the collusion came unstuck, but often it put prices up by 20 percent or more, and profits up by hundreds of millions of dollars.[15]

Twenty-nine companies and 45 of their officers, including General Electric and Westinghouse and 16 of their officials, pleaded guilty or offered no defense in 20 criminal suits. Seven officers spent brief periods in jail. The total fines were only $1.9 million, but 1,900 treble-damage suits were filed. One by Consolidated Edison of New York was for $100 million and another by Commonwealth Edison of Chicago was for $75 million. (Note: No private utility had earlier complained of

---

[15]The defendants had allocated contracts, selecting the low bidder by drawing names out of a hat, by rotating them in alphabetical order, and by making allotments according to a formula based upon the phases of the moon. The low bidder had then informed the others regarding his bid, and they had adjusted their prices accordingly. The conspirators had met under assumed names in luxury hotels in various cities, in motels, in mountain-top retreats, in cabins in the Canadian woods, and at a Milwaukee bar known as "Dirty Helen's." To maintain secrecy, they had used codes in referring to the companies and their executives, called one another from public telephones, sent letters in plain envelopes without return addresses to their homes rather than their offices, and destroyed these communications when received.

overcharging or helped start the suit. And the damage claims were widely regarded in the trade as moderate.[16])

In the first suit tried, Philadelphia Electric proved damages of $9.6 million and was awarded the trebled amount of $28.8 million. The companies then settled the rest privately. The payments ultimately totaled some $405 million, though a special tax ruling—defining these payments as the "normal" costs of doing business and therefore tax deductible—reduced the net impact upon the firms. The structure of the industry was not changed to increase competition. Tacit collusion soon followed, as will be discussed in Section III below.

In 1969, 15 of the country's largest manufacturers of plumbing fixtures were found to have met in a hotel room in Chicago to set the prices of bathtubs, toilets, and sinks. Also, three of the leading pharmaceutical houses were found to have agreed upon the prices to be charged for antibiotic "wonder drugs." Agreements restricting competition in national markets have been prosecuted in scores of other cases, ranging from eyeglasses to explosives and including such important products as soap, cheese, watches, electric lamps, typewriters, ball bearings, newsprint paper, stainless steel, fertilizers, and various chemicals.

Topco Associates.[17] Dividing up the market also comes under strict Section 1 prohibitions. Topco was a cooperative association of small grocers, banding together in the 1950s and 1960s as a joint purchasing agent in order to get price discounts. Since its members had only 1.5 to 16 percent of sales in local markets (the average was 6 percent), these discounts would help Topco members compete with larger grocery chains.

Topco licensed its members, assigning them territories. This was market splitting, which could limit competition. Topco claimed that this small sacrifice of intrabrand competition was justified by helping Topco members survive to put competitive pressure on the large grocery chains. On balance, this claim was almost certainly true, and competition was increased.

However, the Supreme Court prohibited even this small abridgment of (intrabrand) competition under the per se rule. Although this strict-

---

[16]They could pass on the extra costs to their customers. See F. M. Westfield, "Regulation and Conspiracy," *American Economic Review,* 1965, pp. 424–43, and Chapter 14 for further discussion. A lively account of the conspiracy is in R. A. Smith, *Corporations in Crisis* (New York: Doubleday, 1963), pp. 113–66. For an excellent review of the process by which the damages were set, see Charles A. Bane, *The Electrical Equipment Conspiracies* (New York: Federal Legal Publications, 1973).

[17]This section benefited from discussions with Charles E. Mueller, editor of the *Antitrust Law & Economics Review.*

ness probably tended to sacrifice competition here, on balance, it retained the clarity of the per se rule as a precedent for other markets.[18]

Folding-Carton Case. A classic large case caught some 23 major makers of paperboard boxes, who had fixed prices during 1960–74.[19] The boxes were used for foods, drugs, household supplies, and textiles. The firms held 70 percent of their market, and some 50 of their officials were also caught. The criminal suit resulted in nolo contendere pleas by nearly all of the firms and officers. A trial resulted in convictions of the rest. The volume of business was over $1 billion a year.

The practices were familiar: Price information was shared, and winning bids were rotated, while the rest put in deliberately high bids. Also, the firms agreed to make uniform price increases to customers they shared. The Division used the case to announce new tough guidelines for price-fixing penalties: an average 18-month jail term and an average $50,000 fine, plus fines on the company equaling 10 percent of sales in the product. Adjustments up or down would depend on the individual circumstances. But the judge in this case refused, setting only light sentences. The new stiff felony penalties for price fixing have often been replaced by "creative sentences" that require community service (including speeches against price fixing) instead of jail time.

Of the two elements of enforcement—the probability of getting caught and the severity of penalty—both can be important in deterring violations.

Who Can Sue? The Illinois Brick Case. The question of who can sue price fixers is significant. The Supreme Court held in June 1977 that final consumers of bricks were only "indirect" purchasers who had bought from wholesalers.[20] Only wholesalers, the direct purchasers, could sue, Justice White explained for the 6–3 majority, because otherwise the price fixers would face "multiple liability," and there would be "whole new dimensions of complexity" in settling the correct damages. The issue had important economic content. If wholesalers could pass on the price increases, they would suffer no harm, but the harmed final consumers would be unable to recoup by filing antitrust claims. Unless wholesalers chose to sue—which would be unlikely if their "pass-on" were complete—the final consumers would have no recourse.

---

[18]Afterward, the parties settled the suit by Topco's agreement to soften its geographical limits on members. Therefore, the end result did recognize the value of Topco in promoting effective competition.

[19]See *U.S.* v. *Alton Board Co.*, 76 CR 199, N. D. Ill., and *ATRR*, March 22, 1977.

[20]*Illinois Brick Co.* v. *Illinois*, 431 U.S. 720 (1977). See also Robert G. Harris and Lawrence A. Sullivan, "Passing on the Monopoly Overcharge: A Comprehensive Policy Analysis," *University of Pennsylvania Law Review*, December 1979, pp. 269–360.

The basic issue was whether damage suits would be stimulated too much or discouraged too much. The Court claimed that direct purchasers would have full incentives and knowledge to sue. Critics argued that they would often fail to sue because they feared future reprisals from the suppliers. Final purchasers might have less knowledge, but the triple-damage feature would balance that gap by giving higher rewards for damage claims. In contrast to that, the Court's defenders urged that triple damages *over*stimulated final buyers to sue and only the direct purchasers have about the right balance of incentives.

Therefore, the debate turns on unknown degrees of incentives and knowledge. Evidently, the *Illinois Brick* decision could undercut the force of damage claims in many price-fixing cases. But the optimal policy is not known.

The Professions. In the 1970s, there was growing antitrust pressure against rules preventing competition in certain professions—lawyers, doctors, stockbrokers, accountants, druggists, architects, engineers, and others—which had long been informally accepted. In these "learned professions," one did not even announce one's prices or skills, much less engage in competitive bidding to get contracts. Certain persuasions might be used privately, but the "ethical" codes usually ruled out the explicit information and efforts that effective competition requires.

Since 1908, state bar associations had recommended, and the local bar associations had adopted, "suggested minimum fee schedules" for certain standard tasks. Checking the deed for a house buyer is one such task, and the lawyer's fee is usually a fixed percent of the house's value, even though some searches take much more effort than others. In Fairfax County, Virginia, in 1971, the fee was 1 percent ($600 for a $60,000 house) regardless of the actual effort required. Lewis H. Goldfarb, a house buyer, sought out 37 lawyers, none of whom would budge from the fixed fee. His suit against these price fixers won by an 8–1 vote in the Supreme Court in 1975.[21] Through the fee schedule was only "advisory," the Court noted that it was effective and that the Virginia Bar Association equated price cutting with misconduct. Goldfarb did not need to show that the fees were raised; that "the fee schedule fixed fees" was enough to clinch the violation.

Professional engineers' prohibitions on competitive bidding for contracts were struck down in 1978.[22] In addition, the FTC, in particular, has challenged a range of professional groups. For example, the Mari-

---

[21]*Goldfarb* v. *Virginia State Bar,* Docket No. 74–70, June 16, 1975. A related case was *Bates & O'Steen* v. *Arizona State Bar,* S.C. 76–346 (1977).

[22]*National Society of Professional Engineers* v. *U.S.,* 435 U.S. 679 (1978).

copa Foundation for Medical Care, a nonprofit doctors' group with some 70 percent of doctors in Maricopa County, Arizona, set the maximum fees that its members could charge.[23] Arizona state officials sued, charging that the fees functioned in practice to *raise* and stabilize the average level of fees. This general effect has been common, as in airline regulation before 1978, when price ceilings customarily had the effect of price floors.

The Supreme Court held the scheme to be illegal, rejecting this effort to chip away at the per se prohibition on price fixing. The professions were not different from ordinary markets, it held, and it found the foundation's attempted justifications to be weightless.[24]

The same reasoning was applied to dentists in Indiana, whose association led them into a boycott, refusing to submit X rays to dental insurers for use in setting patients' benefits.[25]

In the financial sector, the stock exchange's fixing of stockbrokers' fees was ended by the Securities and Exchange Commission in May 1975, after seven years of pressure from the Antitrust Division and certain large-scale brokers. Fees dropped by about 25 to 60 percent, and the brokerage business became more efficient.[26]

Matsushita. The new conservative majority on the Supreme Court drew back moderately in a case involving Japanese firms selling television sets in the United States.[27] This case is most important as a precedent about "predatory" actions, discussed in Chapter 10. Here, the relevance is that Japanese firms jointly arranged to sell television sets after 1953 at prices that were lower than would have maximized

---

[23]*Arizona* v. *Maricopa County Medical Society*, 457 U.S. 332 (1982).

[24]Justices Powell, Burger, and Rehnquist dissented, saying that the plan was new, noncoercive, and in the public interest. They attempted to apply a rule of reason to this case, saying that only "naked restraints of trade with no purpose except stifling of competition" should be found per se unlawful. Their view would open the way to full hearings in each case on the supposed purposes of price-fixing systems.

[25]*FTC* v. *Indiana Federation of Dentists*, 476 U.S. 447 (1986). The association involved 85 percent of dentists in Indiana, and their boycott was designed to prevent insurers from applying alternative payment plans for dentists' services. The plain effect was to raise dentists' fees.

[26]By 1977, the commissions charged to buyers were sharply below the old rates, by as much as 66 percent. The effects are appraised in Aharon R. Ofer and Arie Melnick, "Price Deregulation in the Brokerage Industry: An Empirical Analysis," *Bell Journal of Economics* 9 (Autumn 1978), pp. 633–41; see also Seha Tinic and Richard G. West, "The Securities Industry Under Negotiated Brokerage Commissions," *Bell Journal of Economics* 11 (Spring 1980), pp. 29–41.

[27]*Matsushita Electrical Industrial Co.* v. *Zenith Radio Corp.*, 475 U.S. 574 (1986). See also Kenneth G. Elzinga's chapter on the case, "Collusive Predation: *Matsushita* v. *Zenith*," in *The Antitrust Revolution*, ed. John E. Kwoka, Jr., and Lawrence J. White (Glenview, Ill.: Scott, Foresman, 1989), chap. 9.

their short-run profits.[28] The purpose was to "build market share" in the United States, and, in fact, most U.S. producers were driven out.

The Court saw only that prices had been *lowered*, not raised. The Japanese firms had no real motive for doing this, they said, and so no real conspiracy existed. This view fitted the majority's willingness to deny that the Japanese firms may have had a long-run plan, which involved a phase of collusive price cutting.

Sports. Each major sport—baseball, football, basketball, and hockey—has been run as a form of cartel managed by the owners of the teams.[29] Each has prevented bidding by the teams for each other's stock of players or for the yearly stream of new players. The owners also control the number and location of teams. These key controls are surrounded by others. The whole effect has been to keep players' prices below their competitive levels.

Baseball has been formally exempt from antitrust since 1922, by tradition. In the other sports, since 1965, various private suits, reinforced by new leagues and other pressures, have weakened the restrictions, and basketball players' pay in particular has risen. Even baseball was forced by court decisions to permit bidding for "free agents" after 1975. There has been a reduction of price fixing in the major sports, yet the main controls remain. (Should they? Do they protect the integrity and balance of the leagues? Of the sport as a whole?)[30]

A major private case opened up competition for televising collegiate sports, providing the rich array of games now offered on television. Before 1984, the NCAA had controlled all televising of games involving its 276 Division I colleges, as well as 574 others. Complex rules limited the volume of games broadcast, and they broadened the coverage to include at least 82 member teams within each two-year period. The leading teams (e.g., Oklahoma, Georgia) wanted more exposure and revenues, and so five major conferences banded together in the College Football Association (CFA), after some jockeying, and sued in 1981 to break the NCAA's monopoly.

The CFA won in 1984 in the Supreme Court, ushering in the large flow of collegiate sports broadcasting that is now routine.[31] The effects

---

[28]The American producer, Zenith, sued in 1974, after some two decades of the Japanese pricing activity. Such an interval does raise questions whether the Japanese firms' approach really was a short-run phase of a long-run strategy. See Chapter 10.

[29]See, among others, Roger C. Noll, ed., *Government and the Sports Business*, rev. ed. (Washington, D.C.: Brookings Institution, 1985).

[30]For an argument in favor of retaining baseball's exempt status, see Jesse W. Markham and Paul V. Teplitz, *Baseball Economics and Public Policy* (Lexington, Mass.: D. C. Heath, 1981).

[31]*National Collegiate Athletic Association* v. *University of Oklahoma*, 468 U.S. 85 (1984).

of this victory do include a negative side: the further commercializing of big-time collegiate sports and a narrowing of broadcasting coverage to the most famous teams. However, the Sherman Act merely enhances competition, leaving it to other policies (e.g., by the colleges themselves) if other purposes need to be served.

Reagan Policies in the 1980s. The flow of cases, large and small, continued to rise on into the 1980s. However, the Reagan administration, as part of its general cutback of antitrust, reduced and narrowed the enforcement of Section 1. Many prosecutions came to be focused on bid rigging in highway construction in Appalachian states. Bid rigging on public contracts is one of the oldest and easiest violations to treat. The total number of cases, inflated by these minor ones, remained roughly the same, but the effectiveness of Section 1 declined markedly. State enforcement activities expanded, partly to fill that vacuum, but the total scope of price-fixing enforcement has receded, despite the Chicago-UCLA doctrinal opposition to collusion.

Reagan officials also sought to remove the per se treatment of several forms of price fixing, particularly those involved in vertical restraints (which are covered in Chapter 10). Therefore, the 1980s witnessed a diluting of antitrust's treatment of price fixing, as well as in other antitrust areas.

Importance of the Per Se Treatment of Price Fixing. Since 1899, the agencies have won many hundreds of standard price-fixing cases, either by trial or by consent decree. There are usually at least 20 or 25 in process at any time, and (except in cases testing marginal issues) the agencies usually win. With good reason, many company lawyers tell their executives *never* to discuss prices with competitors.

The per se rule on simple price fixing is an efficient policy. Virtually all price fixing creates social costs and no social benefits. To evaluate the costs and benefits in all cases would invite confusion, costly proceedings, and delay. The cases possibly offering social benefits ("dying" industries?) are few and usually small. Any true social benefits can often be gained by other programs. In fact, many sectors have indeed been exempted or given other special treatments.

So the per se rule is clear and efficient, and its coverage of sectors may be roughly correct. It can be so strict partly *because* there are many exemptions.

2. Resale Price Maintenance

All policies have their shaded edges, where the balance of decisions may be more complex. Chicago-UCLA economists and Reagan officials have tried to make resale price maintenance (RPM) into such a marginal case, arguing that the general prohibition on price fixing should be reversed in this area. RPM is both horizontal and vertical in nature, because the manufacturer is involved in setting prices for retailers to observe. RPM's vertical aspects are covered in the next chapter, but its horizontal features need discussion here.[32]

RPM occurs when retailers apply ("maintain") the prices that the goods' producers have set. It arose in the 1930s, when small retailers lobbied for protection from large-scale price discounters. By 1941, most states passed laws permitting manufacturers to enforce retail prices, and in 1937 the Miller-Tydings Act exempted vertical price fixing from the Sherman Act, Section 1, in states with such "fair-trade" laws. In 1952, the McGuire Act was added; it permitted manufacturers to enforce RPM on all retailers, including those who would prefer to cut prices.

So RPM can function as price fixing among retailers, reaching out to force mavericks into line (so-called "nonsigners," who had refused to sign RPM agreements). Sometimes, instead, the manufacturers themselves prefer RPM, rather than just going along with retailers' interests. However, the balance of interests is often impossible to discern in practical cases.

Many familiar items have been fair traded, such as books, cameras, and various appliances. Indeed, "suggested" retail prices are a widespread custom, ranging from automobiles to toothpaste. Most suggested prices have no force, and many are used by retailers mainly as a device to claim that they are offering bargain prices. But certain types of goods seem to encourage enforcement of RPM: expensive, complex items, such as cameras and stereo sets, where dealer assistance and quality can be valuable. Therefore, the problem is rather limited, instead of universal. Yet the issue has stirred strong claims and numerous articles, and Chicago-UCLA analysts mounted an intense effort in the 1980s to evaluate RPM on a rule-of-reason basis.

The economic aspects are complex, and the efficiency effects can go either way. If one focuses strictly on static efficiency, RPM can either

---

[32]This section benefits from Scherer and Ross, *Industrial Market Structure and Economic Performance,* chap. 15. See also Lester Telser, "Why Should Manufacturers Want Fair Trade?" *Journal of Law and Economics* 3 (October 1960), pp. 86–105; Ward S. Bowman, Jr., "The Prerequisites and Effects of Resale Price Maintenance," *University of Chicago Law Review* 22 (Summer 1955), pp. 825–73; and the summary in Thomas R. Overstreet, Jr., *Resale Price Maintenance: Economic Theories and Empirical Evidence* (Washington, D.C.: Bureau of Economics, Federal Trade Commission, November 1983). The same logic applies to a variety of vertical restraints, including territorial restrictions (see Chapter 10) as well as resale price maintenance.

For balanced evaluations, see William S. Comanor, "Vertical Price Fixing and Market Restrictions in the New Antitrust Policy," *Harvard Law Review* 98 (March 1985), pp. 983–1102; and F. M. Scherer, "The Economics of Vertical Restraints," *Antitrust Law Journal* 52 (September 1983), pp. 687–718.

raise or lower output, depending on the way that demand shifts in response to higher-quality service induced by RPM's higher prices. However, it is virtually impossible to know which demand conditions apply
in which cases.

The core issues are (1) dealer services and (2) product reputation.
High-quality dealers offer extra services, such as advice and repairs,
but they may be eliminated by cut-rate discounters. Chicago-UCLA analysts have stressed that this free-rider problem is large, but in most
markets it is probably small. Important extra services should be able to
be offered and priced separately.

Also, many customers explicitly prefer to deal with high-quality retailers, who offer continuing support and advice. In addition, only a
relatively few expensive, complex items lend themselves to significant
free-rider problems. This effect usually lasts only during the early years
of a new product, before it has spread from premium status to mass
marketing. That helps manufacturers maintain a quality brand image,
by avoiding low-quality mass marketers.

All of these elements might be evaluated in a full-blown rule-of-
reason approach to RPM. Every case could be considered on its merits.
Instead, RPM laws were repealed in 1975, and RPM has been treated
largely as horizontal price fixing. That has permitted discounters wide
latitude to spread price cutting, even though some manufacturers seek
to cut off supplies to them. Such cutoffs have bred numerous private
suits by discounters, claiming that pressure from other retailers led to
the cutoffs. Courts have treated such cases as violations of Section 1,
though the cutoffs themselves (without proof that other retailers forced
them) are permitted.

As part of their campaign to apply Chicago-UCLA doctrines, Reagan
officials sought to use the *Spray-Rite* case in 1983 to establish the principle that RPM could be beneficial.[33] For decades up to 1968, the
Spray-Rite company was a retailer of Monsanto's herbicides to farmers,
and it was known as an energetic price discounter. Yet Monsanto had
an enforced program of RPM for its products.

In 1968, Monsanto terminated Spray-Rite as a dealer, forcing it out
of business (by 1972), and Monsanto pressured other dealers to maintain resale prices. Spray-Rite sued Monsanto on antitrust grounds. Reagan officials filed an advisory brief in the case, urging the Court to
declare agreement with its view that all RPM should be weighed under
the rule of reason, but the Supreme Court did not comply. In 1984, it
upheld the conviction of Monsanto for cutting off Spray-Rite, though it
tightened the burden of proof that a plaintiff would have to meet.

---

[33]The case was *Monsanto Corp.* v. *Spray-Rite Service Corp.*, 465 U.S. 752 (1984). See also
Frederick Warren-Boulton's chapter on "Resale Price Maintenance Reexamined: *Monsanto* v. *Spray-Rite*," in *The Antitrust Revolution*, ed. Kwoka and White, chap. 13.

In 1988, in the *Sharp* decision, the Court went far toward putting RPM under a rule of reason. Sharp Electronics had terminated one of its dealers of electronic calculators in Houston in 1972. That dealer was a price cutter, and Sharp acted after its other dealer complained. Justice Scalia's majority opinion was based on the Chicago-UCLA belief that price fixing is fragile and difficult, and so there must be strong proof that enforcing RPM would actually raise prices. He flatly rejected the idea that RPM reflects normal horizontal restraint among dealers. Only if the plaintiff had proven that Sharp and its other dealer specifically raised prices would the rule of reason be met.

The minority termed the action "a naked agreement to terminate a dealer because of its price cutting," saying that it was per se illegal as a horizontal restraint. The majority had set a precedent on RPM, requiring a balance of evidence that it would reduce competition, in each case.

RPM is recognized to be only a specific part of the nation's monopoly problem, though it can reduce the scope of discounting in a range of products. The scope of the impacts in actual markets are not yet clear.

3. Comparisons Abroad

Some other countries have been stricter against RPM than the United States had been before 1975, notably Canada after 1951, Britain after 1964 (though books and proprietary drugs were excepted), and West Germany after 1973.

Until the 1950s, however, the United States was far stricter against conventional price fixing than were other countries. West Germany permitted cartels, and they could be enforced by the courts. Britain's cartel craze of the 1930s established price fixing in most industries. During 1948–55, Britain had a Monopolies and Restrictive Practices Commission, but it did little more than make studies.[34] Meanwhile, price fixing had spread even further.

Then the Conservative government cracked down; the 1956 Restrictive Practices Act required all agreements among competitors to be reported and dropped, unless a positive case for them could persuade the new Restrictive Practices Court to approve them. By 1959, some

[34]See D. C. Elliot and J. D. Gribbin, "The Abolition of Cartels, and Structural Change in the United Kingdom," a chapter in *Welfare Aspects of Industrial Markets,* ed. A. P. Jacquemin and H. W. de Jong (Leiden: Martinus Nijhoff, 1978). This excellent paper surveys the patterns of price fixing and the effects of removing them. See also Dennis Swann, Denis P. O'Brien, W. Peter J. Maunder, and W. Stewart Howe, *Competition in British Industry* (London: Allen & Unwin, 1974); and John Agnew, *Competition Law* (London: Allen & Unwin, 1985).

2,240 agreements had been filed (up to 2,875 by 1972), from a very wide range of industry and trade. They covered about 55 percent of all industry, an increase from 26 percent in 1935. Some 30 were defended in proceedings during the 1960s, but only 11 were approved. In about 60 percent of the industries, competitive activity visibly increased, typically with 10 to 20 percent price drops. In 1968, information agreements were also restricted.

The Restrictive Practices Court applies a broad rule-of-reason approach, with several gateways through which price-fixing agreements can obtain permission. The gateways involve possible benefits of price fixing, such as supporting export earnings, balancing the power of supplying firms, and avoiding local unemployment. Although a number of price-fixing agreements have been excused through these gateways, they are few, and the general policy against price fixing is rather strict.

During 1960 to 1980, British prohibitions on price fixing were about as tight as those in the United States. After 1980, as U.S. enforcement narrowed down mainly to bid rigging on small government contracts, British policies could be said to be stricter than U.S. treatments. There is some concern that U.K. price fixers have simply modified their actions to make them more informal, but that is identical with the problems that have arisen in the United States.

On the continent, the European Community prohibits explicit price-fixing schemes, but it excuses them if there are benefits to customers and if competition is not entirely stopped. After 1969, some strict actions were attempted, but subsequent enforcement can be regarded as mixed.[35]

In West Germany, formal prohibitions against price fixing have generally been strengthened by successive revisions of the original 1957 law. Industries can be exempted on grounds that the price fixing promotes efficiency or that the firms involved have less than 15 percent of the market. Some penalties for price fixers have been substantial.

Japan has officially supported depression cartels, which supposedly only prevent disarray in industries undergoing short-run drops in demand.[36] The MITI department (the Ministry of International Trade and

---

[35]For instance, in 1986, the Commission penalized polypropylene producers for rigging prices and production levels. But in 1986 the Commission also permitted a network of joint ventures in optical fibers which controlled a 48 percent share of the European market. See Henry W. de Jong, "Competition Policy in Europe: Stimulus, Nuisance, or Drawback?" a chapter in K. Groenveld, J.A.H. Maks, and J. Muysken, eds., *Economic Policy and the Market Process: Austrian and Mainstream Economics* (Amsterdam: North-Holland, 1990), pp. 131–32.

[36]See Scherer and Ross, *Industrial Market Structure and Economic Performance,* 1990, pp. 334–35; also Merton J. Peck, Richard Levin, and Akira Goto, "Picking Losers: Public Policies toward Declining Industries in Japan," *Journal of Japanese Studies* 13 (Winter 1987), pp. 79–123.

Industry) has supported many such cartels, which have covered 15 to 28 percent of Japanese industry at various times. The Japanese Fair Trade Commission has sought to apply its formal powers to numerous cartels, but MITI has prevented that on many occasions.

III. TACIT COLLUSION

Section 1 applies cleanly when there is concrete evidence of price-fixing activity. Tacit collusion avoids such evidence, so the coordination must be inferred. After the 1930s, there arose pressure to do something about tacit collusion. Several cases during 1939–53 seemed to bring it under Section 1, but no penalties were imposed and action lapsed. Interest revived in the 1960s, stimulated by Kaysen and Turner's influential book, followed by two major cases in the 1970s: electrical equipment and cereals.[37]

The attempt to treat these cases has largely lapsed again, partly because economists have turned toward game-theoretic analysis of *noncooperating* duopolists. This analysis rules out quasi-direct collusion and gives little guidance for policies toward such collusion. Also, the decline of tight oligopoly in the U.S. economy since 1960 has made the problem less important.

1. The Problem

Tacit collusion has probably been effective in many industries. High concentration and high entry barriers are the structural basis for it. Mature industries often evolve it, as firms learn to coexist and attune their planning to each other. Coordination then crystallizes, but tacitly, in "parallel pricing." These three criteria—concentration, barriers, maturity—plus parallel pricing behavior help identify "shared monopolies" for treatment. However, they are not infallible criteria. Some tight oligopolies are highly competitive, at least on occasion. Even for collusive ones, hard proof is lacking, and the firms assert they are just responding quickly to each other's moves.

Remedy is even more difficult to arrange. Usually, no oligopolist has over 40 percent of the market, and so dividing up the firms seems too radical and not effective. Economies of scale will be claimed by the firms and must be disproved (if possible). Several firms, not just one dominant firm, must be treated. Against this complexity, the possible gains may seem small and uncertain.

---

[37]Kaysen and Turner, *Antitrust Policy*.

2. Early Cases

During 1939 to 1953, economists' new ideas about tight oligopoly were applied by the Supreme Court. Parallel behavior could now be defined and convicted as a Section 1 conspiracy.

In the *Interstate Circuit* case in 1939, the operator of a chain of movie houses in Texas had entered into separate contracts with eight distributors of films, agreeing to show their pictures for an admission charge of 40 cents on condition they not be rented later to be shown for less than 25 cents or run on a double bill. There was no evidence that the distributors had consulted one another or agreed among themselves. Such evidence, said the Court, "was not a prerequisite to an unlawful conspiracy. It was enough that, knowing that concerted action was contemplated and invited, the distributors gave their adherence to the scheme and participated in it. . . . Acceptance by competitors, without previous agreement, is sufficient to establish an unlawful conspiracy under the Sherman Act."[38] A similar position was taken in the *Masonite* case in 1942. Here, a manufacturer of hardboard had signed an agency agreement with each of his competitors, authorizing them to distribute his product and fixing the prices at which they could sell. And here, again, there was no evidence of agreement among the other companies, but the Court found the plan to be illegal, holding that each of them must have been "aware of the fact that its contract was not an isolated transaction but a part of a larger arrangement."[39]

In these cases, there was evidence that plans had been proposed by Interstate and Masonite; the inference of conspiracy among the other companies was drawn from their adherence to these plans. In the second *American Tobacco* case, a criminal suit against the three leading producers of cigarettes, decided in 1946, no such proposal was in evidence. Instead, statistics of purchases, sales, and prices were relied upon for proof. In buying tobacco, it was shown, these companies had purchased fixed shares of the supply, each of them paying the same price on the same day. In selling cigarettes, they had adopted identical price lists, changing their prices simultaneously. In other practices, too, there was striking uniformity. "There was not a whit of evidence that a common plan had even been contemplated or proposed. The government's evidence was admittedly wholly circumstantial."[40] The reliance on inferential evidence did not deter the Court. Conspiracy, it said,

---

[38]*Interstate Circuit Co.* v. *U.S.*, 306 U.S. 208, 226–27.

[39]*U.S.* v. *Masonite Corp.*, 316 U.S. 265, 275.

[40]William H. Nicholls, "The Tobacco Case of 1946," *American Economic Review* 39, no. 3 (1949), pp. 284–96, especially p. 285.

"may be found in a course of dealings or other circumstances as well as in an exchange of words."[41] This was a strong position indeed.

The doctrine was carried furthest in the case of *Milgram* v. *Loew's* in 1950. Here, eight distributors of motion pictures had been sued by a drive-in movie for refusing to supply it with first-run films. A district court found the distributors guilty of conspiracy, holding that their common refusal to supply first runs could not have been due to independent business judgment but was sufficient, in itself, to establish violation of the law. A meeting of minds need not be proven; identity of behavior was all that was required.[42]

Conviction, however, was not followed by basic remedies. Much of the structure and habits remained. After 1952, the boldness in inferring conspiracy disappeared both from the FTC and the Court. In decisions involving investment banking (1953), movie distribution (1954), and meatpacking firms (1954), the Court firmly reversed itself and abandoned parallelism—and the broad use of "inferential" evidence—in Section 1 cases.[43] The experiment with tacit collusion was abandoned.

3. Recent Issues

The issue persisted. In 1959, Kaysen and Turner urged amending the Sherman Act so that high concentration would be a "rebuttable presumption" that a shared monopoly exists and violates Section 2.[44] Turner himself was head of the Antitrust Division during 1965–68 but failed to bring any shared-monopoly actions. About every three years, the agencies have announced new investigations into parallel pricing by various industries, usually including steel, automobiles, or oil. The filing of path-breaking shared-monopoly cases is said to be imminent.

In 1972, the FTC did start an experimental shared-monopoly case against the leading cereals firms (recall Chapter 7), but it was ultimately dropped.

The pricing in the cereals industry deserves a brief mention here. Scherer and Ross conclude from the voluminous case evidence that price leadership was "sufficiently robust to permit price increases in times of both booming and stagnant demand," and informal shading of prices was "totally absent."[45] Kellogg usually led price increases, in-

---

[41]*American Tobacco Co.* v. *U.S.*, 328 U.S. 781, 810.

[42]*Milgram* v. *Loew's, Inc.*, 94 F. Supp. 416.

[43]*U.S.* v. *Morgan*, Civil No. 43-757, District Court of the U.S., Southern District of New York, October 14, 1953. *U.S.* v. *Armour & Co.*, Civil 48-C-1351, discontinued March, 1954. *Fanchon & Marco* v. *Paramount Pictures*, 100 F. Supp. 84, certiorari denied, 345 U.S. 964. *Theater Enterprises, Inc.* v. *Paramount Film Distributing Corp.*, 346 U.S. 537, 540.

[44]Kaysen and Turner, *Antitrust Policy*.

[45]Scherer and Ross, *Industrial Market Structure and Economic Performance*, p. 258.

cluding 12 out of 15 during 1965 to 1970. The others usually followed; only once did neither major rival firm follow. The firms' own memoranda reflect a strong recognition of mutual interests in avoiding price cuts.

General Electric–Westinghouse. The main recent action is the *General Electric–Westinghouse* consent decree of 1976. It stopped a system of tacit collusion that those two leading firms had started right after the great electrical-equipment price conspiracies were broken in 1960 (recall Section II above). There was strong price competition in the turbine-generator market from 1960 to 1963. Then, in May 1963, General Electric announced a new system of pricing with four parts: (1) It greatly simplified the formulas for setting prices and published its method in detail. (2) It added a simple multiplier (.76, to be precise) for converting book prices to actual bids. (3) A "price protection" clause was to be put in all sales contracts. If GE lowered price for any customer, it was bound to extend the discount—retroactively—to all sales during the preceding six months. This self-penalty assured Westinghouse that GE would not give selective discounts. (4) All orders and price offers were to be published so that Westinghouse would not fear secret price cuts.

This ingenious plan surrendered all of the secret methods and strategies of price competition that make oligopoly competition work. Westinghouse immediately copied GE's plan and even the precise numbers in it. Each firm now could coordinate confidently with the other. From 1964, the firms used the same multiplier applied to identical book price levels. There was no price cutting, no flexibility.

The system went beyond simple parallel pricing but stopped a little short of explicit price fixing. GE intended the system to make collusion work, as shown by internal GE documents. Yet the Division ignored it, until an electric utility—American Electric Power—sued both firms in 1971. The Division then developed a strong case, but it was later scared off from filing the suit by Westinghouse's uranium price troubles in 1975–77. It settled for only a consent decree in December 1976.[46] The pricing scheme was withdrawn, but there were no penalties or damages for over eight years of tacit price fixing, nor was the underlying cause—the duopoly structure—changed.

After 1980, the Chicago-UCLA presumption that price fixing is weak and transient has excluded any interest in preventing tacit collusion, which is even weaker. Airline pricing offers strong indications of tacit collusion, but no action is contemplated or discussed.

---

[46]*U.S.* v. *General Electric Co. and Westinghouse Electric Corp.,* D.C. for Eastern District of Penn., Civil No. 28228, December 9, 1976. In 1977, American Electric Power also settled its case, to return to a normal customer relationship with the two suppliers.

Airline Price Structures since 1983. When U.S. airlines were de-regulated during 1978–83, pricing became extremely flexible and "fare wars" broke out repeatedly (recall Chapter 3). Prices reflected a mix of demand and cost conditions, over thousands of city-pair routes and differing competitive situations.

To quell this pricing anarchy, American Airlines announced on March 14, 1983, a new fare structure. It replaced thousands of different fares with four basic fare steps based on the distance traveled. Within a week, virtually all other airlines had adopted American's fare structure.

Further adjustments and discounting occurred, and then American announced new standard discounts. Two of the main discounts were called "supersavers" and "max-savers"; they had rigid conditions (over-Saturday stays, etc.), and each was either nonrefundable or only partly refundable. Once again, American's fare structure was copied by other airlines, and it continues to this day as the solid structure of all airline fares.

No direct collusion has been alleged or proven in these pricing episodes, but the new fare structures radically changed the flexible nature of airline pricing. In installing these fare systems, the few leading airlines achieved a high degree of tacit coordination, not just among themselves but among all airlines. (Chapter 10 discusses the price discrimination embodied in these fares.)

IV. CONNECTIONS AMONG FIRMS

There are often softer links among competitors. They can take many forms, and the effects on competition are often debatable. Three main types of links are included in this section.

1. Interest Groupings and Interlocks

Interest groupings exist quietly in many forms. Large blocks of shares in competing firms are owned by a family group, or a bank trust department, an investment bank, an insurance firm, or pension fund. Similarly, accounting firms, security underwriters, law firms, engineering firms, and others deal intimately with competing firms. This tissue of interests is extensive and intricate in many major industries. It softens independence and inculcates a degree of uniformity. But it is beyond the reach of antitrust policy, or indeed of any policy control now existing.

Interlocking directorates were common before the Clayton Act, Section 8, made them illegal in 1914. Direct interlocks—one person on the boards of two competing firms—mostly disappeared long ago. There are many indirect interlocks, where two officers of a bank, law firm, and so forth, sit on boards of competing firms. But these are also mainly ignored, because their effects are likely to be small.[47]

2. Joint Ventures

A *joint venture* is created by two or more firms, usually for some stated technical purpose (such as to mine ores, do research, or make sales in new foreign markets). When set up by competing firms, joint ventures obviously make for common interests and may reduce competition in all the firms' activities. The defense is usually that, instead, they make possible large benefits while leaving competition unabated. As in other antitrust issues, one compares the real benefits and costs. The benefits are often quite accessible without the joint venture.

The most pervasive joint ventures are in metal ores, especially steel and copper, where ore supply is vital to competitive strategy. In practice, joint ventures are often extended into by large firms, not small ones. Therefore, the possible anticompetitive effect is significant, while the technical need for the combined ownership is less, perhaps minimal. That many joint ventures do have social costs has been shown by research.[48] Generally, the social cost is greater when (1) the parent firms have a high share of the market, (2) the joint venture is in a highly concentrated market, (3) the joint venture's purpose can be met by the firms separately, and (4) there are additional restrictions attached to the joint venture.

Before 1980, U.S. policies were roughly in the direction of these economic criteria, but enforcement was limited. Most cases invoked the Sherman Act, Section 1, against conspiracy. Horizontal joint ventures were found illegal whenever there was cartel behavior or boycotts and exclusion of competitors. If the result was price fixing—either inherent in the joint venture, or ancillary to it—the joint venture was illegal. Remedy then depended on the market share of the parents of the joint venture. If the shares were large, the joint venture was dissolved.[49] If

[47]U.S. House Subcommittee on Antitrust, *Interlocks in Corporate Management* (Washington, D.C.: U.S. Government Printing Office, 1965); and U.S. House Subcommittee on Domestic Finance, *Commercial Banks and Their Trust Activities* (Washington, D.C.: U.S. Government Printing Office, 1968), 2 volumes. See also Peter C. Dooley, "The Interlocking Directorate," *American Economic Review* 59 (June 1969), pp. 314–23.

[48]See Jeffrey Pfeffer and Philip Nowak, "Patterns of Joint Venture Activity: Implications for Antitrust Policy," *Antitrust Bulletin* 21 (Summer 1976), pp. 315–39. For an extensive review of legal and economic issues, see Joseph Brodley, "Joint Ventures and Antitrust Policy," *Harvard Law Review* 95 (May 1982), pp. 1521–90.

[49]Landmark cases in which the joint venture was dissolved include *Lee Line Steamer* v. *Memphis H & R Packet Co.*, 277 F. 5 (6th Circuit, 1922); *U.S.* v. *Imperial Chemical Industries*, 100 F. Supp. 504 (S. D. N. Y., 1951); *U.S.* v. *Paramount Pictures*, 334 U.S. 131 (1948); and *Citizens Publishing Co.* v. *U.S.*, 394 U.S. 131 (1969).

the shares were small, the joint venture could continue, *if* it stopped the price fixing.[50]

Around this core of clear policy were large twilight zones: (1) A joint venture formed to enter a new market was illegal *if* the two parents themselves had been on the verge of entering. Of course, such potential entry is difficult to judge, and so few cases were brought. (2) Any explicit geographic limits on competition among the parents or their joint venture were illegal. But only if their market shares were large was the joint venture dissolved. (3) If the joint venture clearly served a useful purpose, it permitted real latitude in restrictions and behavior. (4) If a joint venture controlled a natural monopoly, it could stand as long as it offered fair access to all comers.[51] (5) Certain vertical joint ventures were proscribed. Until 1948, the main movie makers jointly held many theaters as part of a massive set of restrictions on movie bookings.[52] The Court dissolved them because they reduced competition among the parents and excluded other theaters from fair access to films. Only if the parents had a small share would their vertical joint venture survive scrutiny.[53] (6) Virtually all conglomerate joint ventures—between unrelated firms—were outside any policy constraint.

Most joint ventures came under a balancing (rule-of-reason) approach, with the burden of proof set against the public agencies. After 1980, policy shifted toward permitting virtually all joint ventures. The leading case was in the automobile industry.

General Motors–Toyota Joint Venture.[54] The issues were posed dramatically and controversially by the joint venture in 1983 between General Motors, the largest U.S. automobile producer, and Toyota, the leading Japanese car maker. General Motors sold about 44 percent of new cars in the United States in 1982, while Toyota's market share was 7 percent and rising. Toyota was clearly the leading potential entrant into U.S. car production under the incentive of the "voluntary" limits on imports of Japanese cars.

The joint venture would (and actually did, later) produce Nova cars in GM's then-idle plant in Fremont, California. GM would gain experience with superior Japanese methods for lower cost and higher quality.

---

[50]Cases of this sort include *U.S.* v. *Sealy, Inc.,* 388 U.S. 350 (1967) and *U.S.* v. *Topco Associates,* 405 U.S. 596 (1972).

[51]The classic case of such bottleneck joint ventures is *U.S.* v. *Terminal Railroad Association,* 224 U.S. 383 (1912). Such situations are rare in practice.

[52]*U.S.* v. *Paramount Pictures,* 334 U.S. 131 (1948).

[53]That was the case in the "Screen Gems" case; *U.S.* v. *Columbia Pictures,* 189 F. Supp. 153 (S. D. N. Y., 1960).

[54]The merger aspects of the case were discussed above in Chapter 8.

Otherwise, it claimed an inability to compete in small cars. Toyota would gain direct access to the U.S. market.

Intense controversy ensued, and the FTC investigated thoroughly. Lee Iacocca of Chrysler denounced the joint venture as anticompetitive. It would indeed reduce competition, in three possible ways: by deterring each partner from expanding its own production directly, by softening price competition between the two firms, and by facilitating exchanges of information. The FTC negotiated several safeguards that would reduce these hazards, but the core effects toward cooperation could not really be removed.

The FTC then approved the venture, as one of the most dramatic and resolute instances of its Chicago-UCLA orientation. However, the project has not fulfilled its promise, having lower production and higher costs than were forecast. GM claims to have gained good experience, as planned, but the benefits have not spared GM a steep drop to a market share below 35 percent in 1988–90. Meanwhile, all leading Japanese automobile makers have built or bought plants in the United States.

Therefore, the venture has probably not strongly reduced the rise of Japanese production in the United States, but it has probably delivered little of the efficiency gains for GM that were confidently predicted. It fits the general criterion: Small ventures by large competitive firms probably reduce competition, on balance, while adding little directly to efficiency.

The same criterion applies to joint research ventures among U.S. firms, which the Reagan administration moved to legalize by amending the antitrust laws.[55] The provision is meant as a response to some promotional activities in Japan and elsewhere, but the policy is merely permissive, letting firms cooperate in varying degrees while hoping that innovation would increase. Approval is based on judgments about the possible impacts on competition and innovation. Little is known about the net effects of the act. There are, in any event, no protections against excess cooperation and inferior results.

3. Trade Associations

Most industries have associations, which range from extensive secretariats down to little more than a mailing list. Their activities are diverse, and the periodic trade meetings do give opportunities for illegal discussions and fixing of prices. Before the 1950s, many trade-association activities tended to reduce competition, and, abroad, trade associations

---

[55]The National Cooperative Research Act, 15 U.S.C. Sections 4301–5, 1984.

were the nucleus for tight cartels in hundreds of industries, in many countries.

Price-reporting systems highlight the leading antitrust issues. They disseminate information about recent transactions, such as the amounts and prices (and sometimes the names of the parties) of sales contracted during the previous week. Such systems, by increasing the amount of knowledge available to traders, might lessen the imperfection of markets and enhance competition.

Price reporting may improve market functioning when the market (1) has low concentration and entry barriers, (2) homogeneous output, (3) elastic demand, and (4) stable demand. This describes a textbook competitive market. In others, price reporting is likely to support agreement and quicken pressure against price cutters. To help competition, a reporting plan will need to (1) be fully available to all sellers *and* buyers, (2) not identify traders, (3) cover only past sales, not present or planned ones, (4) avoid circulating average prices (focal points for new price agreements), and (5) be free of any controls or penalties on sellers.

The lines of policy have come to fit the economic criteria reasonably well. Four seminal cases in the 1920s involved lumber, linseed oil, maple flooring, and cement.[56] The Court held against pervasive reporting schemes that violated the first four conditions just above: access, anonymity, past sales, and no averages. Where an anticompetitive tendency could be seen, the system was rejected. In 1936, an even vaster scheme in the sugar industry was also enjoined from violating the five conditions.[57]

And in 1969, the treatment was confirmed in the major *Container Corporation* case.[58] Cardboard box sellers in one region had a system allowing each seller to call up any other seller and demand the price of that seller's most recent sale. This system was struck down: (1) because it would "chill" competition by exposing price cutting more quickly, and (2) because buyers did not have equal access to the prices.

V. INTERNATIONAL MARKETS

There are two main parts: (1) collusion among U.S. firms as exporters and (2) collusion among foreign firms (and possibly U.S. firms) that

---

[56]*American Column and Lumber Co.* v. *U.S.*, 257 U.S. 377 (1921); *U.S.* v. *American Linseed Oil Co.*, 262 U.S. 371 (1923); *Maple Flooring Mfrs. Assn.* v. *U.S.*, 268 U.S. 563 (1925); *Cement Mfrs. Protective Assn.* v. *U.S.*, 268 U.S. 588 (1925).

[57]*U.S.* v. *Sugar Institute*, 15 F. Supp. 817 (1934); *Sugar Institute* v. *U.S.*, 297 U.S. 553 (1936) 601.

[58]*U.S.* v. *Container Corp. of America*, 393 U.S. 333, 1969.

affects imports into U.S. markets. Generally, U.S. policies apply to actions that clearly affect U.S. markets, no matter where the actions occur, but enforcement is often erratic and unable, in fact, to reach much beyond U.S. borders.

1. Export Cooperation

For 60 years, the Webb-Pomerene Act has permitted "associations entered into for the sole purpose of engaging in export trade." Such associations are not exempt as they may affect domestic trade, but the foreign trade exemption is not trivial. The FTC is given jurisdiction over them, but the supervision has been nominal. There have been only about 30 such associations, which have handled less than 5 percent of the goods exported from the United States. The exemption offers possible public gains; the associations may offset foreign cartels or achieve economies in the handling of foreign sales. These and other possible benefits are likely to be relatively small.

2. Foreign Collusion Affecting U.S. Markets

International markets are often rigged in ways affecting U.S. consumers. After 1901, the world's cigarette markets were divided into three separate preserves, which, though fading, have persisted all the way down to the 1970s. U.S. chemical firms split world markets with British and German firms before World War II, so that competition was avoided. DeBeers Central Selling Organization has long marketed at least 90 percent of the world's diamonds. Among other current cartels, the OPEC oil cartel stands out for its awesome impact since 1972.

Antitrust's formal coverage of these cartels has had little substance. Especially when foreign governments directly comprise or back the cartel, the problem can be reached only by diplomacy, if at all. Indeed, other U.S. agencies are often busy creating international cartels, rather than breaking them up (see Chapter 16). Certain members of the 1960s' quinine cartel were indicted in the United States in 1968, but by 1977 the case had petered out and the Division was ready to withdraw the suit as being old and impractical to pursue.

Ironically, antitrust does have an influence on many small issues of foreign activity, such as joint ventures, patent restrictions, know-how licenses, and so on. Thus, contracts to exchange know-how between U.S. and foreign firms must avoid any agreements not to compete in each other's areas. International joint ventures come under the same rules as joint ventures in the United States, but the enforcement is even looser abroad. A 1974 case forced certain U.S. and U.K. book publishers to stop agreeing not to sell English-language books in each other's markets.

In short, antitrust grapples lengthily with certain marginal practices abroad, with some effect, but it has little power over large-scale international collusion.

VI. SUMMARY

The long trend has been toward clear, severe lines against price fixing and related kinds of collusion. There remain certain twilight issues and areas, especially the enigma of implicit collusion. Yet the large center of per se policy remains, and it closely fits the economic criteria for efficient policy. For eight decades, it has been the United States's most distinctive and successful single policy toward market power.

Much collusion still persists, both underground or in alternative forms, and in the many exempted sectors (including many local markets). Important international price fixing also affects certain U.S. markets. Policy toward collusion is still largely trench warfare, on many fronts. Progress is often only by inches, and there is a steady stream of new problems to cope with.

QUESTIONS FOR REVIEW

1. "Short-run price cutting can be more severe than long-run costs would permit." True?
2. "Many price conspiracies collapse quickly." True?
3. "Uniform bids prove the existence of collusion." True?
4. "If bids aren't uniform, competition is fully effective." True?
5. Officers of competitors A through Z meet in a hotel room and agree on a new price schedule. Yet they can't make the new prices stick. Are they guilty? What economic evidence is needed to decide?
6. Will stiff penalties deter price fixers? How stiff should they be?
7. How would you resolve the "indirect purchasers" problem?
8. Which professions and sports should be exempt from antitrust law?
9. What categories of cost and benefit should be used in judging whether the per se treatment of price fixing is wise?
10. Locate five products that carry suggested prices. Are these prices above the competitive level?
11. Is there presently any policy toward tacit collusion or parallel pricing. What action should there be?
12. Could the GE–Westinghouse tacit collusion method have been modified to make it noncollusive?

13. How can two firms in the same market create a joint venture without reducing competition in some way? Could Toyota and General Motors have done so?

14. What kinds of price-reporting systems promote competition rather than reduce it?

15. If collusion occurs outside U.S. borders, is it genuinely outside the reach of U.S. antitrust policy?

C·H·A·P·T·E·R 10

**Restrictive Practices:
Price Discrimination and
Vertical Restrictions**

Instead of colluding with its rivals, a firm can reduce competition by two main classes of unilateral actions taken *against other firms:* price discrimination and vertical restriction. Each class requires a careful economic analysis, for the issues are often complicated and obscure. Each has had a checkered history of policy actions. Policies toward both classes of action continued to evolve in recent decades amid extensive debates.

I. PRICE DISCRIMINATION

First we analyze price discrimination in Section 1. Then we evaluate policies toward its main forms in Section 2. Tie-ins are a special type of discrimination; they are reviewed in Section 3.

Price is a sharp weapon which can be deployed in many ways.[1] Prices can be structured, changed in sequences over time, and used selectively so as to gain in the competitive fray, in some cases by damaging or removing other firms. Price discrimination can be a powerful strategy, but it is only part of the whole spectrum of devices.[2] Other

---

[1]See W. G. Shepherd, *The Economics of Industrial Organization,* 3rd ed. (Englewood Cliffs, N.J.: Prentice-Hall, 1990), chap. 12; F. M. Scherer and David Ross, *Industrial Market Structure and Economic Performance,* 3rd ed. (Boston: Houghton Mifflin, 1990), chap. 13; and Louis Phlips, *The Economics of Price Discrimination* (Cambridge: Cambridge University Press, 1983).

[2]See Basil Yamey, "Predatory Price Cutting: Notes and Comments," *Journal of Law and Economics* 15 (April 1972), pp. 129–42, for a lucid, well-rounded analysis of the wide range of tactics and weapons.

devices include product changes and announcements, overspending, advertising blitzes, and patent litigation. Pricing strategies often mingle with these (for example, a selective price revision timed with a change in product), rather than exist in isolation.

1. The Analysis of Price Discrimination

Price discrimination occurs very widely, in such common products as magazines, copiers, theater tickets, groceries, electric and telephone services—indeed in virtually all retail and industrial goods. It can either reduce competition or promote it. The task is to learn how discrimination's effect depends on its setting.

As always, *price* means the "whole" price, allowing for all dimensions of the purchase.[3] This clarifies the many cases where bare price is only part of the terms of the entire transaction.

The core concept is simple: Price discrimination is a difference among the price-cost ratios in the selling of like goods to different customers.[4] Prices are set in line with *demand* instead of cost. Such demand-based discriminatory pricing occurs when (1) buyers have differing demand elasticities, which the seller can discover, (2) the seller can fit different price-cost ratios to these differing elasticities (high price-cost ratios for inelastic demand, low price-cost ratios for elastic demand), and (3) the buyers cannot resell the good to each other. The seller "creams" off high profits from the "best" parts of the market—the customers that have little or no choice. In the "skim" parts of the market, the seller makes do with prices that are close to cost levels.

Price discrimination has been given a variety of names: charging what the traffic will bear, price discounting, demand-based pricing, selective pricing, value-of-service pricing, loss leaders, price sharpshooting, pinpoint pricing, Ramsey pricing, and inverse-elasticity pricing. They all share the key feature: variation among price-cost ratios for a seller's related goods.

Examples are widespread and familiar. Magazine prices vary widely by various subscription rates and newsstand purchases, probably more than the costs vary. On an airline flight, you may pay $216, the executive on your left may pay $473, while your child pays $108 (half of your fare). Grocery ads are full of special discounts, which mostly con-

---

[3]Other dimensions include the quality of output, the terms of payment, time of delivery, and degree of security of supply.

[4]See also, for early classic discussions, Joan Robinson, *The Economics of Imperfect Competition* (London: Macmillan, 1933); and A. C. Pigou, *The Economics of Welfare* (London: Macmillan, 1920). For analysis of extensive discrimination in regulated industries, see Alfred E. Kahn, *The Economics of Regulation*, vols. 1 and 2 (New York: John Wiley & Sons, 1971; Cambridge, Mass.: MIT Press, 1988).

Table 10–1   Some Types of Discrimination

Personal Discrimination

Haggle-every time.   Common in bazaars and private deals. Also cars, pianos, antiques.
Give-in-if-you-must.   Shading off list prices. (Widespread.)
Size-up-his-income.   Fit the price to the customers. Doctors, lawyers, and other professionals have long done this.
Measure-the-use.   Even if marginal costs are low, charge heavy users more. Xerox and IBM have used this strategy.

Group Discrimination

Kill-the-rival.   Predatory price cutting to drive out a competitor. Said to have been commonly done by American Tobacco and Standard Oil before 1900, and frequently claimed to occur now in other industries.
Dump-the-surplus.   Selling at lower prices in foreign markets (where demand is more elastic) has occurred for drugs, steel, TV sets, and others. But complaints about dumping are often inaccurate.
Promote-new-customers.   Common in magazine subscriptions; this lures in new customers.
Favor-the-big-ones.   Volume discounts are steeper than cost differences. Endemic in many industrial markets.
Divide-them-by-elasticity.   The general result, common in utility services.

Product Discrimination

Pay-for-the-label.   The fancy (premium) label gets a high price, even if the good is the same as a common brand.
Clear-the-stock.   "Sales" are used to stabilize inventory. Any town has scores each year in retail stores.
Peak–off-peak differences.   Prices may differ by more or less than costs do, between peak-hour congested times and slack off-peak periods. Becoming increasingly common in utilities.

Source: Adapted from Fritz Machlup, *The Political Economy of Monopoly* (Baltimore: The Johns Hopkins Press, 1952)

stitute discrimination. Most hotel rooms, car rentals, and utility prices involve discrimination.

An amusing classification of the variants of discrimination was prepared by Fritz Machlup long ago. This classification is condensed in Table 10–1, which covers many kinds but by no means all of the variants of discrimination.

Simple Discrimination. In the simplest case, there is one identical good going to two buyers (or groups of buyers). Under competition:

$$\frac{\text{Price to buyer 1}}{\text{Cost}} = \frac{\text{Price to buyer 2}}{\text{Cost}}$$

Indeed, price is driven down to cost, so that all ratios are 1.0. The equality is replaced by an inequality when discrimination occurs. For example, buyer 1 might be retail purchasers of a medical drug (who have low elasticity of demand because they buy whatever drug the doctor tells them to) while buyer 2 is a group of large hospitals (who have high elasticity because they are well-informed large-scale buyers who can turn to alternative suppliers). Cost might be $1 per bottle. The ratios might then be:

$$\frac{\$10}{\$1} \neq \frac{\$2}{\$1}, \text{ and } 10 \neq 2, \text{ so that } \frac{P_1}{P_2} = 5$$

That is fairly steep discrimination. Actual discrimination is usually milder, but it can go even steeper if the conditions are right. (Even small, benign instances of discrimination, such as children's half-price theater or airline tickets, often involve sharp price differences.) The firm gets profits from both parts of the market, but one part is much "creamier" than the other. Consumers are made to pay partly in line with their ability to pay, rather than in line with cost levels.

The simple economic analysis is shown in Figure 10–1. There is just one good, whose average costs are assumed to be constant (for example, a pill that can be made at a constant $1 per dozen). When average costs are constant, then marginal cost is also constant and identical to average cost.

There are two distinct customer groups, shown by the two different demand curves. The firm can sell separately to each group, but one group cannot resell the product to the other group. For each of the down-sloping demand curves, there is a corresponding marginal-revenue curve, as shown.

The firm treats each customer group separately, setting output and price at levels that will maximize its total profits. For the inelastic group A, the profit-maximizing price (where marginal revenue equals marginal cost) is as shown at output A, and the resulting price is price A. For the elastic group B, the corresponding results are output B and price B. Price A is over twice as high as price B, and the ratio of prices to the marginal cost differs accordingly. Price discrimination exists, reflecting the differences in demand, despite equal costs.

The sharpness of discrimination depends on the three preconditions: (1) the ability to identify differing elasticities; (2) the differences among the elasticities; and (3) the prevention of reselling by low-price customers to high-price customers. A deficiency in any one of these conditions can limit the sharpness and profit yields of discrimination. Also, obviously, the existence of alternative supplies at low prices can prevent discrimination.

Figure 10–1   The Simplest Case of Price Discrimination: One Good with Uniform Costs and Two Groups of Buyers

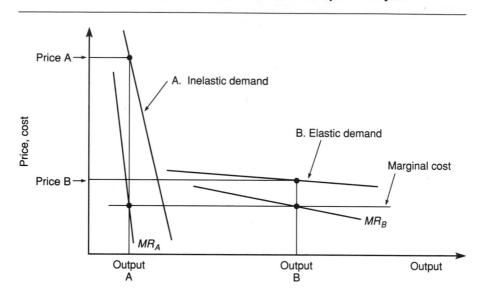

Generally, *the ability to discriminate varies with the firm's market share.* A pure monopolist can discriminate more fully, *ceteris paribus,* than firms with lesser shares. Firms with small shares will scarcely be able to discriminate at all. All of their customers will be able to choose other suppliers at competitive prices. No group of inelastic-demand buyers will exist. Competition will press all of their prices tightly down toward costs.

Degrees of Discrimination. A monopolist can often discriminate with utmost precision, segregating each customer individually and extracting all consumer surplus. This is called *first-degree discrimination,* following Pigou's terms. Third-degree discrimination is much cruder. The seller can only arrange two or three large groups, rather than fine-tune the pricing. The simple two-group case in Figure 10–1 is an example of third-degree discrimination. The intermediate cases of, say, 5 or 10 groups are second-degree discrimination. All of these "degrees" fit the same analysis: Sellers subdivide the market, and their price-cost ratios vary inversely with demand elasticities.

The product need not be precisely uniform. The firm can offer a product line with a range of products appealing to different "levels" of the market (examples are automobiles, from subcompacts up to luxury limousines; and computers, from small to large systems). Differing price-cost ratios among these items will be discriminatory. Alternatively, the same physical product may be sold in regional markets, with varying transport costs.

In still another case, if costs vary, then *uniform* prices are discriminatory. If any costs vary, or prices vary, or both prices and costs vary, discrimination remains simply a difference in the price-cost ratios among like or related goods. If prices vary *in proportion to costs,* there is no discrimination. Costs, therefore, are a key element in judging whether discrimination exists.

Costs may differ for various reasons. (1) There may be economies of scale for the supplier, which permit it to offer price discounts for larger purchases. (The question is whether the prices accurately fit the true cost differences; often, instead, the discounts are bigger or smaller than the cost differences.) (2) The products may differ (for example, some are bigger, or better, or transported further, or supplied with greater security, or supplied at peak or off-peak times). The task is to measure the cost differences accurately so that price-cost ratios can be compared. Usually, long-run marginal cost is the correct concept of cost, but for time-based products (such as peak-load air fares or new products), short-run marginal cost may instead be the right concept.

Costs are often extremely difficult to measure, and often they can only be guessed at. Firms rarely measure their marginal costs, and frequently the precise nature of the good and its costs is debatable. Sellers can often allocate their accounting costs so as to justify a price structure that actually is discriminatory.

If there are large overhead costs in the firm, the discrimination will be even steeper and harder to detect. The marginal costs of each unit will tend to be low, and large floating costs can be assigned among products at the seller's will. In such cases, it may be difficult for outsiders even to discover how steep the discrimination is.[5]

Three Effects of Discrimination on Competition. Discrimination is a method for *extracting* the maximum total profit from a market position. If only one price were permitted, profits would be lower (confirm this by trying a single price in Figure 10–1). Discrimination can also serve two other purposes: to help *create* market power and to help *maintain* it. By adroitly manipulating prices in parts of its markets, at different times, a firm can often beat competition. The extreme of this is a kind of sharpshooting using prices, where the firm selectively cuts prices to

[5]For rigorous theoretical discussion of such multiproduct cost situations, see William J. Baumol, John C. Panzar, and Robert D. Willig, *Contestable Markets and the Theory of Industry Structure* (San Diego: Harcourt Brace Jovanovich, 1982).

injure, discipline, threaten, or even drive out a rival firm in part of the market.[6] The firm merely cuts prices deeply where demand is most elastic—in other words, where the competition is keenest. It can selectively meet or beat competition, especially if it can draw on its profits from the "creamy" submarkets.

There are limits to this: Price cuts sacrifice profits, and merger or other techniques may be cheaper and more effective methods to get the same result. Yet selective price cutting can often be an efficient way to build up market share. Note that it is perfectly rational and natural; firms always fit pricing to the market conditions.

Discrimination can also be used to defend a high share, by keeping new firms out or smaller firms down. The selective pricing is only part of the whole arsenal of tactics, as we noted: Nonprice tactics are often powerful, too. All these tactics can be used to scare off competitors; more precisely, the dominant firm may be able to threaten future losses for rivals, without actually having to cut prices all the way to cause those losses. All it does is change expectations, which then govern behavior.

These uses of discrimination involve "hard" competition, in which firms' strong efforts may injure or eliminate rivals as part of a relentless competitive process. Chicago-UCLA economists accept such discrimination as normal and healthy. If these actions are carried even further and are done by dominant firms with large advantages over their rivals, then they may become genuinely anticompetitive. They hurt not only competitors but the viability of the competitive process itself. These anticompetitive instances are only one category within the larger domain of discrimination.

Discrimination is not always a unilateral choice by the seller. Discrimination also arises from vertical pressures applied by buyers. Large buyers may demand special prices and be able to play oligopolist sellers off against each other. Bilateral oligopoly is often suffused with price discrimination, arising from pressures on both sides. Even a virtual monopolist may be under strong buyer pressures. Indeed, discrimination can even occur under coercion by a third party (see below). So one must be sophisticated in judging the causes and motives in actual cases of price discrimination.

---

[6]See Scherer and Ross, *Industrial Market Structure and Economic Performance,* chap. 13; Shepherd, *The Economics of Industrial Organization,* chap. 12; Yamey, "Predatory Price Cutting"; Philip Areeda and Donald F. Turner, "Predatory Pricing and Related Practices under Section 2 of the Sherman Act," *Harvard Law Review* 88 (February 1975), pp. 697–733, and Scherer's rebuttal and further exchange, *Harvard Law Review* 89 (March 1976), pp. 869–903; and Oliver E. Williamson, "Predatory Pricing: A Strategic and Welfare Analysis," *Yale Law Journal* 87 (November 1977), pp. 284–340.

Judging the Competitive Impacts. From these features of price discrimination comes the basic method for judging whether price discrimination is *anticompetitive* or *procompetitive*. There are two crucial criteria: (1) the market position of the firm and (2) how systematic and rigid the discrimination is. The larger the firm's market share, compared to its rivals, the more likely it is that discrimination will suppress competition. It helps increase and harden the dominance. High market shares often cover a wide variety of demand elasticities, which permit segmenting the market and setting different price-cost ratios. Small-share firms have only limited scope, and any success they achieve merely intensifies competition, not reduces it.

The more systematic the discrimination by a firm, the more it blocks competitors and extracts high profits. That too tends to harden the dominance. Small-share firms, in contrast, usually have little opportunity to apply rigid discrimination.

The two criteria—market share and rigidity—are combined in Figure 10–2. To assess any specific discrimination, try to locate it in this diagram according to the firm's market share and the rigidity of the discrimination. Done flexibly by a small-share firm, the discrimination is in Area A, in the lower left-hand corner. It is procompetitive, indeed the lifeblood of effective competition.[7]

In area B, where a dominant firm does it systematically, it generally suppresses competition. The firm pinpoints the significant rivals, cuts prices against them, but retains higher prices elsewhere. If small rivals alter prices, the dominant firm merely matches or exceeds their cuts, while drawing revenues from other sales at maintained prices. If there are any imperfections in the market (from customer loyalties, lags, imperfect information, or the like), then the small firms may be overcome, with little revenue sacrifice by the dominant firm.

Strict Chicago-UCLA analysts do not accept this view. They assume that markets have few imperfections and regard all price discrimination as promoting efficiency (see below). The market, according to them, is self-limiting and self-correcting, because small competitors can do their own discriminating, focusing their price cutting on any products that have high prices; therefore, dominant firms cannot succeed at it. Their conclusion is that price discrimination cannot be harmful to competition. The more moderate Chicago-UCLA supporters would admit that pricing in zone B might reduce competition, but they would require a rule-of-reason judgment on each instance.

---

[7]Sporadic discrimination "like a high wind, seizes on small openings and crevices in an orderly price structure and tears it apart." See Morris A. Adelman, "Effective Competition and the Antitrust Laws," *Harvard Law Review* 61 (1949), pp. 1289–350, especially pp. 1331–332.

**Figure 10–2   Price Discrimination May Increase or
Reduce Competition**

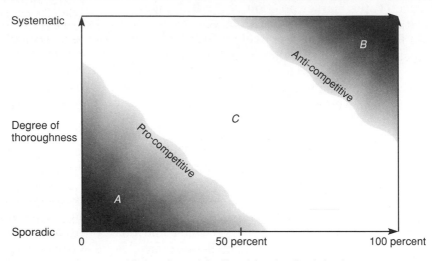

Market share of the firm doing the discrimination

Criteria for Assessing Price Discrimination and "Predation"

In fact, three specific criteria have been prominent in the debate: price-cost comparisons, effects, and intent. We consider them in turn.

Price and Cost. An influential article by Areeda and Turner in 1975 recast the literature and sharply affected court decisions.[8] Areeda and Turner argued that actions might reduce competition only if the aggressor firm set its price below cost (that is, if it incurred a definite financial loss, in order to accomplish a strategic gain). If no loss is suffered, then the action has not gone too far, and so it is innocent.

Therefore plaintiffs must bear the burden of showing that price was set below cost. Attention focuses strictly on the aggressor firm's price and cost. Areeda and Turner seemed to offer an objective, efficiency-based test of anticompetitive actions. Their rule stirred wide debate, and it was quickly adopted in a number of court decisions.

Yet the rule is too narrow, focusing on short-run conditions in just one product, whereas the real struggles among firms typically cover a

---

[8]Areeda and Turner, "Predatory Pricing."

number of products over the long run.[9] A simple, narrow test may give definite answers which miss the real problem.

Moreover, which cost is the right test? Long-run marginal cost is generally the correct basis. But such costs are often difficult to measure, especially when the firm has many outputs with shared overhead and joint costs. Therefore, in practice one often uses average variable costs to estimate marginal costs. Even then, the measures are often imprecise.

Moreover, Areeda and Turner's price-cost test ignores the critical role of relative market shares and rigidity. It cannot be anticompetitive for a small firm to challenge a larger firm by using deep price cuts, particularly if the cuts are flexible and sporadic. That can only intensify competition, by making the firms more equal. Yet the Areeda-Turner test would condemn such pro-competitive price cutting by lesser firms.

Used carefully, with attention to market shares, the Areeda-Turner price-cost test can be part of an evaluation of competitive impacts. But it is not definitive by itself.

Effects. One can use the effects of the pricing in testing whether it is pro- or anti-competitive. If the target firm is only lightly affected, then perhaps the pricing tactic is innocent.

Yet effects are actually an impossible criterion. As was noted earlier, all firms try to eliminate their rivals in order to succeed, and so markets are constantly filled with strong impacts. What threshold can be defined to judge when the effects go "too far"? Moreover, the facts about the effects are often murky and disputed. And worse, the effects are always mingled with questions about the competence of the target firm. Thus, when Firm A complains that Firm B is killing it with strategic pricing, Firm B can be counted on to retort that Firm A is merely inept and is trying to blame its failures unfairly on Firm B.

Such cases would clog the courts with endless debates and testimony about firms' quality and wisdom. And they would ignore, again, the critical role of market positions and the rigidity of pricing patterns.

Intent. Third, the courts might focus on the aggressor firm's intent: Did it really intend and try to put the target firm out of business? The plaintiff would need to provide information about the aggressor firm's

---

[9]For assessments of the rule, see Scherer and Ross, *Industrial Market Structure and Economic Performance,* 1990, pp. 472–79; William J. Baumol, "Quasi-Permanence of Price Reductions: A Policy for Preventing Predatory Pricing," *Yale Law Journal* 89 (November 1979), pp. 1–26; Joel B. Dirlam, "Marginal Cost Pricing Tests for Predation: Naive Welfare Economics and Public Policy," *Antitrust Bulletin* 26 (Winter 1981), pp. 769–814; and Charles W. McCall, "Rule of Reason versus Mechanical Tests in the Adjudication of Price Predation," *Review of Industrial Organization* 3 (Spring 1988), pp. 15–44.

intentions. If no intent to kill can be shown, then the aggressor firm would merely have been adopting healthy, hard competition.

Yet that approach makes neither logical nor practical sense. All firms naturally intend to defeat their rivals, and their actions mostly are part of healthy competition. Trying to judge when intent goes too far would be impossible. Actions can be anti-competitive even when they seek only to cripple or intimidate a small rival, without trying to kill it outright.

Again, the market positions and pricing patterns are crucial: If the rivals are on an equivalent footing, then their intent is irrelevant. If the market positions are highly unbalanced, then intent is also irrelevant. In any case, intent is usually a complex mixture of attitudes that are nearly impossible to assess objectively. And, once again, intent could be anti-competitive only when a larger firm is using systematic pricing strategies against a smaller rival.

Levels of Price Discrimination

As a separate matter, the competitive effect of discrimination can occur on *two different levels,* which come up frequently in antitrust cases.

1. *Primary line* effects are at the level of *the discriminator and its rivals.* (Example: Acme Cup Corporation strengthens its own market share and profitability by discriminating. Its rival cup makers are prevented from competing effectively.)
2. *Secondary line* effects are at the next level, *among the buyers.* (Example: A railroad sets discriminatory rates for oil shipments. The lower rates paid by Strand Oil Company enable it to raise its market share at the expense of its rival oil companies.)

Discrimination by a dominant firm—even very steep discrimination—can in theory improve the static allocation of resources. It will yield a total output higher than a single-price monopoly output.[10] That is illustrated in Figure 10–1, where the total of output in the two parts of the market exceeds the output sold under any single price. In certain natural monopoly situations, discrimination might be necessary in order to make the firm viable at all (Chapter 13 considers that case).

This result has recently been labeled *Ramsey prices,* to denote the ability of price discrimination to maximize static efficiency in the multiproduct firm. Overhead costs shared by the many outputs may then mean that marginal costs are below average cost. Setting prices strictly equal to just those marginal costs would leave no revenue to cover the

---

[10]See Scherer and Ross, *Industrial Market Structure and Economic Performance,* chap. 13; Robinson, *The Economics of Imperfect Competition;* Philips, *The Economics of Price Discrimination;* and Baumol, Panzar, and Willig, *Contestable Markets and the Theory of Industry Structure.*

overhead costs. Therefore, strict marginal-cost pricing would result in financial losses. To stay alive, the firm must do some discriminating, and Ramsey prices purport to give the best set of discriminatory prices.

Ramsey prices are in fact merely full-blown discrimination, fitting the *inverse-elasticity rule:* Price-cost ratios vary inversely with elasticity. Prices are relatively higher where elasticities are lower. That is precisely what Figure 10–1 illustrated. Ramsey prices have the same effects on competition as all other forms of discrimination. Their possible relevance to regulated utilities will be noted in Chapter 14.

2. Policies toward Discrimination

Several categories of discrimination often reduce competition: (1) true predatory pricing, in which prices go *below* costs on some outputs but not others; (2) systematic discrimination by dominant firms; and (3) tie-ins by dominant firms. U.S. policies have been roughly efficient toward categories (1) and (3), while most dominant-firm discrimination since 1970 has been scarcely constrained at all. Since tie-ins are a special form of discrimination, they will be given a more complete treatment in a separate section.

Before the 1970s, U.S. policies tended to restrict the more harmful kinds of discrimination. The main policy lines addressed the anticompetitive discrimination illustrated in Figure 10–2. This systematic discrimination by dominant firms was a sign of monopoly abuse under Section 2 (for example, in the *United Shoe Machinery* case and in the 1973–75 FTC action against Xerox). Brazen predatory pricing, to eliminate a specific small rival, was often resisted, commonly in suits brought by supposed victims. The "intent" to eliminate competitors was often considered, but of course that is difficult to know or prove. And intent to defeat rivals is a natural part of strong competition. Hundreds of suits were filed by private plaintiffs and the FTC against price discrimination, and many of the suits succeeded.

The 1970s brought a tightening of the criteria for determining whether pricing is predatory. After 1980, Reagan officials deliberately avoided actions against discrimination. Private suits dwindled as the courts turned chilly toward plaintiffs' allegations of predatory actions. As of 1990, discrimination has been largely unrestrained, under the reasoning that it is merely part of hard competition.

The basic laws that are invoked in cases against price discrimination are the Sherman Act, Section 2, against "monopolizing" actions, and the Robinson-Patman Act of 1936, which replaced Clayton Section 2 (recall Chapter 5). Under the first, price discrimination may show a firm's intent to monopolize or be evidence of an abuse of monopoly power. True predatory pricing may be sufficient by itself to convict a firm for monopolizing. This was noted in Chapter 6 and will be enlarged on below. The Robinson-Patman Act places various limits on price discrimination in order to protect small firms.[11] This act shifts concern from primary- to secondary-line effects in order to protect small retailers against chain stores that could get their goods from wholesalers at price discounts. Still, the precedents operate at both levels.

A firm accused of price discrimination can first try to show that costs also differed in proportion or that the goods differed in their grade and quality; hence, price differences did not constitute true price discrimination. Beyond that, there were two main economic defenses against a charge of discrimination: that the prices (1) only met competitors' prices in good faith or (2) did not substantially lessen competition. The act is often blamed for preventing effective competition by limiting price cutting. However, in practice, neither its good nor its bad effects are probably very strong. Primary-line effects are the main issue in the following review, though secondary-line effects will be noted at the end.

Predatory Pricing and Related Actions. Brazen predatory pricing has long been a Section 2 offense. Standard Oil Company had used selective prices in at least two ways. One was selective price cutting in local areas to force small competitors into more favorable merger terms. The other was Standard's coercion of railroads to give special freight rates, including a rebate to Standard for each barrel of oil shipped for its competitors. The pricing played a vital role in the creation of Standard's monopoly, and it was abusive.[12] For American Tobacco and the Du Pont Gunpowder Trust, too, predatory pricing was a count in the monopoly offense.

From 1914 to 1936, the FTC issued only eight effective orders against price discrimination (four others were appealed and reversed by the Supreme Court). Under Robinson-Patman, the activity multiplied, with

---

[11]Good reviews of the act and its enforcement are in Corwin D. Edwards, *The Price Discrimination Law* (Washington, D.C.: Brookings Institution, 1959); Scherer and Ross, *Industrial Market Structure and Economic Performance*, pp. 510–16; and a symposium of papers marking the 50th anniversary of the Robinson-Patman Act, in the *Antitrust Bulletin* 31 (Fall 1986).

[12]John J. McGee has suggested that none of Standard Oil's tactics were truly predatory, "Predatory Price Cutting: The Standard Oil (N.J.) Case," *Journal of Law and Economics* 1 (October 1958), pp. 137–69. Predation would have been too costly to Standard Oil to make sense. He searches the trial record in the antitrust case and finds no persuasive instance of predation. However, his approach is narrow, as Burns has noted. See Malcolm R. Burns, "Outside Intervention in Monopolistic Price Warfare: The Case of the 'Plug War' and the Union Tobacco Company," *Business History Review* 56 (Spring 1982), pp. 33–53; Burns, "Economies of Scale in Tobacco Manufacture, 1897–1910," *Journal of Economic History* 43 (June 1983), pp. 461–74; and Burns, "Predatory Pricing and the Acquisition Cost of Competitors," *Journal of Political Economy* 94 (April 1986), pp. 266–96. See also Scherer and Ross, *Industrial Market Structure and Economic Performance*, pp. 388–91.

430 cases resulting in 311 cease-and-desist orders by 1957; of the 23 that were appealed, 19 were upheld.[13] By 1978, the total of orders had gone over 1,400, about two thirds of them in food-products markets. The Antitrust Division also brought many actions, over a wider range of markets. Usually, the firm offers little defense, preferring merely to change the pricing. The act specifies five different types of violations, all of which boil down to differences among "whole" prices that are not based on costs or that show intent to exclude rivals.

Predation has also been alleged in various Sherman Act monopolizing cases brought by private plaintiffs as well as the Antitrust Division. From this welter of case activity and hair splitting over fine points, a few main lines of precedent stand out.

1. The agency must show that price discrimination occurred and that it did injure competition.

2. "Cost" is now usually defined as long-run marginal cost, which includes a normal return on the capital used in producing the good.

3. A dominant firm cannot cut price below cost if that reflects an intent—and does have the effect—of increasing its market share. If price covers cost, the firm is innocent, even though other firms are killed off. The firm bears the burden of proving that price did not go below cost, validly measured. The evidence is often murky and inconclusive, since costs can be defined and measured in many ways. Small-share or new firms *can* use such "loss leaders" to build up their positions.

4. Leading firms can only "meet" competitors' price cuts, not cut below them in a way that increases their market share. As with cost, the defendant bears the burden of proving that it did not go below competitors' prices. Small firms can, as before, go below that in order to get established.

5. Much true predatory pricing slips by, particularly since 1976, when courts began adopting the Areeda-Turner cost standard, and, after 1980, when the agencies stopped applying the Robinson-Patman Act.

6. On the other side, some procompetitive pricing has been incorrectly charged as predatory (especially actions taken by firms that do not hold dominant shares). Such cases have virtually ceased since 1976, under the narrower rules.

On balance, the stream of Robinson-Patman cases has probably provided some protection for efficient small firms in resisting strategic pricing by dominant rivals. It has been applied inappropriately in some cases, but defendants can usually adjust the pricing easily so that "wrong" restrictions have little serious impact on efficiency.

---

[13]Edwards, *The Price Discrimination Law,* chap. 4.

Against this view, Chicago-UCLA analysts sternly denounce all Robinson-Patman cases, and they regard these cases as a serious threat to hard competition.[14]

The older precedents have not been crystal clear, because the cases often raise confusing evidence and the decisions have often contained economic error.

Anheuser-Busch (A-B). Anheuser-Busch is now the leading U.S. brewer, but its industry share in the middle 1950s was only about 7 percent.[15] During 1954–55, A-B cut prices on Budweiser beer in the St. Louis area, but not in other markets, and so there was a price difference not based on costs. A-B had been fourth in St. Louis in 1953 with 12 percent of the market, behind Falstaff, GW, and GB. A-B's share rose to 39 percent, but then fell back to 17 percent after the price cutting was over. Despite the discrimination, A-B was exonerated in a court case because (1) it had responded to valid causes (sales losses during 1953); (2) its prices were not shown to be below costs; (3) its competitors in the St. Louis area still made profits; and (4) A-B's share slipped back after the price cuts were ended. Note also that A-B was only a poor third in the St. Louis market after the episode. In short, A-B was in zone A of Figure 10–2.

Utah Pie. In 1957, three national companies—Continental Baking, Pet Milk, and Carnation—shipped in all the frozen pies sold in Salt Lake City, Utah. During 1957–58, a new, small local firm named Utah Pie Company seized 67 percent of this market by cutting prices and saving on transport costs. The three then cut prices below their average total cost levels *and* below Utah's prices, and this dropped Utah's share to 34 percent.[16] Though Utah's share went back up to 45 percent in 1961, and though Utah was able to get and hold its prices below the other firms' prices, the Court inferred a predatory intent from the three big firms' actions. This intent was also shown by other actions, including industrial spying. The Court held that the intent was likely to harm competition if it were permitted to take effect, and so Utah's private suit won.

This decision took the broader view, with prices only part of the whole predatory sequence. It was sharply criticized by some economists for ignoring the dominance of Utah Pie Company after 1957.

---

[14]Chicago-UCLA specialists focused particularly strong attacks on the Robinson-Patman Act after 1975, seeking outright repeal. For one instance of the criticisms, see Richard A. Whiting, "R–P: May It Rest in Peace," *Antitrust Bulletin* 31 (Fall 1986), pp. 709–32.

[15]The case is *FTC* v. *Anheuser-Busch, Inc.*, 363 U.S. 536 (1960), 289 F.2d 835 (1961).

[16]For a full evaluation of this case, see Kenneth G. Elzinga and Thomas F. Hogarty, "*Utah Pie* and the Consequences of Robinson-Patman," *Journal of Law and Economics* 21 (1978).

The new, permissive line on predation emerged in the 1970s' "IBM cases," a series of some 20 private suits against IBM attacking its pricing and product strategies. Small, specialized makers of disk drives, plotters, and other peripheral equipment claimed that IBM had resorted to excessive price cuts and product redesigns, which made them unable to compete vigorously. IBM responded with fierce litigation, using the Areeda-Turner rule to claim that it had not cut prices below cost and therefore had not injured competition. Judges quickly applied the new rule, and IBM escaped any convictions for predation. Given IBM's severe actions, its exoneration opened wide precedents for future pricing by dominant firms.

The precedent was a wide one, for new competition often leaves the established firm with excess inventory, which has low marginal cost. Indeed, a rational monopolist could plan always to have excess capacity, so that its marginal costs were low, leaving it free to make deep price cuts against any newcomer.[17]

The fullest acceptance of predatory pricing occurred when Reagan's antitrust chief dropped the Division's *IBM* case in 1982. IBM's prices had been set below cost on three parts of IBM's 360 line: the 360/44, 360/67, and 360/90 models. Other actions had reinforced the effects of the selective pricing. By accepting these actions by a dominant firm, the official dropped virtually all limits on pricing tactics.

In short, recent actions have given dominant firms virtually a free run in price-cost tactics. This is a clear departure from criteria based on economic efficiency.

Systematic, Continuing Discrimination. Toward systematic discrimination—without specific predation—policy has been lenient in primary-line cases but strict on secondary-line ones.

The leading primary-line cases involve a few dominant firms whose deep price discrimination has been challenged in a Sherman Section 2 monopolizing suit. The conviction of United Shoe Machinery Corporation (USM) in 1956 rested partly on USM's extensive price discrimination, including the bundling of repairs into the machinery price. This discrimination may not have been predatory, but it had reduced competition and reflected USM's intent to do just that, in Judge Wyzanski's opinion.

In three other big Section 2 cases since 1968—*Xerox, Matsushita,* and *AT&T* (recall Chapter 7)—price discrimination was a major ele-

---

[17]Average costs decline at output levels below capacity, and marginal costs are below average costs. That is a prime implication of having idle capacity: The out-of-pocket costs for additional production are low.

Excess capacity as a barrier to entry is discussed in A. Michael Spence, "Entry, Capacity, Investment, and Oligopolistic Pricing," *Bell Journal of Economics* 8 (Autumn 1977), pp. 534–44.

ment. Xerox refined its discrimination, with three-part tariffs, special large-user plans, and frequent revisions to respond to changes in demand. Its pricing became a labyrinth of discounting, systematically giving discounts amidst strong competition, and setting high profit margins where competition was weak. This was a part of the FTC's 1973–75 case against Xerox, but the settlement left it untouched. As with IBM's predatory pricing, systematic discrimination was becoming immune to challenge.

In 1986, in the *Matsushita* decision, the Supreme Court adopted the Chicago-UCLA view that predatory pricing is unlikely to occur.[18] The Court argued that, while Japanese TV-set producers may have set low prices, the later recoupment of profits probably could not be expected. Therefore, the Japanese firms were exonerated of any harm to competition, largely by assumption, not factual proof. The precedent immunizes virtually all other supposed predatory action in other markets.

AT&T's long-distance telephone service provides a bellwether current case. When new competition entered in the 1970s, AT&T sharpened its discrimination to discourage MCI and other new rivals, but its specific price cutting was still restrained by FCC regulation. By 1989, AT&T's pressure to discriminate grew strong, and the FCC effectively removed the limits. Even though AT&T's market-share advantage was very large, it was given full pricing freedom. By 1990, it had reached major customized pricing deals with over 30 major customers, providing steep discounts unrelated to costs. The discrimination helped AT&T stop the decline in its market share, keeping it over 70 percent.

Secondary-Line Effects. Here the treatment was stricter, and the precedents are more fully developed. Only the main lines and leading cases are noted here.

The *A&P* case, begun soon after the Robinson-Patman Act was passed, charged A&P with all the counts of discrimination in the act. The appeals court in 1949 based its conviction mainly on secondary-line effects: A&P, *as a buyer,* had forced suppliers to discriminate, thereby enabling it to beat out competitors at the retail level. Possibly some of the price differences reflected true efficiencies achieved by A&P, but many did not. The whole judgment in the case was sound (and was not appealed by A&P).[19]

---

[18]*Matsushita Electrical Industrial Co. v. Zenith Radio Corp.,* 475 U.S. 574 (1986).

[19]From the intense debate on the case, see Morris A. Adelman, *A&P: A Study in Price-Cost Behavior and Public Policy* (Cambridge, Mass.: Harvard Univ. Press, 1959), for criticism of the case; see Joel B. Dirlam and Alfred E. Kahn, "Antitrust Law and the Big Buyer: Another Look at the A&P Case," *Journal of Political Economy* 60 (April 1952), pp. 118–32; and Dirlam and Kahn, "A Reply," *Journal of Political Economy* 61 (October 1953), pp. 441–46, for analysis on the other side.

In *Morton Salt* (1948), the price of table salt had varied inversely and substantially with the size of orders, over a 15 percent range.[20] The discounts were not "cost justified." Only five large chain stores had ever bought enough salt to get the lowest price. They could resell the salt at prices lower than small grocers could buy it. Evidence showed that the price disparities had caused retail prices to differ. Conviction followed routinely.

In later cases, price ranges as low as 5 percent were held to be "substantial" enough to reduce competition and violate the law.[21] Cost defenses were of course permitted, but they usually had to show that prices cover total costs, including a correct portion of overhead costs. Since 1975, the standards have shifted to marginal cost, which is usually much lower. Since the defendant bears the burden of proof, and cost disparities must cover *all* of the price differences, the cost defense is often too complex or costly to make in these small-scale cases. The courts are not finicky, and many thousands of price differentials are never brought to trial, so policy does not stamp out the common run of petty price discrimination.

"Meeting competition in good faith" is the second line of defense. It has prevailed in some cases, and it has an intrinsic validity.[22] Competition requires that firms be able to respond, if not to overreact. Yet "good faith" has usually been too elusive to judge firmly, so the policy is only a rule of thumb: A larger firm usually cannot slash below a smaller firm's price in order to chill competition.[23]

The Robinson-Patman Act continues to attract criticism and proposals for repeal. Yet its broad role is probably economically sound, or at least not strongly harmful. More urgent than its reform is the need to develop policy toward complex discrimination by leading dominant firms.

3. Tie-Ins

Tie-ins are a form of price discrimination. A tie-in requires you to buy product *B*, which you don't want, in order to get product *A*, which you do want. The tying product (*A*) is often patented or a popular branded

---

[20]*FTC* v. *Morton Salt Co.*, 334 U.S. 37 (1948).

[21]The cases include *American Can Co.* v. *Bruce's Juices* 187 F.2d 919, 924, modified, 190 F.2d 73, 74 (5th Cir.), cert. dismissed, 342 U.S. 875 (1951); and *Foremost Dairies, Inc.* v. *FTC*, 348 F.2d 674 (5th Cir.), cert. denied, 382 U.S. 959 (1965).

[22]The leading case is *Standard Oil Co. (Indiana)* v. *FTC*, 340 U.S. 231 (1951). It abounds in legal fine points, but the main lesson is that the firm can use good-faith meeting of competitors' prices as a way of justifying price discrimination.

[23]Note that IBM was able to cut below the PCM firms' prices in 1971–72 and still escape conviction (recall the *Telex* case).

item. The tied item may be a new product or an inferior one, or simply a complement. The firm holds more market power for product A than for product B. Tying is an ancient custom, though a rather specialized one which crops up only in certain situations. Market processes usually undermine tie-ins, as new firms offer the tied goods separately. While it lasts, tying can: (1) extend market power from the tying product into the tied product and/or (2) serve as a form of price discrimination to extract more profit.[24] That is, it increases the profits the firm can extract from product A.

Tying has limits, of course. The firm gains by selling more of product B, but it will probably sell less of product A. The firm will need to balance its gains on B against its net losses on A. The outcome depends on the demand elasticities for the two products and also on the cost curves for the two. Only when A's demand is much more inelastic than B's is tying clearly profitable. This leads some writers to say that tying cannot extend monopoly from A to B. The total profits available from A to B, sold either separately *or* together, are a fixed amount, they say.

However, this Chicago-UCLA view has validity only in a perfect market setting. Tying by dominant firms (especially those with patents or some other special advantage in product A) can foreclose much or all competition in product B's market. Even if such leverage is not strong, the tie may raise entry barriers by forcing any new entrants to offer both products, not just one.

Some social benefits of tie-ins are also possible, though less likely. The joint sale might realize cost savings in ordering, shipping, or servicing. Also, tying makes it hard to identify the separate prices of the tied goods. An oligopolist might use tying as a device for quietly offering concealed price cuts, thereby increasing profits.

The general economic rule is that tying's anticompetitive effects are correlated to market share. Tying by small-share firms is neutral or procompetitive; only when market share in the tying good is substantial can tying tend to reduce competition. An efficient policy will only bar tying when market shares are over about 20 percent, and the severity of policy actions will increase at higher market shares.

Actual policies have not fit this criterion closely. During the 1950s to the 1970s, the Court ostensibly had a per se rule against *all* tying. That would be too strict, because tying is surely harmless when product A's

---

[24]See Carl Kaysen and Donald F. Turner, Jr., *Antitrust Policy* (Cambridge, Mass.: Harvard Univ. Press, 1959); and Donald F. Turner, "The Validity of Tying Arrangements Under the Antitrust Laws," *Harvard Law Review* 72 (November 1958), pp. 50–75; also Richard A. Posner, *Antitrust Law* (Chicago: University of Chicago Press, 1976), pp. 171–84. For example, in the 1960s when Xerox held a patent-based monopoly of plain-paper copiers, it refused to sell rather than lease them; and it required customers to use only Xerox toner and ink, on which it set very high price-cost margins. This extended market power, *and* it attained thorough price discrimination.

market share is below about 10 percent. This per se approach drew scornful criticism, but, in fact, the cases rarely involved market shares below 10 percent. A discussion of several leading cases follows.

Tie-ins can violate Sherman Section 1 (an unreasonable restraint) or Sherman Section 2 (attempt to monopolize), but it is Clayton Section 3 that specifically prohibits tie-ins if they "substantially lessen competition." Before 1914, sellers of machines could prevent machine users from using supplies, or other machines, from other sellers.[25] Clayton Section 3 made most tie-ins illegal, and the *IBM* case in 1936 confirmed the policy. IBM made its customers use only IBM cards, and it had overwhelming dominance (over 90 percent) of tabulating machines (product *A*). The Court rejected IBM's claim that other cards would jam the machines or cause errors.[26]

International Salt Company (another dominant firm) had required users of its patented salt-processing machines to use only its salt in the machines. It claimed that only this could protect the machines from malfunctioning. Though there were competitive machines and the effect of foreclosure was only "creeping," rather than "at a full gallop," the Court convicted International in 1947 on a per se basis.[27]

Block booking of movies had long been a packaging device by which Hollywood studios forced theaters to take inferior films in order to get the best ones. This tie-in was found illegal in the 1948 *Paramount* case, along with other conditions (recall Chapter 7).

American Can (also dominant) required users of its patented can-closing machines to use only its cans in them. When a major monopolization case against it and Continental Can was settled in 1949, a central clause was the prohibition of this tie-in.[28] The action worked; by 1956, competition had risen sharply. In 1956, an Antitrust Division action challenging Eastman Kodak's dominance and its tying of film processing to film purchases was settled. The tie was broken, and henceforth film buyers could have a choice of processors.

For many decades, Northern Pacific Railway had sold or leased its land-grant holdings of 40 million acres with "preferential-routing" clauses. The land user had to ship all its products over that railway. This clause was struck down in 1958, as a foreclosing device.[29]

---

[25]The case of *Henry* v. *A. B. Dick Co.*, 224 U.S. 1 (1912), involved supplies to be used with a potential duplicating machine; see also *Heaton Peninsular Button-Fastener Co.* v. *Eureka Speciality Co.*, 77 F.288 (1896).

[26]*International Business Machines Corp.* v. *U.S.*, 298 U.S. 131 (1936). By 1956, IBM still had over 90 percent of the card business.

[27]*International Salt Co.* v. *U.S.*, 332 U.S. 392 (1947).

[28]The case is *U.S.* v. *American Can Co.*, 87 F. Supp. 18 (N.D. Cal. 1949); see also James W. McKie, *Tin Cans and Tin Plate* (Cambridge, Mass.: Harvard Univ. Press, 1959). American and Continental together held 86 percent of both levels (machines and cans).

[29]*Northern Pacific Railway Co.* v. *U.S.*, 356 U.S. 1 (1958).

The *Jerrold* decision in 1961 held that a supplier of cable TV receiving systems could not prevent users from buying parts of their systems from other firms.[30] Jerrold had pioneered cable TV technology during 1948–55, and its exclusive rule helped it protect quality and grow. After that initial phase, the "infant-company" excuse lost its force, especially because Jerrold now dominated the industry. The effort to sell only complete systems had ceased to be reasonable and was not anticompetitive and, therefore, illegal. This special infant-company escape has rarely been used since then.

The *Loew's* decision about block booking in 1962 involved movies.[31] The owners of a large library of old films had required the TV networks to take packages of films, rather than let them select among separately priced films. Thus, for example, "The Man Who Came to Dinner" was tied to "Gorilla Man" and "Tugboat Annie Sails Again." Loew's claimed that old movies were less than 8 percent of all TV offerings and, therefore, a minor competitive factor. The device was primarily aimed to maximize profits, rather than extend the firm's market power. Yet it, too, was held to be illegal per se. Note that Loew's was a large factor in the old-movie sector of the entertainment industry.

In a 1984 decision, the Court reaffirmed that tie-ins reduce competition only when done by firms with substantial market shares.[32] The Jefferson Parish Hospital had an exclusive contract with an anesthesiology firm that provided all anesthesiology services for the hospital. This excluded all other anesthesiologists, one of whom sued to break the contract.

The Court found that this hospital had only a small share of hospital services in the New Orleans area. Therefore, any exclusion could not reduce competition significantly, and so the tie-in embodied by the contract was legal. A high market share would have created monopoly effects and made the tie-in illegal.

Altogether, the per se rule against tie-ins *by dominant firms* is consistent and sound. A rule-of-reason approach to all cases would—as it would in price fixing—mire the process in unworkable delays and confusion. There are calls for liberalizing the policy, but any social losses from the present strict line are probably small.[33]

---

[30]*U.S.* v. *Jerrold Electronics Corp.*, 187 F.Supp. 545; 365 U.S. (1961).

[31]*U.S.* v. *Loew's Inc.*, 371 U.S. 38 (1962).

[32]*Jefferson Parish Hospital District No. 2* v. *Hyde*, 466 U.S. 2 (1984).

[33]Including Posner, *Antitrust Law*, pp. 171–84; and Ward S. Lowman, Jr., "Tying Arrangements and the Leverage Problem," *Yale Law Journal* 67 (November 1957), pp. 19–36.

II. VERTICAL RESTRICTIONS ON COMPETITION

Among the many kinds of restrictive devices and actions, *vertical* limits on dealers are a large portion. There are two main types. First are limits on what and where the dealers may *sell*. Second are restrictions on what the dealers *buy*. A complicated set of policies toward these practices has evolved, and litigation has recently flourished. To evaluate the policies, one must first understand the peculiar economics of dealerships and franchising.

1. Analysis

Retailing methods are extremely diverse. At one extreme are discount houses offering a wide variety of products under one roof. At the other extreme, some other products are retailed by the manufacturer itself (such as many computers and copiers). Close to that extreme are chains of specialized franchised dealers, who are quasi-owned and controlled by the manufacturer. Examples include some gasoline stations and stereo-equipment sellers, McDonald's and many other fast-food chains, and most soda-pop bottlers. The degree of control varies. The supplier or parent firm will often try to restrict its retailers' choices. Alternatively, the dealers may cooperate horizontally with each other to force the producer to impose, though reluctantly, the vertical restrictions. In either case, competition among dealers is likely to be reduced.

There are many kinds of restrictions: on dealers' selling in each other's local areas, on dealers' carrying of other companies' brands, on dealers' pricing actions, and so forth. Many of these specific controls are interchangeable with each other, serving much the same purpose. Some of them reduce competition sharply, while others do not.

Intrabrand and Interbrand Competition. The restrictions (1) reduce *intrabrand* competition in *selling* or the dealers' choice in *buying* their supplies, in order to build up the brand and, therefore, (2) increase *interbrand* competition and the manufacturer's profits. For example, Coca-Cola prohibits its franchised bottlers (one in each town) from selling in each other's areas. That stops *intra*brand competition. But by making each bottler more profitable and secure, it may strengthen their ability to compete against other pop brands, in *inter*brand competition. The policy problem is to identify these effects and weigh them. Only where the loss of *intrabrand* competition is small, while *interbrand* competition is strongly raised, should the restriction be permitted.

The issue affects many thousands of producers, as they select among many different methods of marketing, and millions of retailing firms, including over 500,000 franchisees. Automobiles, gasoline, flowers, shoes, bicycles, hotels, film developing, machinery, stereo equipment, income tax preparation, and, of course, fast foods are among the many familiar items so affected. The franchisee or authorized dealer promotes, sells, and services the product. For this it gets the franchise and other sorts of support from the supplier.

Close vertical relationships arise under certain conditions: (1) the product is complex, and so users need assurance of quality; (2) the product is important enough to be a major activity of a dealer (for example, there are auto dealers but not safety-pin dealers; shoe dealers but not shoestring dealers); and, (3) the producer has a distinct status, from a patent, brand image, or simple market share, and dealers can both benefit from this identity and help maintain it. The product or service may gain a higher price when marketed through "high-quality" dealers than through mass discounting, and so the maker may take great efforts to keep it out of discounters' hands.

Producers and Dealers. There are inherent conflicts of interest between the producer and the dealers. The producer wants intensive sales coverage; each dealer wants a large exclusive sales area to itself. The producer wants each dealer to focus only on its product; the dealer wants to add new products, even though they would dilute the maker's brand image. The producer wants the dealer to buy only from itself; the dealers often want a free hand. Yet both sides also gain from mutual support.

The producer generally extracts what monopoly profit it can in its own price and then prefers that the retailing of its product to final customers be as extensive and cheap—that is, as competitive—as possible. The maker would be willing to sacrifice this beneficial competition only (1) during an initial growth and building-up phase, (2) to foster dealer loyalty and excellence in sales and service, or (3) when coerced by dealers to help reduce competition at their level.

Here, the free-rider problem may be significant, as noted by Chicago-UCLA analysts. For certain types of products, the producer may gain by reducing competition among its dealers. The dealers, because they are getting more profits from the products, will promote them more and provide better service. The logic is clear, though the benefits involved may be small.

Market Share Is Crucial. As in other topics, *the crucial condition is the firm's market share*. When shares are substantial, the anticompetitive effects tend to prevail, but restrictions by small-share firms can only be neutral or procompetitive. Two main kinds of restrictions have drawn the most attention. One is geographic limits on the areas where dealers may *sell* (so-called territorial restrictions). These limits *do* cut intrabrand competition among the firm's dealers and *may* raise interbrand competition by strengthening those dealers. The balance between the two effects depends mainly on the producer's market share. For dominant firms, the social loss prevails; for lesser firms, there may be a net rise in competition if the restrictions help them to build up their positions against larger rivals.

The second category is clauses binding the dealers to buy their supplies from the franchiser (so-called requirements contracts). They *do* exclude competition from the suppliers' market, but they *may* assure quality at the retail level. So here, too, the net effect on competition hinges on the producer's market share.

Therefore, the broad lines of efficient policy are reasonably clear. *Dominant firms would be prohibited from both kinds of restrictions.* Dealers would instead have free choice among suppliers and customers. By contrast, producers with small market shares would be largely free to adopt vertical restrictions.

Private and public suits on these matters have proliferated in recent years. The main lines of policy do fit the efficiency criteria fairly well.

2. Geographic Limits on Sales

The restrictions vary. The tightest categories are territorial restrictions and customer limitations. Exclusive franchises and location clauses are of medium force. Other restrictions only discourage intrabrand competition rather than prohibit it. Policy has developed toward a per se rule against the tightest and medium-force categories, but a 1977 decision has limited that coverage to dominant firms with a large economic impact. The key question is the threshold market share for a per se treatment. It has been moved about in the 5 to 25 percent range. Meanwhile, the remaining two milder restrictions are presumed to be legal under a rule-of-reason approach.

The evolution of the policies has been fairly complex, with several leading cases. In *Bausch & Lomb* in 1944, the Supreme Court held that a vertical territorial restriction that was part of an agreement to fix prices is illegal per se.[34] The Antitrust Division then announced in 1948 a per se basis: It would challenge any vertical restraints that close off intrabrand competition. For 15 years, it got many consent decrees stopping them. Its first litigated case was *White Motor Company*. The district court held White's restrictions to be illegal per se in 1961, but the Supreme Court reversed in 1963 and remanded for further study and trial.[35] By 1967, both the FTC and the Antitrust Division had drawn

---

[34]*U.S. v. Bausch & Lomb Optical Co.*, 321 U.S. 707 (1944).

[35]*U.S. v. White Motor Co.*, 194 F. Supp. 562 (N.D. Ohio 1961), reversed and remanded, 372 U.S. 253 (1963).

back; territorial restraints were only presumptively illegal, not illegal per se. The firm could try to show that, on balance, the restrictions promoted competition. In *Schwinn* in 1967, the Supreme Court took a tougher line, nearly to a per se basis. In the 1950s, Schwinn had kept its wholesalers from selling to dealers outside their fixed territories or to nonfranchised dealers, on threat of termination. The Court held that such restrictions on reselling the bicycles were illegal, even though Schwinn's market share had fallen to 12 percent by 1960.[36]

This decision triggered a flood of suits, many strict lower-court opinions, and much criticism. Then, in 1977, the Court's decision in the *GTE* case appeared to raise the threshold market share for a per se treatment.[37] The intrabrand and interbrand effects were to be weighed after all. Yet, in fact, the decision fitted the presumption that restrictions will be prohibited where market shares are sizable. When it enforced geographic restrictions on its deals, GTE had only a 2 percent market share, which then rose only to 5 percent. Probably, a market share of 15 or 20 percent would have been too high. So the basic approach is not changed; vertical geographic restrictions by significant firms are likely to be stopped.

The leading exception is the soda-pop industry. For many decades, Coca-Cola, Pepsi-Cola, and other leading firms have set and enforced the local areas within which their franchised bottlers may deliver. The larger firms, with market shares between 25 and 45 percent, clearly reduce competition by these restrictions. The FTC ruled in 1978 that both *intra*brand competition and *inter*brand competition were reduced.[38] The firms then obtained from Congress an antitrust exemption for the restrictions, and so the practice now continues without restraint.

The same issues arise in the beer industry, where Anheuser-Busch sets rigid limits on bottlers' delivery areas in many states. Given A-B's 43 percent share of the industry, the reduction in intrabrand competi-

---

[36]*U.S.* v. *Arnold, Schwinn & Co.,* 388 U.S. 365. Perhaps the key passage in Justice Fortas's opinion was: "Once the manufacturer has parted with title and risk . . . his effort thereafter to restrict territory or persons to whom the product may be transferred . . . is a per se violation of Section 1 of the Sherman Act" (at p. 382). The government's brief had explicitly abandoned the contention that the restrictions were illegal per se, asking instead only for a rule-of-reason decision.

[37]*Continental TV, Inc.* v. *GTE Sylvania, Inc.,* No. 761-15 (1977).

[38]FTC docket no. 8885. For varying views on the matter, see Robert Larner, "The Economics of Territorial Restrictions in the Soft Drink Industry," *Antitrust Bulletin* 22 (Spring 1977), pp. 145–55; Barbara G. Katz, "Territorial Exclusivity in the Soft Drink Industry." *Journal of Industrial Economics* 27 (September 1978), pp. 85–96; and Louis W. Stern, Eugene F. Zelek, Jr., and Thomas W. Dunfee, "A Rule of Reason Analysis of Territorial Restrictions in the Soft Drink Industry," *Antitrust Bulletin* 27 (Summer 1982), pp. 481–515.

tion is substantial. Officials in several states have challenged the restrictions, but Reagan officials during the 1980s displayed no concern about it.

3. Restrictions on Purchases and Related Tie-Ins

Requiring one's dealers to carry only (or mainly) the franchiser's products is an old practice, one which has been gradually limited by the courts.[39] Such "exclusive-dealing" issues are closely related to "requirements contracts" in which the buyer is forced to buy more of a product, to contract for a longer period, or to buy more related goods, than it wishes. In each case, the seller excludes others from competing to supply the goods. The practice involves tying, but here in a special vertical context. The producer may set rigid requirements or may only try to "persuade." That rigid requirements do have anticompetitive effects is clear if the supplier/franchiser has a significant market share. Whether persuasion for tie-ins reduces competition is debatable. Again the precedents have developed gradually, and the producer's market share has been the key test.[40]

In the *Standard Fashions* and *Butterick* cases in 1922 and 1925, respectively, firms making two fifths of the dress patterns sold at retail excluded their competitors from the best stores in the cities and from the only outlets available in many smaller towns.[41] In the *Eastman Kodak* case in 1927, a firm producing more than nine tenths of the motion picture film made in the United States entered into an agreement with its customers, through an association of laboratories making motion picture prints, forbidding them to purchase film imported from abroad.[42]

In the *Carter Carburetor* case in 1940, the principal manufacturer of carburetors gave discounts to dealers who bought exclusively from it and denied them to those who bought from its competitors.[43] In the case of the *Fashion Originators' Guild* in 1941, an association of dress manufacturers, whose 176 members made three fifths of the dresses sold at retail for $10.75 and up, sought to prevent "design piracy" by

---

[39]Familiar examples are the franchised gas station that is required to carry certain brands of tires or accessories and fast-food shops that must buy their meats or containers from the franchiser.

[40]*FTC* v. *Sinclair Refining Co.*, 261 U.S. 463; and *Pike Mfg. Co.* v. *General Motors Corp.*, 299 U.S. 5 (1936).

[41]*Standard Fashion Co.* v. *Magrane-Houston Co.*, 258 U.S. 346; *Butterick Co.* v. *FTC*, 4 F.2d 910 cert. denied, 267 U.S. 602.

[42]*FTC* v. *Eastman Kodak Co.*, 247 U.S. 619.

[43]*FTC* v. *Carter Carburetor Corp.*, 112 F.2d 722.

signing contracts with 12,000 retailers and forbidding them to buy from imitators.[44]

In all of these cases, exclusive dealing was enjoined on the grounds that its use by a dominant seller had substantially lessened competition and tended toward monopoly. In later cases, a less rigid criterion was employed.

In the *International Salt* case, where a contract tying the sale of salt to the lease of a patented salt dispenser was found to be illegal in 1947, the Supreme Court went on to say that "it is unreasonable per se, to foreclose competitors from any substantial market."[45] Note the key term *substantial*. This reasoning was applied to exclusive dealerships in the *Standard Oil of California* case in 1949.[46] Standard Oil, producing 23 percent of the gasoline sold in seven western states, contracted with some 6,000 independent dealers, handling less than 7 percent of the gasoline sold in the area, to fill all of their requirements for petroleum products and, in some cases, for tires, tubes, batteries, and other accessories. The lower court held Standard's contracts to be illegal on the grounds that competition is substantially lessened when competitors are excluded from "a substantial number of outlets."[47] The Supreme Court affirmed the lower court's decision. It is enough, said Justice Frankfurter, to prove "that competition has been foreclosed in a substantial share of the line of commerce affected." Standard's contracts created "a potential clog on competition."

This precedent was followed in the *Richfield Oil* case in 1951. Richfield's exclusive contracts with filing stations on the Pacific Coast accounted for but 3 percent of the gasoline sold in the area, but the rule of quantitative substantiality was applied and the contracts were condemned.[48] In the light of these decisions, it appeared that exclusive arrangements were to be outlawed per se, but later developments point the other way.

During the 1950s, the FTC declined to proceed against exclusive arrangements that appeared to be harmless, confining its orders to cases in which the probability of actual injury to competition could be shown. Then, in 1961, in the case of *Tampa Electric Co.* v. *Nashville Coal Co.*,[49] the Supreme Court modified its earlier position. Tampa had contracted to purchase from Nashville, for 20 years, all of the coal required for one

[44]*Fashion Originators' Guild* v. *FTC*, 312 U.S. 457.

[45]*International Salt Co.* v. *U.S.*, 332 U.S. 392, 396.

[46]*Standard Oil Co. of California* v. *U.S.*, 337 U.S. 293.

[47]*U.S.* v. *Standard Oil Co. of California*, 78 F. Supp. 850, 857.

[48]*U.S.* v. *Richfield Oil Corp.*, 99 F. Supp. 280 (1951), sustained per curiam 343 U.S. 922 (1952).

[49]16, 365 U.S. 320.

of its generating stations. Since this affected only 1 percent of the Nashville-area coal market, and did give both partners a degree of security, the contract was let stand. In *Loew's* (1962) and *Perma Life Muffler* (1968), the Court rejected rigid tie-ins, but said that the suppliers could use "persuasion."[50]

In the 1970s, several decisions further defined the range of permitted vertical tie-ins. Chicken Delight, Inc., had required its franchisees to take its chickens and supplies, even at prices above alternative suppliers. These were only a few essential items that helped to make the retail food distinct. Though Chicken Delight had no large market share, the appeals court held in 1972 that it was distinct in the market and that trade had been restrained.[51] In 1973, the FTC's *Chock Full O'Nuts* decision affirmed that a franchiser of chains can't make franchisees buy from itself or from designated suppliers, although the franchiser could try to show that the tie-in is needed to ensure quality.[52]

In this whole area, further cases might refine precedent within a narrow zone, where persuasion shades over into packages and rigid tie-ins. However, no final answers are likely, since the devices and pressures can vary so subtly and widely.

III. SUMMARY

The behavior to be "controlled" comes in many forms and shadings, often raising complex points of economics and law. The agencies may often have pressed Robinson-Patman and vertical restriction issues beyond the efficient limits.

Despite the dropping of action in certain directions, the basic patterns continue. Exclusionary actions are harmless when done by small-share firms, but they may be illegal when done by dominant firms. This policy roughly fits the economic effects. Selective pricing below cost is effectively banned, except for firms with small market shares. Tie-ins are illegal, except for small-share firms. Likewise, vertical restraints on sales and purchases also are under a correctly tilted rule, which is stricter on firms with larger market shares. These rules are not only in the right direction but are applied strictly (except for the soda-pop industry). After a flurry of case activity in the 1960s, policy seems to have stabilized.

---

[50]*U.S.* v. *Loew's Inc.*, 371 U.S. 38 (1962); and *Perma Life Mufflers, Inc.*, v. *International Parts Corp.*, 392 U.S. 134 (1968).

[51]*Siegel* v. *Chicken Delight, Inc.*, 448 F.2d 43 (9 Cir. 1971), cert. denied, 405 U.S. 955 (1972).

[52]The FTC did accept Chock Full O'Nuts' argument for coffee and baked goods, which were more important for the brand image of the chain (634 ATRR, A-22).

The clear gap in policy is systematic price discrimination by dominant firms. Recent decisions have permitted dominant firms to price-discriminate sharply, even to the point of killing off rivals, as long as their prices did not provably go below costs. This neglects the fact that bare pricing is only part of a larger range of strategies that can exclude competition.

QUESTIONS FOR REVIEW

1. "Price discrimination simply means differences in prices." True?
2. "Price discrimination can help create and maintain market power, as well as help to extract maximum profits." True?
3. "Price discrimination is procompetitive when it is done systematically by a dominant firm." True?
4. "In the 1970s, dominant firms have been given wider latitude in using pricing tactics against small or new rivals." True?
5. "Tie-ins are harmful to competition only where the tied product has a high market share." True?
6. "By preventing intrabrand competition among its dealers, a producer may be able to increase interbrand competition in the market as a whole." True?
7. "Territorial restrictions seemed to be illegal per se after *Schwinn,* but now a rule-of-reason basis applies." True?
8. Is present policy too strict on price discrimination by small firms? By dominant firms?
9. If you are a dominant firm wishing to drive out a small rival who has lower costs than yours, what devices can you use—including pricing—and still escape an antitrust challenge?
10. Are vertical restriction cases by public agencies likely to be both numerous and of little net social value, as is often said? What criteria should be used by the agencies in deciding whether to bring such cases?
11. Draw up a balanced critique of the Robinson-Patman Act, including its main probable costs and benefits. What reforms might be warranted?

C·H·A·P·T·E·R 11   Antitrust Appraised

The established antitrust policies of the United States radically shifted in the 1980s toward minimal enforcement in line with strict Chicago-UCLA doctrines. It seems unlikely that enforcement will return to previous levels, because the laissez-faire doctrine is still in place and the staff resources can only be rebuilt slowly. Moreover, the judiciary has been shifted toward conservatism by the Reagan appointment of new judges, so the courts would probably resist any major efforts to expand antitrust activity.

Yet it is important to consider what antitrust has done to the economy and might still do. Section I of this chapter appraises the larger patterns of the 1890–1980 period. Section II summarizes mainstream antitrust's main effects. Section III considers the alternative procompetition policies that could be tried.

I. CRITERIA FOR ANTITRUST

The correctness of past policies depends on the nature of the conditions to be cured. Before 1980, there was a broad consensus that many markets contained imperfections, which gave rise to monopoly that is *not* justified by efficiency. Therefore, monopoly was generally to be reduced or prevented, unless strong, exceptional evidence could be found to exonerate it.

The 1980s brought an opposite outlook, in which Chicago-UCLA analysts simply denied that imperfections are significant. Moreover, they said, new entry is powerful, able to nullify most existing dominance or restrictions. Therefore, monopoly was largely to be welcomed, not resisted, in their view.

Your judgment about all past antitrust actions—during 1899 to 1970 and the contrasting actions since 1980—depends on your view about these economic issues. What concepts do apply? How important are imperfections? How great are the efficiencies of monopoly and the power of entry?

II. THE EFFECTS OF ANTITRUST

Now consider the main effects of past antitrust actions. The prohibition of collusion has reduced price fixing and related cooperation in most of the economy. Collusion must now be covert and is undoubtedly weaker than it would otherwise be. Tacit collusion remains untouched, and resale price maintenance and other vertical restriction probably have widespread but moderate effects. Large areas of the economy are exempted from Section 1, either formally or informally. Like a Swiss cheese, Section 1 is firm but has large holes.

Horizontal and vertical mergers were rather tightly constrained from about 1962 to 1980, but the limits largely dissolved for the next 10 years. The result was an extensive restructuring of scores of markets, which is continuing at a lesser pace. Also, many firms acquired heavy burdens of debt during buyouts or in resisting takeovers. The efficiency losses from this have been substantial, but were not restrained by 1980s' policies.

No new Section 2 actions were started after 1980. The AT&T divestiture proved that major Section 2 cases are still entirely feasible. However, the lapse in enforcement is deliberate, and it may continue indefinitely. Private cases can restrain dominant firms, but current Supreme Court precedents prevent them from leading to changes in structure. The moratorium on Section 2 may be appropriate if (1) Chicago-UCLA doctrines are correct and/or (2) there are few important candidates for action. Again, your own judgment about these points is your best guide.

Altogether, the century of U.S. antitrust has had enormous, widespread, and largely positive effects. The economy's structure is less concentrated, its behavior is less collusive, and its performance is undoubtedly more efficient, innovative, and fair. The broader effects toward openness, diversity, and healthy democracy have also been large.

These positive effects suggest a need to keep antitrust strict and effective so as not to lose the hard-won benefits. However, one can instead draw the opposite conclusion: Widespread competition is here to stay even if antitrust is kept at minimal levels, so that little enforcement is needed. This conclusion is the Chicago-UCLA case against antitrust, and it derives from a belief in powerful world competition and entry in concentrated markets. It also reflects a judgment that government actions are bumbling and/or harmful.

The Political Context

By now you can reach your own tentative judgment about the quality and effectiveness of antitrust actions. There have been some errors, which are natural in the crucible of pressures and interest groups. However, the Division, in particular, has largely been a compact and forceful agency for promoting competition, with a higher quality of staffing and activity than most public agencies.

Its critics often represent specific commercial interests (such as IBM and AT&T during the 1970s and 1980s), and they often overstate the supposed mistakes and harms of antitrust. Also, some supposed antitrust "excesses" often arise instead from Supreme Court decisions and political interferences.

American antitrust may be remarkably effective, even increasingly so. Or at the other extreme, it may be largely a pawn, controlled rather than controlling. The appraisal is determined by one's view of (1) the economic conditions needing treatment, (2) the real effects of policies, and (3) the *realpolitik* surrounding policy. And these trace back, once again, to the natural rate at which market power diminishes.

Yet there is wide agreement that the procedures are usually slow and contain bias; that the agencies are small compared to their tasks; that officials often lack expertise; and that mistakes and waste occur. It is also agreed that antitrust is likely to continue largely as is, a system in political and economic equilibrium. There are few powerful groups seeking change. Most industrial interests that might be deeply hurt by antitrust have been exempted, formally or de facto. Nearly all sides engaged in the antitrust process find something to gain from it—some very much indeed. Even the dominant firms that face Section 2 treatment gain legitimacy by the existence of agencies that might be able to treat them but don't. If that were not so, the citizenry might demand something more effective.

By comparison, a few antitrust policies abroad have had real substance. Britain's agencies have sometimes been comparable to U.S. ones, and their procedures are more brisk. They have adopted a wider array of techniques, including price controls, and direct changes of various sorts. Yet, during the Thatcher 1980s, British antitrust has also been cut back sharply.

III. POSSIBLE REFORMS

The most obvious possible reforms would be to restore the agencies' resources and raise their quality. Larger budgets, in line with the expanding and increasingly complex economy, would permit more effective coverage of problems. Appointees, especially to the FTC, could be more skilled and enforcement-minded. Powers to get information and create basic changes could be added.

1. Fines and Damages

At a more technical level, two experiments could be tried.

Using Fines More Precisely. The use of economic penalties is now crude and haphazard. The economic objective is to set penalties and probabilities of conviction just high enough to induce optimal choices of behavior and structure by the firms. Optimal fines, therefore, can be lower if enforcement is more thorough, and, for some offenses by small firms, fines are already steep enough. However, for major offenses by very large firms, fines are presently too small. Even if used imaginatively by judges (for example, X thousand dollars *per day* and per individual offense), they often leave a convicted offender with large monopoly gains for every day the infraction lasted. One alternative approach would fit fines to the degree of harm caused or the firm's ability to pay, or both. This could be a percent of monopoly profits, or of all profits, of the firm.[1] At present, fines are too small to be efficient in treating many problems, and their incidence—hitting smaller firms harder—often is quite unfair.

Change the Rules about Treble Damages. The Sherman Act's provision for treble damages for private victims has its merits, but it does accentuate some problems of Section 2 action. By opening up large damage claims, it encourages effective private suits. However, it also stimulates fanatical efforts to resist, and that has helped to cause the current problems. There are several possible revisions, but none is clearly best. The trebling feature could be revised downward (but how far is not clear). The groups eligible to collect damages could be narrowed. Criteria for calculating damages could be limited.

Such revisions would need great care, for the damages provide a powerful, effective mechanism for compensating victims and inducing self-corrective action against monopoly. Reagan officials in the 1980s

---

[1]See Kenneth G. Elzinga and William Breit, *The Antitrust Penalties* (New Haven, Conn.: Yale University Press, 1976).

urged the dropping of trebling for all but the most acute infractions, but their broad attack had no effect, partly because they had no evidence that trebling had caused harm.[2]

2. Private Suits

Private suits offer an important force against monopoly power. The growth in private litigation since 1960 is an experiment in the effectiveness of the approach. Repeatedly, private actions have been prepared earlier, filed sooner, and litigated more effectively than agency actions. In some areas, private actions have really been "making the law," by posing new claims and evoking landmark decisions. To some observers, this may go too far, bypassing the official agencies in forming the ruling precedents of "public" policy.

There is little danger that private action might go too far. Small plaintiffs are still often brushed off by the massive legal resources of dominant firms. Private suits are either lacking or unsuccessful against the leading dominant firms, as well as many lesser ones. Class-action suits offer a way to mobilize the interests of numerous victims who have suffered small individual losses. They are brought by one victim on behalf of the others, seeking penalties that can justify the cost of the action. The courts have resisted class-action suits, but perhaps legislation authorizing them would be appropriate.

3. Sound and Dubious "Reforms"

Several other ways to supplement antitrust have been noted, especially in Chapters 5 and 7. Trade barriers could be cut. This would affect several industries, but it is not a promising or general solution. Patents could be revised. This would affect a rather wide set of industries, but prospects for it are even less favorable. Nor would it abate the cases of settled market structure already created under patents.

Finally, there are several "reforms" that seem more likely to be *harmful* than efficient.

Abolition. This is occasionally suggested, on grounds that antitrust is (1) too powerful and harmful, or, at the other extreme, (2) weak and ineffectual, merely a tool of corporate power. Sheer abolition, with no

---

[2]For extensive discussion of possible changes in the trebling of damages, see Lawrence J. White, ed., *Private Antitrust Litigation* (Cambridge, Mass.: MIT Press, 1988). This book reports on a large-scale study that was launched in the expectation of finding substantial wastes from private antitrust suits. In fact, the possible wastes were found to be minor, and the case for reducing treble damages did not emerge as strong.

alternative, would surely lead to far more collusion and concentration, plus possibly rather more flexibility in structure. Until other alternatives have been more fully tried, simple abolition seems extreme and crude.

Performance Criteria. It is urged occasionally that antitrust act only where performance is poor, rather than treat market structure and behavior directly. Thus, price fixing and monopoly would be treated only if performance could be shown to have been hurt. Chapter 4 helps us see that this proposal simply shifts the burden of proof and alters its content. Since performance data are hard to interpret and are controlled by the firms themselves, this proposal would bring antitrust nearly to a standstill and increase the load on the judiciary. In fact, it is precisely because performance questions have seeped into most Section 2 actions that they have slowed to a crawl and become nearly unmanageable in court. To increase their role would paralyze antitrust policy behind a facade of economic rationality. Performance is already influential in policy, perhaps *too* influential in diverting attention from the existence and costs of market power.

More Consent Decrees. Compromises do get half-loaves of remedy while sparing agency resources for other uses. Greater use of them could spread antitrust treatments further. Yet consent decrees have drawbacks (noted in Chapter 5) that caution against a shift toward them. *First,* they are often ineffective. They are routinely ignored after a few years by the firm, courts, and the agencies themselves. Soon after a case is settled, the staff experts on it are gone or preoccupied elsewhere, so that a threat to reopen the case is often empty. Practices change to soften the decree's limits.

Second, they stifle private treble-damage suits. No conviction is obtained, so private suits must start from scratch. They are also hobbled by the fact that the agency has not pressed for a conviction. Therefore, a decree often throws away the one tool for treating the problem. *Third,* a decree immunizes. It legitimizes the situation so that further action is presumed to be inappropriate for at least a number of years or decades. *Fourth,* it leaves policy unresolved (as in conglomerate mergers in 1971). Precedential multipliers are not applied.

Antitrust reform is a popular pastime, but it contains more hazards and illusions than is usually realized. Some reforms are clearly unwise, no matter how one appraises the present effectiveness of antitrust. Others are surely needed but are unlikely to occur. Still others are untried and speculative. Devising optimal antitrust is a test of analytical skill, ingenuity, and sophistication. One can expect the topic to persist unresolved for the next several decades, at least.

QUESTIONS FOR REVIEW

1. "Antitrust only hardens dominant positions. Therefore, it should be abolished." True?
2. "The effects of U.S. antitrust policy have long been pretty well known." True?
3. "The agencies win the remedies, while the firms win the decisions." True?
4. "British antitrust policies are similar to U.S. policies in kind but far weaker in degree." True?
5. "Private antitrust suits have not appreciably affected many of the leading dominant firms." True?
6. What effects do you think that U.S. antitrust policies have had on market structures?
7. What incentives of Section 2 policy most need correcting? How could it be done?

P·A·R·T T·H·R·E·E   **UTILITY
                         DE-REGULATION
                         AND REGULATION**

C·H·A·P·T·E·R   12   The De-Regulation
of Markets

The years 1975–85 were a major period of de-regulation in the United States. A variety of controls were removed from a number of industries, including airlines, railroads, intercity buses, natural gas, long-distance telephone service and some local telephone services, cable television services, wholesale electricity supply, and various financial markets. The actions have often been dramatic, and their results have often been spectacular and controversial.[1]

To many mainstream economists, the changes have merely been sensible adaptations to new industrial conditions. To many conservatives in the Reagan administration, de-regulation was, instead, more of a crusade, designed to free markets from the dead hand of government controls. As the 1990s begin, the debates continue and the boundaries of regulation are still shifting, with possible changes in airline policies and the likely re-regulation of cable television.

De-regulation fits between antitrust and classic utility regulation, because it is the transition from regulation to effective competition. The

---

[1]The de-regulatory experiments since 1975 have bred a lively literature. General references include Leonard W. Weiss and Michael W. Klass, *Deregulation: What Really Happened* (Boston: Little, Brown, 1987); Almarin Phillips, ed., *Promoting Competition in Regulated Markets* (Washington, D.C.: Brookings Institution, 1975); Robert E. Litan and William D. Nordhaus, *Reforming Federal Regulation* (New Haven, Conn.: Yale University Press, 1983); and Stephen Breyer, *Regulation and Its Reform* (Cambridge, Mass.: Harvard Univ. Press, 1982). See also Alfred E. Kahn, *The Economics of Regulation,* vols. 1 and 2 (New York: John Wiley & Sons, 1971; Cambridge, Mass.: MIT Press, 1988); Bruce Owen and Ronald Braeutigam, *The Regulation Game* (Cambridge, Mass.: Ballinger, 1978); and Murray Weidenbaum, *The Benefits of Deregulation* (St. Louis: Center for Study of American Business, Washington University, 1987).

standard patterns of regulation itself are covered in the next two chapters. In this chapter, we will see what de-regulation involves and then study several cases of actual de-regulation.

At this point, the student needs to know only that utility regulation involves mainly (1) the franchising of a single natural-monopoly supplier and (2) the setting of limits on that monopoly firm's prices in order to prevent monopoly abuses. De-regulation means the removal of both the franchise and the controls on prices. Such de-regulation can successfully occur *if* the technology has evolved toward "natural competition" so that there is enough room for competition (recall Chapters 2 and 3). Ideally, the minimum efficient scale is less than one fifth of the total market size so that at least five comparable rivals can compete vigorously. Competition can then be let in to enforce the competitive results, and regulation can be removed.

A second kind of de-regulation can also occur in oligopoly markets that have *not* been natural monopolies. In a number of such industries (e.g., airline, banking, railroads, and buses, before the 1970s), competition has been blocked, on the rationale that competition would be destructive. Removing those regulatory barriers can introduce competition easily, because the regulation of prices has previously been minor and the natural-competition basis for effective competition already exists. If enough new firms come in and mergers are restrained, then competition becomes spontaneously effective.

In fact, both problems are part of one unified challenge in seeking effective de-regulation: to replace government controls with fully effective competition. That requires large changes, moving from (1) full monopoly down through (2) single-firm dominance *and* then down through (3) tight oligopoly so as to reach (4) fully effective competition. More broadly, effective de-regulation involves two policy goals: reducing the dominant firm to below 50 percent of the market while at least four other strong rivals emerge, and installing protections against mergers or other methods for regaining dominance. De-regulation must occur, *and* the effective competition must be maintained against the pressures to backslide toward renewed monopoly power.

No de-regulation of a complete monopoly has yet accomplished this full change. Most de-regulations so far have been "easy" cases that merely opened up an officially protected oligopoly group (such as in the airlines and railroad industries). As a result, many economists regard the de-regulation of classic regulated monopolies as a complex, difficult process.

Chicago-UCLA analysts are more optimistic. They are satisfied even if the former monopolist remains as a highly dominant firm. In their view, no monopoly effects will occur as long as there is some competition, plus open entry. The main task is to remove the state's propping up of monopoly so that competitive forces can prevail.

I. GENERAL PROBLEMS

The mainstream economic analysis of issues covered in Chapters 2, 3, 5, and 10 applies here as fully as it does to antitrust issues. Market shares, entry, and strategic pricing are all important. Moreover, there are usually conditions of bottleneck controls lingering from the previous regulated-monopoly situation. Therefore, de-regulation usually needs to be managed carefully, in a cautious sequence, rather than rushed with a hasty removal of constraints, before effective competition is established.[2]

1. Guidelines for Effective De-Regulation

Mainstream analysis suggests four guidelines for effective de-regulation.

1. Market Share below 50 Percent. As Chapters 2, 5 and 10 noted, market dominance usually prevents effective competition. Accordingly, the dominant firm's market share must usually sink below 50 percent, and there must be at least four comparably strong competitors, before regulation can be removed safely. Otherwise, the dominant firm can employ selective pricing and its continuing advantages as the established firm so as to suppress the emergence of comparable rivals.

Chicago-UCLA analysis permits a higher degree of dominance, possibly with market shares over 75 percent, as long as there are no market imperfections and entry is free.

2. Remove Bottleneck Controls. Competition cannot survive independently if there are bottleneck controls by which one or several firms can exclude others or overcharge them for access to the market. Such bottlenecks must either be removed or placed in outside hands, or regulation must remain in order to assure that access is kept open and that the prices for access are fair. Once effective competition has evolved or is imminent, then regulatory controls on the formerly dominant firm can be withdrawn. Implicit in this guideline is the third guideline.

3. Avoid Premature De-Regulation. Regulatory controls are to be removed *after* effective competition is established. Premature de-regulation is the cardinal error of de-regulation.

After de-regulation, the market is often still a tight oligopoly, which can easily move back to dominance. Therefore, there is a need for strict antitrust policies.

---

[2]See Harry M. Trebing, ed., *New Regulatory and Management Strategies in a Changing Market Environment* (East Lansing, Mich.: Institute of Public Utilities, Michigan State University, 1987).

4. Strict Antitrust. Mainstream analysis indicates that mergers must be carefully screened and selective pricing tactics must be limited, so as to prevent a reversion to dominance. Entry barriers need to be kept low. That would fit the established, pre-1980 lines of U.S. antitrust policies. Chicago-UCLA analysts would instead tolerate these conditions and tactics.

2. De-Regulating Monopoly

The transition from complete monopoly to effective competition is particularly difficult and has, in fact, not yet been fully completed in any industry. The monopoly has a full set of complex prices, it knows its evolving technology thoroughly, and it is well situated to exploit every advantage to retain its monopoly as best it can. Its prospective monopoly profits may have been capitalized into the market price of its common stock, giving it added pressure to retain as much dominance as possible so as to avoid a fall in that price. Its customers regard it as *the* supplier; for example, AT&T is often regarded as *the* phone company. The incumbent firm is also usually politically powerful and astute from its many decades of operating in the policy setting.

Accordingly, the de-regulation of a utility monopoly faces severe problems of access to information, strategic advantages, and political influence. The former monopoly firm will demand that full de-regulation occur immediately. However, premature de-regulation would merely permit the firm to retain its dominance. Even if one or several small rivals do get established, they will tend to seek survival with the dominant firm. To protect themselves, these little rivals will favor policies that put any further entrants at a disadvantage.

If premature de-regulation does occur, then the market may be frozen into a very lopsided tight oligopoly, containing a heavily dominant firm and a few weak rivals. Competition will exist, but it is likely to be unbalanced and ineffective. The dominant firm's complex strategic pricing may keep its small rivals passive and prevent newcomers from entering. Once the regulatory constraints are removed, it is usually extremely difficult to apply them again in the fact of the firms' resistance.

3. Specific Issues under De-Regulation

Five issues usually complicate the progress of de-regulation, as follows.

Price Discrimination. The regulated monopoly firm has been using price discrimination to maximize its profits, and it will want to expand its discrimination so as to meet and beat the new competitors. Those entrants will naturally choose to focus on the most lucrative services, where the price-cost ratios are highest. The process creates complex price discrimination and strategic actions, sometimes straying over into predatory actions, as analyzed in Chapter 10.

The newcomers will complain that they are being hit by predatory pricing, while the dominant firm will demand the right to compete fully.[3] Is competition effective, or is selective pricing endangering the little rivals and entrants?

The criteria outlined in Chapter 10 are the basis for assessing these claims. When selective pricing is done systematically by a dominant firm, it is usually anticompetitive; but done flexibly by firms with small market shares, it is usually procompetitive. Therefore, dominant firms need to avoid deep selective price cutting until their market shares go below 50 percent and comparably strong rivals have developed.

Relying on Antitrust Agencies. Under de-regulation, the industry is the responsibility of the antitrust agencies, to deal with selective pricing, mergers, collusion, and the other problems covered in Part II. Unfortunately, the agencies are often unequal to the task, particularly during the initial years.

The de-regulated sector is usually unfamiliar to the agencies, and the antitrust treatment is weakest precisely during the early period when it is most critical. De-regulation immediately stirs problems of selective pricing and mergers (as in the airline industry during 1984–88), but the agencies typically are unprepared to treat them adequately.

Indeed, dominant-firm situations are the agencies' weak spot. The policy tools are narrow. The agencies can only bring lawsuits to stop specific actions or conditions. They cannot exercise continuing formal or informal controls over complex conditions.

Moreover, since 1980, Reagan and Bush officials have pursued minimal antitrust policies and simply applied a moratorium on Section 2 cases. Even during its stricter periods, antitrust policy had only scant resources compared to its large responsibilities. Adding major de-regulated sectors has stretched those resources further, at a time when enforcement choices are narrow. Antitrust is no longer a steady policy to rely on.

Effects on High Regulation-Induced Costs. Because regulation tends to foster higher costs, as Chapter 14 will explain, de-regulation can cause

---

[3]The firm will assert that it is merely following Ramsey pricing, in which price-cost patterns fit the inverse-elasticity rule. Under certain conditions, that pattern can provide for efficient allocation. But the assumptions are narrow, and there are important exceptions. See William J. Baumol, John C. Panzar, and Robert D. Willig, *Contestable Markets and the Theory of Industrial Structure* (San Diego: Harcourt Brace Jovanovich, 1982). The point is covered in the next two chapters.

shocks when new competitors are leaner and tougher. Under regulation, cost inflation takes three main forms: (1) more capital is used, (2) more current inputs are used (labor, materials, and the like), and (3) the wages paid to labor are higher. De-regulation and competition, therefore, put the existing firms under severe pressure to cut costs, both by trimming employees and other inputs, and by forcing wages down for those workers who remain. Often, too, the services must be revised, to offer cheaper, lower-quality services.

For example, regulation induced airlines to have too many planes and workers, with pilots working easy schedules at salaries over $130,000, providing fancy service at high prices. Competition since 1978 forced cuts in pay, employment, and equipment, and services became more diversified toward cheaper, no-frills versions. The pre-1984 Bell System displayed the same patterns, especially in its Western Electric equipment factories. Because most of those factories could not meet new efficient competition, they have been closed down.

The shock of competition has often been severe, causing sharp adjustments, but they are an appropriate corrective to the X-inefficiency that regulation induces. They give added force to the need to get effective competition established before regulation is removed. Otherwise, the X-inefficiency may continue.

The Threat to Small-Town Service. De-regulation commonly stirs complaints that it will cause service to small-town users to close down. For instance, when the telephone, bus, truck, railroad, and airline industries were de-regulated, there were claims in each case that small-town services would disappear.

The incumbent sellers contend that they have been "cross-subsidizing" the costly small-town services with profits from their profitable, high-density main routes. New competition will fasten upon the profitable denser routes, they say, and skim that cream, so that the unprofitable small-town routes will either have to be closed down or priced much higher. Thus is competition portrayed as a threat to the Jeffersonian values of a democratic small-town America. In political terms, the thousands of smaller towns in rural regions throughout the country that feel threatened by de-regulation often wield disproportionate influence in elections and legislatures.

The danger has some analytical validity. As shown in simplified form in Figure 12–1, the average cost of service may decline with the size of the route. Thus, on high-density truck and telephone routes, average costs per unit are often much lower than on the sparsely used peripheral routes to (and among) small towns out in the countryside.

Suppose that the price per unit of service is kept largely uniform in order to be "fair," as is illustrated by price A in Figure 12–1. That has often been done simply to avoid accusations of favoring one group of

**Figure 12–1   Cross-Subsidizing between High-Volume
and Low-Volume Routes**

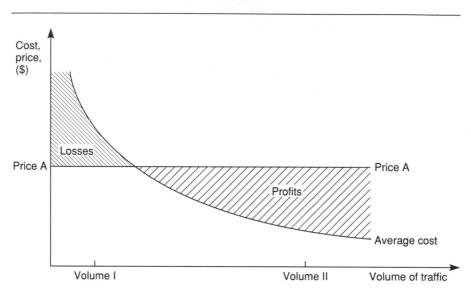

customers over others. Then big losses will occur on small routes (volume I), and big profits will be gained on the high-traffic routes (volume II). If all routes are part of a monopolist's single system, then a pooling of the losses and profits can maintain the whole system at zero excess profits while assuring "universal" service. Letting competition enter the dense markets will take away the profits that maintain the whole system's "integrity." Small-volume routes will be closed, or else prices for them will have to be raised prohibitively high to cover the true costs, as shown in Figure 12–1.

This problem of vulnerable cross-subsidization has been used to resist de-regulation in virtually every instance so far. Often, the services to small towns do dry up, unless regulators forbid abandonment, as was done with railroads from the 1930s to the 1970s.

Yet the real threat is frequently much smaller than is claimed. The costs of small-town service may not be as high as the monopolists assert and often are debatable because of joint and overhead costs. Additionally, many times, the "rural" groups turn out to be well-to-do gentry living in affluent suburbs rather than poor farmers or artisans.

Moreover, the technology of supply often adjusts to maintain small-town service at lower costs and prices. In air travel, for example, the main airlines have cut back their flights by full-size jet aircraft to smaller airports, but smaller "commuter" planes have emerged to take their place on many thin routes, at costs lower than those for partly filled large jets. Therefore, the actual costs have been much lower for small-town traffic than the curve in Figure 12–1 suggests. Much the same may be possible in other industries.

Where small-town service does involve some financial losses, they may be measurable and compensable by direct public payments. Those payments will probably be small compared to the benefits of X-efficiency and innovation that competition will deliver.

The issues are not simple, but experience so far suggests that this supposed danger is frequently an illusion invoked by incumbent firms to defend their monopolies.

The best regulatory approach has two parts. The first carries out independent studies of the actual costs on thin routes, covering alternative technologies where possible. (Do not rely on the monopolist's cost estimates, for they reflect not only self-interest but also narrow technological choices based on a monopoly-oriented system.) The second part weighs any provable small-route losses against the benefits competition is likely to provide. Small losses in a few locales can often be covered in order to realize the large gains from competition throughout the industry.

Diversifying. As de-regulation proceeds, firms often make ambitious moves to diversify, even into markets wholly unrelated to the original utility services. Regulators often resist this, for several important reasons. First, diversification can divert managerial attention and commitment from the established activities. Also, it adds financial risks to the whole enterprise and may cause the firm's cost of capital to rise. In addition, if a financial crisis does occur, it may undercut the firm's ability to meet its utility responsibilities. This problem is aggravated if the pooling of finances between the old and new activities makes it hard for the regulators to assess the firm's actual financial soundness in its utility operations. Moreover, the firm may be able to use its market power in the utility lines so as to gain unfair advantages in the new lines. Prudent regulators therefore tend to resist all diversifying.

The correct criterion, though, is more specific, following directly on the earlier analysis of dominant firms. *Only dominant firms may raise problems by diversifying. Fully competitive firms can be left free to diversify as they choose.* Diversifying by dominant firms may indeed endanger the basic service responsibility and frustrate regulation, as well as threaten effective competition in the new markets. Regulators may therefore properly require that risky, unrelated lines not be added by a dominant firm and that the finances of utility and other operations be kept separate. As in other matters, the firm will gain freedom from these limits only when it loses its dominance.

Summary. Altogether, de-regulation is not the quick, easy solution that is often claimed. It poses sophisticated issues in judging when competition is effective so that regulation can safely be removed. One must assess skeptically: (1) the room for competition, (2) the degree of actual competition, (3) the role of selective pricing, (4) the effects on high costs, (5) the effectiveness of antitrust agencies, (6) the impacts on small towns, and (7) the effects of diversifying by the dominant firms into other markets.

All this occurs amid controversy and partisan claims. De-regulation is a long, complex process, requiring caution, skill and the avoidance of hasty actions.

II. CASE STUDIES OF DE-REGULATION

Six brief case studies follow: airlines, railroads, trucking, intercity buses, bulk electricity supply, and telephone service. The lessons are often tentative, because the de-regulation is not yet complete.

1. Airlines

The industry's history and de-regulation were summarized in Section V of Chapter 3.[4] Here, only several features of de-regulation need to be noted.

The industry has been naturally competitive throughout its life, so that competition could have been effective whenever the Civil Aeronautics Board was removed. The CAB acted mainly to boost airline growth, rather than restrain airline actions. It served the airlines' interests, freezing a monopolistic structure for nearly 40 years. It restrained airline fares only mildly at best. And the quasi-regulation tended to foster large rises in costs, by diverting competition to service quality.

Estimates of the excess costs are summarized in Table 12–1. In addition, Keeler showed that fares ranged from 20 to 80 percent over long-run marginal costs on a range of routes. Therefore, de-regulation was

---

[4]See Richard E. Caves, *Air Transport and Its Regulators* (Cambridge, Mass.: Harvard Univ. Press, 1962); William A. Jordan, *Airline Regulation in America: Effects and Imperfections* (Baltimore: The Johns Hopkins Press, 1970); Elizabeth E. Bailey, David R. Graham, and Daniel P. Kaplan, *Deregulating the Airlines* (Cambridge, Mass.: MIT Press, 1985); Alfred E. Kahn, "Surprises of Airline Deregulation," *American Economic Review* 78 (May 1988), pp. 316–22; Melvin A. Brenner, "Airline Deregulation—A Case Study in Public Policy Failure," *Transportation Law Journal* 16, no. 2 (1988), pp. 179–228, and his "Rejoinder to Comments by Alfred Kahn," *Transportation Law Journal* 16, no. 2 (1988) pp. 253–62; and "The Big Trouble with Air Travel," *Consumer Reports*, June 1988, pp. 362–67.

Table 12–1   Estimates of the Economic Impact of Civil Aeronautics Board Regulation

Author	Estimate Relates to	Estimated Effect of Regulation on Prices	Estimated Welfare Loss from Regulation	
			Total	As a Percent of Revenue
Jordan	1960s	30% higher	$1.5 billion	20%
Douglas and Miller	1969	4% to 6% higher	$0.3 billion	4
Keeler	1974	30% to 50% higher	$1 billion to $3 billion	10 to 30

Sources: William A. Jordan, *Airline Regulation in America: Effects and Imperfections* (Baltimore: The John Hopkins Press, 1970); George Douglas and James C. Miller III, *Economic Regulation of Domestic Air Transport* (Washington, D.C.: Brookings Institution, 1974); and Theodore E. Keeler, *Domestic Trunk Airline Regulation: An Economic Evaluation,* part of *A Framework for Regulation,* U.S. Senate Government Operations Committee (Washington, D.C.: U.S. Government Printing Office, 1978).

likely to reduce costs substantially, as well as force prices down closer to costs.

De-regulation was therefore decidedly overdue when it finally occurred during 1977–81. It did cut costs and force costs and prices down during the 1978–83 period when the new competition was sharpest. New airlines were numerous and forceful, and all carriers switched flexibly among routes. Price cutting was aggressive, and new, maverick airlines undercut much of the established leaders' fare structures.

Yet the industry contains an enormous variety of conditions, submarkets, and imperfections. Major customer groups have inelastic demand; business passengers, in particular, have compelling travel needs and are on expense accounts. Major airports have been congested so that new entry to them has been blocked. All maverick lines are now gone or absorbed into the leading airlines.

Therefore, de-regulation has had some classic effects, but it has also encountered the classic problems. Consider them now, in turn.

Costs have been directly affected as X-inefficiency has come under pressure. The leading airlines (United, American, etc.) responded by trimming staff and by putting new employees on lower pay scales. To some extent, de-regulation provided an occasion for attacking union protections.

The cost-cutting process has not been completed, however. In the mid-1980s, Continental Airlines attained the lowest costs by declaring bankruptcy, dropping its union contract, and rehiring workers at much lower rates of pay. It then set lower fares, which put pressure on the other airlines to cut their costs. But in 1988, Continental shifted explicitly to a higher-yield pricing basis, and so the pressure for cost cutting was removed. There are still major differences among the airlines' costs, and substantial X-inefficiency in some.

Price discrimination is rampant; much of it is procompetitive, but much of it is not. The fare structure since 1984 has settled into rigid patterns which target most business travelers for higher fares (recall Chapter 3, Section V). Generally, fares on routes to hub cities with one or two dominant airlines have been 20 to 30 percent above other fares. Some instances of predatory pricing have also occurred, and any new entrants would have to face the probability of drastic, selective fare cuts by the established airlines.

Therefore, strategic price discrimination has occurred as predicted, and it reduces competition in major parts of the industry. There appears little likelihood that it will be moderated.

Antitrust agencies did little to restrain the pricing or the 1985–88 mergers. The CAB's expert resources were dispersed, and the agencies had neither the resources nor the authority to replace them. There were some attempts to resist two of the mergers, but they were ineffective. There is virtually no antitrust role in studying or affecting the pricing strategies.

Local service has not been drastically reduced in general, and some smaller cities now have improved service. However, many cities have less service than before, and much of the small-city service is now by small commuter airplanes, which give a lower quality of ride (noise, bumpiness, less safety, no in-flight meals, etc.). Also, fares on thin routes tend to be substantially higher than before.

In 1990, there was intense controversy about airline performance and possible re-regulation. Yet the system is now hardened into place, and no easy ways exist to restore the free-wheeling 1978–84 competition. Hub dominance is set, fare structures are solid, and no new entry is in sight. De-regulation was a clear success for about six years, and then the predictable reconcentrating efforts were able to prevail. The industry therefore illustrates clearly the need not only to de-regulate but also to block the later pressures to restore monopoly power.

2. Railroads

Railroads were the first industry put under regulation, when the Interstate Commerce Commission (ICC) was created in 1888. In 1980, that long-running, often ineffective regulatory experiment was largely ended.

The de-regulation was long overdue in most parts of the country, because competition with trucks, buses, and airplanes had eliminated much of the railroads' power. Railroads had slipped from being the dominant form of transport in the 1880s, to facing road competition after 1920, to being merely a secondary carrier for most traffic. To assess railroads and their de-regulation, one approaches them as just one part of the transport sector.

Basic Economic Issues in Transport.[5] Each mode has a network of routes among points. Traffic includes goods and passengers, taking infinite varieties of trips under varying conditions of speed, size of load, safety, and so forth. As markets shift and technology alters, the networks and their traffic will evolve. From the old canals, rivers, and highways of 1800–40, through the Railway Age of 1840–90, to the mixed sector of the present day, there have been major shifts with large impacts on the country. The social objective is the optimal mix and format of transport at each point of time.

The social objective might be achieved by open competition, or instead, competition may be so unstable that regulation must intercede to guide pricing and allocation.

Natural Monopoly. There are many pockets of natural monopoly and areas of "natural oligopoly," but most of the sector is naturally competitive. Competition can occur between modes (for example, trucks competing against railroads, and airlines against buses), as well as among firms within each mode. The main natural-monopoly parts are in some western railroads in handling certain commodities. In these cases, there is only one railroad, and trucks cannot match the low costs of large-volume rail loads. Otherwise, there are several or more direct competitors in almost all transport submarkets.

Costs differ among the modes, because technology differs. Railroads have large costs for fixed patterns of roadbed. Trucks have larger elements of variable costs, with great flexibility in routes. Cost structures are hard to unravel, but the basic patterns fit common sense. Costs for freight favor trains for high-bulk, large-scale, long-haul cargo going more than 200 miles at intermediate speeds. Trucks do best at moving high-value goods in small quantities for short hauls with diverse destinations. Water carriers are superior for slow, large-scale, high-bulk

---

[5]Good sources on the economic issues include John R. Meyer, Merton J. Peck, John Stenason, and Charles Zwick, *The Economics of Competition in the Transportation Industries* (Cambridge, Mass.: Harvard Univ. Press, 1959); National Bureau of Economic Research, *Transportation Economics* New York: Columbia University Press, 1965); chapters 2–4 in Almarin Phillips, ed., *Promoting Competition in Regulated Markets* (Washington, D.C.: Brookings Institution, 1975); James T. Kneafsey, *Transportation Economic Analysis* (Cambridge, Mass.: Ballinger, 1975); Theodore E. Keeler, *Railroads, Freight and Public Policy* (Washington, D.C.: Brookings Institution, 1983); Ann F. Friedlaender and Richard H. Spady, *Freight Transport Regulation: Equity, Efficiency and Competition in the Rail and Trucking Industries* (Cambridge, Mass.: MIT PRess, 1981); and Stephen Glaister, *Fundamentals of Transport Economics* (New York: St. Martin's Press, 1981).

items along certain routes. Airline costs favor rapid, long-distance carriage of high-value goods to diverse destinations. In many cases, a shipment needs to go by more than one mode (such as some rail cargo that is delivered by truck to the final destination).

Each mode is superior for certain conditions of trip length, speed, type of cargo, and geography. The optimal transport mix will fit these advantages. It will usually involve a division of traffic among modes and many firms, rather than a natural monopoly of one firm in one mode.

Price Discrimination. Some degree of price discrimination is common in the sector, for three main reasons. First, shippers vary in demand elasticities. Second, some modes have high overhead costs, which leave room for variety in cost allocation. Railroad-track costs have been the prime example of this, for the same track will carry both freight and passenger trains under differing degrees of congestion. Third, these are networks, with shared costs among many routes. This leaves still more room for price discrimination.

In railroads during 1850–1920, the scope for such discrimination was very large on many routes. The rise of trucks, buses, and airlines greatly reduced it.

Unequal Subsidies. If the net subsidies are unequal among modes, then prices based on the private costs will bias traffic choices away from the unsubsidized mode. That has been the railroad's complaint since the 1920s: that the other modes get subsidies and tax privileges. There are investment and operating subsidies for some modes more than for others. Truckers reply that fuel taxes and other charges offset their seeming advantages.

Shrinkage. Railways have had to cope with shrinking demand since the 1930s in the eastern part of the country. The problem was caused by a combination of natural limits on the rate of depletion of railway capital, external limits on the railroads' efforts to drop services and close down routes, and poor management. During the shrinkage to an efficient network, financial deficits were appropriate. They put many eastern and midwestern railroads into bankruptcy, and they continue under the Amtrak and Conrail systems created in 1969–71. The ICC's pricing policies during 1930–70 permitted the railroads to set higher, discriminatory rates. This improved the short-run finances but made the declines in traffic even sharper.

The Interstate Commerce Commission. Early railroad growth in the United States during 1830–80 was by private ventures, with little planning and much turbulence. In the West, there was much monopoly along major lines; in the East, powerful competition was common among two or more railroads along most routes.

As the network grew toward maturity in the 1880s, the ICC was established to "regulate" it. Several forces created the ICC. One was Granger resistance by the Granger movement to western railroad monopoly. Another was the desire of eastern railroads to stop mutual rate-cutting competition.[6] The ICC was thus born of uncertain parentage.

The Supreme Court soon emasculated its powers to put ceilings on rates. More than 20 years passed before Congress gave the ICC authority to get data and to set effective ceilings on prices. During this interval, the ICC did help to keep rates up against railroad price cutters. However, not before 1906–10 did the ICC possess more than shadow powers to *reduce* railroad rates. Therefore, when railroads were most powerful, regulation was a mere pretense or even a prop for railroad cartels. When the need for strict regulation had passed, by the 1920s, it began.

World War I brought an interval of government operation of the railroads. Then railway regulation was markedly tightened with the Transportation Act of 1920, which gave the commission new authority over service, securities, and rates.

Weaker railroads were to be assisted. They were now encouraged to pool their resources or even merge. During 1921–29, the ICC prepared a comprehensive plan for consolidating stronger and weaker railroads in a system of about 20 competing railroads. However, the stronger systems, instead, merged with the better of the weak systems, leaving the main problem unsolved.

The Great Depression hit the railroads hard. From 1929 to 1932, gross revenues were cut in half. World War II restored traffic for a while, but the long-term malaise persisted, and the new interstate highway system—mostly complete by 1965—plus the spread of airline travel, further eroded the position of most eastern railroads.

Regulation was extended in 1935 to trucking, airlines, and waterways. The methods were conventional, but the motivation was different: to contain competition, not constrain monopoly. Also, the rate bureaus, which had long served as private railroad cartels, were legalized in 1948 by the Reed-Bullwinkle Act.[7]

The "railroad problem" worsened during 1945–70, as trucking and airlines grew rapidly. The ICC was slow to let beleaguered railroads cut prices toward marginal cost in order to meet competition.

---

[6]See P. W. MacAvoy, *The Economic Effects of Regulation: The Trunk-Line Railroad Cartels and the Interstate Commerce Commission before 1900* (Cambridge, Mass.: MIT Press, 1965); Gabriel Kolko, *Railroads and Regulation* (Princeton, N.J.: Princeton University Press, 1965); and Keeler, *Railroads*.

[7]Rate bureaus were regional cartels run by the railroads and their larger customers. Any proposals to change railroad rates went through a process of consensus in these bureaus. In practice, the bureaus' recommended rates were mostly rubber-stamped by the ICC.

Table 12–2   Alternate Estimates of the Loss Caused by ICC Regulation of U.S. Railroads

Author	Estimate Relates to	Estimated Welfare Loss (current $)	Welfare Loss as a Percent of Freight Revenue
Harbeson	1963	$1.1 billion to $2.9 billion	12% to 32%
Friedlaender	1969	$2.7 billion to $4.2 billion	24% to 36%
Boyer	1963	$125 million	1.37%
Levin	1972	$53 million to $135 million	0.3% to 0.8%

Sources: Kenneth D. Boyer, "Minimum Rate Regulation, Modal Split Sensitivities, and the Railroad Problem," *Journal of Political Economy* 85 (June 1977), pp. 493–512; Anne F. Friedlaender, "The Social Costs of Regulating the Railroads," *American Economic Review* 61 (May 1971), pp. 226–34; Robert W. Harbeson, "Towards Better Resource Allocation in Transport." *Journal of Law and Economics* 12 (October 1969), pp. 321–38; and Richard C. Levin, "Allocation in Surface Freight Transportation: Does Rate Regulation Matter?" *Bell Journal of Economics,* (Spring 1978), pp. 18–45.

By 1959, it was clear the de-regulation of railroad prices was in order for much or all of the railroad sector. Yet the ICC resisted such a change; it shifted its policies toward mergers after 1958, to permit almost all railroad mergers, ignoring their possible anticompetitive effects.

By the 1970s, the ICC proved to be incapable of applying an efficient set of controls.[8] It had blocked competitive pricing but permitted a number of anticompetitive mergers. It cost about $70 million per year in direct expenses. It also imposed various economic costs of inefficiency in transportation. Estimates of this burden are summarized in Table 12–2; they ranged as high as $4 billion per year in the 1960s.

By 1975, the ICC's costly, obstructive role was clear and railroads were eager to compete, so de-regulation finally began. The Railroad Revitalization and Regulatory Reform Act of 1976 allowed greater freedom in pricing, along with financial support, easier merger approvals, and easier dropping of unprofitable services. Railroads could change prices sharply on routes where they did not have "dominant" market positions. This freedom turned out to be minor, because competition limited it when dominance was absent.

---

[8]In contrast, de-regulated Canadian railroads have been much more efficient. See Douglas W. Caves, Laurits R. Christensen, and Joseph R. Swanson, "Economic Performance in Regulated and Unregulated Environments: A comparison of U.S. and Canadian Railroads," *Quarterly Journal of Economics* 96 (November 1981), pp. 559–81.

The Staggers Rail Act of 1980 greatly widened the railroads' degree of choices in pricing and dropping services. Railroads quickly adjusted many prices and services, and, by 1984, the de-regulation process was largely complete. Efficiency and profits both rose markedly, with a greater focus on such specialized hauls as coal, ores, and chemicals.[9] The ICC also permitted major mergers to occur. Competition with trucking and barges in most areas appears strong enough to prevent important abuses.

Altogether, railroad de-regulation has succeeded rapidly because (1) competition was already vigorous in most markets and (2) the railroads welcomed it, as the only way to regain profitability.

3. Trucking

Trucking is a classic instance of a naturally competitive market. Scale economies are slight, and free entry can bring in thousands of new competitors. Large nationwide firms are a distinct part of the market, but they are numerous enough to give effective competition to each other.

In 1935, regulation was imposed on trucking, supposedly to help the railroads. It mainly resulted in cartel pricing, restricted competition, and inefficiency. The ICC's regulation of trucking was weak and a morass of bureaucracy. By controlling prices and entry, the ICC created great economic harm.

Entry. Applicants for new operating authority, for alternate routes, and for extensions of existing routes were required to prove that the proposed service was really needed, that the services already available

---

[9]Costs may have fallen by some 23 to 29 percent during the four years after the Staggers Act; see Tenpao Lee, C. Phillip Baumel, and Patricia Harris, "Market Structure, Conduct, and Performance of the Class 1 Railroad Industry." *Transportation Journal* 26 (1987), pp. 54–66.

Savings were estimated at $93 million per year by Kenneth D. Boyer, "The Costs of Price Regulation: Lessons from Railroad Deregulation," *Rand Journal of Economics* 18 (1987), pp. 408–16; Christopher C. Barnekov and Robert A. Taggart, Jr., in "The Costs of Railroad Regulation: A Further Analysis," Working Paper no. 164 (Washington, D.C.: Federal Trade Commission, 1988), estimate the efficiency gains in the billions of dollars.

Perhaps the most optimistic assessment is in Clifford Winston, Thomas M. Corsi, Curtis M. Grimm, and Carol Evans, *The Economic Effects of Surface Freight Deregulation* (Washington, D.C.: Brookings Institution, 1990). They rate the gain from de-regulating railroads and trucks at some $18 billion per year. About $6 billion would be from improved railroad efficiency.

Note that this estimate is well above those by Boyer and others. The assumptions and research methods are controversial. Note also that some gains (including one third of those estimated in trucking) come from reducing employees' wages, rather than just from pure efficiency gains.

were inadequate, and that adequate service could not be provided by carriers already in the field. They were asked to justify their applications in detail: to defend the financing they proposed, the equipment they intended to use, and the schedule they planned to follow. For small concerns, the obstacles created by this procedure were almost insurmountable. Decisions could be delayed for months or years.

Where operating rights were granted, they were strictly limited. Operators were often confined to hauling particular goods between particular points. They were often required to follow circuitous routes, forbidden to serve intermediate points, and denied the right to carry cargo on the return haul.[10]

Pricing. Changes in motor-carrier rates, as with the railroads, were agreed upon in rate bureaus before being proposed to the ICC. Here, the burden of proof was on the carrier who proposed to cut a rate. The Commission's effort was largely to prevent price cutting. It tended to raise prices, by approving the collusive proposed rates.

De-regulation began in 1978 by a reversal of ICC policies, toward permitting some entry and price cutting. The Motor Carrier Act of 1980 greatly increased the scope for competition and entry. Some 18,000 new truckers were granted operating rights. Their total impact was small, but larger firms began competing much more fully. The monopoly value of the old operating certificates vanished almost overnight. Over $100 million in these rights was written off by large trucking firms in 1980.

Much inefficiency stopped quickly, such as the empty hauls resulting from ICC restrictions. Routes and traffic flows improved, and prices rose less than they would have under regulation. Older Teamster pay rates (largely over $30,000 per year) were forced down by the inroads of nonunion truckers and owner-operators. Meanwhile, predictions that service to small towns would shrink turned out to be wrong.[11]

---

[10]In one instance, a carrier operating between New York and Montreal had to detour 200 miles via Reading, Pennsylvania; a carrier operating between the Pacific Northwest and Salt Lake City could carry cargo eastward but not westward. Walter Adams, "The Role of Competition in the Regulated Industries." *American Economic Review* 48, no. 2 (1958), p. 531.

[11]Shipping rates may have fallen over 20 percent after de-regulation; Theodore E. Keeler, "Deregulation and Scale Economies in the U.S. Trucking Industry: An Econometric Extension of the Survivor Principle," *Journal of Law and Economics* (1990), in press. The sharp impacts on the wages of union drivers is shown by Nancy L. Rose, "Labor Rent Sharing and Regulation: Evidence from the Trucking Industry," *Journal of Political Economy* 95 (1987), pp. 1146–78.

See also John S. Ying, "The Inefficiency of Regulating a Competitive Industry: Productivity Gains in Trucking Following Reform," *Review of Economics and Statistics* 72 (May 1990), pp. 191–201, where gains in productivity are estimated at over 15 percent.

As with railroads, de-regulation succeeded because it came long after the basis for effective competition existed. The gains were immediate and large, enough to show that regulation had been a vast economic mistake.

4. Intercity Buses

Bus travel among cities was also regulated by the ICC. Most service was provided by the Greyhound Corporation, but there were a number of other carriers, such as Trailways and Peter Pan. De-regulation swiftly removed ICC controls in 1982, leading to major adjustments.

Greyhound has continued as the one nationally operating system. It has used the new freedom to condense its service coverage toward the larger routes. As in airlines, there has been some filling of thin routes by smaller, regionally based companies, but the coverage of small towns has been reduced.

In 1988, Greyhound bought out Trailways, its one nationally operating competitor. Permission was given by the Department of Transportation on the same grounds—contestability theory—that it used to justify the airline mergers of 1985–88. The theory may be slightly more valid in this case, because there is no critical bottleneck, such as airport capacity, that can keep out new entrants. Moreover, many customers can resort to driving as a substitute for bus travel.

In principle, new bus lines can easily designate new routes and pick-up points. However, that is less true in the major cities, where space in downtown station areas is difficult to acquire. Therefore, the threat of new entry is largely confined to medium- and small-sized cities and towns.

Thus, the industry now has major elements of market dominance, restrained only moderately by small regionally based rivals and threats of new entry. During strikes by Greyhound workers, service has been cut off to many areas.

The net effects of de-regulation have been mixed. The industry is more efficient, from reducing its staffing, wages, and route coverage. Some elements of service quality are improved, while others have been reduced. As of 1990, there is no serious effort under way to restore any important elements of regulation.

5. Bulk Electricity Supply

The electricity industry has three stages: generation in electric plants, transmission from plants to cities, and local distribution to final customers. The first two stages comprise the supply of bulk electricity. From 1880 to about 1975, these stages were regulated under geographical controls, which prevented free choices. Since then, active markets for bulk electricity have developed, and a quiet shift toward de-regulation has occurred.

It is now well recognized that meaningful bulk electricity markets exist in various regions and could be opened up for competition.[12] Many of them are capable of effective competition, with relatively low concentration and a variety of comparable-cost sources of supply. Moreover, there would be a variety of buyers of power, many large enough to exert strong pressure against any tendencies to collusion among the sellers.

However, vertical integration between the transmission and retail-distribution levels currently blocks the emergence of effective competition. The integrated private companies are both (1) the major suppliers of bulk power at the transmission level and (2) powerful rivals of publicly owned systems at the retail level. This permits the private systems to control their retail rivals' access to bulk supplies and to set or manipulate the prices they charge those rivals for their key input. Accordingly, the playing field is not level.

Only if integration were dissolved would bulk supply markets have a chance to become effectively competitive. Some initial steps in that direction may be emerging in areas involving Chicago, Virginia, and New York. Moreover, there have been experiments in bulk supply marketing in the Southwest, and monopsony pressure is being developed by public systems' pooled buying in other regions. However, it will take added changes, such as divestiture, to set the basis for fully effective competition.

Even if that happens, regulators will still need to define markets and retain controls on firms that hold dominant positions. Electric markets may be difficult to define sharply, because power can be transmitted over long distances at graduated cost differences. Therefore, dominance may be hard to identify and control.

It may be necessary, instead, to treat transmission as a core service, dividing it out to be coordinated in a separate nationwide transmission entity, or possibly in several regional systems. Access could then be open and fair, and dominance in bulk supply would cease to be a problem.

Dominance in retail distribution of power would remain, however, and the standard criteria would apply. Price constraints would still be

---

[12]The classic articles are by James E. Meeks, "Concentration in the Electric Power Industry: The Impact of Antitrust Policy," *Columbia Law Review* January 1972, pp. 64–130; and Leonard W. Weiss, "Antitrust in the Electric Power Industry," in *Promoting Competition in Regulated Markets*, ed. Almarin Phillips (Washington, D.C.: Brookings Institution, 1975). See also Paul Joskow and Richard Schmalensee, *Electric Power Markets* (Cambridge, Mass.: MIT Press, 1984).

needed, and service responsibility and obligations to serve peripheral areas would continue to apply. Diversification would be restricted, including takeovers by firms located in other markets.

Since competition in both bulk and retail electricity is still limited, the practical criteria for de-regulating either level have to be imprecise at this point. However, if competition does develop, the basic criteria will provide useful guidelines for the eventual de-regulation.

6. Telephone Service[13]

De-regulation has affected both long-distance service, throughout the United States and within a number of states, and local service in a number of states. Most the changes came during the 1980s, as after-effects of the 1984 divestiture of the Bell Telephone system and as part of the crusade for de-regulation within the FCC and in many states. For decades, the Bell System lived with regulation and largely controlled it. After 1980, it accepted the pressures for divestiture, and its offshoots took advantage of the new de-regulatory climate to help eliminate most regulation.

Chapters 3 and 7 noted some landmarks of AT&T's history and competitive status. Before 1975, it provided local service in most cities and areas and all of the United States' long-distance service. It used its control over access to cities' local networks (often called the *local loop*) to block all efforts at new competition. At that time, it was believed (partly under AT&T persuasion) that the whole country formed one big natural monopoly; competition was alien and destructive.

The situation is illustrated in Figure 12–2. In each city, the many local subscribers were connected by a network and central switching, which connected and carried their calls. Cities were connected by lines or satellite transmission, as shown by the lines between cities in Figure 12–2. New rivals might create intercity transmission networks, but AT&T's refusal to let them connect to their local loops simply blocked

---

[13]Valuable references include Peter Temin, *The Fall of the Bell System* (New York: Cambridge University Press, 1987); Alvin von Auw, *Heritage and Destiny: Reflections on the Bell System in Transition* (New York: Praeger Publishers, 1983); and David S. Evans, ed., *Breaking Up Bell* (New York: North-Holland, 1983). See also Paul W. MacAvoy and Kenneth Robinson, "Winning by Losing: The AT&T Settlement and Its Impact on Telecommunications," *Yale Journal on Regulation* 1 (1983), pp. 1–42; Gerald W. Brock, *The Telecommunications Industry* (Cambridge, Mass.: Harvard Univ. Press, 1981); Manley R. Irwin, "The Telecommunications Industry," a chapter in *The Structure of American Industry,* 8th ed., ed. Walter Adams (New York: Macmillan, 1990); Fred Henck and Bernard Strassburg, *A Slippery Slope: The Long Road to the Breakup of AT&T* (Westport, Conn.: Greenwood Press, 1988); and Peter Huber, *The Geodesic Network,* 1987 Report on Competition in the Telephone Industry (Washington, D.C.: Antitrust Division, U.S. Department of Justice, 1987).

Figure 12–2   Telephone Service: Connections among and within Cities

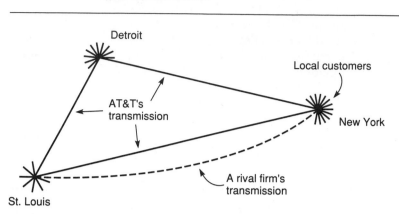

the rivals from operating at all; they could not connect their customers in one city with customers in another city.

In 1968, the FCC finally decided to permit competition by requiring AT&T to interconnect with any new rivals. AT&T resisted, and only after a Supreme Court decision in 1978 did competition seriously begin. AT&T did provide physical access, but it still held advantages from its long-established dominance and widespread customer loyalties. By 1990, AT&T's extreme dominance in most of the long-distance market continued, as shown in Chapter 3. Moreover, the Bell operating companies continued to hold total or virtual monopolies over service in their cities and states.

De-regulation involved two dimensions: (1) intercity traffic, and (2) local switched service within cities. We consider both below.

Long-distance Service. As AT&T's market share has receded to about 70–75 percent, it has responded in classic fashion.[14] Its costs have come under increasing pressure, and significant amounts of the earlier X-inefficiency has been eliminated. AT&T has also adopted increasingly complex and aggressive pricing strategies, offering selective price cuts in order to retain important customers. In addition, AT&T has demanded that the remaining regulatory limits on it be dropped, claiming that competition is now fully effective.

AT&T stresses that the market is largely "contestable," which prevents any possible abuse of its pricing ability. Entry is indeed free in

[14]See William G. Shepherd and Robert J. Graniere, *Market Dominance and Oligopolistic Competition in the Telecommunications Market* (Columbus, Ohio: National Regulatory Research Institute, 1990).

the simple physical sense of switched access to the networks. Entrants can gain access, and customers can switch freely between AT&T and its several rivals.

Yet entry is not near to being contestable in an economic sense, because important imperfections continue to exist. Many AT&T customers retain loyalties and resistance to change, which AT&T's familiar advertising messages reinforce. AT&T has many more access points for customers, which are closer to their premises and therefore cheaper.

These conditions have permitted AT&T to keep its prices generally higher than its rivals, without losing market share rapidly. Selective pricing permits AT&T to keep many major customers without eroding its standard price structure. AT&T has gained high profit rates on long-distance service, while its small rivals have generally absorbed losses or minimal profits. Moreover, few rivals have actually entered. After the second-tier competitors—MCI and US Sprint—there are only a handful of tiny third-tier competitors that own their own capacity. There are scores of tiny firms that merely resell capacity that they lease from these firms.

In short, the market's actual evolution clashes with the contestability predictions. Prices have not been forced down to low profit levels; entrants have been few; and the dominant firm is able to resist competitors by using complex pricing strategies.

Yet the FCC largely eliminated its remaining regulation during 1989. It adopted "price caps," which give AT&T a wide range for adjusting individual prices (they are discussed in Chapter 13 below). Also, regulators in a number of individual states removed their regulation of AT&T's intercity services within their states. These changes were made under strong pressure from AT&T, in hearings and in advertising to the public.

Much of the changes appear to be premature de-regulation, given AT&T's high continuing dominance. The market's evolution during coming years will indicate whether the changes were wise or premature.

Local Service. The local Bell operating companies have also pressed for de-regulation of their local services on the grounds that traditional regulation is ineffective and burdensome (see Chapters 13 and 14). Many states have complied, either dropping all restraints or adopting variations of price caps.[15]

---

[15]At least 11 states had made these changes by June 1990; see National Regulatory Research Institute, *Regulation and Deregulation of Local Telephone Service,* Columbus, Ohio, 1990.

These actions have no basis either in actual or potential competition. The local services are still complex monopolies. Moreover, they have been permitted to diversify into a range of other activities, including equipment supply and other services unrelated to telephone operations. Therefore, they pose the same dangers of mingling monopoly and competitive services that led to the breakup of the Bell System in 1984.

The states are merely relying on trust that the Bell firms will not abuse their positions. Some regulatory supervision is retained so that commissioners could act if prices and profits go too high. Yet profits actually have been ample, leading to nearly a doubling of the Bell firms' stock prices since 1984. Moreover, any attempts at re-regulation will be difficult.

Therefore, these states' de-regulation of local services is decidedly a gamble. Future experience may show whether it was premature or reasonable.

QUESTIONS FOR REVIEW

1. "De-regulation is premature when it removes the regulatory restraints before effective competition is established." True?
2. "Many classic regulated monopolies have been de-regulated to a state of fully effective competition." True?
3. "Price discrimination can impede the emergence of effective competition as de-regulation proceeds." True?
4. "Trucking is a natural monopoly, because only the large fleets can provide full service." True?
5. "De-regulation always harms service to small towns." True?
6. Explain why effective de-regulation is often a long and complex process, rather than a simple sweeping away of controls.
7. What difficult antitrust problems usually arise during and after de-regulation?
8. Make the case that airline competition is not effective in much of the industry. Then make the opposite case, that the competition is fully effective.
9. What instances of bottleneck controls are there in the airlines, electricity, and telephone-service industries? Please explain.
10. What practical policies could be applied to limit the now-de-regulated firm's use of price discrimination to retain its dominance?
11. How have commuter airlines altered the conditions in Figure 12–1 so as to make small-town service more viable?

12. Does trucking provide totally effective competition to railroads so that no railroad can set monopoly prices on its traffic?

13. Discuss how useful the idea of contestability has been in choosing de-regulation policies toward airlines, railroads, and telephone service.

14. How soon would you de-regulate AT&T in long-distance service, and in what specific ways?

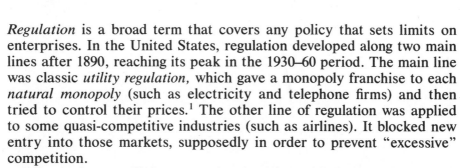

C·H·A·P·T·E·R 13 The Coverage and Methods
of Regulation

Regulation is a broad term that covers any policy that sets limits on enterprises. In the United States, regulation developed along two main lines after 1890, reaching its peak in the 1930–60 period. The main line was classic *utility regulation,* which gave a monopoly franchise to each *natural monopoly* (such as electricity and telephone firms) and then tried to control their prices.[1] The other line of regulation was applied to some quasi-competitive industries (such as airlines). It blocked new entry into those markets, supposedly in order to prevent "excessive" competition.

Like antitrust policies, natural-monopoly regulation has been a peculiarly U.S. experiment. In other countries, most utility sectors have been owned by the government as public enterprises.[2] U.S.–style regulation is economically attractive, especially when it performs well. Private sources voluntarily provide the capital and management under

---

[1] The leading treatises on it have included Alfred E. Kahn, *The Economics of Regulation,* 2 vols. (New York: John Wiley & Sons, 1971; Cambridge, Mass.: MIT Press, 1988); and James C. Bonbright, *Principles of Public Utility Rates* (New York: Columbia University Press, 1961). More recent theoretical treatments include Richard Schmalensee, *The Control of Natural Monopolies* (Lexington, Mass.: Lexington Books, 1979); William W. Sharkey, *The Theory of Natural Monopoly* (New York: Cambridge University Press, 1982); and Daniel Spulber, *Regulation and Markets* (Cambridge, Mass.: MIT Press, 1989).

See also Harry M. Trebing, "The Chicago School versus Public Utility Regulation," *Journal of Economc Issues* 10 (March 1976), pp. 97–126; and Kenneth Nowotny, David B. Smith, and Harry M. Trebing, eds., *Public Utility Regulation: The Economic and Social Control of Industry* (Boston: Kluwer Academic Publishers, 1989).

[2] Yet the 1980s brought a wave of "privatization" of public firms, particularly in Britain. That privatizing is covered in Chapter 15.

incentives to be efficient. The public pays only the modest costs of a supervisory commission, which merely collects data, holds hearings, decides how much profit the utility firm deserves, and sets the maximum prices that can be charged.

Ideally, the method is flexible and complete, giving effective public control at a minimum of public cost and effort. The low average costs of the natural monopoly are achieved. Prices are kept down to those efficient levels of cost, and the amount of investment flowing from private sources is adequate. The firm's technology is progressive, and consumers are protected from being overcharged for service by the monopoly. The regulatory method is applied only to natural monopolies, and it is removed when the technology evolves toward natural competition.

In practice, of course, regulation is less than perfect, and every part of it has always been controversial. It first began in 1888, when the Interstate Commerce Commission was created to regulate the railroads. It spread to other sectors during 1907–40, and it reached its fullest extent during 1950–70, but it came under harsh criticism after 1970. Regulation was sharply reduced after 1975 in the general campaign to remove government controls. The same Chicago-UCLA doctrines that inspired the removal of most antitrust policy in the 1980s swept away much regulation too.

Many Chicago-UCLA analysts denounce "traditional" regulation as a prime instance of government-created monopoly, and they churn out proposals to rely on competition instead. But has regulation mostly failed? It can be imperfect: ineffective, too rigid, and a cause of economic waste. However, the real question is how well it usually does in practice *compared* to the alternatives of laissez-faire or public enterprise. Moreover, there are many gradations and types of regulation, rather than just crude yes-or-no choices.

Regulation therefore poses sophisticated questions about its methods and effectiveness. This chapter lays the foundation by reviewing the economic concepts and standards of regulation. Section I presents the standards for deciding what industries ought to be regulated. Section II covers the core economic issues: how regulation controls prices and how that may cause inefficiency. Section III reviews actual regulation, and Section IV focuses on the history of regulation as it has developed since 1888. Chapter 14 will focus in more detail on actual regulation, particularly in the electricity and telephone industries.

I. WHAT SHOULD BE REGULATED?

Regulation involves interference with the market, in creating the monopoly franchise and in trying to control the monopoly firm's prices.

Regulation is suitable only where technology really does dictate a natural monopoly so that regulation may improve efficiency. This section summarizes this condition and then reviews the industries that *are* regulated in practice.

1. Natural Monopoly

Suppose that the underlying technology of electricity, for example, yields the average-cost curve shown in Figure 13–1. The lowest point on the average-cost curve (minimum efficient scale; recall Chapter 2) is at a large output, marked Q_N, that supplies the whole market. Accordingly, there is room for only one firm in this market. In electricity, it is easy to see that one set of wires in a town is cheaper than three sets of wires would be if there were three electricity suppliers.

To see that, suppose instead that there are three equal-sized firms, each with one third of Q_N output. Their costs will each be at AC_O, reflecting the duplication of wires, which is much higher than AC_N. As they compete, one of them will get ahead, achieve lower average costs, underprice the others, and take over the entire market. There will be just one system, with one set of wires. Monopoly is therefore natural and inevitable. Wise policy will accept it and control it.

Figure 13–1 shows a simple, ideal case, where demand intersects average cost precisely at the MES level. Capacity is nicely aligned with demand. Price can equal marginal cost *and* average cost. If price is set at that level, then the efficient result where price equals marginal cost occurs. Moreover, the monopoly firm obtains enough total revenue to cover total costs so that it earns a barely competitive rate of profit. It stays in business, but it does not gouge the public.

However, the firm would urgently prefer to set the monopoly price P_M, which is at the output level (Q_M) where marginal revenue equals marginal cost. As noted in Chapter 2, the monopolist cuts output below the competitive level and raises price. Most utilities provide services that are heavily relied on by customers (electricity, telephone service, water, cable TV), and so the demand for them is relatively inelastic. That means that the monopoly price is sharply above the efficient price, as shown in Figure 13–1. Therefore, the natural monopoly is a threat to its customers because it seeks to charge high prices. Only regulation prevents that.

Another danger is that the monopolist will adopt extensive price discrimination. We saw (Chapters 2 and 10) that such discrimination can be extensive when market shares are high. Utility monopolies are the extreme case, where the monopolist sells to the whole array of consumers and has direct physical connections to them. It is able to prevent

Figure 13–1 Simple Natural Monopoly

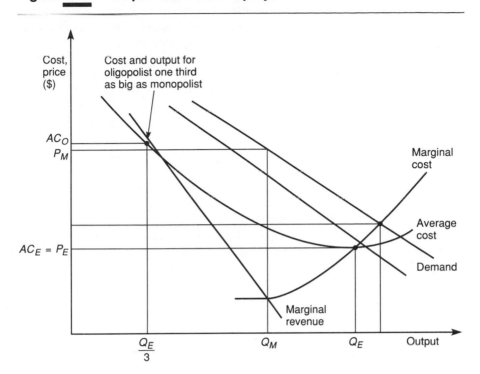

reselling by the low-price customers to the high-price customers, because it holds a legally enforced monopoly franchise.

Therefore, the natural monopoly would adopt pricing even more ex-
ploitative than the one-price diagram shown in Figure 13–1. The customers most reliant on the output, with the least elastic demands,
would be the most heavily overcharged.

Regulation therefore faces a daunting task. It must prevent the established franchised monopoly firm from setting high prices, against the
firm's deep incentives to get those high prices. The firm may have complex conditions of cost and demand across the whole array of business
and residential customers in a rapidly changing industry. The regulators
must obtain the necessary data, reach clear decisions, and enforce
them tightly against the knowledgeable firm that actually comprises the
industry.

The objective—setting prices in line with marginal costs—is reasonably clear, but, in practice, there are often three conditions that reduce
the clarity:

1.   Scale economies may fall short of a clear natural monopoly, in either of two ways. First, the cost gradient may be shallow, rather than steep as in Figure 13–1. Then the monopoly's cost may be only a few percent lower than for a small firm. The monopoly gives a tiny cost gain, while it may impose high prices. It may be better to try for competition instead, which will enforce higher X-efficiency and innovation. Those gains may easily offset the slight average-cost difference, yielding a better total result.

Second, the MES level may be below a monopoly, even perhaps at half the market size rather than 100 percent. The policy choice is then difficult, because monopoly is no longer necessary. However, the market is not naturally competitive, and a two-firm situation is merely an extremely tight oligopoly that may give monopoly pricing much of the time.

2.   Natural monopoly conditions often exist only in part of the utility sector. Moreover, this mixture often changes over time, as technology evolves. Fitting the utility franchise only to the true natural-monopoly parts becomes a ticklish job. Telephones, electric power, and railroads pose this problem especially.

3.   Actual cost conditions are often hard to measure. This is acute where the utility produces outputs from a central capacity or network. Determining true costs is then a prime regulatory task.

2. Other Conditions of Utilities

In addition to natural monopoly, most regulated firms meet three other criteria that add to the need for regulation.

1. Demand Elasticities Vary. This permits price discrimination, which can go to extremes (recall Chapter 10). Customers with inelastic demand face high price-cost ratios, and high excess profits can be earned. Customers with elastic demand are more fortunate; the prices they face involve low price-cost ratios, and so the efficiency benefits of competition occur. There is distortion of allocation, as well as unfairness between the two sets of customers. Discrimination is especially likely where a common service is sold to greatly varying customer groups. Some cases of discrimination may actually encourage efficient allocation, but a full monopoly is likely to carry it too far.

2. Output Fluctuates Sharply and Regularly. The system faces pulses of high "peak" demands and low off-peak demands, by hours, days of the week, and seasons. Examples are rush-hour bus loads, electricity loads, and telephone traffic during business hours versus 1:00 to 5:00 A.M. This makes cost and demand conditions very complicated, raising the need to supervise the firm's pricing choices.

3. Physical Connections. Users are often directly hooked up to the supply system, by wires, pipes, access roads, or other means.[3] Users, therefore, cannot change suppliers easily, nor can they resell the utility output among each other. Then enhances the supplier's ability to set monopoly price levels and to price discriminate.

Regulation is also facilitated if the utility product is uniform and slowly changing. Uniformity does not call for regulation, but it is nearly essential for regulation to work. Otherwise, the seller can manipulate the nature and quality of the product.

These criteria boil down mainly to *scale economies plus the danger of too much price discrimination.* They make a single producer "natural," and this increases the power to exploit some or all users. The unregulated monopoly outcome would be both inefficient and unfair.

The criteria do not neatly mark off a clear set of utilities for regulating. The criteria often conflict with each other. Often their conditions are only weak and marginal. The conditions usually evolve as time passes (see Section IV below). The conditions can be misrepresented, either to fend off regulation or to extend it too far. Setting the lines of regulation is an intensely controversial activity. The economic criteria do not provide crystal-clear answers.

Yet the real conditions do exist, regardless of the difficulties in discovering them. At each point in time, there is an array of sectors; some strongly need regulation, while many other sectors have no "regulatable" features at all. This array evolves over time as technology changes, and so regulation needs to be added to some sectors and withdrawn from others. The set of industries needing regulation in 1990 differs from those of 1900 and 1950, and those of the year 2050 will probably differ, too.

3. What Is Actually Regulated?

The rugged political process, not refined criteria, is what creates regulation. The coverage has shifted, especially since 1975.

Sectors. There are four broad sectors that have had "regulated utilities": energy, communications, transport, and urban services. In each sector, only part should clearly be regulated, while the rest could nearly or definitely be competitive. There has been intense debate over which parts are which. Table 13–1 outlines the sectors and parts. Actual regulation may stray from the appropriate areas. Telephone service and electric power have been the classic cases of needed and actual regu-

---

[3]Examples include wires for electricity, telephones, and cable TV, and pipes for water and gas.

Table 13–1   Traditional Utility Sectors and Their Current Status

Primarily Monopolies	Primarily, Partly, or Potentially Competitive
Local telephone service	Long-distance telephone service
Local electric-power distribution	Specialized postal services
Local natural-gas distribution	Railroads
Basic postal services	Waterways
Cable television	Oil and gas pipelines
Urban transit	Airlines
Water and sewage	Broadcasting
	Hospitals
	Trucking

lation. Some sectors are under public ownership (for example, some urban systems and postal service); their policy issues are treated in Chapter 15.

The sectors generate less than 5 percent of national income. Since they are capital intensive, their share of national investment is about 15 percent (the share of all business investment is even higher, at 27 percent). This share is probably growing gradually, for telephone and urban investment have risen especially rapidly in recent years. By contrast, the share of all civilian employment is below 3 percent.

II. THE ECONOMIC TASKS AND EFFECTS

Regulation involves complex—often delicate—relationships and tasks. The aims are the basic economic goals of maximum efficiency, fairness, and social contribution (recall Chapter 1). With regulation, these boil down to several specific practical matters (Chapter 14 gives more detail). Regulated firms have *rights* and *duties,* as in a "social contract":

Rights. (1) They are entitled to "reasonable" prices and profits. (2) They are given complete or partial protection from competition (via a franchise). (3) They can exercise eminent domain in acquiring property, even by coercion. (4) Rules governing them must be reasonable.

Duties. (1) Prices and profits are to be no more than "reasonable." (2) At those prices, all demand must be met, even at peak times. Service must be adequate in quantity and quality. (3) All changes in services (adding *or* dropping them) must be approved in advance. (4) The safety of the public is to be protected.

The firm is given a franchise (often an exclusive monopoly), but it is still a private firm owned by its shareholders. The firm naturally strives to maximize its profits, by actions both in the market and toward the regulators. Indeed, it directs much of its effort toward influencing the regulators' decisions.

The franchise enlarges and reinforces whatever natural monopoly there may be, and it excludes entry. The firm is shielded from actual *and* potential competition. The franchise raises the value of the enterprise, but the commission strives to keep the value from rising to contain large monopoly rents.

1. Tasks

In this situation, the regulators have three main tasks: to restrain price and profit *levels,* to get an efficient and fair *structure* of prices, and to get efficient internal management and correct input combinations.

The Level of Prices and Profits. The main effort of regulation has been to restrain total profits to the efficient—the usual term is *fair*—rate of return on the utility's investment. The basic choice is in these terms:

$$\text{Fair rate of return} = \frac{\text{Total revenue} - \text{Total cost}}{\text{Capital (the ``rate base'')}}$$

Capital is the rate base. It is supposed to include all fixed assets actually used (and necessary to use) in supplying the utility service. The rate of return includes the return to all investors, in both equity and debt. The firm's costs and capital are to be kept to the minimum for each level of output.

The regulators then try to set the firm's prices just high enough to yield total revenues that will cover the costs, including the cost of capital. Usually, the fair return (after taxes) is somewhere between 8 and 15 percent, just above the rate on "riskless" Treasury securities. A "fair" return would just cover the cost of the capital used. Typically, the commission estimated the cost of capital and then sets the fair rate of return just above that level. Although these concepts are discussed in great detail at the hearings, the whole process of decision making is usually just a compromise between proposals by the company and the commission's staff.

The Structure of Prices. The second task is to get an efficient structure of prices. Utilities supply many different *consumers,* in residences, shops, industry, offices, and so on. The *outputs* themselves also vary, in times, amounts, and terms of supply; but they are usually supplied via direct physical connections to the users. The utility usually has a lot of room to price discriminate, setting different price-cost ratios in line with demand elasticities.

A main task of regulators is therefore to prevent discrimination, except in unusual situations where it may be justified. This usually means *setting prices in line with the true costs of service; that is what efficient allocation means* (recall Chapter 1). These real costs, properly defined, are marginal costs (which may be hard to measure in practice. Chapter 14 analyzes marginal cost in some detail).

The broad objective is to set each price equal to the marginal cost of service. In a simple formula:

$$\text{Price} = k \text{ (Marginal cost)}$$

where k is some ratio that is similar among outputs and that is as close to 1 as possible. The utility firm wishes to violate that result; it wishes k to vary, setting it highest where demand is most inelastic, so as to maximize its profit and avert new competition. Various customer groups at rate hearings will demand lower rates. Caught between consumers and the utility managers, who know their own cost and demand conditions best (though not always very well), the regulators usually settle on compromises that reflect both cost and demand conditions. Alternatively, they may just leave these complex issues to the utility firm to decide, acquiescing in most or all of the proposed rates.

Internal Efficiency. The regulators also need to prevent inefficiency in the firm. This task requires care and thoroughness. X-inefficiency is likely to occur, because (1) the firm's monopoly power insulates it from market pressures and (2) the regulatory constraints themselves may cause inefficiency (as we will shortly see). Regulators need to define the efficient cost levels and then see that the firms attain them. Instead, regulators have often done little to monitor or enforce efficiency.

2. Does Regulation Induce or Permit Inefficiency?

In theory, regulation can foster serious wastes.

1. Enlarged Operating Costs. Under regulation, the firm can gain by padding its costs in several ways: (1) by *accounting methods* that make utility costs look bigger than they are—accounting methods often leave much room for choice; (2) by *transferring nonutility costs* onto the accounts of the utility operations—this can be done outright or, more subtly, when the firm's overhead costs include both utility and nonutility items; and (3) by *actual waste* (raising the levels of inputs)—waste can arise in many forms, since utility managers have wide discretion over technology and operations. Costs of any or all types (workers, capital items, purchased inputs, and so on) may not be minimized, and specific types of costs—managers' rewards and perquisites, benefits for favored groups—may be enlarged.

In the "typical" utility, expenses divide roughly as follows, as percents of revenue: labor costs, 25 percent; purchased materials and services, 25 percent; depreciation, 20 percent; and taxes, 10 percent. Consider how these groups may be altered.

The problem of operating costs has been recognized at least since 1892.[4] Many commissions scrutinize costs and try to disallow inflated or unnecessary items. Usually, the burden of proof is borne by the commission, to show that managers' choices are wrong or abusive. Most commissions simply accept most utility expenses as valid.

Depreciation offers much discretion to managers in setting their accounting levels of cost. Assets decline in value as time passes, mainly from (1) wear and tear (physical depreciation) and (2) obsolescence, as innovations render an old plant inferior and, therefore, destroy its value. Yearly depreciation is a valid cost of business. It is entered as a cost: Its summed totals appear in the balance sheets, where total fixed assets minus accrued depreciation reflects the *net* value of assets actually in use.

Note this *key point:* The level of *costs* is thus connected to the rate base via depreciation. A high rate of depreciation (for example, writing off an investment in 5 years, rather than 20) will *increase* the current cash flow—permitted profit plus yearly depreciation, but it will also keep the rate base *lower* in later years. The utility optimizes this dual choice by choosing a depreciation method that attunes present cash flows versus its future rate base, in line with the firm's motivation. The standard method of rate-base regulation favors keeping a high rate base, and so slow depreciation—with long assumed asset lives and small yearly amounts of depreciation—is common.

Also, the choice of accounting methods can sharply affect the recorded values. Depreciation involves (1) salvage value, (2) asset life, and (3) the method of write-off during the life. A short life with no assumed salvage value will give large present write-offs. A long life with high salvage value gives small yearly write-offs. Accounting methods—straight-line, declining-balance, and sum-of-the-years' digit are three common ones—give further choice.

Despite its seeming dullness and obscurity, depreciation is intensely controversial and keenly argued. It is mostly guesswork put into "objective" formulas. Engineers can try to measure the useful physical life on a piece of equipment (10, 30, even 40 years), but these are really

---

[4]In the decision *Chicago & Grand Trunk Railway Co.* v. *Wellman*, 143 U.S. 339 (1892).

only rough estimates. And innovation can falsify them quickly, as can changes in demand and in official requirements.

2. The Rate-Base Problem: Gold-Plating? The utility is permitted to earn profits on the full value of whatever assets are included in the rate base. Regulators need to prevent the rate base from being padded or overstated: to limit it strictly to "prudent investment" actually needed for utility service.

The rate base can be enlarged in two main ways, similar to those affecting costs: (1) accounting devices that overstate its value, and (2) actual expansion of real investment.

Accounting valuation is, again, partly a matter of optimum depreciation strategy by the utility. It was also–during 1898 to about 1940—a morass of empty dispute about reproduction versus original cost of assets.[5]

Not until 1944 did the *Hope Natural Gas* case lay it firmly to rest.[6] The rate base could at last be settled, and attention could rightly center on the rate of return.

This detour is now mostly closed, though many states use "fair value," a mix of original and replacement (or reproduction) cost. It did deep damage to regulation while it lasted, and it ensured that regulation had little effect on railroads, telephones, electric and gas utilities until well into their mature stages.

Actual investment may also exceed efficient levels, either by mistake, design, or as a natural response to regulatory incentives. Justice Brandeis urged during the 1920s that only "prudent investment" be allowed, excluding unwise, extravagant, or fraudulent investment. Most commissions made little effort to reinforce such investment, but in the 1960s the problem was reasserted by economists.[7]

---

[5]Reproduction cost appears to fit economic analysis, since it seems to reflect what the assets are *now* worth. Yet it ignores the bedrock fact that the regulators *make* the value of the assets by their own decision. And reproduction cost invites endless differing estimates. The assets can't actually be sold to anybody, because they are installed and highly specialized. And estimates of cost can be made in at least four different major ways, which give varying values. That the Supreme Court was willing even to entertain the sophistry of reproduction cost during 1920–40 was bad economics.

[6]*FPC v. Hope Natural Gas Co.*, 320 U.S. 591 (1944).

[7]The landmark analysis of this is H. Averch and L. L. Johnson, "Behavior of the Firm under Regulatory Constraint," *American Economic Review* 53 (December 1963), pp. 1052–69. A stream of later articles has left its main point intact and given it empirical support. See E. E. Zajac, "A Geometric Treatment of Averch-Johnson's Behavior of the Firm Model," *American Economic Review* 60 (March 1970), pp. 117–25; Elizabeth E. Bailey, *Economic Theory of Regulatory Constraint* (Lexington, Mass.: Lexington Books, 1973); and Robert M. Spann, "Rate of Return Regulation and Efficiency in Production: An Empirical Test of the Averch-Johnson Thesis," *Bell Journal of Economics* 5 (Spring 1974), pp. 38–52.

Managers usually have a wide degree of choice in designing their systems and in innovating new technology. They also gain profits by having a larger rate base, as was noted earlier. Therefore, *rate-base regulation often induces these choices to favor higher capital intensity*. The effect shifts the margin of choice toward capital-intensive plants. By making capital cheaper, in effect, regulation may induce some extra use of it.

The research consensus is that the rate-base effect is often significant but rarely very large. It may enlarge investment by several percent, typically, but rarely by more than 10 percent. Also, the effect may have its good side. Kahn has noted that it may promote innovation and overcome the monopoly's tendency toward restrictive behavior.[8] It adds to the amount of current investment, which tends to use the latest technology. It also assures that there will be adequate capacity for use at peak times.

How severe are the expansions of operating and investment costs under regulation? Most observers regard them as no larger than moderate, especially since regulators grew more sensitive to them in the 1960s. They have stirred efforts to apply "incentive" regulation to eliminate the wastes.

3. Possible Reforms

1. Incentive Regulation. There is no easy way to inject incentives for efficiency while also keeping regulation effective. Of course regulation can simply be removed, but that leaves the monopoly unrestrained. In the 1960s, there were efforts to apply two kinds of formal incentive devices.

One method was simply to order outside audits of managerial quality and cost efficiency. Management-consulting firms were hired to study the firm's operations and investment patterns so as to discover and publicize any wastes. Even the threat of such an audit could energize managers to take more efficient actions. Many such audits were ordered in the 1970s by state commissions, with beneficial results. There are limits to these audits, because some inefficiencies are too subtle and ingrained to be clearly detectable, and the consulting firms are not infallible.

The second method was to determine which firms were more efficient and then reward them by permitting higher profit rates. Some of this was tried in the electricity industry, where econometric studies could suggest which firms' costs were higher than their conditions justified. However, the measures were controversial, and the rewards were difficult to apply precisely.

---

[8]Kahn, *The Economics of Regulation*.

Since 1975, the de-regulation movement has led to more direct methods of incentive regulation, amounting largely to removing most regulatory limits. One version sets a reasonable target rate of return for the utility firm, such as 13.5 percent on the rate base for an electricity firm. Any higher profits are shared between the firm and its customers, for example, with 75 percent of the profits above the 13.5 target rate being paid to the buyers. A second approach is *price caps*. They set a target rate of average price increases for the firm, using a formula that reflects likely cost trends. The firm is supposed to keep its average price below that target increase; any excess is refunded to the buyers.

Both approaches let the firm adjust its individual prices freely. Therefore, they abandon the effort to regulate price structures. Such a situation would be acceptable when the firm has little monopoly power, but, when it does have dominance or total monopoly, then the incentive effects are achieved at the cost of permitting monopoly exploitation of some customers. Moreover, the price discrimination can block the emergence of effective competition (recall Chapters 10 and 12).

Therefore, the 1980s' versions of incentive regulation rest on the faith that monopoly power will not be abused. That faith may be in error. Moreover, the attempts to calculate the target rates of profits and the rate of sharing excess profits are always hazardous and controversial. So are the attempts to set the target rate of price increases when price caps are being used (as noted in the next section). Therefore, the new incentive regulation methods are open to serious doubt.

2. Bidding for Franchises. Drawing on an idea from John Stuart Mill in 1848, some Chicago-UCLA economists have suggested that the government should simply auction off natural-monopoly franchises to the highest bidder.[9] In setting its winning bid, the winner would have to yield up all of the prospective monopoly profits that it hopes to gain, in order to get the franchise. Those profits would go to the people, and, henceforth, the firm could only earn competitive profits. Moreover, the firm would voluntarily adopt the efficient structure of prices; its discriminatory pricing would fit the inverse-elasticity Ramsey pricing rule.

Unfortunately, the idea has distinct limits, and it has been tried only a few times, especially in the early years of regulation, around 1900. The main problem is that there may not be effective competition in the bidding, because one firm may have overwhelming advantages or simply

---

[9]See Richard Schmalensee's review of the idea in his *The Control of Natural Monopolies* (Lexington, Mass.: Lexington Books, 1979); see also Harold Demsetz's version of the proposal, "Why Regulate Utilities?" *Journal of Law and Economics* 11 (1968), pp. 55–65; and Dennis W. Carlton and Jeffrey M. Perloff's discussion in *Modern Industrial Organization* (Glenview, Ill.: Scott, Foresman, 1990), chap. 23; see also the effective critique by Trebing, in "The Chicago School versus Public Utility Regulation."

because not many firms may be qualified to take over the particular utility operations. Also, there may be imperfect knowledge of the conditions so that the authorities could not know that the winning bid is, in fact, just equal to the future monopoly profits.

Moreover, the resulting prices would probably be inefficient if the utility is a declining-cost case.[10] The firm would avoid setting prices at the low, money-losing levels of marginal cost, preferring instead to price-discriminate in order to maximize profits. Indeed, the regulators would need to maintain close supervision of the firm's pricing in order to avoid the standard forms of demand-based pricing.

III. THE PROPOSAL FOR PRICE CAPS

Parallel to deregulating competitive services, dominant firms have recently begun requesting to be set under price caps in place of traditional rate regulation. Old regulation, it is said, is obsolete and discredited as causing inefficiency. Price caps are said to be more effective and less harmful.

The idea is borrowed from recent British experiments. The Thatcher government has privatized a number of utility firms (such as British Telecom, the telephone system), which are still monopolies (see Chapter 15).[11] Some constraint on these monopolies is needed, but the British had heard the criticisms of rate-base regulation and wished to avoid them.

So they invented the price cap. One virtue of it is simplicity, since it merely limits the average of the firm's price increases to the rise of a general price index (such as the Consumer Price Index), minus a factor to reflect productivity gains. The following formula embodies the price cap idea:

$$\frac{\text{Permitted rate}}{\text{of price rise}} = \frac{\text{Rate of rise of}}{\text{a general price index}} - X$$

or

$$\Delta\text{Price} = \Delta\text{GPI} - X$$

---

[10]See Lester Telser, "On the Regulation of Monopoly: A Note," *Journal of Political Economy* 77 (1969), pp. 937–52; Oliver E. Williamson, "Franchise Bidding for Natural Monopolies—In General and with Respect to CATV," *Bell Journal of Economics* 7 (1976), pp. 73–104; Schmalensee, *The Control of Natural Monopoly;* and Carlton and Perloff, *Modern Industrial Organization,* chap. 23.

[11]The influential version of the proposal is in Stephen C. Littlechild, *Regulation of British Telecommunications' Profitability* (London: HMSO, 1983) see also Michael Beesley and Stephen Littlechild, "Privatisation: Principles, Problems, and Priorities," *Lloyds Bank Review,* July 1983, pp. 1–20.

where X is some percent designed to squeeze the firm a little so as to maintain efficiency.

The price cap avoids the cost-plus and rate-base effects toward inefficiency (recall Section II). It permits the firm to select the array of prices, rather than to follow external controls. This permits flexible adjustments to new conditions and innovations. It may also yield an optimal set of discriminatory (Ramsey) prices, under certain limited conditions, as Section II also noted. It lets the regulators withdraw—regulating only lightly—as competition is growing. It may even be suitable for franchised monopoly utilities.

Yet the method has limits and defects, too. Ironically, the method has been largely discredited in Britain, for the reasons I will cover shortly.[12] But in the late 1980s U.S. regulators were urged to accept this new method nonetheless. A number of states have done so, and the FCC adopted it in 1989 for AT&T in long-distance service.

One basic fault is that price caps permit the dominant firm a wide latitude to take selective actions. Those actions, as we have noted, can be critical in enhancing dominance and in exploiting customers who have no alternatives. Price caps can be a license for widespread anti-competitive actions.

On more specific points, the formula's basis is unreliable. It accepts the current prices as valid, seeking to constrain only any additional increase in them. Yet some or all of the utility's prices may be at inefficient levels at the outset. There may be elements of X-inefficiency in the firm's costs, or the utility's overall profits may be too high or low. If there are such errors, the price cap is unable to correct them. Instead, it builds them in as permanent conditions. Or, if the firm eliminates the inefficiencies, the firm keeps all of the savings as profits, while customers still pay too-high prices.

Each specific element of the formula is also weak or defective. The permitted rate of average price rise ignores individual price changes. Therefore, it is appropriate only when there is just one output price to be constrained. That simple case is not true in significant regulatory cases.

A general price index is the wrong index to use. Instead, an index based on the utility's own *costs* is appropriate. Only if prices are rising from outside influences does the firm deserve to raise its prices. But such a narrow cost index can be difficult to measure, because the weights among inputs usually change over time.

---

[12]See also Cento Veljanovski, *Selling the State* (London: Weidenfeld and Nicolson, 1987), especially Chapter 7; "The Privatization of Public Enterprises—A European Debate," *Annals of Public and Co-operative Economy,* Special Issue, April-June 1986, especially the paper by Heidrun Abromeit; and the many sources cited in footnotes 1 and 16 in Chapter 15.

If the price cap applies only to some of the utility's outputs, then the task is virtually impossible. Overhead costs cannot usually be assigned by clear economic criteria, and the utility firm can move its accounting costs so as to frustrate the constraints. These problems are at the core of the utility problem, and the resort to price caps will not make them go away.

The third element in the price-cap equation—the X factor—also poses serious problems. Its proper size is largely guesswork, because it requires a judgment about the coming technological trends and opportunities of the industry. How much is autonomous technological progress likely to reduce costs, as innovations emerge? The question involves sophisticated, complex judgments about multidimensional trends of technology. Moreover, correct judgments may lead to unexpected and difficult results, such as an X level high enough to require price *reductions* rather than increases.

In short, the price caps will require much detailed attention to prices and costs, perhaps as extensive as established regulation has been forced to provide. In addition, it requires judgments about technological trends which current regulation is largely able to avoid. The problems appear to make price caps at least as difficult as traditional regulation.

If price caps are attempted, economic analysis suggests that they should take the following dual form. First, the formula should be:

$$\frac{\Delta \text{ Price}}{\text{of outputs}} = \frac{\Delta \text{ Cost}}{\text{of inputs}} - \frac{\text{Savings from autonomous progress}}{} - X \text{ (squeeze factor)}$$

The input cost index must be correctly weighted and adjusted for shifts. The savings from autonomous progress must be decided after thorough evaluations of the industry's technological opportunities; it may also need frequent change as events develop new opportunities. The squeeze factor is needed in order to apply incentives to maintain tightness in costs and innovation. How large it should be is a matter of delicate judgment, for which there are no simple criteria.

But this applied formula is not enough in itself. A second level of constraint is needed on individual prices. Because selective actions will inevitably be taken by the dominant firm, the regulators may often need to prevent them. That requires constraints comparable to the traditional price-structure restraints that traditional regulation is supposed to apply. Because price caps permit the firm to take these selective actions, regulators must specifically prevent them.

Altogether, price caps are illusory, promising an escape from regulatory reality that cannot, in fact, be made so easily. In some ways they may be more burdensome and less effective than conventional regulation, with all its faults. They are appropriate only when (1) the outputs are few, (2) competition is already effective, (3) reliable input cost indexes can be constructed (with little or no overhead costs shared between capped and uncapped outputs), (4) technological opportunities are accurately known, and (5) a correct squeeze factor can be applied.

The price cap literature and British policies have understated these problems and implied that solutions are direct and simple. Instead, a rise in staffing, in the complexity of regulatory tasks, and in the intensity of public complaints may well occur. Or the price-cap regulation may simply be a label for lifting regulation altogether.

IV. REGULATION IN PRACTICE

Regulation is usually carried out by a commission (for example, in most states by a "Public Service Commission"). There are three to seven members, with a permanent staff including accountants, engineers, and economists. Hearings on price increases and other matters are held, and legally binding decisions are issued.

What are these regulators accomplishing? To "regulate" has at least three definitions. One is strict and unilateral: "to govern or direct according to rule." Another refers to compromise and smoothing over: to reduce to order . . . to regularize. And another is superficial, perhaps empty: to make regulations. Actual regulation varies among these: sometimes strict, sometimes trivial or even controlled by the regulated firms themselves.

1. Theories of Regulation

Before one learns details of actual regulation, it is helpful to consider three main theories about regulation's true nature.

Compromise. Commissions arrange compromises. A private utility firm sells goods to customers, while seeking to benefit its shareholders. The conflict between customers and shareholders is usually quite direct. Higher prices (and profits) transfer money from buyers to the shareholders, and so the firm's stock price rises. Other groups also are affected. Utility workers' wages may rise and the number of people employed by the utility may increase. Suppliers of fuel, equipment, and other items hope to sell more to the utilities, and at higher prices. There are clashes among customer groups, too, such as in setting higher prices for residences than businesses, or higher prices for some residences than others, and so on.

Precisely because these conflicts are so sharp, an agency is needed to resolve them. Some abstract guidelines are helpful in setting the decisions, such as to "set the rate of return at the cost of capital" and to "set prices in line with marginal cost." But there is often much disagreement about the facts, and so the commission has much room and much urgency for compromise.

Indeed, much regulation *is* merely compromise. Hearings provide one process; a forum for all to be heard and for issues to be joined. The decisions normally strike a balance among the interests, not systematically denying any significant group. The usual decision takes the middle ground. For example, a company requesting a 10 percent rise can usually expect to get about 5 percent. Or if it claims the fair rate of return to be 14 percent while the opposing experts assert it to be 8 percent, a commission will surprise nobody by deciding it is 11 percent.

Knowing this, all sides may overstate their case, expecting to get only half of what they claim to be absolutely necessary. They deny this tendency to exaggerate, naturally, but it is a natural one. It permits all sides to look partly successful. The company gets what it really needed, the commission is able to look strict, and the consumer representatives can feel that they restrained the price rise. Of course, this means that the debates and results are partly shams, but no great harm is done, and the inevitable compromise occurs amid a sense that issues have been vigorously aired and fairly heard.

Motives of Regulators and Firms. Specific motives have also been explored by economists, to see how they may tilt the decisions.

Regulators are normal people, working within a specific set of pressures and rewards. Their success comes from continuing in office or moving to higher positions. This they achieve by avoiding two things: (1) appearing too lenient toward the firms, and (2) any breakdowns of supply (for example, blackouts, stoppages). Their motivation is defensive, to avoid trouble, to pacify. To this end, they will seek larger budgets for fuller staffing. They will also encourage the utility to have higher degrees of reserve capacity so as to avoid service breakdowns.

Utility managers face unusual constraints and rewards. Their monopoly is strong but may contain marginal areas of competition. The firm's profits are regulated, but not tightly. Profits can be raised by manipulating the commission as well as by actions in the market.

The prime objectives of utility officers are three. *One* is to raise the permitted profit ceiling. Such increases can have potent effects on shareholder capital, since a "mere" one point rise in the rate of return—say, from 8 to 9 percent—can sometimes add as much as 10 or 20 percent to the price of the company's stock. A *second* motive is to set low prices where there is actual or potential competition, covering the balance of costs from its more captive markets, where demand elasticity is low. This minimizes long-run risk and enlarges the rate base upon which profits can be earned. The *third* motive is to avoid, at almost any cost, a service failure (for example, a blackout), for that stirs public resentment and endangers the utility's privileged status.

Several traits of behavior are likely to follow. First, the managers are likely to self-select into a group of relatively conservative, risk-avoiding people. The premium is on avoiding trouble, rather than aggressive innovation. Second, they will be preoccupied with reinforcing their monopoly position, by choices about price structures, technology, and other issues. Third, like the regulators, they will prefer to have high degrees of reserve capacity in order to avoid service breakdowns.

Both groups share the motive of making regulation seem to work. Otherwise, their security is removed. This joint motivation underlies all of their surface arguments. It unites them against most outside efforts to change or replace regulation.

Capture. Chicago-UCLA economists argue that regulators are usually captured by the utility firms.[13] A regulated firm's interests are highly focused and intense. It can enrich its shareholders by millions of dollars by "winning" a rate case. It has staffing and funds organized to get its way, and it knows the technical facts and issues thoroughly. Customers' interests are more diffuse. Each may have only a few dollars per month at stake, and none is well versed in the facts and issues.

So regulation can be a tool of the regulated firm. Moreover, the company may also control the selection of commissioners and influence the legislators to give inadequate funds for the commission's activities. The firm can also use advertising to win the populace to its side and mollify customers. Even if the commissioners are honest, they may serve largely as agents of the firms. Indeed, electric and railroad companies lobbied during 1885–1930 to have regulation put over them. It gave them protection from competition, while the controls could be kept weak.

Each commission may have some element of capture, and some have been passive, largely rubber stamping the firm's decisions. Yet some regulators are aggressive and independent, at least for intervals.

Life Cycles of Utilities and Regulation. Utility sectors commonly proceed through four stages. In *Stage 1,* the system is invented, often lead-

---

[13]See George J. Stigler, "The Theory of Economic Regulation," *Bell Journal of Economics* 2 (Spring 1971), pp. 3–21; Richard A. Posner, "Theories of Economic Regulation," *Bell Journal of Economics* 4 (Autumn 1974), pp. 335–58; and Sam Peltzman, "Toward a More General Theory of Regulation," *Journal of Law and Economics* 19 (Autumn 1976), pp. 211–40.

Table 13–2   Stages of Utility Life Cycle: Approximate Intervals

	Stage 1	Stage 2	Stage 3	Stage 4
Manufactured gas	1800–20	1820–80	1880–1920	1920–50
Natural gas	1900–10	1910–50	1950–	
Telegraph	1840–50	1850–1916	1916–30	1930–
Railways				
All	1820–35	1835–1910		
Passenger			1910–35	1935–
Freight			1910–60	1960–
Electricity	1870–85	1885–1960	1960–	
Street railways	1870–85	1885–1912	1912–22	1922–
Telephone				
Local	1875–80	1880–1947	1947–	
Long distance	1880–90	1890–1960	1960–83	1984–
Airlines	1920–25	1925–60	1960–75	1975–
Television	1935–47	1947–65	1965–75	1975–
Cable television	1950–55	1955–75	1975–	

ing to control by patents. This period is usually brief but decisive for the future form of the system.

In *Stage 2,* the system is created and grows, often displacing a prior utility (for example, buses replace trolleys, telephone displaces telegraph). Cross-subsidies among users and a separation of creamy and skim markets become embedded in the price structure. The new service *seeks to get itself regulated* in order to achieve permanence, legitimacy, and market control. The new regulators act as promoters, doing what they can to make the service available to all households and businesses.

In *Stage 3,* the system becomes complete as a matter of technology and market saturation. It now shifts from an offensive to a defensive stance. Competing new technologies arise, able to substitute for it in its basic and peripheral markets.

Finally, in *Stage 4,* the system is ready to revert back—no longer a true, natural-monopoly utility—to conventional competitive processes. Or, in certain cases, a degree of public ownership may be adopted.

Table 13–2 estimates very roughly the stages for a number of present and past utilities. Regulation usually starts in Stage 2, in harmony with the preexisting interests of the utility and its larger industrial customers. The structure of mutual interests, the profit expectations, and the basic terms of exchange (especially the supplier's rate level and structure) therefore *precede* regulation. Thus, placed atop the preexisting situation, regulation tends to legitimize these interest-group compromises. Rate structure is not thoroughly assessed and changed.

Table 13–3   The Main Federal Commissions

Commission (and the year it was formally established)	Number of Members	Number of Staff Members	Expenditures Fiscal Year (1984, estimated in $ millions)	Jurisdiction
Interstate Commerce Commission (1887)	5	1,063	$60	Railroads; motor carriers; water shipping; oil pipelines; express companies; etc.
Federal Energy Regulatory Commission (1934)	5	1,707	92	Electric power; gas and pipelines; water-power sites.
Federal Communications Commission (1934)	7	1,975	88	Telephone; television; cable TV; radio; telegraph.

Sources: U.S. Government, *Budget, Fiscal 1985* (Washington, D.C.: U.S. Government Printing Office, 1984), Appendix volume.

Factors Are Usually Mingled. The wise student looks for all four elements (compromises, motives, capture, and life cycles) in judging actual commissions. In the heat of de-regulation after 1970, there has been much cynicism that regulation is weak, shallow, and costly. It does fall short of the ideal, but it can also be superb, and it may usually be better than the alternatives.[14] Often it is at least roughly in line with economic criteria or can be pressured to improve its results.

2. Actual Regulation

The typical commission has members, a staff, a budget, and various legal powers. It is usually hard pressed to deal fully with its problems. Most state commissions, in particular, have slender resources and a great variety of tasks.

The main federal commissions are summarized in Table 13–3. Federal units deal only with *interstate* operations. The line between them and *intrastate* activities is often obscure, because much of a utility's

[14]For reasoned defenses of the strengths of regulation, see Kahn, *The Economics of Regulation;* Bonbright, *Principles of Public Utility Rates;* and Trebing, "The Chicago School versus Public Utility Regulation."

capacity may be involved in both operations. For example, several Bell operating companies and many electric and gas firms spread over a number of states; each state commission must somehow regulate only a part.

Commission resources are often absorbed mainly by secondary duties and housekeeping chores (monitoring service, inspecting railroad crossings, answering complaints, and so forth). Most commissions are underfunded. The staffs often include brigades of clerks and accountants but few well-trained economists.

As in antitrust, the top officials come and go, often rapidly, while the career staff work on along conventional lines.[15] Also, as in antitrust, the private side's resources routinely dwarf those of the agencies.

Procedures. Commissions act by hearings and decisions. Usually, the hearings are precipitated by the utility firm requesting a price change or a change in service offerings. The typical sequence is summarized in Figure 13–2. It involves (1) open hearings, offering opposing rationales for a decision; (2) setting the range of possible compromise; and then (3) deciding the specific amount and explaining it by one or more rationales. The hearing process, as outlined in Figure 13–2, is an adversary proceeding, conducted by lawyers following legal rules. Economists are used mainly in preparing some features of the staff proposal; some may also be used as expert witnesses by one side or another.

Also, much is done informally between commissions and firms, in negotiating small (and even large) issues of pricing and service. This can be quicker and smoother than full-dress public cases, but the process is covert, and the issues are not openly raised and settled. There is little "public responsibility," which is what regulation is supposed to provide.[16]

The process inserts a degree of delay and uncertainty into the utility firm's pricing and profits. This is often called regulatory lag. The economic effect differs sharply between inflationary and other times. During *inflation,* delay squeezes the utility's profits, as price increases lag behind cost increases. This gives the commission great power. By contrast, if costs are falling, the firm can sit pretty, earning excess profits while the commission tries to catch up by starting cases to cut the prices. Roughly speaking, the process involved falling costs

---

[15]For a lively account of the foibles of actual officials and agencies, see Louis M. Kohlmeier, Jr., *The Regulators* (New York: Harper & Row, 1969); also Bruce Owen and Ronald Braeutigam, *The Regulation Game* (Cambridge, Mass.: Ballinger, 1978).

[16]For one extreme instance, the FCC chose to regulate the telephone industry informally—by so-called continuous surveillance—from 1938 to 1965. Some state commissions in the 1950s and 1960s went for five to eight years without a formal hearing.

Figure 13–2   The Conventional Process of Regulation

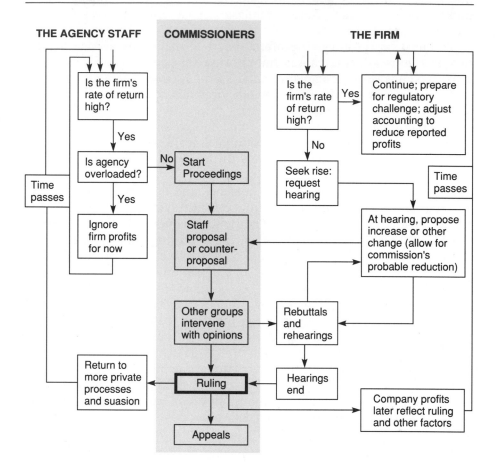

during 1930–65 but then reversed to rising costs after 1965 for most utilities. This dramatically raised the power of the commissions over the firms.

V. A BRIEF HISTORY OF REGULATION

Regulation has developed slowly and fitfully—and often stormily—during the last 100 years.

1. Early Origins

Variants of regulation—giving favor to an enterprise and setting limits on it–trace back into prehistory. Then, during 1400–1700, monopoly grants by the sovereign came to carry varying rights and duties. The great laissez-faire purge of such interferences during 1750–1850 cleared away many quasi-regulatory devices.

The legal origin of modern regulation traces back to 1670, when Lord Chief Justice Hale in Britain summarized the law of businesses "affected with a publick interest."[17] Speaking of ferry boats, as well as port facilities, he noted that they were not merely private, because—as monopolies—they had public effects and public duties. This concept of *pubic interest* has been the pivot upon which all later setting of *public* constraints upon *private* capital have turned.

During 1820–70, there was much local experience in the United States with rate regulation: for example, private wharves, chimney sweeping, bread, and horse-drawn transportation in Washington, D.C., and in other cities.[18] By 1860, five eastern states had tried advisory commissions for regulating railroads: They relied on competition plus supervision. By 1870, a variety of small-scale utilities—gas works, water works, railroads, and so on—existed and were being loosely treated in many ways. Competition was still commonly part of the approach.

2. Modern Regulation Begins

It was railroads and the newer utilities—electricity, telephones, and city transit, all of which began during the 1870s—and all of which crystallized the modern regulatory method during 1880–1920. Transcontinental railroads evolved during 1850–70. They had great bargaining power in the Midwest in dealing with individual farmers. In contrast to many eastern lines, where a degree of competition was possible, farmers out on the plains usually had no alternative ways to get their products to the market. Grain elevators also exercised monopoly power, often tied directly in with the railroads. Therefore, by the mid-1870s, an extensive set of discriminatory practices had been developed by the railroads. The resulting wave of opposition took form as the grass-roots Granger movement, a middle-western protest based on local Granges, and was the origin of "prairie populism."

By 1874, many midwestern states had created regulatory commissions to control railroad rates. Most of them quickly became passive, for railroad power was really a regional problem. The landmark *Munn v. Illinois* case in 1877 established that states could assert regulatory

---

[17]Sir Matthew Hale, *De Portibus Maris* and *De Jure Maris* (London, 1670).

[18]See C. L. King, ed., *The Regulation of Municipal Utilities* (New York: Appleton, 1912); and M. H. Hunter, "Early Regulation of Public Service Corporations," *American Economic Review* 7 (September 1917), pp. 569–81.

authority over trades (in this case grain elevators) "affected with the public interest."[19] The criteria of public interest were: (1) *necessity* of the service and (2) *monopoly*. The decision set the general precedent that regulation can be applied wherever a public interest can be perceived. Yet it fatefully set *monopoly* as the prime target of regulation, and that still persists in the orthodox image.

By 1887, pressure had risen to redress the monopoly power of midwestern railroads. This meshed neatly with the eastern railroads' wish to create a cartel device to prevent periodic bouts of price competition among them.[20] The result was the Interstate Commerce Commission. Despite its apparent position of control, the fledgling ICC was blocked by the courts from setting effective rate ceilings until about 1910. By the 1920s, the railroads were already under heavy new competition from road carriers. The ICC, therefore, failed to regulate when it was appropriate and then did regulate after it became largely unnecessary. It has lingered on through the 1980s and into the 1990s.

3. Regulation Spreads

By 1900, electric and telephone utilities were already well advanced and evolving toward regional and national scope. Initially, open franchising had been the rule, with cities often having several or more little utility systems, but then the doctrine of natural monopoly took hold. During the watershed period of 1907–30, most states created public-service commissions to franchise and regulate these private firms.[21] In many cases, the firms lobbied hard to create state regulation, as preferable to public ownership or federal regulation. Most state commissions had little leverage until the 1930s. Powers and resources were lacking, and firms created long, sterile controversy over the proper rate base, and these staved off action during the 1920s.

Federal regulation of electric power and telephones was formally established only in the 1930s in reaction to severe scandals from utility-stock manipulations during the 1920s stock market craze. In 1934, the Supreme Court opened the criteria for regulated industries to include

---

[19]In *Munn* v. *Illinois* (94 U.S. 113), the Court approved a law, enacted by the state of Illinois, controlling the charges made by grain elevators and warehouses.

[20]See Gabriel Kolko, *Railroads and Regulation, 1877–1916* (Princeton, N.J.: Princeton University Press, 1965); and Paul W. MacAvoy, *The Economic Effects of Regulation* (Cambridge, Mass.: MIT Press, 1965).

[21]There was also much experimenting with hybrid forms of franchises, incentives, sliding scales, and other regulatory devices. See King, *The Regulation of Municipal Utilities;* Martin G. Glaeser, *Outlines of Public Utility Economics* (New York: Macmillan, 1927); I. Bussing, *Public Utility Regulation and the So-Called Sliding Scale* (New York: Columbia University Press, 1936); and John Bauer, *the Public Utility Franchise* (Chicago: Public Administration Service, 1946).

any industry the public wished to regulate.[22] The federal commissions often conflicted with state agencies over jurisdiction. State commissions have sided with the firms, against what is seen as the common threat of the (marginally) stricter federal commissions. State regulation has also been used as a haven from federal regulation in insurance and other trades.

In short, the concept and legal basis for effective regulation ripened in good time—in 1877, before electric, telephone, and other modern utilities emerged. However, actual regulation has lagged behind by decades, and it has been applied to existing structures of firms and interests. Actual regulation has really only been tried for several decades. Most commissions have had limited resources. Also, the utilities have gained by using obtuse doctrines and procedural tactics to congest and fend off regulatory efforts. In the early 1920–35 period, this led to a morass of stupefyingly complex debates over reproduction cost as the value of the rate base. This has made much regulation ineffective.

Still, an image of adequate regulation persisted after 1940. New sectors evolved (natural gas, airlines, TV, cable TV, and the like), each with mixed motives toward being regulated. Slight though its known effectiveness was, regulation was extended to new areas. By the 1950s, it covered—formally—nearly the whole of the economic infrastructure of the U.S. economy. This was probably the peak coverage of conventional regulation.

Yet, by the 1950s, research had not shown in detail or depth what the effects of regulation had been and how well they conformed to the public interests. During the 1960s, the more searching economic questions about regulation began to be asked again. The possibility that regulation was a charade, a cloak for utility interests, or itself a source of unnecessary monopoly came to the fore.

4. New Stresses and an Era of De-Regulation

The 1940–65 "golden age" was marked by a downward drift of average costs in electricity and telephones. Problems became benign and re-

---

[22]The concept of a peculiar category of industries affected with a public interest was abandoned, in 1934 when the Court handed down its decision in the *Nebbia* case (*Nebbia* v. *New York,* 291 U.S. 502). The state of New York had set up a milk control board and empowered it to fix the retail price of milk. The board had fixed the price at nine cents per quart. Nebbia, a grocer in Rochester, had sold two quarts for 18 cents and added a loaf of bread as a bonus. When sued for violating the law, he argued that the milk business was competitive, rather than monopolistic, having none of the characteristics of a public utility, and that the state was, therefore, powerless to regulate the prices that it charged. The Court, in a 5 to 4 decision, rejected this defense. Henceforth, regulation could be applied wherever legislatures voted it.

solving them routine. Then several new problems converged with severe jolts. Inflation forced up costs, and fuel prices jumped after 1972. Ecological problems came to the fore, preventing the use of choice power station sites and slowing the use of nuclear energy. Poor planning caused the first serious breakdowns ever in Bell System service during 1969–71 in New York City and elsewhere. After 1965, the whole promotional ethic of utility managers ran squarely against the new scarcities of urban and national life.

New research after 1960 showed that regulation may have weak "good"effects and important costly side effects on efficiency (see Section II).[23] This stirred political efforts to de-regulate, especially in airlines, railroads, trucking, broadcasting, and natural gas. These efforts have gone far. Struggles over de-regulating natural gas have been a leading congressional issue. Airlines passenger and cargo service were de-regulated during 1978–84. Buses, railroads, and trucking have been mostly de-regulated. Almost all regulation of radio broadcasting has been lifted, while television broadcasting and cablecasting retain only some restrictions. The antitrust splitting of the Bell System let competition replace some regulation of telephone service, and the FCC has dropped most regulation of AT&T. Many states also removed most restraints on local telephone pricing.

The 1968–85 period was a great watershed for regulation, and the domain of price and entry controls is still shrinking. Yet, amid this flux, the basic economic criteria remain valid. They occupy the next chapter.

APPENDIX: A GLOSSARY OF REGULATORY TERMS

Affected with the Public Interest: Defined by the legislature as being eligible for public regulation. The grounds for inclusion are almost limitless.

Common Carrier: A franchised utility required to serve all customers at the regulated prices.

---

[23]There is also much intriguing folklore about regulation. For example, only a handful of utility regulators stand out as being effective and forceful, from among the vast numbers of those that have held office down the years. Among state commissions, a few are known to be strict or at least creditable. Meanwhile, there is a rich folklore about utility performance and management. For example, electric power managers since the 1930s are agreed to have been relatively stodgy and insular; hence, their severe difficulties in meeting the new problems after 1965. Bell System management was widely regarded as thorough, conservative, and tenacious in its defense of the Bell System's monopoly. During the 1920s, there were widespread efforts by utilities to influence academic and public discussion of utility interests. In some cases, this reached the level of open scandal. Since then, utilities have been more careful to avoid even the appearance of trying to twist debate their way. Nonetheless, utilities are also anxious to have a favorable image, and the Bell System in particular cultivated academic and public approval in a wide variety of ways. The persuasive and social power of these large, settled enterprises can be great.

Cream Skimming: Entering the most lucrative part of the market. Alleged by the utility against newcomers.

Fair Rate of Return: The criterion the regulators are supposed to meet: avoids confiscation of owner's value while not gouging consumers.

Franchise: Legal term for a common carrier's market position. It usually excludes some or all competitors and is enforced by public agencies.

Just and Reasonable Rates: The ideal price structure; blending several considerations.

Marginal-Cost Pricing: Setting price strictly in line with specific marginal costs (not in line with demand differences). Peak-load pricing is one variant.

Natural Monopoly: In concept, a case in which average costs decline over such a wide range of output that only one firm will survive.

Original Cost: The value of utility investment when first installed. (Now commonly used instead of reproduction and historical cost.)

Price Discrimination: Prices set in line with demand. Often called value-of-service pricing.

Public Utility: Vernacular phrase for a common carrier. May be privately or publicly owned.

Rate Base: The asset value that a commission accepts as a utility firm's investment, for rate-setting purposes.

QUESTIONS FOR REVIEW

1. "Natural monopolies are defined by economies of scale. Therefore, regulation is found where, and only where, there are great economies of scale." True?

2. "Utility sectors change, making it hard to keep regulation in line with the ideal coverage." True?

3. "A physical connection between utility and customer increases the scope for price discrimination." True?

4. "Regulation is often merely a forum for hammering out compromises among the interested groups." True?

5. "Since the 'correct' rate of return is usually in the 15 to 20 percent range, regulation can't really go seriously wrong in setting profit levels." True?

6. "Utility firms are tempted to enlarge their rate requests, knowing that the commissions will cut them back." True?

7. "Cost-plus regulation will always induce great X-efficiency." True?

8. "Rate-base regulation tends to encourage inflation of the firm's real and accounting capital." True?

9. "Regulation induces cautious behavior and a desire for excess reserve capacity, both among regulators and utility officials." True?

10. "It usually is hard to assign credit and blame for performance between the regulators and the firm." True?

11. "Regulation has existed since 1888 at least, but it was forcefully applied only for a few decades." True?

12. Which criteria ought to govern in deciding what to regulate?

13. If regulation is merely a form of compromise rather than clear direction, is it then useless?

14. What old utilities need to be de-regulated? What new sectors need to be put under regulation?

C·H·A·P·T·E·R 14   Regulation in Practice

In practice, regulators apply two criteria: Profits and price levels are to be "fair," and the price structure is to be "just and reasonable."[1] In other markets, a competitive process usually gives these efficient outcomes. Here it is to be done by scrutiny and price ceilings. If things go well, there will result (1) precisely the efficient level of capacity and output in each part of the utility and in its total; (2) no X-inefficiency; (3) the optimal rate of innovation, no more, no less; and (4) a fair division of burdens and rewards among investors, consumers, managers, and others.

Commissions must try to do most of this indirectly, as they decide rate cases about price levels and structures. These decisions and controls may bring about the good economic results. However, that is not assured, as Chapter 13 noted: mistakes may occur, the indirect influence may not be tight enough, or the regulatory process itself may insert new biases. Additionally, one goal may conflict with another; for example, prices that maximize *efficiency* may not be *fair*. A more basic problem is that firms in competitive markets must struggle to reach the competitive results; the *utility* firm's main struggle is with the regulatory commission.

---

[1]For more advanced analyses of these core economic issues, see Alfred E. Kahn, *The Economics of Regulation,* 2 vols. (New York: John Wiley & Sons, 1971; Cambridge, Mass.: MIT Press, 1988), especially vol. 1; James C. Bonbright, *Principles of Public Utility Rates* (New York: Columbia University Press, 1962); Richard Schmalensee, *The Control of Natural Monopolies* (Lexington, Mass.: D.C. Heath, 1979); and Daniel Spulber, *Regulation and Markets* (Cambridge, Mass.: MIT Press, 1989). For detailed coverage of the ongoing flow of practical issues and actual regulatory decisions, see the research reports and Quarterly Bulletins of the National Regulatory Research Institute, Columbus, Ohio.

So we consider controls on price levels and structures in this chapter. In both sections, we first define the optimum constraint and then compare it with what is done in the electricity and telephone-service industries.

I. SETTING PRICE AND PROFIT LEVELS: ECONOMIC CRITERIA

1. The Problem

Assume first that the utility's price *structure* is correct. At what *level* should that whole structure be set so that the total profit rate is consistent with efficient allocation? Recall from Chapter 2 that a firm's net profit is:

$$\text{Net profit} = \text{Total revenue} - \text{Total Cost}$$

In more detail:

$$\text{Net profit} = \left(\begin{array}{c}\text{Output} \\ \text{prices}\end{array} \times \begin{array}{c}\text{Output} \\ \text{quantities}\end{array}\right) - \left[\left(\begin{array}{c}\text{Input} \\ \text{prices}\end{array} \times \begin{array}{c}\text{Input} \\ \text{quantities}\end{array}\right) + \begin{array}{c}\text{Annual} \\ \text{depreciation}\end{array}\right] \quad (1)$$

The profit *rate* on investment is simply the profit divided by the amount of investment, often called the rate base.

$$\text{Profit rate} = \frac{\text{Total revenue} - \text{Total cost}}{\text{Rate base}}$$

$$\text{Profit rate} = \frac{\text{Total revenue} - \text{Total cost}}{\text{Original value} - \text{Accrued depreciation}} \quad (2)$$

The commission decides the prices of all the outputs to be sold to final customers at the end of the hearing on the rate increase. This is supposed to combine with the other elements to permit the firm only a fair rate of profit on its rate base. The commission can try to scrutinize each of the other items in the full equation (2), by looking through the utility's records and quizzing the managers during the hearings. It can try to judge whether the amounts of inputs used by the utility, or the prices paid for them, are too high. If they are, there is X-efficiency, and total costs are too high. The same goes for the rate base, which may be inflated. The commissioners can also debate and decide whether the firm's chosen rate of depreciation is too low or too high. If so, that would affect both the yearly profits and the rate base itself, as Chapter

13 noted. The commissioners can also adopt a different basis for figuring the rate base. For example, they may use a *present value* (based on reproduction cost or replacement cost) instead of the original prices paid for the capital.

At any rate, this is *rate-base regulation*. The standard rate case and decision focus only on the output prices, but they are evidently just one element in a complex set of variables. The key choice is usually about the fair rate of return which will be set. How high should this profit-rate ceiling be set? The firm cares intensely about this. The market value of the firm (that is, the price of its stock) will rise if the profit rate can be raised, even by just a little.[2] The utility firm will be willing to use large resources—and virtually any line of argument—to persuade the commission to raise the ceiling on the profit rate. There is a range within which reasonable profit-rate ceilings (π) could fall: 8 to 15 percent is a good estimate.

The main issue boils down to the conditions shown in Figure 13–1. The monopoly firm strongly prefers to set its output where its marginal revenue equals marginal cost. At that output level, the equilibrium price is at P_M and average cost is AC_M. By setting price well above average cost, the monopoly reaps large profits.

Regulation's job is to prevent that result by forcing price down to the efficient level, where price is just equal to marginal cost. In the special case shown in Figure 13–1, demand happens to intersect both the marginal-cost and the average-cost curves where average cost is at its minimum level. Therefore, the Efficient price = Marginal cost result can be obtained while price also just covers average costs. The firm's profits are sufficient, neither too much nor too little; in short, the *competitive* profit rate is obtained. This ideal result occurs when capacity (the output level where average cost is lowest) is so well planned that it coincides with demand. The exact result is hard to arrange, but a reasonable approximation is commonly reached.

So regulators strive to define and enforce the price P_E, while the company tries instead to get the price up to P_M. Even a slight rise above P_E can be worth millions of dollars to the firm, and so the struggle recurs incessantly in scores of commissions, year after year.

---

[2]Consider as an example a utility with $2 billion in total asset value and a permitted profit rate (π) of 10 percent (there are more than 50 actual utility firms larger than this). The firm's capital is covered half by bonds and half by common stock, and the current market value of the stock is $1 billion, or 8.3 times the net income flow of $120 million per year (that is, a price-earnings ratio of 8.3: quite normal). Interest on bonds is at 8 percent, and the estimated cost of equity is 12 percent

Now suppose the commission raises the permitted rate of return on all assets to 11 percent, up a mere one point. Net income will rise by $20 million per year (1 percent of $2 billion). This will capitalize at a price-earnings ratio of 8.3 into a stockholder gain of $166 million, or 16.6 percent. Just that small rise in the profit rate has enriched the stockholders by $166 million. The leverage of a small change in profit rate can be strong.

2. Criteria for the Rate of Return

What *should* π be? Answer: It should be at the level that attracts the efficient rate of new investment into the firm. The utility's profit rate is to be fitted within the efficient allocation of resources among all markets. If profit rates elsewhere are high, even for secure firms, then this regulated firm's rate of profit should perhaps be raised. Otherwise, the firm will go begging for funds and will soon be below its optimal capacity. Thus arises the conventional regulatory concern about the cost of capital and capital attraction; company lawyers try to scare the commission with forecasts that capacity will lag and breakdowns will occur if the rate of profit is set below the cost of capital.

Specific criteria therefore include:

1. *The cost of capital.* The measured average cost of acquiring investment funds to make necessary investment in the system.
2. *Capital attraction.* Returns on capital high enough to induce capital markets to supply at least the efficient level of new capital.

These seem sensible and mutually consistent, but they present some tricky theoretical and practical problems. They are circular and perhaps empty, though commissions regularly seek to apply them.

3. Defects of the Criteria

Circularity. The criteria are circular because the commission cannot "find" the economic conditions of risk and return and then fit the profit rate to them. Instead, the commission itself sets much of the utility's risk and performance conditions. The commission can force low profits, onerous service burdens, and even new competition on the utility. Such risks may exceed the "innate economic risks" of the monopoly firm.

Impracticality. The criteria don't yield easy, clear answers in practice. The cost of *new* capital is difficult to measure. The cost of *existing* capital is easier to pin down, but it is not the correct basis to use because it is backward-looking (though commissions do use it; see below). Capital attraction implies that there is a specific correct level of investment, but there are no precise ways to measure that level.

Depletion or Growth? The correct growth rate for a utility may be high, low, or negative, depending on its life-cycle stage. Capital may need to be depleted or held constant, rather than attracted. This, in turn, may prescribe negative or low profit rates for the shrinkage of "overbuilt" utilities. Alternatively, there may need to be high profit rates if the utility faces excess demand or super-rapid growth. Only for a "normal" growing utility—with capacity in line with demand—will capital attraction require a profit rate in the normal range of 8 to 15 percent.

Profits Are Given, Not Earned. The earnings of the firm should come from attaining higher efficiency, not from a guaranteed rate of return. Instead, the two criteria give the profits as a right, regardless of efficiency or innovation. That has been a fallacy of regulation; by making the profit results *look* like competition, the other results of competition—efficiency, equity, innovation, and so on—could be attained. A truly economic criterion for profits would vary with the firm's performance.

In light of all this, the intelligent commission will treat various sophistries about criteria with good-humored skepticism. Normally, the rate of return should fall somewhere in the 8 to 15 percent range. The reasonable commission will consider the following, without pretending to have a rigid formula or crystal ball:

1. The general financial condition of the utility.
2. The recent trend of the utility's stock price.
3. How well the utility has been performing (a composite of many things: service complaints, adequacy of capacity and expansion plans, trade commentary on managerial and service quality, and so forth).
4. General price and wage trends, by comparison with the utility.

Single criteria can give some guidance and clarity, but good decisions also draw on a variety of present and future conditions, weighed carefully but informally.

4. Setting the Rate of Return in Practice

The correct π is never crystal clear. It needs to be above the rate on riskless assets (for example, the Treasury prime rate), for utilities have some risk (depending on their life-cycle stage and regulatory treatment). But how much higher?

Commissions usually look to the *cost of capital*. Estimates of the cost of past capital are prepared.[3] There are also guesses about the cost of new capital. And the commission usually adds a safety margin. The resulting figure, artificial and inelegant as it is, does give an approximation roughly in line with reasonable judgments.

---

[3]The method uses weighted averages of the cost of debt and equity capital. The process can grow arcane, with formulae for finding the cost of equity capital, in light of dividend payout ratios, growth rates, and so forth. But it all boils down to reasonable guesses within the traditional range.

The resulting estimates of fair return lack clear guidance.[4] The rates actually allowed by the commissions and the courts have usually been conventional or arbitrary. They have usually been based on expert testimony and rules of thumb. The allowed return differs from state to state and from industry to industry, and it varies over time.

Averages and Dispersions. Regulated profits often seem to reflect a degree of restraint, but there is naturally much variety. In recent decades, utility rates of return on equity have been about the same as those in other sectors. Gross exploitation has been avoided, but profit rates are not tightly limited.

Actual rates of return do not follow the ceilings rigidly; some of them shift or stay above, while others move below. Most utility firms actually get returns on equity in the range of 11 to 15 percent.

The spread reflects utility life cycles and relative efficiency, as well as regulatory limits. Broadly, the mainline utilities have had returns surprisingly close to the average for all large firms, and some have done even better. Others have done poorly—eastern railroads, many electricity firms since 1975 because of nuclear plant problems and slow growth—not only from errors but also because of underlying life-cycle determinants.

Regulatory Lag. During about 1945–65, average costs in some utilities (for example, telephones, electricity, airlines) were stable or declining, as scale economies were explored. This was the golden age of regulation: few rate hearings, steady or falling utility prices, good service quality, simple issues, and handsome profits. Rate hearings lagged behind the falling costs.

The regulatory lag favored the firms, and the excess profits were not recaptured. However, it seemed not to matter, for utility finance, per-

---

[4]One example shows how the estimates can vary. In a telephone-rate case in New Hampshire, five witnesses gave these estimates:

	Debt Ratio	Cost of Equity	Cost of Capital
McIninch	—	9.5–10%	—
Conrad	35%	10–11	8.0%
Barker	35	10	7.75–8.5
Lowell	35–40	10–11	8.0
Kosh	45–50	6.95–8	5.5–6.05
Commission decision	45	7.75	6.11

Source: New England Telephone & Telegraph Co., 42 PUR 3d 57, 60–61, summarized in Charles F. Phillips, Jr., *The Economics of Regulation,* rev. ed. (Homewood, Ill.: Richard D. Irwin, 1969), p. 286.

formance, and price trends all seemed favorable. There was even a boom in AT&T stock and many other utility stocks during the 1950s.

Since 1965—and especially during the 1970s—regulatory lag has put great pressure on the firms. Rapidly rising costs forced rapid price rises, faster than commissions were used to acting. The pressure of events forced a drastic shortening of the old regimen of rate hearings, often from many months to just a few weeks.

In the 1980s, inflation abated, and so the regulatory process could resume its earlier stately pace, but many commissions also loosened their regulation, as Chapter 13 noted. Companies were permitted to keep some or all extra profits gained above the old regulated rates. In these cases, deliberate regulatory looseness was adopted in hopes of giving the same results as the older regulatory lag.

To some extent, this merely permitted monopoly pricing at excess profit levels. However, to the extent that it did encourage lower costs and higher innovation, it fostered greater efficiency.

II. RATE STRUCTURE: ECONOMIC CRITERIA

We now turn to the inner *structure* of prices. The problem is important and complex. The utility—private or public—usually has much latitude in designing its prices. A great variety of price structures will be consistent with any single profit rate for the entire firm. Some of these structures are socially "best"; others can be grossly unfair and inefficient.

1. Marginal Cost as the Basis for Prices

As usual, there is a core of relatively simple concepts, which can be refined down to the point of hair splitting. The basic objective is clear: *Individual prices should normally be as close to marginal cost as is reasonably possible.* This harmonizes with the basic criteria of efficiency and fairness. In Chapter 13's simple equation, the aim is to reach:

$$\text{Price} = k \text{ (Marginal Cost)} \tag{3}$$

where k is to be at or close to 1. The k ratio will not, in any case, vary sharply among the utility's outputs and customers. Though marginal costs are often hard to define and measure, they are the correct basis.

The firm invariably wishes instead *to discriminate in prices,* varying k inversely with demand elasticity on each output (recall Chapter 10). It calls this *value-of-service pricing,* or *ability-to-pay pricing,* or some other nice name, but it is still discrimination. Demand is inelastic where the users have strong minimum needs for the output and where there are no alternative sources of supply. Demand is elastic for those customers who have less urgent needs or can choose among rival suppliers. The firm can discriminate extensively; doing so will maximize its profits while minimizing its long-run risks from new competition.

The two sides are at loggerheads: The commission's objective is to line up prices with marginal *costs*, while the firm wants to fit prices to *demand* conditions. In some parts of the utility, costs and demand conditions are parallel, so that marginal-cost pricing and discrimination are also parallel.[5] Efficient pricing then may occur voluntarily, though supervision is still needed. However, costs can differ in *contrast* to demand differences, so that the correct price ratios differ even more sharply.

Regulation has often been created in reaction to brazen price discrimination. So commission decisions on price structure can be an acid test of their effectiveness. Yet, until 1960 or so, rate-level questions largely crowded out rate structure from regulatory attention. The 1960s reawakened interest, and the 1970s thrust price structure to center stage in electricity, telephones, and other sectors.

Marginal cost *is the key concept.*[6] *It is the true cost of supplying the additional (or "incremental") unit, at a given level of output. Long-run marginal cost* is defined for the future, letting all inputs vary (including fixed capital). *Short-run marginal cost* assumes some costs as given (usually fixed capacity costs, or overhead costs), and therefore, includes only those costs which can be changed (roughly, "out-of-pocket" costs). The ideal criterion is long-run marginal cost, since it reflects the basic pattern of future resource choices. Also, regulators try to fix prices for a period of years, rather than have them jump about. Yet the long run is series of short runs, and so pricing often needs to fit short-run variations in cost.

Marginal costs vary in two broad categories: (1) by *output types* and (2) by *time*.

1. Outputs vary in physical type, location, and other conditions of service. (Examples: electricity at high and low voltages; local versus long-distance telephone calls; and mailing a 1-ounce letter versus a

---

[5]Thus, long-distance telephone rates reflect the structure of costs, both by distances and by time of day (for example, low night and weekend rates). Airlines may offer discounts for late-night travel and stand-by service, where costs are lower.

[6]For more advanced discussion of marginal costs, see Kahn, *The Economics of Regulation,* vol. 1, chap. 3–5; Bonbright, *Principles of Public Utility Rates,* chap. 4, 16, 17, and 20; James R. Nelson, ed., *Marginal Cost Pricing in Practice* (New York: Prentice-Hall, 1964); and Harry M. Trebing, *Assessing New Pricing Concepts in Public Utilities* (East Lansing, Mich.: Institute of Public Utilities, Michigan State University, 1977); and Spulber, *Regulation and Markets.*

20-pound package.) The costs vary because of identifiable differences in the resources used. Overhead costs may blur the measurements, but the concept of differing outputs is clear.

2. Outputs vary by time of use: by time of day, day of the week, and season of the year. When output cannot be stored, peak-load costs may differ sharply from off-peak costs.

Figures 14–1 and 14–2 sum up the key points. Use fluctuates, and so costs vary. Figure 14–1 simplifies down to two periods, peak and off-peak. Demand for each period is in a different range of marginal costs. These correspond to peak conditions commonly found in the electricity, transit, telephone, and other sectors.

How can marginal costs vary so sharply among periods? There are three main causes:

1. The last margin of capacity is used only at peak, and so the total costs of installing, depreciating, and maintaining it year-round are focused on just a few units of use. This cost properly falls on peak-load use, which is responsible for requiring the capacity.

2. Utilities use their best capacity for base load, holding their worst units (old buses, inefficient generators) for use only at peak times. Their variable costs may be high.

3. At off-peak times, fixed (capacity) costs are zero and variable costs may be low (for example, slight costs from using an idle telephone exchange or line).

Figure 14–1   Efficient Price Structure: Prices Are in Line with Marginal Costs at *B* and *C*

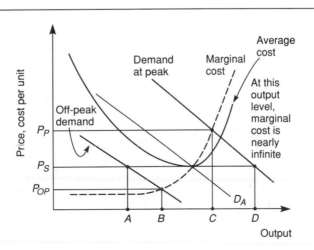

Figure 14–2   Efficient Pricing Often Can Smooth Loads and Reduce Needed Capacity

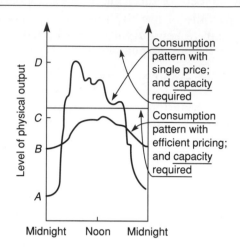

These factors can set peak costs at a multiple of off-peak costs. A telephone call, an extra subway ride, a light switched on, or a letter, at peak times, is much more costly than off-peak. Moreover, external costs are often much higher at peak periods. (Examples: old smoky generators, old fume-emitting and noisy buses are used only at peak times. They increase pollution disproportionately.) Therefore, social costs would be shown by curves above those in Figure 14–1 tipping up extra sharply at the right-hand end.

These short-run cost differences are parallel to long-run costs, for a succession of capacity-straining peaks ultimately means that peak costs are high in the long run.

If a utility is on an efficient growth path, it will usually have peak and off-peak conditions similar to Figure 14–1. Its aggregate revenues from all periods will balance out to cover total costs. Marginal-cost pricing will not cause chronic deficits or surpluses unless the utility gets seriously overbuilt or short of capacity. *Normally, marginal-cost pricing is compatible with private ownership and fair rates of return.*

For efficient allocation, price should be in line with marginal cost for each individual class of output. This results in a peak level price at P_P which is much higher than the off-peak price P_{OP} When costs differ, prices should differ in line with them. If demands are at all elastic, efficient pricing will smooth fluctuations and raise the load factor (as in both Figures 14–1 and 14–2. If D_A represents some kind of average demand conditions and the commission required a single price to be set at P_S, the resulting levels of output demanded would diverge sharply and perhaps disastrously from the efficient levels, as shown in Figure 14–1. Peak-level demand would be far to the right, straining capacity so severely that true marginal costs would be almost infinitely high. In practical terms, the utility would be short of capacity and some demand would *not* be met. Meanwhile off-peak usage would be less than optimal.

Evidently, marginal-cost pricing can be of critical importance, for it may avoid gross and chronic overload on the system. Before 1970, this point often fell on deaf ears; the 1970s' scarcities drove it home. *Without it, the inherent tendencies of regulated utilities to overinvest will be aggravated.* Therefore, peak-load pricing is an essential offset to the other distortions that regulation may induce.

Marginal-cost pricing, in practice, faces difficult problems in defining peak-load responsibility and cost. Still, the principle is clear: During peak-load periods, pricing should be up in line with costs, while off-peak prices should be relatively low.

2. The Declining-Cost Case

There is one special case that may require modifying strict marginal-cost pricing. That is the classic declining-cost case, where marginal cost is everywhere below average cost. This is illustrated in Figure 14–3, for one output. Fixed costs of the system are large, causing average total costs to be high. Yet marginal cost is low (and constant, in this case). Average total cost declines as output rises, because the fixed cost is spread out over larger volumes, but marginal cost is always lower than average cost.

The efficient price is P_{MC}, equal to marginal cost at the point where the demand curve intersects the marginal-cost curve. But at that price, the firm incurs a loss of L per unit, giving the total loss that is shown by the shaded rectangle. The firm can just survive financially if price is set at P_{AC}, where the demand curve intersects the average total-cost curve. That, however, deviates from the price-equals-marginal-cost condition of efficient allocation. Meanwhile, the monopoly firm prefers to set the price at P_M. That gives the output level where marginal cost equals marginal revenue, as shown.

Therefore, the regulators are caught with a dilemma. The efficient price (P_{MC}) puts the firm in bankruptcy, while the firm itself tries to obtain a much higher monopoly price (P_M) Unless the regulators have accurate cost and demand information, the firm may get its monopoly price. Even if the regulators can somehow get accurate information, they still cannot bring about the efficient price and output levels.

The discussion above relates to the single-output case. The declining-cost problem can occur equally well for a firm with many outputs, such as a telephone system; its single system of switching and intercity

Figure 14–3   The Declining-Cost Case

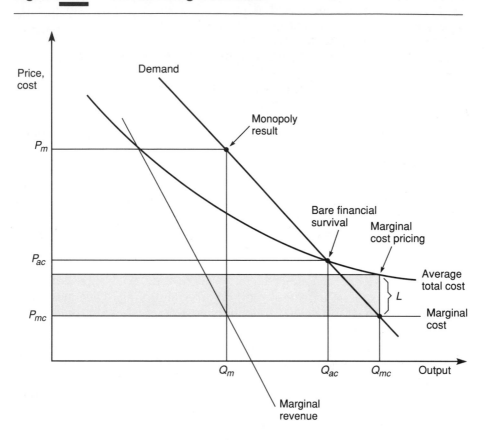

transmission carries calls by many different customer groups, at varying times of day. Those are distinct products, with differing costs.

The costs of the whole system are overhead costs, which are *not* specific to the individual outputs. To that extent, a set of prices that are equal to all the individual marginal costs will not add up to enough revenue to cover the marginal costs *plus* the overhead costs. Marginal-cost pricing will leave the firm with a financial loss, just as in the single-output case.

Earlier writers focused on the single-output case and struggled to find a way out, to reconcile efficient marginal-cost pricing with keeping the firm in business.[7] Their standard idea was to pay the firm a subsidy large enough to cover the financial loss.

---

[7]See Kahn, *The Economics of Regulation,* for a review of this literature of the 1930s.

More recently, Sharkey and Baumol, Panzar, and Willig have focused on the multiproduct case, coining the term *subadditive* to describe the case of a natural monopoly with multiple products.[8] They recommend the Ramsey inverse-elasticity rule in place of marginal-cost pricing (recall Chapter 10). They correctly note that the rule will generate the necessary revenues with the least distortion in allocation among the multiple outputs. Consumer surplus will be maximized.

However, the approach has limits:

1. Many utilities are not declining-cost cases. If total capacity has been expanded just in line with demand, then the standard U-shaped average-cost curve will apply. Marginal cost will equal average cost at the level of capacity, and the sum of revenues will equal the sum of costs. In more technical terms, many utilities are not subadditive. Their arrays of marginal costs can generate sufficient revenues, because not all of them are low; some marginal costs are "high" (e.g., at peak-load times).

2. Often the overhead-cost elements can be isolated and charged at separate prices. For example, the wires to connect a house can be covered by a separate access charge, rather than treated as just part of all overhead costs.

3. Ramsey prices are efficient only when the firm earns a bare competitive profit rate. But the firm will instead try to generate monopoly profits from the discriminatory prices. Constraining the firm so as to avoid monopoly profits—while permitting complex price discrimination—may be nearly impossible for the regulators to accomplish. At the least, it will be extremely difficult.

4. When any competitive elements are present in the situation, Ramsey pricing is ideally suited to *prevent* the emergence of competition. Therefore Ramsey prices are suitable for only the pure franchised-utility case. But most utilities tend instead to evolve toward dominance under emerging competition.

3. Sustainability

The emergence of competition can pose a related problem: The Ramsey efficient prices may be vulnerable to entry by new firms that produce only one or several of the outputs. That entry would force the existing firm to change to other prices, reflecting the new competition on the

[8]William W. Sharkey, *The Theory of Natural Monopoly* (New York: Cambridge University Press, 1982); and William J. Baumol, John C. Panzar, and Robert D. Willig, *Contestable Markets and the Theory of Industry Structure* (San Diego: Harcourt Brace Jovanovich, 1982). See also Spulber, *Regulation and Markets;* and Dennis W. Carlton and Jeffrey M. Perloff, *Modern Industrial Organization* (Glenview, Ill.: Scott, Foresman, 1990), chap. 23.

one or several outputs. The lesson of "sustainability" theory has been firm: Prevent the entry so as to protect the set of efficient prices.[9]

However, the dilemma is not as troubling as it seems. The sustainability problem does not threaten the existence of the firm itself. It merely calls for adjusting the set of prices from the current Ramsey prices to a new set of Ramsey prices, based on the new elasticities. The incumbent firm merely cuts prices where new entrants are giving it pressure. That, in fact, is the natural result of the entry process, as cream skimming attacks inelastic-demand goods and raises their elasticities. Therefore, sustainability does not pose a radically new issue or difficulty.

III. ELECTRICITY PRICING

Now we consider some economic features of classic regulated sectors. This section focuses on electric service (telephone service will be covered in the next section). In both, there is a core of natural monopoly allied with other parts that could have a competitive structure.

The electricity industry has several unusual features. There are three levels of operations, which are usually joined together by vertical integration. The supply of electricity at the final level is usually a local monopoly. But the conditions that have traditionally seemed to require vertical integration and local monopoly are debatable. Electricity pricing has been a classic natural-monopoly topic, but the conditions of natural monopoly may be disappearing.

1. The Sector

Levels. Electricity is a three-stage sector.[10] The first stage is *generation,* the production of electricity by rotating large electric motors backwards so that electric power comes out. The driving force may come from conventional sources of heat, such as coal, oil, and gas, or from water power. Recently, nuclear energy has begun to be a signifi-

---

[9]Sharkey, Baumol, Panzar, and Willig were working for AT&T when they developed these ideas. The lesson they drew (to bar new competition against AT&T) was in line with AT&T's interests.

[10]For good summaries of the sector see Russell E. Caywood, *Electric Utility Rate Economics* (New York: McGraw-Hill, 1956); Edwin Vennard, *The Electric Power Business* (New York: McGraw-Hill, 1962); and Federal Power Commission, *National Power Survey,* 4 vols. (Washington, D.C.: U.S. Government Printing Office, 1970); Sanford V. Berg, ed., *Innovative Electric Rates: Issues in Cost-Benefit Analysis* (Lexington, Mass.: D.C. Heath, 1983); and Paul L. Joskow and Richard Schmalensee, *Markets for Power* (Cambridge, Mass.: MIT Press, 1984).

cant generation source. By now, most of the good hydroelectric sites are occupied, and the future sources of power lie mainly between coal and nuclear fission (using uranium)—with possibly fusion (using water) and solar heat further ahead.

Transmission is the bulk carriage of electricity from generating sites to final-use areas. The huge towers that march across the countryside carry these high voltage power lines. Increasing scale has lengthened the distances that power can be carried with little loss. That has made competition possible over great areas of the country. As transmission scale has increased, the country (and certain sources in Canada) has become partly interconnected, but there are a series of about 170 separately owned systems, coordinated only to a degree.

The *distribution* systems are local: from the substation to the final users. This involves wires to a great variety of users, including residential, commercial, industrial, and public agencies. These are the end points of electricity supply, which require much servicing and change, as customers and uses shift.

Technology. There are relatively slight economies of vertical integration. More important are the economies of scale at each level. At both the generation and transmission levels, the scale economies have been large, favoring an increasingly large size of apparatus during the last several decades. However, it is *distribution* at the local level where natural monopoly most clearly exists. There the inefficiency of duplicating the network of wires seems to be clear and compelling. Distribution is *the* core of natural monopoly in electricity supply.

In *generation,* the last four decades have seen a rise in size of units and a reduction of average costs. This was not strictly a technological advance, but rather the realization of preexisting economies of scale. In the 1960s, it became apparent that the limits of scale economies were being reached.[11] Therefore, generation is characterized by economies of scale that are definite but limited.

Transmission has been increasing in scale also, and further economies seem to be large. Large-scale transmission offers major new opportunities for carrying bulk supply over long distances and in high volume. This could lead either to new competition in wholesale electricity or to more unification in a national grid. Transmission is, therefore, the most sensitive area for future adjustments in the scope of local monopoly and regulation.

On the whole, the technology is evolving and will permit realignments of the old service areas and competitive strategies, as Chapter

---

[11]Federal Power Commission, *National Power Survey,* vol. I; M. Galatin, *Economies of Scale and Technological Change in Thermal Generation* (Amsterdam: North Holland Press, 1968); and Joskow and Schmalensee, *Markets for Power.*

12 noted. The core of natural monopoly at the distribution level will continue, but the pressures for detaching it from the rest of the sector—so new structures can evolve—are growing. Electricity is currently at a watershed from which new structures and regulatory treatments could evolve.

2. Earlier Pricing

Until the 1970s, commissions rarely tackled rate structures thoroughly. In a standard rate-level case, prices were often increased equally across the board. Only when new services were offered, or a specific price was challenged, did commissions try to allocate costs in setting a price. Yet such treatment is piecemeal and infrequent. Commissions often avoided the divisive issues of price structure by simply accepting what the firms proposed.

Despite this, regulation's broad effect has been to reduce price discrimination. The pricing for broad customer groups—such as residential, commercial, and large industry—often is less discriminatory than it would be if left free, but much discrimination remains, particularly in railroad pricing.

Until about 1965, there was little careful action. Pricing had come to be mainly *promotional,* with volume discounts for higher use (so-called declining block and two-part tariffs). This promoted use and growth, but it probably overstimulated peak-load use and involved widespread discrimination. Many utilities voluntarily used marginal-cost pricing, but only for some services.

After 1970, major efforts began toward time-of-use rate restructuring, especially in electricity and telephones. Federal commissions and the better state commissions have tried a variety of experiments.[12] This has been reinforced by the utilities' own interests in avoiding excess investment and peak-load breakdowns. Yet action so far has been only a beginning. Concepts and methods are still formative. Peak-load use is still underpriced in most utility systems, and price discrimination among customer groups continues to be important.

3. Shifts toward Marginal-Cost Pricing

Electricity pricing presents the issues of regulatory treatment most clearly, as shown by the following details.

---

[12]See Leonard W. Weiss, "State Regulation of Public Utilities and Marginal-Cost Pricing," in *Case Studies in Regulation: Revolution and Reform,* ed. Leonard W. Weiss and Michael W. Klass (Boston: Little, Brown, 1981); and Schmalensee, *The Control of Natural Monopolies.*

Table 14–1   Illustrations of Electricity Rates

Declining Block—for Residential Customers	Rising-Block Variant
1. Monthly customer charge: $1	2.0¢ for the first 200 kwhr.
2. Energy charge per kwhr.	3.5¢ for the next 300 kwhr.
7.85¢ for the first 50 kwhr.	4.5¢ for all additional kwhr.
4.29¢ for next 100.	
1.95¢ for ncxt 200.	
1.67¢ for next 500.	
1.50¢ for all additional kwhr.	

Two-Part Tariff—for Industrial Customers (at 4,800 to 120,000 volts)

  1. Demand Charge per kw.
    $8.00 per kw. for the first 200 kw.
    $6.50 for next 800.
    $5.50 for next 500.
    $5.00 for all additional kw. of demand.
    (Demand measured by the maximum load of the customer at any time during the previous month.)

  2. Energy charge: 1.5¢ per kwhr. plus fuel adjustment per kwhr.

After intensive debates in the 1890s, electricity pricing soon evolved into two basic rate structures: the *declining-block* tariff for residential customers and the *two-part* tariff for commercial and industrial customers.[13] After 1970, the declining-block tariff was converted into flat-rate or "rising-block" rates by many commissions, for reasons to be given shortly. Otherwise, the basic pricing approaches are little changed.

The basic forms are illustrated in Table 14–1 and Figure 14–4. The block-based tariff merely sets differing prices for various volumes of electric power taken. When charted in Figure 14–4, these prices appear as blocks.

A two-part tariff sets (1) a monthly "demand" charge, based on the customers' maximum load on the system and (2) an encrgy charge per kilowatt hour, to reflect the cost of fuel. In theory, those two payments cover the capacity and the fuel used by the customer.

The declining-block rate is a *promotional* rate, because it sets successively lower prices for taking larger amounts. These volume discounts were meant to encourage families to use more power. Indeed, in the 1960s, a special low-price block was added for "all-electric" houses, where the family used electricity for all fuel needs (with no gas or oil).

---

[13]See Ralph K. Davidson, *Price Discrimination in Selling Gas and Electricity* (Baltimore: The Johns Hopkins Press, 1955); Charles J. Cicchetti and John Jurewitz, eds., *Studies in Electric Utility Regulation* (Cambridge, Mass.: Ballinger 1975); and Caywood, *Electric Utility Rate Economics*.

Figure 14–4   Illustration of Declining-Block and Rising-Block Tariffs for Electricity

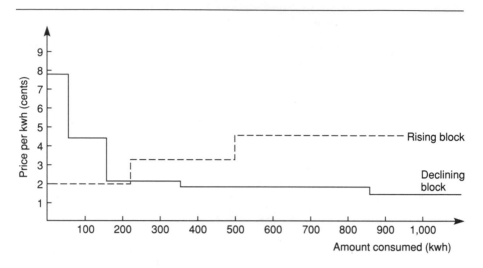

These discounts made sense when power costs were falling in line with greater economies of scale, up to 1968, but then conditions quickly reversed, for several reasons. The economies of scale in generation stopped increasing. Rising prices and interest rates made new equipment more expensive. Generating sites became scarcer and more costly. Fuel prices rose drastically after 1972. Therefore, discounts needed to be replaced by rising-block tariffs, to reflect the new patterns of costs.

This has been done in some states; thus, flat or rising blocks are more common than declining blocks. However, there are few sharply rising cases. Another important feature is "lifetime rates." They give the first moderate amount of electricity per month (enough for "basic service") at a lower price, such as 3¢ per kilowatt hour. The rest is on a flat-rate basis, such as 6¢ per kilowatt hour. This bargain rate is meant to help the poor afford basic service—as a matter of fairness, rather than of efficiency. It is a "social" adjustment, rather than one of cost. After intense battles over lifetime rates during the late 1970s, a minority of states adopted them.

Time-Based Pricing. The 1970s brought widespread efforts to set prices in line with differing costs at different times of the day, of the week, and of the year.[14] Electricity load fluctuates between peak and off-peak levels, as Figures 14–1 and 14–2 noted and as Figure 14–5

---

[14]The literature on peak-load pricing is extensive. See among others, Jan Paul Acton and Rolla Edward Park, *Response to Time-of-Day Electricity Rates by Large Business Cus-*

Figure 14–5   Typical Daily-Load Patterns

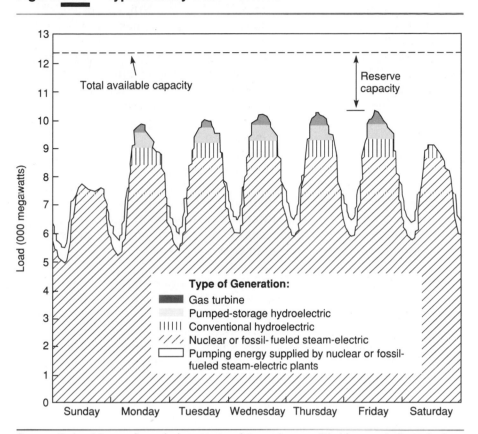

Source: Federal Power Commission, *National Power Survey,* (Washington, D.C.: U.S. Government Printing Office, 1970), p. 1-7-5.

tomers: Reconciling Conflicting Evidence, R-3477-NSF (Santa Monica: The RAND Corporation, August 1987); Dennis J. Aigner and Lee A. Lillard, "Southern California Edison's Time-of-Use Experiment," in *Award Papers in Public Utility Economics and Regulation,* MSU Public Utilities Papers, ed. Harry M. Trebing (East Lansing, Mich.: Institute of Public Utilities, 1982); Michael A. Crew and Paul Kleindorfer, *The Economics of Public Utility Regulation* (Cambridge, Mass: MIT Press, 1986); Michel Francony, Bruno Lescoeur, and Philippe Penz, "Updating the French Electricity Tariffs," in *Award Papers in Public Utility Economics and Regulation,* MSU Public Utilities Papers, ed. Harry M. Trebing (East Lansing, Mich.: Institute of Public Utilities, 1982); Hendrik Houthakker, "Principles of Efficiency in Relation to Electricity Tariffs," *Economic Journal,* 1954; Roger McElroy, Timothy Pryor, Russell Profozich, Amy Garant, and Kaye Pfister, *Marginal Cost Ratemaking for Cogeneration, Interruptible, and Back-Up Services* (Columbus, Ohio: National Regulatory Research Institute, 1981); Bridger M. Mitchell, Willard G. Manning, Jr., and Jan Paul Acton, *Peak-Load Pricing: European Lessons for U.S. Energy Policy* (Cambridge, Mass.: Ballinger Publishing, 1978); Asher Tischler, "The Industrial and Commercial Demand for Electricity Under Time of Use Pricing," *Journal of Econometrics,* December 1983; and Ralph Turvey, *Optimal Pricing and Investment in Electricity Supply* (London: Allen & Unwin, 1968).

shows for daily hours, and for months of the year. Costs are higher at peak times, often by a multiple of off-peak costs. Efficient prices would reflect those costs, with high prices during the business hours and during seasonal peaks.

U.S. rates, however, have largely been uniform, regardless of the fluctuations. The French first developed peak-load rates in the 1950s, followed by the British in the 1960s. Only when severe pressures of costs and supply arose in the early 1970s did U.S. commissions turn to peak-load pricing. Congress passed a law encouraging it, and new time-based rates have been adopted in about 15 states.

Their main features are illustrated by a Wisconsin tariff shown in Table 14–2. Time periods are defined, ranging from the highest peak times (7:00 A.M. to 7:00 P.M., Monday through Friday in the summer) to the lowest off-peak periods (7:00 P.M. to 7:00 A.M., Saturday and Sunday, in the spring and fall). Prices vary to reflect loads, from 7.69¢/kwhr. down to 3.41¢ for residences. The research on these price experiments points to sizable savings in costs.

Discrimination. The structure of electricity prices has long been highly differentiated. Different classes were established for residential use, commercial light and power, industrial power, and the like. The typical utility now has 4 to 8 rate categories, each with different prices.

Demand conditions encourage sharp discrimination. Elasticities vary, with businesses generally having higher elasticity of demand than residences. Electricity is essential for lighting—that is, demand is ine-

Table 14–2   Illustrations of Time-Of-Use Electricity Prices

Residential Rate

Customer charge per month	$2.75
Meter charge per month (for a time-of-day meter)	2.50/meter
Water heating credit (applicable in all months)	1.50/month

Energy charge (high-use hours: 7:00 A.M. to 7:00 P.M., Monday through Friday, inclusive)

	Billing Periods		
	Summer July– September	Winter January– March	Base All Other Months
First 500 kwhr./month	7.69¢/kwhr.	5.10¢/kwhr.	3.71¢/kwhr.
Over 500 kwhr./month	7.69¢/kwhr.	4.50¢/kwhr.	3.41¢/kwhr.
Energy charge (low-use hours: all other hours)			
All months	0.94¢/kwhr.		

lastic—so all households need some electricity. For appliances (stoves, water heaters, air conditioners), demand for electricity is fairly elastic. The key fact is that businesses can often generate their own power or substitute other fuels for power in their industrial processes. Discrimination would prescribe the basic pattern of rates that has evolved: higher prices for residences, declining blocks to induce the use of electric household appliances, and demand charges that ignore system peaks.

Are rates cost based or discriminatory? The answer is both, and there are three reasons. First, broad cost patterns (in the regional price of fuel, in obvious customer costs, and so forth) are bound to show through in rates. Thus, sharp state differences in typical utility bills mainly reflect such cost differences. Second, cost and demand conditions are parallel in some areas: For example, most households cost more per kwhr. to supply than most businesses. Third, regulation has had some effect, but nobody can be sure how much. The role of costs as a price criterion is probably increasing.

IV. TELEPHONE-SERVICE PRICING

The core natural monopoly is local telephone service, familiar to everyone.[15] The other, newer parts—such as long-distance traffic and large-scale business services—are growing faster. U.S. telephone capacity is more advanced than most other countries, both in the coverage of households and in the quality of service provided.

1. The Sector

To understand conditions since divestiture in 1984, one must recognize how the old Bell System functioned (recall Chapter 7). The telephone system is actually just part of a wider set of telecommunications markets. There are two main levels: (1) the *production* of equipment and (2) the *operation* of equipment. From 1881 to 1984, AT&T combined both levels, in a virtually closed, vertically integrated system. Its Western Electric Company supplied nearly all of the important equipment to its 21 operating companies (BOCs). However, in the whole sector, and even in parts of the AT&T domain, there was a growing amount of competition and choice.

---

[15]Most of the recent literature on the sector relates to competition and the divestiture of AT&T. For a lucid review of regulatory policies, see Harry M. Trebing, "Telecommunications Regulation—The Continuing Dilemma," in *Public Utility Regulation: The Economic and Social Control of Industry,* ed. Kenneth Nowotny, David B. Smith, and Harry M. Trebing (Boston: Kluwer Academic Publishers, 1989), and the sources listed therein.

Production of Equipment. These producers were divided into two categories: (1) those owned by regulated carriers, such as AT&T and General Telephone and Electronics; and (2) all other equipment-making firms, large and small. Firms in the second category generally innovated and marketed their equipment under competitive, or at least rivalrous, conditions.

Western Electric did not compete in these markets. There are many buyers of broadcasting equipment (networks and individual stations), even though one buyer is owned by a major producer (General Electric owns the National Broadcasting Company). Since the networks' earnings are not regulated, rate-base preference is not a factor in their purchasing policies. Many items were affected by competition from European and Japanese firms. Market structure came to be particularly competitive in the smaller, peripheral products, such as terminal attachments for data transmission.

In short, AT&T stuck out as a large zone of monopoly in a competitive sector. AT&T (and GTE) were, in fact, the main vertically integrated utilities in the country (compare electricity, gas, railroads, airlines, cable TV, the postal service, and various urban services). This vertical integration turned out to be unnecessary and a source of monopoly. Divestiture has largely cured the problem (recall Chapter 7).

Operations. Telephone operations involve three main parts.

1. The core is the *local system* of lines and a central switching office. This core natural monopoly would be more costly if duplicated by competitive systems. Switching is done by electrical or, more recently, electronic equipment. (Try to locate the central switching office in your town.)

2. *Transmission among cities* involves a network of long-distance facilities, including complex routing equipment. Signals travel by several modes, such as cable, land-based microwave, and terrestrial satellites. Messages include both voice and data, each requiring specific levels of quality transmission. Some intercity transmission is done within the 21 operating systems (for example, from Albany to New York City within New York Bell). Traffic among these systems—and among all other independent systems—is handled by the AT&T Long Lines Department. New competition in long-distance service in recent years has reduced AT&T's market share to between 70 and 75 percent.

3. *Terminal equipment* is what the user has on its premises, such as a telephone set or two in the home or store, a private exchange system of 50 telephones in a business or college, feed-ins for data, printing devices, and display units. From the old uniform black telephone of 1900 to the 1950s, these proliferated in the 1970s to a great variety,

once newcomers were permitted to compete with Bell. These markets have little or no natural-monopoly conditions.

The local-service monopoly has been apparent from the industry's start about a century ago. It is the nub of the basis for regulation. The other two parts were added as parts of AT&T's actual monopoly. Yet terminal equipment is separable and naturally competitive. Transmission is also separable and may have room for substantial competition. The scope of natural monopoly in the sector is limited and debatable.

Technology. A telephone system does need to function well as a whole. Reliability may be enhanced by having the equipment produced by a branch of the system itself. Yet full monopoly is not preordained, and indeed the "system" has many separable parts. The key word is *choice:* choice in the technical design of the system itself and choice about the scope and form of the company.

Telephone technology offers much room for choice in designing equipment and coordinating it throughout the system. Even before 1920, there was variety in switching equipment, handsets, office exchanges, and so forth. Since then, the range of choice has widened sharply. Long-distance cables were supplemented by microwave towers after 1945, and then satellites, while cable capacity itself was being vastly improved and increased. Further alternatives—wave guides, lasers, and so on—are being developed. Local switching by electromechanical devices has gradually been replaced by electronic, computer-based switching since 1965. Local lines and long-distance lines, now mostly of metal, began to be displaced by optical fibers during the 1980s, and terminal equipment developed after the 1960s into a profusion of alternatives.

The old vertically integrated Bell System controlled these choices, in ways that enhanced its monopoly position in the entire sector. Now competition is permitting technology and product variety to evolve more freely in line with costs and consumer choices.

2. Pricing Patterns

Bell officials have pressed for value-of-service pricing, which is their name for price discrimination. Since 1970, they have also used marginal-cost pricing arguments for some prices. This partly reflects a genuine shift toward more efficient pricing. In other areas, however, this is just another way of rationalizing price discrimination to head off new competition. Certain new Bell services have been provoked by new entry and then priced low to prevent the entry. The FCC and some state commissions have, instead, leaned toward "fully distributed costs" as the basis for prices. This rough method would prevent price cutting in response to competition, to prevent predatory discrimination, but it might also miss some of the valid patterns of marginal cost. Since Bell costs have been so slippery and easily manipulated, it is not clear which criterion is best for practical uses.

Local pricing has mainly followed conventional lines. This pricing—your phone bill—has mostly been promotional, with a flat monthly fee and a *zero* price for each call. This has induced extra use at peak times and let people be indifferent to the length of the call. When you talk with a friend across town for a half hour during the daytime busy hours, the true cost of your call may be as much as $1, even though you get it free. Figure 14–6 illustrates the inefficiency of such pricing. This also erodes revenues, by reducing the average revenue per unit as growth occurs. The degree of inefficiency depends mainly on the elasticity of demand and on the cost gradients.

After 1965, the burden of this was gradually recognized, and "message-unit" pricing has spread from business use in large cities down to residence use in medium-sized cities. Message-unit pricing sets a smaller monthly fee and roughly a five cent charge per call; the rates

Figure 14–6   Illustration of Local-Service Telephone Pricing

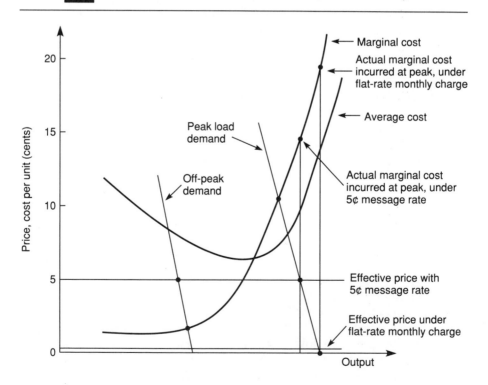

now fit cost conditions more closely, but they still usually ignore the timing and length of calls, so that peak use is still enhanced.

In most European systems, pricing has long been more efficient. Metering is usually precise, so that prices can be closely fitted to the true costs of peak and off-peak use. The meter clicks every 12 seconds, for another penny. During busy hours, it is set to click more frequently, so the price is higher. Only now are U.S. metering equipment and pricing beginning to move toward the sophistication that has long existed abroad.

In the United States, prices also vary between business and residential users (business rentals are higher) and among basic and optional service.[16] Discrimination is common. The monthly rentals charged for added equipment, for instance, were based not on costs but on the subscriber's inelasticity of demand. Business users are charged more than domestic users because they find the service indispensable. Domestic users are charged more for single-party lines mainly because they are willing to pay for added convenience. Recent revisions of rates have made them even more complex. The remaining degree of discrimination is hard to appraise, but it is not small.

Long-distance services have long been priced with a structure that reflects peak–off-peak cost differences. Your local phone directory displays these prices. During weekday business hours, prices are highest. Evenings (except Saturday) are a medium period, while nights (11:00 P.M. to 8:00 A.M.) and most of the weekend have low off-peak prices. The differences are sharp: Calls in the evenings are at a 35 percent discount, while night and weekend calls go for 60 percent less than the daytime rates. These differences reflect cost differences, and so this degree of marginal-cost pricing is familiar and important.

Price discrimination may also be present in all dimensions of this price structure. The differentials include: (1) among peak, mid-peak, and off-peak, for the first minute; (2) between the first and later minutes (why *is* the first minute more expensive?); and (3) by distance. Costs may justify these exact price differentials, or discrimination (in line with demand elasticities) may be involved.

It is likely that the off-peak discounts are too small. Peak use is supposed to bear all capital costs plus the relevant operating costs; off-peak costs on a partly idle system are probably very low. The only condition that might justify these seemingly high off-peak rates would

---

[16]Also, rates have long been higher for cities than towns, with steep gradients across the range of sizes. This made good political sense, but it did not fit cost patterns. Recently, these differences have been narrowed, but small-town users still typically pay only about 75 percent of big-city rates.

be if heavy data transmission is done at night by businesses, so that nighttime traffic is substantial rather than low.

Another key aspect is that competition from MCI and Sprint is stronger on the longer routes. Therefore, AT&T has responded by setting relatively low price-cost ratios on those longer routes to meet that competition. Again, that is pricing in line with demand elasticities.

QUESTIONS FOR REVIEW

1. "The prices of outputs are only one part of the whole regulatory equation." True?
2. "In some cases, a regulated firm should not attract capital for investment." True?
3. "One can easily prepare figures for the cost of capital, but the true cost of capital is difficult to define and measure." True?
4. "If regulation were efficient, the utility would have to earn its rate of return rather than be given it as a right." True?
5. "Cost-plus regulation will always induce great X-efficiency." True?
6. "A high depreciation rate gives low cash flow now, but it pays off by providing a higher rate base in later years." True?
7. "Rate-base regulation tends to encourage inflation of the firm's real and accounting capital." True?
8. "The correct basis for rate structure is marginal cost, perhaps with some price discrimination for special conditions." True?
9. "Cost and demand conditions sometimes give parallel results for price structures." True?
10. "Correct peak-load pricing can help to avoid overexpansion of the rate base." True?
11. "Price discrimination is lessened by regulation, but much of it remains." True?
12. "Regulatory lag can restore incentives for efficiency." True?
13. "Peak-load costs of electricity may be 5 or 10 times as high as off-peak costs." True?
14. "Electricity prices do fit cost patterns in some respects." True?
15. Explain why the regulators' search for "the" fair rate of return is circular.
16. Regulation often tries to enforce a competitive-looking outcome (low profit, prices near costs). Explain why such a simulation does not guarantee efficiency and fairness, the ultimate economic objectives.

P·A·R·T F·O·U·R

PUBLIC ENTERPRISE AND SPECIAL CASES

C·H·A·P·T·E·R 15   Public Enterprise: Concepts and Cases

Public enterprises are integral and important in modern economies. Their role varies from country to country, and the firms come in many forms and varieties. There are gradations of public ownership, of market positions, pricing policies, and internal management. They provide a rich set of experiments in many sectors.[1]

The United States has long had thousands of public enterprises, many of them as familiar and American as apple pie. The private-enterprise ideology of the country causes them to be ignored and belittled, and, indeed, some public enterprises do perform badly. Yet many are efficient and innovative. They are important and varied, at any rate, and they illustrate many fascinating lessons about policies.

Public enterprise is more widespread abroad, but dramatic changes have been occurring in Britain and some other countries since 1980, toward privatizing many of these public firms. Therefore, this chapter is about both public enterprise and the phenomenon of privatizing.

---

[1]There is no comprehensive treatment of the economics of public enterprise. Good sources include W. G. Shepherd and Associates, *Public Enterprise: Economic Analysis of Theory and Practice* (Lexington, Mass.: Lexington Books, 1976); and William J. Baumol, ed., *Public and Private Enterprise in a Mixed Economy* (New York: St. Martins' Press, 1980).

See also Yair Aharoni, *The Evolution and Management of State-Owned Enterprises* (Cambridge, Mass.: Ballinger, 1986); R. Rees, *Public Enterprise Economics* (New York: St. Martin's Press, 1984); Ralph Turvey, *Economic Analysis and Public Enterprise* (London: Allen & Unwin, 1971); Stuart Holland, ed., *The State as Entrepreneur* (White Plains, NY: International Arts and Sciences Press, 1973); Annmarie Hauck Walsh, *The Public's Business: The Politics and Practices of Government Corporations* (Cambridge, Mass.: MIT Press, 1978); J. Redwood and J. Hatch, *Controlling Public Industries* (Oxford: Basil Blackwell, 1982); and J. Vickers and G. Yarrow, *Privatization and the Natural Monopolies* (London: Public Policy Centre, 1985).

First, we consider the economic elements of public enterprise in Section I. Then, Section II reviews the actual patterns of public firms, and it shows their historical roots. Next, Section III presents several case studies: electricity firms, the U.S. Postal Service, and state lotteries. Finally, Section IV discusses privatizing and some of its results.

I. ECONOMIC CONCEPTS

The critical difference between private and public enterprise is simple: The public firm does not issue shares of stock to private investors. Its owner is the public, not private investors. All other features of the public firm can be identical to private firms: the technology, capital, hiring of workers, the products made, and prices set, even the pursuit of a maximum profit. However, maximizing profit is no longer the *necessary* goal. The public firm can, and often does, pursue social purposes, rather than merely profits.

1. Public Enterprises Can Reach the Competitive Outcome

The similarity of public and private firms led economists to a great insight in the 1930s: A whole economy can be organized in *public* firms and still yield the efficient outcomes of a *private* competitive system.[2] To grasp this "Lange-Lerner solution," first imagine that an economy consists of private firms in effectively competitive markets. Competition forces them all to the efficient outcomes, where price equals marginal cost and average costs are at their minimum (recall Chapter 2).

Now wave a magic wand and convert them all into public firms, by replacing their common stock with (nonvoting) stock or bonds. The government instructs all firms to keep producing at levels where price equals marginal costs. Antitrust is continued and thus prevents monopoly from forming.[3] The whole outcome is efficient allocation as before, but now under *public* ownership. Even if economic conditions change, the firms will adjust to give new efficient results in line with the new situation.

Therefore, public enterprise can equal private enterprise's efficiency, in theory, and the same criteria apply in both cases. Public enterprises are to be judged by their pricing, X-efficiency, and innovativeness. By following commerical guidelines of maximum profit, public enterprises can perform as well as private ones.

---

[2]Oskar Lange and Fred M. Taylor, *On the Economic Theory of Socialism* (New York: McGraw-Hill, 1938).

[3]Any natural monopolies can be instructed to set price equal to marginal cost.

2. The Social Element

Public firms are often created not just to copy private results but rather to serve some social purpose that private firms are *not* meeting. The social elements are usually controversial, but they can be real and important.

Among the main kinds of such social purposes are:

1. **Security and responsibility for supply.** Certain services may seem so crucial that the public wishes to have direct control over their supply. Utility services are so regarded in most countries outside the United States: electricity, telephones, railroads, and so on. In the United States, many urban services are publicly owned: water, sewer, buses, and subways are examples. The basic postal service is public everywhere.

2. **Social values and public goods.** Education, national parks, libraries, and the postal service provide fundamental values that private markets would skimp. The result is education, books, and parks for all, and a postal service connecting the whole country. When needy people would otherwise lack supply (as of health care), the public firm can provide universal service.

3. **Inadequate private supply.** A new industry or project may often seem too large and risky for private firms to carry out. They will ask for government grants, guarantees, or other subsidies. It may seem more efficient to create the capacity and production by direct public ownership.

4. **Salvaging firms.** The public often rescues failing firms by buying out their capital and supporting their rehabilitation. This saves the firms, the jobs, and the products.

5. **Controlling private power.** Some banks or firms have great social and economic power. These "commanding heights" (such as large banks and major industrial firms) can be taken over and thus put the power under public control.

6. **Sovereignty.** A small country may take over the local branches of large international companies in order to control their power and prevent outside dominance.

These social elements can be large, but they are often hard to assess and hotly debated. Conservatives rate these values as low or fully provided, or both, by private markets. Liberals see certain social needs, which public firms may serve efficiently.

The typical public firm, at any rate, has a *social element* to serve, which is apart from its usual commerical goals of producing its services efficiently and selling them at prices that fit cost and demand conditions. For example, a public-enterprise local bus line is supposed to provide reliable service throughout the city, on a more extensive schedule than a strictly commercial bus line would provide (especially because it would be a monopoly).

The social element is usually debated intensely, both its nature and its extent. What social element is provided by the postal service, for instance? And does it require daily deliveries, including Saturday? Should "junk mail" be subsidized? If so, to what extent? There are ongoing controversies over Amtrak's services, library hours, parks, Medicare, and city-owned sports stadiums used by private professional teams. Quieter debates continue constantly about city services, public schools and universities, airports, golf courses, state liquor stores in 16 states, and all other public enterprises. In every case, the questions are: What is the valid social element? How much of it should the public pay for?

3. Commercial and Social Activities

The firm's activities range between strictly *commercial* (for example, producing electricity, or airplanes, or tools) and *social*. The social part may be dominant, and the output or service may be provided free. If the commercial part dominates, then prices covering much or all of the costs may be charged.

Most public enterprises have both commercial and social activities. For clarity, these need to be disentangled. Ideally, the social part is subsidized directly by the public, while the commercial part is paid for by the customers through prices that cover costs. In practice, the two parts are hard to keep clear.

Subsidies and Efficiency. The public pays for the social element by means of subsidies, which come from government tax revenues. The subsidy can be of any amount, ranging from 0 to 100 percent. Thus, the public schools are subsidized totally from taxes, while local water supply is paid for by the users. Most public universities are in-between, supported partly by government subsidies and partly by students' tuition payments.

The subsidy ought to be fitted precisely to the social element of the public firm. *A small social effect requires little or no subsidy, while a large social element might justify a total subsidy*. Total subsidy means that the direct users pay nothing; the taxpayers pay for it all.

There are two dangers from subsidies to public firms.

Size. One danger is that the subsidy will simply be too large, giving the users an undeserved free ride. Should library users, or local golfers on the public course, or bus riders, or students at public universities be subsidized heavily? Does the service meet a special social need? Are the users really needier than the cross section of tax payers?

Incentives. The second risk from subsidies is that they will weaken the enterprise's incentives to cut costs. Whenever costs can be covered without effort, the firm may let them rise. The subsidy can become a self-creating device. Public firms as diverse as city transit, the postal service, and Medicare are regularly accused of such wasteful and demoralizing subsidies.

These dangers are real, and they have no universal solution. Society must struggle along with its public enterprises, trying to fit the subsidies to the true social element and trying to avoid wasteful incentives. If the political process works well, it may supervise the firms effectively and trim their subsidies to just the right patterns. Public enterprises can go beyond the narrow limits of profit to serve genuine public needs, but this capacity needs constant control to keep the firms from wasteful mistakes.

Efficient Pricing. Public enterprises come under the same rules for efficient pricing that private firms do. Their prices should be aligned with their marginal costs (including social costs), just as for regulated utilities. Many public firms do, in fact, adopt efficient price structures, carefully measuring marginal costs and setting prices in line with them. The task is easier because the firms are not subject to the special biases from cost-plus-profit regulation that privately owned utilities have.

4. Publicness

There are three main economic dimensions to the "publicness" of public enterprise. One is *ownership,* the traditional criterion. Public firms may be totally publicly owned, and many are. Yet the public may hold only part of the ownership, in all gradations from 0 to 100 percent. So ownership is not the only criterion.

Second, the public may *subsidize* the public enterprise, in some degree. The firm may show financial losses on its operations, which are covered by payments of public funds. Put the other way around, the firm may charge prices that cover none, some, all, or even a lot more than all of its operating costs. The firm's capital needs may also be met by the government. A public firm whose operations and investment are heavily subsidized is more "public" than one that earns a profit and raises its own investment funds.

Third, the closeness of public *control* over the firm affects its publicness. This control can range from tight down to nil. Some so-called public firms are quite independent of outside guidance. At the other extreme, some units are parts of the government itself, closely involved with the "state." Note the basic point: A public enterprise is not necessarily controlled by the government.

Whenever studying a public enterprise, *first try to appraise where it fits in these three dimensions.* Generally, public subsidy without public control is the worst of both worlds.

5. Policies for Public Firms

Once a public firm exists, it should follow efficient policies, of course. This divides into four topics, as follows.

Efficiency. The public firm should of course avoid X-inefficiency. The problem can become severe when the social element is large. It can confuse the usual commercial tests of profit making. Moreover, the social objectives themselves may be complicated and hard to evaluate.

There should be the "correct" amount of subsidy for the social element of operations. Also, the subsidy should be so designed that it does not become a prop or an excuse for slacking off on the commercial part. Often, instead, the public firm comes to count on the subsidy as a way of covering any inefficiency it has.

Pricing. The basic criterion for prices is still long-run marginal cost. Users should pay the true cost of what they consume. Of course, this is to be adjusted for (1) external effects and (2) needy users who are to be deliberately subsidized. However, these are only specific departures from the fundamental rule.

The price structure should avoid harmful discrimination, which public firms may be tempted to do, just like private firms. Only "socially valid" discrimination is to occur, in line with the firm's special objectives. Cross-subsidizing is normally to be avoided. If subsidies of some parts are needed, they should usually be defined openly and paid directly by the public.

Profit Objectives. Capital has an opportunity cost, which is usually in the range of 8 to 15 percent. Public firms need to fit within that range, except where there are strong social reasons for a departure. There are two costs of straying very far from the 8 to 15 percent range. First, low rates of return may induce the public firm to expand to too much output and capacity; and vice versa for too-high profits. Second, X-efficiency can be hurt. Big financial deficits often demoralize the managers and workers, spreading a sense that normal efficiency is hopeless. Conversely, high profits may breed complacency and slack.

Usually, the public firm is set a profit *floor* (such as a rate of return of *at least* 8 percent). This contrasts with the profit *ceilings* placed on private utilities under regulation (such as *no more than* 8 percent). Both targets are in the same range, but they are in different directions. They may have contrasting effects, even though, in practice, they are not airtight.

Two specific problems are common. *First,* public firms are often guaranteed by the government against going out of business. With its risks thus artificially reduced, the firm aims for a low profit rate, or even losses. Instead, it should set prices to make a higher profit rate in line with its true business risk. *Second,* public firms usually pay no taxes and get capital at low interest rates. Such assistance is bitterly criticized by private interests for giving the public firms unfair advantages. The firms should run higher profit rates to offset these advantages, it is charged, so they will be on an even footing with private firms.

There is no clear guideline for picking the "right" rate within this wide range, from roughly 8 to 15 percent. Such indeterminacy is not a bad thing, for it leaves room for the government to align the profit policy with its social objectives. But it can lead to debate and misunderstandings. A low profit rate will anger any private competitors of the public firm. A high profit rate will seem unfair to the public firm's customers.

So the profit policy for public firms can be intensely debated and will often lack a unique guideline.

Investment. The familiar investment criteria apply to public firms, too: Invest up to the point where marginal expected returns are equal to the firm's cost of capital. Often public enterprises have avoided such a rate-of-return screening. Yet informal rules or informal judgment can come close to the same results. The social factor also needs to be included, and it may not be so easily calculated. Indeed, even the "commercial" screening of investment often involves guesswork underneath the neat, precise figures.

Public firms are often accused of investing too much, because they get capital "too cheaply." Sometimes, the government provides investment funds directly, at low interest rates. Alternatively, the public firm may float bonds, but with a government guarantee that reduces the interest rate it has to pay. Such "cheap" capital might then induce the public firm to invest too much. Note that this corresponds to the rate-base effect, which induces regulated *private* firms to invest too much (recall Chapter 13). Still, the overinvestment by public firms may be limited. The lower interest costs may scarcely affect the choices, and the government often controls the investment funds directly, thereby perhaps keeping wasteful tendencies in check. Overinvestment might occur, but one needs to appraise it case by case.

6. Performance

The familiar performance criteria apply, plus whatever specific social objectives are to be met. The rate of profit is only one part of the whole evaluation.

Success can only be appraised in light of the external support and burdens of the firm. If the social tasks are costly but no subsidy is provided, then a firm's most nearly correct choices may involve cross-subsidies and financial losses. Such outcomes may be socially better than a rigidly commerical profit-making result. High profits may merely reflect monopoly and a lack of social effort. Of course, low profits or deficits may also reflect mistaken policies. So one must make a rounded judgment both of the firm *and* of the treatment that it gets from the government.

Comparisons with private firms are useful but hazardous. In most cases, one cannot find really comparable units. This is especially so when one tries to compare (1) across national lines, such as between U.S. private telephone firms and foreign public ones or (2) among sectors, such as between private electricity firms and public railroads in the United States. Also, performance is hard to measure. The quality of service is often a complex, subjective matter, involving many aspects of the service. Prices can be compared, but they, too, usually have many parts and special influences. Costs, too, are complicated. Also innovation can be interpreted in many ways. Above all, the perform-ance within the public firm may be shaped by forces and assistance from outside it. Therefore, the wise student avoids rash, simple com-parisons between public and private enterprises.

Public firms do not automatically find and fit the public interest. They need the right balance of pressure, guidance, and support. Anti-trust policy or regulation, or both, should usually apply to them, de-pending on their market positions. In practice, some are under these healthy policy constraints, while others aren't.

II. ACTUAL PATTERNS AND HISTORICAL ROOTS OF PUBLIC ENTERPRISE

1. Patterns

The United States differs from other Western economies chiefly in the low share of public enterprise in its utilities, industry, and finance. The typical pattern in Western economies is (1) *utilities*—entirely or mainly publicly owned; (2) *finance*—one or several public banks; (3) *insur-ance*—large social insurance programs; (4) *industry*—several major in-

FIGURE 15–1   Share of Public Ownership in Selected Sectors in Selected Countries, 1984

Industrial Sector

(Privately owned: ○   Publicly owned: ◔ 25% ◑ 50% ◕ 75% ● All or nearly all)

Country	Posts	Telecommunications	Electricity	Gas	Railways	Coal	Airlines	Motor Industry	Steel	Shipbuilding	Country
Austria	●	●	●	●	●	●	●	●	◕	na	Austria
Belgium	●	●	◔	◔	●	○	●	○	○	○	Belgium
Britain	●	○	●	○	●	●	○	○	○	○	Britain
France	●	●	●	●	●	●	◕	◑	○	○	France
W. Germany	●	●	◑	◔	●	◔	●	◕	◕	◕	W. Germany
Holland	●	●	◑	◕	●	na	◕	○	◕	○	Holland
Italy	●	●	◕	●	●	na	●	◔	◑	◕	Italy
Spain	●	◔	○	◕	●	◔	●	○	◕	◕	Spain
Sweden	●	●	◑	●	●	na	◑	○	◕	◕	Sweden
Switzerland	●	●	●	●	●	na	○	○	○	na	Switzerland
United States	●	○	◔	○	◔	○	○	○	○	○	United States
Yugoslavia	●	●	●	●	●	●	●	●	●	●	Yugoslavia

Note: The proportions shown are often approximate.
*n.a. = Not available.
Source: Adapted from *The Economist,* March 4, 1978, p. 93, and more recent sources.

dustries under partial public ownership; (5) *social services*—mainly under public ownership; and (6) *distribution*—with little public enterprise. This pattern is reflected in Figure 15–1.

In nearly all countries, the central banks are owned by governments; in some countries, other banks and insurance companies are public enterprises. Almost all of the railroads outside of the United States are public enterprises. Commercial airlines are usually government-owned. Telephone and telegraph services, too, are usually public firms. Radio and television broadcasting is mainly a public enterprise in most countries. Urban transit and electricity are almost always provided by governments. There are important industrial firms, too; some 15 of the largest 200 manufacturing firms outside the United States are public enterprises in a wide range of industries.

Competition between public and private firms is found in many industries, and its extent is growing. It occurs in Canada in railways, airlines, steel, broadcasting, linerboard, pulp and paper, and others. In Britain before 1980, such competition occurred in the steel, automobile, trucking, broadcasting, sugar, shipbuilding, aircraft, and airlines industries. In Italy, it is still even more widespread.

Public enterprise exists in many parts of the U.S. economy. There is a great variety of forms and behavior, as suggested by Table 15–1. It ranges from conventional utility cases, such as TVA, to industrial and service areas, over into certain subsidy programs, and into important *social* enterprises, such as public schools and universities, mental hospitals, the courts, and prisons. Yet these public enterprises tend to be a phantom presence in the United States, not recognized for what they really are.

The Classic Public Utility Form. This is the public corporation. Furthest developed in Britain, it is found in utility sectors throughout Western Europe and less frequently, North America.

This type of public enterprise: (1) is wholly publicly owned; (2) is in a utility sector; (3) is a monopoly in its market; (4) gets all its capital from the Treasury or under a public guarantee; (5) is not regulated, but supervised by a government department; and (6) is required to meet commercial profit targets. The firm is embedded in both economic and political interest groups. Though formally "autonomous," the firm is supervised and given various social objectives to meet. It sells its output and is supposed to avoid financial losses. Yet the social and commercial activities often become mingled.

The firm's board members are public appointees, but they are often virtually identical to their counterparts in private firms. Many of the managers are actually like private managers, drawn from the same pool of talent, and moving between public and private positions. Such officials naturally lean toward commercial policies. Even the lifetime public-firm managers often follow policies that are largely commercial.

The classic public firm often unifies (that is, monopolizes) its industry, sometimes backed by franchise and entry protections as strict as those of private firms under regulation. Its target or *minimum* rates of profit are usually set in the same range (8 to 15 percent) as regulatory *ceilings* on the rates of return of private utilities in the United States. This often leaves the price-*structure* questions at least as indeterminate as they are in private firms under regulation.

At the other extreme are *social enterprises,* such as hospitals, schools, and social insurance. They have a major social purpose and often are heavily subsidized (in contrast to the classic public corporation, which is largely commercial and is expected to get revenues mainly from selling its outputs).

2. Historical Roots

The history of public enterprise is checkered. One line of origin is autocratic, from ancient statecraft through to the organic state of Italy, Soviet-type economies, and other nondemocratic political systems. An-

Table 15–1   Local, State, and Federal Public Enterprises in the United States

Extent of Public Enterprise

1. Local

Utilities

Transit (bus, subway, trolley commuter lines)	All large cities.
Water and sewage	Virtually all large cities.
Garbage disposal	Most cities.
Electricity	Many smaller cities, several large cities.
Ports	Most port cities.
Airports	All large cities.

Social Units

Schools	All cities and towns.
Libraries	Virtually all cities and towns.
Parks, golf courses, pools	Virtually all cities and towns.
Sports stadiums	Many cities.
Museums	Many cities.
Zoos	Some large cities.
Cemeteries	Most cities and towns.
Hospitals	Many cities.

2. State

Prison facilities	All states.
Insurance services	Unemployment, all states; workman's compensation, 18 states.
Parks	Most states.
Liquor retailing	16 states.
Electricity	All Nebraska, a large share of New York.
Ports	Port of New York Authority (transport and urban facilities); New Orleans; other ocean ports
Toll roads, bridges, and tunnels	29 states.
Health care	Mental and old age institutions.
Lotteries	Many states.

3. Federal

Electricity	Corps of Engineers; Bureau of Reclamation; Tennessee Valley Authority: bulk sales to local systems.
Postal service	Variety of services.
Lands	Forest Service; National Park Service.
Commodities stockpiles	Many commodities.
Transport	Military air and sea transport services; St. Lawrence Seaway.
Loans and guarantees	About 100 agencies, including housing, farming, rural electricity, and telephones, Export-Import Bank, Small Business Administration.
Insurance	Many agencies: banks, housing, crops, shipping, foreign investment, stock markets, veterans life and annuity insurance, old age pensions.
Health care	Medicare, Medicaid, veterans hospitals.
Industry	Various: Government Printing Office, Military production, etc.

other is British and continental socialism, which is embodied in national firms in certain utility and sick-industry cases. Still another line is the pragmatic city utility (such as water and bus systems), common throughout history and increasingly widespread in the United States.

Early Origins. From the earliest tribal days, there have been tools and productive units that were held and operated in common. No society has been devoid of them, though few have relied wholly on public units.

In ancient days, many varieties occurred. In the code of Hammurabi and the Old Testament alike are references to various communal workings. However, the ancient lines are often blurred and not easily translated into the modern forms. Athens' theaters were the city's, but many plays were sponsored by wealthy citizens.[4] The mines were state-owned and profitable. Some naval expeditions were sponsored collectively; in others, private sponsorship was central. Public entities were numerous and important; their atrophy coincides with the postclassical decline of Athens.

The Roman Empire at its peak had a variety of "public enterprises."[5] Armaments and defense arrangements were one part. Another was the provision of public facilities for trade, shipping, religion, water and bathing, and, of course, popular games and circuses.

The descent into the Dark Ages was sped by the disintegration of the great public works and enterprises (ports, aqueducts, courts, markets) that had given order and support to the flow of trade and the fabric of society. Only local seigniorage and almonry remained, together with the growing church ownership of lands, and simple production and basic services.

Later, European cities rose and thrived with a variety of public entities and related forms. By the 16th century, kingship had prevailed in much of Europe, and the regional scope of much trade and production was ripe for efforts to induce development.

Mercantilist policy came to stress manufacture and trade, including a range of devices to stimulate new (if primitive) industries. Along with patents, a common device was the state-sponsored factory.[6] The state also commonly made at least some of its own weapons and monopolized trade in such items as salt and tobacco. At the local level, public works and enterprises in the growing infrastructure (ports, highroads, water and sewage, courts, and so forth) helped to induce the rise of early mining and manufacture.

---

[4] See A. Boeckh, *The Public Economy of Athens* (London: John Murray, 1828).

[5] Edward Gibbon, *The History of the Decline and Fall of the Roman Empire*, 5 vols. (1776–88).

[6] C. W. Cole, *Colbert and a Century of French Mercantilism* (New York: Columbia University Press, 1939).

Modern Patterns. As the Industrial Revolution (1770–1850 in Britain) advanced, the relative scope of private enterprise naturally rose, but a variety of new public enterprises also evolved in Europe and the United States. Finance and industry were primarily private, while much infrastructure was public.[7] The post, the mint, and the arsenal were public.

As new utilities evolved during 1830–1900, the European and U.S. choices began to diverge. In railroads, canals, and then electricity, telephone, and city transit, the United States went largely private, while Europe went mainly public. This reflected partly the low state of U.S. political management at all levels during about 1870–1900, in which public enterprises were liable to extensive abuse. However, larger traditions were also at work: collective experience, the free run of private wealth, and differing standards of amenity.

The contrast is only partial. The full scope of Western European public ownership was only reached as late as 1945–50, and much public enterprise has existed all along in the United States. In social infrastructure, Europe developed earlier than the United States: public schools (after 1870 in Britain), social insurance, health care, public housing, and museums are examples.

After 1930, four main further increases in public enterprise occurred: (1) Whole economies were shifted, as in China and Eastern Europe after 1948, and Yugoslavia developed a hybrid set of "worker-managed" enterprises; (2) a nationalization wave in Western Europe rose during the 1930s and crested during 1945–52, touching mainly utility sectors; (3) rising urban and "postindustrial" problems in the United States bred a series of pragmatic new public enterprises (mostly in utilities and social sectors); and (4) many less-developed countries tried new public enterprise for sovereignty, infant-industry, and other reasons.

In Italy, industries were made public less by design than by default.[8] An Institute for Industrial Reconstruction was set up during the depression of the 1930s to manage the assets of scores of failed banks. This agency, with its subsidiaries, came to hold the shares of many Italian companies. These holdings were continued and increased during and after World War II. Despite various adjustments in the holdings after 1970, IRI controls a substantial part of Italian industry, owning nearly all of the stock in shipbuilding, most of that in iron and steel, and a large part of that in the manufacture of transport equipment, electrical equipment, tractors, and machine tools.

---

[7]One example, among many, of important state-owned railroads is detailed in Robert J. Parks, *Democracy's Railroads: Public Enterprise in Jacksonian Michigan* (Port Washington, N.Y.: Kennikat Press, 1972).

[8]See Stuart Holland, M. V. Posner, and S. J. Woolf, *Italian Public Enterprise* (London: Duckworth, 1967).

In addition, the government owned the country's five largest banks, the railroads and the airlines, the telephone, telegraph, radio, and television systems, the motion picture studios, the coal mines, and the petroleum industry. Public enterprise, though adopted without reference to any logical pattern, is thus as extensive in Italy as it is in Britain or in France.

The nationalization program of the Labor Party in Great Britain, adopted in 1946–50, included finance (the Bank of England), Commonwealth communications (civil aviation, cables, and radio), public utilities (gas and electricity), transport (carriers by rail, by water, and by road), a depressed industry (coal), and iron and steel.

In France, the postwar nationalizations included the Bank of France and the 4 largest commercial banks, the 34 largest insurance companies, as much of the coal, gas, and electrical industries as still remained in private hands, the Renault automobile works, and a firm making engines for airplanes. In addition, the government extended its participation in mixed companies in a number of different fields: aviation, shipping, motion pictures, broadcasting, news service, chemicals, and petroleum.

Elsewhere in Western Europe, public enterprise was also expanded in utility areas before 1955. Then patterns stabilized. In the 1970s, there was growth of public banking and social enterprises. Among industries, only sick firms (for example, aircraft, shipbuilding) drew much new public ownership.

After 1979, there were some sharp changes in Britain and France. The conservative Thatcher government promised to "reprivatize" most British public firms. It applied stricter commercial targets for profits, tried to stop financial losses, and it added competitive pressures on some firms. It sold some firms to private investors, in some cases at prices far below the market value of the firm. The whole program has brought radical changes.

In France, by contrast, the socialist Mitterand government in 1981 sharply increased public ownership and control. It took over the rest of the main private banks and leading investment banks, as well as leading industrial groups with large firms in 10 major industries (such as steel, chemicals, and engineering). Broad controls over profits and investment were placed on these firms, but they were left with discretion over detailed operations. The policy was reversed after 1984, toward a moderate privatizing of some public firms. For example, Renault has been shifted toward private profit-maximizing objectives. Its cost cutting generated strong resistance by employee unions, claiming that profit objectives abandoned the proper purposes of public enterprise.

A variety of third-world countries, such as Brazil and Mexico, have found it necessary since 1985 to move major public firms to a private basis. In some cases, the firms had contained large X-inefficiency in the form of bloated payrolls and obsolete technology. Examples include the petroleum monopolies in Mexico and Indonesia. In other cases, the governments merely sought to obtain immediate cash for budgetary purposes.

During 1989–90, large new vistas for choices between public and private enterprise opened up in Eastern Europe and the Soviet Union. The collapse of Communist rule exposed the failures of controlled, state-owned economies. There were immediate campaigns to replace the old systems with free markets. That requires the conversion of public enterprises—most of them monopolies—into private firms, under competitive conditions.

This was largely uncharted territory, but the main lines of the changes could be guided by the analysis and experience covered in this textbook. The shift to private markets is not simple or easy, particularly when the existing markets have full monopolies which are anxious to retain their privileges, and when the countries' political leaders have no experience with competitive economic conditions.

Moreover, many Western advisers are offering simplistic versions of Chicago-UCLA ideas to the emerging democracies, urging that free enterprise and competition will easily triumph. For example, many major Western European companies are forming mergers with state monopolies in the East in order to take advantage of the new market opportunities. Such alliances will pose powerful interests favoring retention of monopoly positions. Pure Chicago-UCLA doctrines would define those mergers as harmless against new competition and market forces. However, they may, instead, prove to be immovable obstacles against effective competition.

As of 1990, the evolution toward private, competitive markets is just beginning, under extremely difficult conditions. Many or most sectors of these economies may require decades to evolve toward effective competition against strong resistance.

The main lessons of history appear to be:

1. Virtually all types and extents of public enterprise have occurred within our cultural mainstreams.
2. The specific set of enterprises in each country is largely a cultural matter, varying widely in line with social traditions and preferences.
3. Few public enterprises are created rationally and carefully. Usually, public enterprises spring from some kind of crisis, which tips the old balance of interests. A major war frequently increases public enterprise, often permanently. Depressions create corporate orphans, which are made into public firms.
4. Resistance to public takeover is mainly a matter of the price offered for the private firm. Almost every private enterprise will agree to becoming publicly owned if the terms are favorable enough. *Ideolog-*

ical battles against public enterprise are often merely a tactic in the underlying *economic* contest over the price to be paid.

5. The economic purposes and operations of public enterprises are highly varied, from high profits to high subsidies and from narrow financial targets to broad social effects.

6. The operating policies and external support of a public firm (*not* its public ownership per se) largely determine its performance.

7. Comparisons of performance between public and private firms are usually difficult and inconclusive.

III. CASE STUDIES

There is space here to discuss a limited number of instances of public firms out of the thousands of fascinating examples in the United States and abroad. They can only suggest the complexity of the problems. In each case, the social element is debatable and the policies have been controversial.

1. State Lotteries and Liquor Marketing

State and national lotteries were popular before 1890, but scandals then caused them to be shunned for some 70 years. Since 1963, state-run lotteries have spread, grown, and thrived again. They are designed to earn a profit for the state, on the order of 45 percent of revenue (which is an astronomically high return on the tiny amount of investment). Essentially a retailing operation, the lotteries operate through existing retail outlets. They have proliferated their brands (for example, into instant and million-dollar offerings) and perfected their marketing skills, as in televised drawings. They have been a solid financial success, though the social contribution—of stimulating gambling against unfavorable odds, much of it by low-income people —is doubtful.

The pari-mutuel systems for race-track gambling in many states are another set of profitable public enterprises. The Off-Track Betting Corporation in New York City has scores of offices and profits of 20 percent of revenue. Each state's gambling operation has a tidy geographic monopoly. Yet each claims to be in competition with illegal gambling.

Liquor retailing has been done by 16 states for many decades. These are large businesses, several with scores of stores and more than $500 million in annual sales. They often have had a statewide monopoly of all sales of liquor by the bottle. They have combined to extract lower wholesale prices from national liquor suppliers. Their

Figure 15–2   Nonfederal Publicly Owned Systems (Municipal, State, County, and Power Districts)

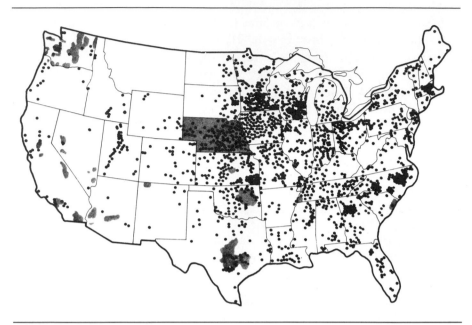

Source: Federal Power Commission.

profits go to the state treasuries. All are profitable, some of them highly so.

Their retail prices are lower than those of private retailers in other states.[9] This reflects their lower wholesale prices, efficiency, and pricing policies in varying degree. State revenues are much larger through the state stores than from taxes in other states. These public enterprises therefore perform well, on the whole.

2. Electricity

U.S. experience is in (1) the Tennessee Valley Authority (TVA) and other federal power programs, (2) New York and Nebraska, and (3) the many local electric systems scattered around the country (see Figure 15–2). Table 15–2 adds detail about them.

Abroad, public enterprise arose first at the local level, during 1890–1930. As national systems matured, national grids became publicly owned. Gas and electricity were publicly provided in more than three

---

[9]See Julian L. Simon, "The Economic Effects of State Monopoly of Packaged Liquor Retailing," *Journal of Political Economy* 74 (April 1966), pp. 188–94.

Table 15–2   Selected Data on Public Power Systems in the United States, 1982

	Assets (net utility plant) ($ millions)	Megawatthours Sold (Millions mwhr.)		Residence Revenues as a Percent of Total
		To Final Users	For Resale	
Federal Systems				
Alaska Power Administration	$108	0	3	0%
Bonneville Power Administration	2,098	0	101.7	0
Southeastern Federal Power Program	1,215	0	6.9	0
Western Area Power Program	920	0	36.0	0
T.V.A.	14,118	32.5	76.0	0
Selected municipalities*	29,428	164.6	96.0	26.1

*Municipalities with annual operating revenues of $5 million or more in fiscal 1982.
Source: U.S. Energy Information Administration, *Financial Statistics of Selected Electric Utilities: 1982* (Washington, D.C.: U.S. Government Printing Office, 1984).

fourths of the cities of Germany and in more than half of those in Great Britain before 1930. Regional systems for the generation and transmission of electricity were operated by governments in Canada, New Zealand, and South Africa. The Central Electricity Board, in Great Britain, was given a monopoly of transmission lines by a Conservative government in 1926. The present patterns were firmly set by 1950. The structure of these units and their policies on profit rates, price structure, and investment have stabilized along lines closely akin to those in private U.S. utilities. Though there are plans to privatize them, action has not yet occurred.

In the United States, thousands of city power systems evolved from the start, followed—mainly in the 1930s—by federal and state agencies. The Tennessee Valley Authority is the leading case of federal power.

TVA.[10] The Tennessee River's large potential for water power was first tapped in World War I at Muscle Shoals. After much sharp controversy, the Tennessee Valley Authority (TVA) was created in 1933 to (1) control floods, (2) assist navigation, (3) generate electric power, and

[10]See G. R. Clapp, *The TVA: An Approach to the Development of a Region* (Chicago: University of Chicago Press, 1955); J. R. Moore, ed., *The Economic Impact of TVA* (Knoxville: University of Tennessee Press, 1967); Richard Hellman, *Government Competition in the Electric Utility Industry: A Theoretical and Empirical Study* (New York: Praeger Publishers, 1972); and James Cook, "Entrepreneurial Power," *Forbes,* March 19, 1990, pp. 83–90.

(4) promote regional growth. The TVA was made a semiautonomous agency, free of Civil Service regulations but financed with Treasury help. It is largely free of regulation or other controls.

It has developed a large power system, based on its dams and on fuel-fired electricity plants (see Figure 15–3). Where possible, it sells its power to public and cooperative nonprofit distributors. After struggles with private utilities, it gained sole rights to generate power in the Tennessee Valley. Though it has built over 20 dams, it now gets over three fourths of its power from fossil-fuel and nuclear generators, rather than water power. TVA is a wholesale supplier, not a distributor to small customers. It sells its power to the Energy Department (partly for enriching nuclear fuels), 50 large industrial users, and some 160 municipal and rural electrification cooperatives.

TVA is a classic case of multiple-purpose development: It promotes the widespread use of power, but its dams also provide flood control and its lakes and parks provide recreational facilities. The power activities involve mainly commercial standards of cost and profit, but its other contributions are in the nature of public goods.

TVA's history divides into two periods: the early phase of successful development and growth during the 1930s to roughly 1970, and the mature era since then, market by severe problems with nuclear-power generators.

The First Phase: Developing Power for All. TVA's first task was to promote improvements in Appalachia by extending cheap power to homes and businesses. Prices were set low, assuming demand to be elastic. As homes were wired and businesses grew, the low electricity prices promoted rapid growth in the use of electricity and in its contribution to more modern technology in the region. At the time, such low-cost promotional pricing was novel, but it served TVA's objectives perfectly. It also applied indirect "yard-stick" competition to private power companies to produce and sell their power as cheaply as TVA.

The low-price policy for residential customers has continued, and it has worked. From 1933 to 1972, the number of farms receiving electricity rose from 3 percent to more than 99 percent. The annual rate of power usage, per customer, rose from 600 kilowatt-hours to 14,040 on average, a figure more than twice as high as the national average.

The Second Phase: Troubles with Nuclear Power. After 1965 TVA plunged deeply into nuclear power, mounting "the biggest, most ambitious, and most disastrously ill-executed nuclear program in U.S. power industry history."[11] Of its 17 nuclear plants, no fewer than 8 were scrapped, and

---

[11]James Cook, "Entrepreneurial Power," *Forbes,* March 19, 1990, p. 86.

5 of them were closed down in 1985 for being unsafe. The errors were common to most private systems too, but in TVA they were deepened by bureaucracy and rigidity as TVA diverged from its original task of social development.

The nuclear fiascos pushed TVA's costs up sharply, forcing its prices up too, at a rate of 10.2 percent per year during 1972–89. Major customers began looking elsewhere in the increasingly competitive regional markets for bulk power.

But in 1988 new management was installed, specifically to rescue TVA by cutting costs along private-enterprise standards. Employment was cut by over 30 percent, and the nuclear plants were refurbished. TVA now appears restored to financial soundness. But its direction is now primarily private and commercial, largely similar to private utilities. In this sense, "privatization" has occurred informally but distinctly.

Subsidies Are Small. It is often charged that the customers of the TVA are subsidized, because the authority does not (1) pay taxes, (2) pay a

Figure 15–3   Extent and Complexity of the TVA System

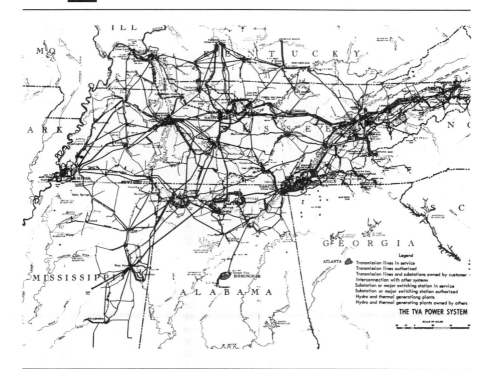

Source: Federal Energy Regulatory Commission.

proper share of the joint cost of the multipurpose facilities or charge to power a proper share of joint administrative costs, and (3) pay the market rate of interest on capital provided by the government. Each of these points requires examination.

The TVA itself pays to state and local governments, in lieu of taxes, 5 percent of the revenue it collects from customers other than the federal government. Its distributors make such payments as the laws of their states require. For example, in 1982, these payments, taken together, amounted to more than $76 million, some 8 percent of total revenue. The taxes paid by neighboring private utilities ranged from 4 to 8 percent of revenue. The TVA does not pay the federal tax on corporate net income, which is a tax on private profit, rather than a cost, but it is repaying the government's investment in its plant, a charge the private companies are not required to meet.

As for the cost of capital, there is probably no major difference. The TVA gets rather lower interest rates; but private utilities get accelerated amortization, which is at least as valuable. Moreover, as noted, the TVA has had to start paying off its $1 billion in debt, something that no private firm would have to do.

City Power Systems. These systems have been under pressure, for power technology has shifted sharply to curtail their discretion. Most systems are now small dependent clients of large private suppliers, merely managing local distribution. In many cases throughout the country, large private joint projects for generating plants have tried to exclude them. This would cause their prices to be higher, and so the private systems could buy them out at lower prices. Public systems have, therefore, continued to face hostile and powerful arrangements. The *Otter Tail* and other court decisions have backed up the public systems' access to some cheap power on fair terms. However, the trends remain.

Meanwhile, the city systems are diverse, but with most of them supplying strictly at cost, as Table 15–2 shows. There is no hard evidence about their efficiency compared to private systems. The continuing inducements to sell off to private utilities applies a steady pressure toward efficiency on many city systems. In many cities, the public power system is active, efficient, and innovative.

3. Postal Service

The basic postal system is everywhere a public enterprise. It is the most familiar and criticized of all public enterprises. The postal service, wrote Adam Smith in 1776, "is perhaps the only mercantile project which has been successfully managed by, I believe, every sort of government. The capital to be advanced is not very considerable. There is no mystery in the business. The returns are not only certain, but immediate."[12] Under the Constitution, a postal system, including 74 post offices, was established by the first Congress in 1789. The system was originally set up as a separate agency under the president. In 1829, the Postmaster General was admitted to the Cabinet, and, in 1872, the Post Office was made a department of the government. In 1971, it was revised into a semiautonomous public corporation, under the Postal Rate Commission. In the early days of the republic, the postal service had a vital function to fulfill. In the absence of modern means of communication, it afforded the only tie that bound the country together, uniting the wilderness with the capital, scattered settlements with centers of trade and finance. It contributed to a sense of national identity, to economic and political unity. It was a basic instrument of public policy.

Today, the Post Office is one of many media of communication. It is a big business with 30,000 offices, over 670,000 employees, and a budget over $30 billion a year. It delivers mail each weekday to nearly every business and household in the land, handling 90 billion pieces each year. Only 14 percent of this is personal correspondence. A tenth is newspapers or magazines. More than a fourth is advertising matter. Over half involves business transactions: orders, invoices, bills, checks, and the like. The volume of such materials is twice as great today as it was 20 years ago, and is likely to keep growing.

In the United States and Britain, it has been converted from department status into a public corporation. The common pattern abroad is for postal services to be combined with telecommunications (the French PPT, the British Post Office, and so forth). This corresponds to combining the Bell System and other telephone independents with the postal service and telegraph service—*but* also splitting it into five small regional systems. Since these foreign systems are all less than one fifth as large as the U.S. system, the total monopoly effect is rather less than it might seem. Also, the services are usually operated, accounted, and evaluated separately.

In the United States, as elsewhere, the postal service is among the country's largest employers. In fact, the postal deliverer on the daily round is part of a network that constitutes the core of natural-monopoly conditions in this industry. Indeed, the local delivery and pickup system is the one clear element of natural monopoly. Of course,

---

[12]*The Wealth of Nations,* Book 5, chap. 2, part 1. Smith was still correct in 1990. Postal costs are 85 percent labor. By contrast, labor costs are only 20 percent in electricity, 18 percent in gas, 54 percent in railroads, 43 percent in airlines, and 47 percent in telephones.

On the monopoly character of the system, see George L. Priest, "History of the Postal Monopoly in the United States," *Journal of Law & Economics* 18 (April 1975), pp. 33–80.

there are the sorting and bulk shipping parts of postal service, but these are more separable and less marked by decreasing costs.[13]

Deficits. Postal services commonly run a financial deficit. This stems from a variety of political and social factors, possibly related to external benefits that postal services may provide. An informed and well-communicating populace is an important precondition for healthy democracy. First-rate postal service may contribute to this, and, therefore, its value may ultimately be greater than the individual users may be willing to pay. This is the rationale behind the subsidies that have been extended traditionally to such postal users as magazines, newspapers, and senders of educational materials.

Yet postal services are overwhelmingly *business* services: 70 percent of all mail is business mail (bills, ads, reports, and so forth). The system routinely subsidizes the circulation of advertising and other strictly commercial items. Therefore, one needs to learn the marginal costs of the different kinds of service and whether social effects justify subsidies to cover these marginal costs.

Cost Structure. The structure of costs arises from the special rhythm of postal activities, primarily in the sorting facilities and the delivery networks.

In every post office, there is a morning and evening peak of activity; these fit the standard analysis of peak-load costs. These peaks are similar to those of other utility services. They cause sharp variations in real marginal costs; peak costs are sharply above off-peak costs. The common schedule of postal rates reflects this, though perhaps not precisely. First-class mail is presumably handled at the peak and is charged a high price (perhaps in line with its true marginal costs) while other types of mail may be set aside for handling during the low-cost, off-peak periods. If postal operations were in fact closely priced, the proper peak level and off-peak costs (that is, basically, first- versus second- and third-class rates) could be ascertained within reasonable boundaries. However, this is not regularly done, and the cost allocations are debatable.[14]

Price Structure. Instead, the tradition of uniform geographic postal rates still governs postal pricing. Designed under Rowland Hill in the early 19th century to foster circulation of messages within the British

---

[13]President's Commission on Postal Organization, *Towards Postal Excellence* (Washington, D.C.: U.S. Government Printing Office, 1968); and Morton Baratz, *The Economics of the Postal Service* (Washington, D.C.: Public Affairs Press, 1955).

[14]See Robert D. Willig, *Welfare Analysis of Policies Affecting Prices and Products* (New York: Garland Publishing Co., 1980).

Isles, the standard "penny post" rate has been extended into the present on the philosophy that all mail should share in covering the costs of the system. Therefore, most postal rates are averaged among users, rather than fitted directly to the real costs involved.

Do first-, second-, and third-class postal rates fit the true costs involved? In all probability, they tend to overcharge first-class mail and to undercharge the lower groups. These prices reflect both actual costs and the political power of those groups that have been able to gain preferential postal rates. The "true" costs patterns are endlessly debated. Good postal price structures could be decisive to the financial health of the postal systems, both in the United States and abroad. Most of the postal deficits arise from handling of high-weight, low-class mail. If there are external benefits from advertisements, they must be very large to justify the subsidy that has been given in the past.

Competition. To some extent, the postal system is under stress from growing competition with telecommunications and package delivery systems.

The handling of parcels is partly a joint product of the main sorting and shipping operations. It can be coordinated with off-peak operations at low costs. Even so, it does not really share in the core natural monopoly of the system—the final delivery and pickup network. Therefore, it is arguably eligible for an open competitive approach. In fact, United Parcel Service Company has long held a private near-monopoly of its own in small, high-value, high-speed parcels. Its high profitability fully reflects its market position. The rise of overnight mail services since 1975 has made this market highly competitive. In this and other areas, the post office "monopoly" is actually under close constraints.

A fair evaluation would be that U.S. postal managers have been emerging from a politicized managerial situation and that many of their more lucrative markets are being skimmed. Beset by inherited deficits and traditions, they are not doing poorly. The moves toward rational pricing, both in the United States and abroad, have to overcome strong pressures.

IV. THE PRIVATIZATION OF PUBLIC FIRMS[15]

The publicness of firms depends on their ownership, the degree of outside subsidy and control, and the kind of policies the firm takes (e.g., strict profit maximizing or pursuing some public purposes). During

---

[15]This section draws on William G. Shepherd, "Public Enterprise: Criteria and Cases," in *The Structure of European Industry,* 2nd ed., ed. Henry W. de Jong (Dordrecht, The Netherlands: Kluwer Academic Publishers, 1988). See also the excellent paper by Richard E.

1950–80, the degree of public enterprise in the United States and Western Europe was roughly stable.

However, the 1980s saw an ideologically inspired program in Britain to put public firms into private hands. The Thatcher government had made major changes by 1986, including privatizing the telephone system, gas supply, intercity buses, British Airways airline, the ports, the airports, and British Steel. As of 1990, there are plans to sell off even the electricity and water systems. This push to privatize was echoed in Japan and certain third-world countries. The United States made only modest changes, despite the ideological leanings of the Reagan administration.

The experience suggests interesting lessons about the methods of privatizing public enterprises and the benefits realized from "getting the government out of the marketplace." The following summary only touches the main points of a large, growing literature.[16]

Privatizing can take either or both of two directions, in economic terms:

1. Ownership can be shifted to private hands; and/or
2. Entry by new private rivals can be permitted.

By itself, private ownership only shifts managements toward a tighter profit orientation. Unless competition is effective, the privatized firm's actions can be doubly harmful: There will be monopoly pricing and retarded innovation, *plus* a withdrawal of the public firm's allowances for social impacts. A pure sell-off is therefore only appropriate when competition will be effective and the social elements are negligible.

The alternative method of privatizing is simply to open up entry in a way that maximizes competitive pressure as new private firms come in. It will succeed only if entry is really free and the new competitors are

---

Caves, "Lessons from Privatization in Britain: State Enterprise Behavior, Public Choice, and Corporate Governance," *Journal of Economic Behavior and Organization* 13 (Spring 1990), pp. 145–69.

[16]See H. Abromeit, *British Steel* (New York: St. Martin's Press, 1986); Y. Aharoni, *The Evolution and Management of State-Owner Enterprises* (Cambridge, Mass.: Ballinger, 1986); Michael Beesley and Stephen Littlechild, "Privatisation: Principles, Problems and Priorities," *Lloyd's Bank Review* (July 1983), pp. 1–20; S. Domberger and J. Piggott, "Privatization Policies and Public Enterprise: A Survey," *Economic Record,* June 1986, pp. 145–62; S. M. Jaffer and D. J. Thompson, "Deregulating Express Coaches: A Reassessment," *Fiscal Studies* 7 (November 1986), pp. 45–68; J. A. Kay and D. J. Thompson, "Privatisation: A Policy in Search of a Rationale," *The Economic Journal* 96 (March 1986), pp. 18–32; J. A. Kay, C. Mayer, and D. Thompson, eds., *Privatization and Regulation: The UK Experience* (Oxford: The Clarendon Press, 1986); R. Molyneux and D. Thompson, "Nationalised Industry Performance: Still Third-Rate?" *Fiscal Studies* 8 (February 1987), pp. 48–82; D. Steel and D. Heald, eds., *Privatizing Public Enterprises: Options and Dilemmas* (London: Royal Institute of Public Administration, 1984); and Vickers and Yarrow, *Privatization and the Natural Monopolies.* See also the symposium of Privatization in the *Journal of Policy Analysis and Management* 6 (Summer 1987).

forceful. Paradoxically, that very situation makes a sell-off unnecessary: The existing tight competition will force an efficient and innovative result even if the firm's ownership remains public. Free entry is therefore both necessary and sufficient for successful privatization, while a sell-off is neither. The British literature has noted the need for competition, but the British government's policies have not succeeded in creating it.

British privatizing since 1979 has shrunk the set of failing firms that had been taken over in earlier rescues. That may provide public benefits, by reducing the costs of covering deficits incurred by poor private management, but the main change has been simply a selling off of ownership that is inspired chiefly by ideology and by pressures from investor groups seeking to make capital gains for themselves. Some privatized firms have indeed faced strong competition: British Rail Hotels and Jaguar (automobiles) are examples. The dominant firms have been much more numerous, however, and they have had it much easier. There are many optimistic predictions of powerful entry into their supposedly contestable markets, and the whole campaign is actually turning into a series of experiments in entry.

Still, in many of these cases, actual entry has been slight and easily repelled. In both telephone service and equipment supply, for example, British Telecom has largely maintained its previous monopoly position. In equipment, it has reputational advantages that have also prevented any large rivals from emerging.

British Gas has had the same experience: Competition against it is ineffective. In inner-city bus travel, the virtual monopoly of the incumbent National Express was not sold off, but new entry was opened in 1980. Though many small chartered bus firms existed as a source of new entry into regular lines, actual entry has been slight. National Express has controlled access to terminals and has applied strategic pricing effectively to minimize the inroads of new bus rivals.

The sell-off of British Airways has also failed to generate effective competition or new entry. The firm faces little competition on its domestic routes, and, in 1987, it actually sought to buy out British Caledonian, its one rival. Its control of airport access in Britain as well as its use of strategic pricing has protected its virtual monopoly, with predictable results in keeping fares at high levels. British Airways has also continued the long-standing collusion with its rivals in international routes so as to resist entry and maintain fare levels.

Taken together, the British experiments demonstrate that effective competition is unlikely to develop in monopolized markets, and so the privatized incumbent is able to sustain monopoly behavior. The U.K. Monopolies and Mergers Commission has had little effect in overcoming these problems, while efforts to apply some form of regulation by government agencies have been largely empty. Therefore, privatization has failed to deliver competitive results in markets with market power.

Moreover, the government has often underpriced the stocks issued to the private buyers, so that private investors have reaped windfall gains at the expense of the public treasury. The pressures to underprice the shares are strong, both from the prospective buyers and from the government's anxiety to ensure that all of the shares are sold.

On the whole, the privatizing programs have provided some improvements for firms operating in competitive markets that have small social elements, but these cases have been the relatively minor ones in Britain, and the selling off of firms with dominant positions (especially in utility markets) has not succeeded in establishing competitive conditions and benefits.

There is a need for variety and experimentation in industrial markets, but the effort to convert utilities into unregulated competitive private firms is an exercise in illusion. It requires a very careful balancing of ownership, entry support, and regulation, under favorable conditions.

QUESTIONS FOR REVIEW

1. "There are at least three elements to public enterprise: control, subsidy, and ownership." True?
2. "The classic form of public enterprise is the utility monopoly getting its capital from the Treasury and trying to meet commercial profit targets." True?
3. "Some public enterprises give their outputs or services away." True?
4. "Public enterprise is rare in the United States." True?
5. "Public firms often have too much monopoly power, just like some private firms." True?
6. "The mingling of commercial and social elements may encourage X-inefficiency." True?
7. "The basic economic criteria for public firms are the same as those for private firms, plus specific social aims." True?
8. "Public firms are specifically designed to run best when incurring large deficits or achieving large profits." True?
9. "A public firm may be a success while incurring a deficit but a failure when achieving profits." True?
10. "Most public firms were carefully planned at the outset, but they are led astray by overly generous subsidies." True?

11. "State lotteries are mistaken ventures, as proven by their high profitability." True?

12. "The TVA is heavily subsidized, and so it gives unfair competition to private power systems." True?

13. "Being a capital-intensive utility, postal service needs only to get cheap capital in order to solve its basic problem." True?

14. "If first-class mail is sorted at peak times, then it should be charged more than lower-class mail." True?

15. Are there natural areas of the economy where public firms are appropriate? How do you define these?

16. Identify five public firms that you deal with routinely. Are they performing well? By what criteria?

17. What are the main risks for society in using public enterprises?

18. Which public enterprises in utility and social sectors are performing pretty well? Why do they do well while others don't?

19. What main revisions or reforms are needed in the U.S. Postal Service?

C·H·A·P·T·E·R 16 Special Departures:
Patents, Barriers, and
Antitrust Exemptions

We now turn to the residual variety of policies that depart from the standard antitrust, regulation, and public-enterprise policies. Ranging from patents to military purchasing and natural resources, each one presents unusual features and each has been intensely controversial.

The first two sections of this chapter discuss several policies that explicitly give exemptions from antitrust or directly promote market power. Section I presents patents, and Section II covers barriers to international trade, agricultural cooperatives, labor unions, and price controls. Then Section III reviews three special types of policies: policies that cover the purchasing of military weapons, farm policies, and policies toward natural resources.

These special cases involve a substantial array of markets, and the policies are often defective or dubious. To that extent, they represent evidence for the Chicago-UCLA hypothesis that the *state* creates monopoly that is often unjustified. In that respect, this chapter can be contrasted with the earlier chapters, which present policies to control monopoly that arises from the *markets* themselves.

I. PATENTS[1]

A patent grants a monopoly right to the investor of an idea, giving control over the production and selling of a new product or technique for

---

[1]See F. M. Scherer and David Ross, 3rd ed., *Industrial Market Structure and Economic Performance* (Boston: Houghton Mifflin, 1990), chap. 17, for a thorough review of the is-

17 years. Recently, over 60,000 patents have been awarded yearly in the United States, and other countries also provide similar protection.

The patent authorizes the inventor to make, use, transfer, or withhold the patented item, to exclude others or to admit them on the patentor's own terms. Without a patent, one might attempt to preserve a monopoly by keeping the invention secret; to get a patent, it must be disclosed.

The policy of promoting invention by granting temporary monopolies to inventors, a policy that had been followed in England for nearly two centuries, was written into the Constitution of the United States. Patents have been obtainable in the United States since 1790 on any useful "art, manufacture, engine, machine," since 1793 on a "composition of matter," since 1842 on "ornamental designs," and since 1930 on botanical plants, and on improvements to any of them. Patents are not granted on methods of doing business or on fundamental scientific discoveries, but otherwise the law is generous in its coverage.

The 17-year patent life is a historical accident. In England in 1643, the duration of a patent was fixed at 14 years, a period sufficient to enable a craftsperson to train two successive groups of apprentices. This term was adopted in the first patent law in the United States. In 1861, however, an effort to extend the term to 20 years resulted in a compromise that fixed it at 17, and 17 years is still the nominal duration of the monopoly conferred by the patent grant.

In most other countries, the patent holder is required to put the invention to work. No such obligations attach to patents issued by the United States. Within the limits laid down by the courts, the owner of a patent may refuse to work it, work it and refuse to license it to others, or license it on virtually any terms.

The Patent Office merely accepts or rejects the applications that are brought before it. Each application must describe, with some precision, the nature of the invention that is claimed. An invention is not supposed to be patented unless it is new and useful and actually works, but the number of applications is so large and the resources available

sues in this section. Other major references include Jacob Schmookler, *Invention and Economic Growth* (Cambridge, Mass.: Harvard Univ. Press, 1966); Edwin Mansfield, *Research and Innovation in the Modern Corporation* (New York: W. W. Norton, 1971); John Jewkes, David Sawers, and Richard Stillerman, *The Sources of Invention*, 2nd ed. (New York: W. W. Norton, 1968); Joseph A. Schumpeter, *Capitalism, Socialism, and Democracy* (New York: Harper & Row, 1942); National Bureau of Economic Research, *The Rate and Direction of Inventive Activity* (Princeton, N.J.: Princeton University Press, 1962); and William D. Nordhaus, *Invention, Growth, and Welfare* (Cambridge, Mass.: MIT Press, 1969). On the patent system's role, see Alfred E. Kahn, "The Role of Patents," in *Competition, Cartels, and Their Regulations*, ed. J. P. Miller (Amsterdam: North-Holland, 1962); William L. Baldwin and John T. Scott, *Market Structure and Technological Change* (Chur, England: Harwood, 1987); and Erich Kaufer, *The Economics of the Patent System* (Chur, England: Harwood, 1988).

for handling them are so small that rigorous standards of appraisal cannot be maintained.

In about 60 percent of patent infringement cases decided, the courts have found that the plaintiff's patent was not infringed or that it was lacking in validity. It is a rare patent, however, that is taken to court, and an even rarer one that is appealed to the higher courts. The "currency" that is issued by the Patent Office thus passes at face value, save in those cases where the courts have decided against it.

The decision to patent often involves close choices, and in numberless cases the choice is for secrecy or some other strategy instead. Patents are a specific strategy fitted to certain conditions, *not* a universal stimulant to progress. They cluster tightly in certain industries, especially in drugs, photocopying, aerospace, and electrical equipment. Over large areas of industry, patents are virtually absent and irrelevant.

1. Economic Issues

Does the system make economic sense? One begins with the basic economics of technical progress. The process divides into various categories:

1. *Invention:* the new idea conceived and tested.
2. *Innovation:* the first application of the idea is production.
3. *Imitation:* spreading of the innovation to other producers.

Innovations are of two types:

1. *Product* innovations: a new product, the same production methods.
2. *Process* innovations: the same product, produced differently (so that the average-cost curve shifts down).

These conceptual distinctions are often blurred in practice, but they clarify the stages and incentives in the process.

Also, new ideas differ in scope. Some are small and specialized: a knob here, a notch there, or stripes in toothpaste. At the other extreme, some are broad and basic concepts, such as the wheel and interchangeable parts. Patents cluster in the middle range: significant ideas whose gains can be temporarily monopolized without intolerable social effects.

The patent grant of a monopoly on an idea need not give much true monopoly power, in an economic sense. The new idea may have substitutes, in some degree. If substitutability is high, the amount of market power may be small. For example, the basic Xerox process had no close substitute until about 1970, and so the monopoly power given by Xerox's patents was very large. However, at the other extreme, a slight design change or a slightly different antibiotic drug (similar to 15 others) may give little market power.

Indeed, most patents give little power or profit, whereas a few strategic ones have been crucial. Moreover, a firm that assembles a number of related patents can often accumulate much more power than the individual patents might give.

Patents have two economic effects: (1) They stimulate invention, by inducing inventors to try harder so as to create valuable patented inventions, and (2) they create monopoly, which may restrict production and raise prices. The critical question is how the two effects compare. Is stimulation or restriction more important?

This issue turns on whether most inventions are autonomous or induced. Many inventions are autonomous, materializing from the general advance of knowledge.[2] Others are induced, occurring only because inventors' efforts are stimulated by the prospect of getting rich.

Patents' only justification is in the inducement effect: in inducing inventions that would otherwise not occur or in speeding them up significantly. Granting patents on autonomous inventions is useless and harmful, because it permits monopolizing but provides no stimulus. Therefore, the patent system rests on one simple belief: that the inducement effect is so strong and prevalent that it offsets the monopoly harms. If inventions are mainly autonomous, and/or if the stimulus is only weak, then patents are an economic mistake, which impedes progress rather than promotes it.

One factual indication regarding the question of patents' inducement effect is a survey of many inventors conducted by the Patent, Trademark and Copyright Foundation. Asked if the availability of patent protection had stimulated their inventive activity, only one fifth said yes, while four fifths said that it was not essential or made little difference. An exhaustive review by Scherer and Ross reports no clear evidence in the literature that patents have made important inventions occur significantly earlier.[3] Moreover, most important inventions have been made by small-scale, independent inventors, rather than by large-scale, corporate, profit-oriented laboratories.

---

[2]For example, the automobile emerged around 1890–1905, using rubber, engines, and other recent metallurgical advances. It could not have been invented before 1860, because oil (for gasoline-powered engines) had not yet been discovered, or indeed before 1880 because metals technology did not yet permit the machining of gasoline engines. After 1890, though, technology made the automobile possible, and it was bound to be invented. Therefore, the automobile was an autonomous creation, requiring no special monetary inducement.

[3]Scherer and Ross, *Industrial Market Structure and Economic Performance,* chap. 17.

Generally, monopoly is an unfavorable setting for invention and innovation, while competition promotes them. Patent-created monopolies can tend to reduce further progress, rather than promote it. Therefore, sound public policies would provide patent grants only to those inventions that are not autonomous, and it would limit the use of patents in creating monopoly positions that might later retard progress. Moreover, it would tailor the life of each patent to the minimum needed to induce the invention without creating unnecessary monopoly.

In practice, the patent system is far cruder than this. It pays no attention to the autonomous-induced distinction, and it permits the accumulation and use of patents to extend monopoly positions. Also, all patent lives are identical (17 years) regardless of the invention's conditions.

The optimum patent life has been analyzed under simplified assumptions.[4] Very roughly speaking, the more sharply a prospective innovation reduces costs, the shorter the optimal life of a patent will be. For a cost reduction of 10 percent and elasticity of demand anywhere in the range of 0.7 to 4.0, the optimal patent life appears to be in the range of three to seven years. Broadly speaking, a long patent life is only optimal for the very largest and costliest innovations.

In short, the patent system lacks any clear economic foundation. It is likely to be retarding innovation in a variety of industries rather than promoting it. For specific inventions, the 17-year patent life probably deviates from the optimal life, perhaps sharply in many cases.

Yet, even though the patent system is merely a historical accident with known defects, there is little likelihood of significant change in it. It has created large property rights and expectations, and it is too valuable to important interest groups. Patent reform is a frequent topic, but little change occurs. The main questions here concern the specific ways in which possible monopoly abuses have been contested in actual patent cases.

2. Abuses of Patents

Suppression. Under American law, the patentee is not required to work its patent. As a consequence, the law may be employed not to promote but to retard the introduction of advances in technology. When suppression of patented inventions does occur, it defeats the fundamental purpose of patent law.

---

[4]The analysis is not simple. See Nordhaus, *Invention, Growth, and Welfare;* and F. M. Scherer, "Nordhaus' Theory of Optimal Patent Life: A Geometric Reinterpretation," *American Economic Review* 62 (June 1972), pp. 422–27.

Accumulation. Many related patents may be accumulated by one or a few large firms or brought together by agreement among them. The large corporation will usually obtain a flow of patents through assignment from members of its own research staff and will supplement them by purchases from outsiders.

A single firm may come to control the methods by which a good may be produced, enabling it to monopolize the technology of an entire industry. Where a few large corporations hold patents that overlap, each often shares its rights with the others through cross-licensing. Such agreements may call for exclusive or nonexclusive licensing, and may cover future as well as present patent rights. The companies participating will usually agree not to attack the validity of patents held by other members of the group. In this way, all of the technology in the field may be brought under unified control.

Patent Warfare. Large firms have sometimes used patents in attacking possible competitors. In addition to "blocking" and "fencing" patents, there are "umbrella," "accordion," and "drag-net" patents, drawn up with claims so broad, so expansible, and so effective as to cover and seize upon extensive areas of industrial technology.

In one view, "The great research laboratories are only incidentally technological centers. From the business standpoint they are patent factories; they manufacture the raw material of monopoly. Their product is often nothing but a 'shot-gun,' a basis for threatening infringement suits and scaring off competitors; or a 'scare-crow,' a patent which itself represents little or no contribution but seems . . . to cover an important part of a developing art and hence permits threat of suit."[5]

Litigation has been deliberately employed as a weapon of monopoly. Between 1877 and 1893, when the first Bell patent expired, the telephone company initiated more than 600 infringement suits. Patent warfare was similarly employed to build the power of National Cash Register, Eastman Kodak, United Shoe Machinery, and many drug firms.

In patent warfare, there is no assurance that the adversary with the better claim will be victorious. Litigation is costly, and the outcome is likely to favor the party with the larger purse.

Restrictive Licensing. The patent holder may fail to work the patent and may refuse to license others to do so. Even if licenses are given, they may be restrictive. Output may be limited by imposing quotas or

---

[5]Kahn, "The Role of Patents."

by charging graduated royalties. A patent holder may also undertake to fix the prices that are charged by subsequent distributors.

Patent Pools. In industries where essential patents are controlled by many firms, they may be brought together in a common pool. Under such an arrangement, patents may be assigned to a trade association or to a corporation set up for the purpose, and licenses granted to each of the participants under all of the patents in the pool.

Patent pooling may be employed either to liberate competition or to intensify monopoly. Improvements resulting from invention are made available to all of the participants, and costs are reduced by eliminating litigation within the group. If unrestricted licenses are granted to all applicants on reasonable terms, outsiders are afforded access to the industry's technology. However, by including in its contracts provisions that restrict the quantity a licensee may produce, the area in which it may sell, and the prices it may charge, a pool may regiment an entire industry.

3. Cases

Most of these abuses have been presented in cases before the courts. In general, the earlier decisions were favorable to the patent holder, but the courts have come increasingly to limit the scope and check the abuses of patent monopoly.

Concentration of Patent Ownership. Where a single company has clearly sought to monopolize an industry's patents as a means of monopolizing the industry itself, its action has been condemned. In itself, however, the ownership of many patents by a single company has not been found to violate the law.[6]

Patent Pools. The leading case on patent pooling, the *Standard Sanitary* case, was decided in 1912.[7] Various patents covering the production of enameled iron bathtubs and other sanitary wares had been pooled with a trade association. Included in licenses issued to firms producing 85 percent of the output of such wares were provisions re-

---

[6]The issue was raised in the *United Shoe Machinery* case. The company held nearly 4,000 patents, about 95 percent of them the product of its own research, only 5 percent of them purchased from others. The government charged that the company "has been for many years, and is now, engaged in a program of engrossing all patents and inventions of importance relating to shoe machinery for the purpose of blanketing the shoe machinery industry with patents under the control of United and thereby suppressing competition in the industry."

[7]*Standard Sanitary Mfg. Co.* v. *U.S.*, 226 U.S.20.

stricting output, fixing prices and discounts, and controlling channels of trade. These restrictions were held to violate the Sherman Act.

In the *Standard Oil of Indiana* case[8] in 1931, a pool controlling patents covering methods of cracking gasoline was allowed to stand. However, many other cracking processes remained outside the pool, licensees under the pooling arrangement did little more than half of the cracking of gasoline, and cracking provided only a fourth of the total supply. The pool, thus faced with competition, was found to be powerless to fix prices and was held to be within the law.

In the *Hartford-Empire* case[9] decided in 1945, Hartford had employed the patents in its pool to dominate completely the glass-container industry, curtailing output, dividing markets, and fixing prices through restrictive licenses; the Court found in Hartford's behavior convincing evidence of unlawful conspiracy.

So, too, with cross-licensing. In the *Line Material* case in 1948, the Court condemned a plan that eliminated competition through cross-licensing.[10] Here, each of two small companies producing patented fuse cutouts had licensed the other and fixed the prices it might charge. Their agreement to do so was held to be illegal per se. In the *Besser* case in 1952, the Court held an agreement between two patent holders to refuse licenses to others to be a boycott and, as such, to be illegal per se.[11] And in the *Singer* case in 1963, where Singer had exchanged licenses with Swiss and Italian manufacturers of zigzag sewing machines and then brought infringement suits against importers of Japanese machines, the Court found the three concerns to be conspiring in restraint of trade.[12]

Patent pooling was an issue in another suit that the government brought against the General Electric Company. The basic patents on the electric lamp had expired, and GE had tried to keep its control of the industry by employing later patents on such parts of the lamp as the filament and the frosting on the bulb. It had formed a patent pool with Westinghouse and granted licenses to four other producers, controlling the output and the prices of all six companies. These arrangements were held in 1949 to violate both sections of the Sherman Act. General Electric, said the Court, had conspired with its licensees and had "unlawfully monopolized the incandescent electric lamp industry in the United States."[13]

---

[8]*Standard Oil Co. (Indiana)* v. *U.S.*, 283 U.S. 163.

[9]*Hartford-Empire Co.* v. *U.S.*, 323 U.S. 386.

[10]*U.S.* v. *Line Material Co.*, 333 U.S. 287.

[11]*Besser Mfg. Co.* v. *U.S.*, 343 U.S. 444.

[12]*U.S.* v. *Singer Mfg. Co.*, 374 U.S. 174.

[13]*U.S.* v. *General Electric Co.*, 82 F. Supp. 753.

An important case involving the operation of a patent pool is that of the Radio Corporation of America. Here, in a civil suit brought in 1954 and a criminal suit brought in 1958, the government charged that RCA had entered into agreements with AT&T, GE, Westinghouse, and with firms in other countries that gave it the exclusive right to grant licenses under more than 10,000 radio-purpose patents in the United States. As a result, other manufacturers of electronic equipment were made to depend upon RCA. In granting licenses, moreover, the company refused to license patents individually, but insisted on licensing all of the patents in a packaged group. RCA pleaded nolo contendere in the government's criminal case, paying a fine of $100,000, and accepted a consent decree in the civil suit. Under the terms of this decree, the company agreed to license its existing radio and TV patents royalty-free, to license its new patents at reasonable royalties, and to permit its licensees to obtain patents individually instead of requiring package deals.[14]

Tying Contracts. Many decisions of the courts have dealt with the efforts of patentees to extend the scope of their monopoly beyond the boundaries of the patent grant. Under the Clayton Act, such tying contracts have consistently been condemned. The courts have struck down contracts, among others, requiring radio manufacturers licensed under RCA patents to buy their tubes from RCA;[15] requiring lessees of International Business Machines to buy their tabulating cards from IBM;[16] and requiring the purchase of rivets by lessees of patented riveting machines.[17] In these cases, the patentee dominated the market for the process or product to which the unpatented commodity was tied. However, tying contracts have also been invalidated in cases where the patentee was far from having a monopoly. Thus, in the *International Salt* case,[18] the Supreme Court held that a contract requiring the users of a patented salt dispenser to purchase salt from its producer was unreasonable per se. Even now, the courts resist the use of tying clauses to extend a patent monopoly.

Restrictive Licenses. Where a patent owner grants a license to use a patented machine or process or to make and sell a patented product, the courts have generally upheld its right to limit the licensee to a certain geographic area or a certain field of industry, to restrict output, and to fix the price of the patented goods.

---

[14]*U.S. v. Radio Corp. of America*, 1958 Trade Cases, Par. 69, 164.

[15]*Lord v. Radio Corp. of America*, 24 F.2d 505 (1928).

[16]*International Business Machines Corp. v. U.S.*, 298 U.S. 131 (1936).

[17]*Judson Thompson v. FTC*, 150 F.2d 952 (1945).

[18]*International Salt Co. v. U.S.*, 332 U.S. 392 (1947).

Surrender of title to a patented good, however, has long been held to terminate the patentee's authority over its subsequent use and sale. The right to control the price at which patented products, once sold, are resold by others has therefore been denied. In the case of *Bauer* v. *O'Donnell* in 1913, it was held that O'Donnell had not infringed Bauer's patent on Sanatogen when he resold it for less than the price that Bauer had printed on the package.[19] This precedent has generally been followed since that time.

Restrictive licensing of another manufacturers has been permitted where it applied to a single licensee, but it has been held to be illegal when employed for the purpose of eliminating competition among many licensees.[20] When each of several licensees accepts restrictive terms on the condition or with the knowledge that others will do so, they are guilty of conspiracy in restraint of trade.

Remedies in Patent Cases. Employment of patents to eliminate competition has repeatedly been restrained by the courts.[21] The Court has also held that a defendant in an infringement suit, brought to enforce a patent that had been obtained through fraudulent representations, could sue the patentor for treble damages.[22]

Judicial actions have also sought to remove barriers to entry. In the *Hartford-Empire* case,[23] the Supreme Court required compulsory licensing for the first time in history.

Royalty-free licensing was first required by a district court in the case of the *General Electric Company* in 1953. The court refused to dismember the company or to ban the agency system; but it did order the licensing of patents, with future patents to be made available at reasonable royalties and existing patents royalty-free.[24]

Similar provisions have been incorporated in consent decrees. Scores of such decrees have been accepted, providing for the licensing of all applicants, many of them for licensing without royalties. Under the typical decree, existing patents must be licensed royalty-free and future patents at reasonable royalties. Royalty charges are determined by agreement between the patent owner and the licensee or, failing this, are established by the courts. A consent decree accepted by General

---

[19]229 U.S. 1.

[20]*U.S.* v. *U.S. Gypsum Co.*, 333 U.S. 364 (1948).

[21]*Morton Salt Co.* v. *G. S. Suppiger Co.*, 314 U.S. 488 (1942); *B. B. Chemical Co.* v. *Ellis*, 314 U.S. 495 (1942); *Mercoid Corp.* v. *Mid-Continent Investment Co.*, 320 U.S. 661 (1944).

[22]*Walker Process Equipment Co.* v. *Food Machinery and Chemical Corp.*, 382 U.S. 172 (1965).

[23]*Hartford-Empire Co.* v. *U.S.*, 323 U.S. 386 (1945). This precedent was followed two years later in *U.S.* v. *National Lead Co.*, 332 U.S. 319 (1947).

[24]*U.S.* v. *General Electric*, 115 F. Supp. 835.

Motors in 1965, in a suit attacking its control of 85 percent of the output of buses, provided for royalty-free licensing of future as well as existing patents. The *Xerox* settlement in 1975 was similar (recall Chapter 7).

II. BARRIERS AND ANTITRUST EXEMPTIONS

1. Trade Barriers

The most ancient and extensive restraints are those of foreign trade. The net effect of a tariff is to exclude competition, and the benefits are reaped by producers at the expense of consumers. For the United States, leading features of these tariffs and physical limits are shown in Table 16–1. Some approach a total exclusion of import competition. The degree of actual protection is often difficult to assess, for it reflects both output tariffs on imported inputs.

Supplementing or substituting for tariffs often are quotas or other physical limitations on imports. These have been most prominent in the oil and steel industries, especially since the middle 1950s. There has existed since 1968 an effective international cartel limiting imports of steel from Japan and Europe to the United States (recall Chapter 9). Since 1980, the United States has imposed or negotiated new restrictions on such goods as bolts and screws, cement and other construction materials, steel products, Japanese light trucks and motorcycles, and textiles from China.

The restraints on Japanese car sales in the United States deserve special mention. Japanese cars flooded the U.S. market in 1978–80, because their quality was higher and their costs were about $2,000 lower per car. As the Japanese market share rose, the United States forced a "voluntary" limit of 1.68 million cars per year, managed by the Japanese themselves. The prices of all cars rose, with Japanese cars selling at a premium. The quota has continued, at 2.1 million cars per year.

The results are the predictable ones. U.S. consumers paid heavily. Prices for all cars sold in the U.S. rose 40 percent during 1980–84, to nearly $11,000 per car. The U.S. firms raised their profit per car from $516 in 1978 to $927 in 1983. Americans paid $5 billion a year more for cars. The Japanese firms naturally sent their most profitable cars, fattening their own profits. They reinvested much of these funds in further improvements, and so their superiority over U.S. firms' efficiency has remained. Also, Japanese firms created major car factories in the United States.

In short, the restraints imposed heavy costs on consumers and gave high profits to U.S. and Japanese firms. The whole episode fitted the

Table 16–1   Selected Trade Restrictions, 1980s

Tariffs	Rate of Tariff as Percent of Value	Tariffs	Rate of Tariff as Percent of Value
Distilled liquors	18%	Steel products	5–15%
Wool fabrics	47	Machinery	5–15
Clothing	20–30	Motors	12
Furniture	11	Appliances	10–12
Organic dyes, etc.	37	Automobiles	6
Shoes	15	Cycles	13
Flat glass	17	Sporting goods	19
Glassware	17	Musical instruments	21

Other Restrictions

Steel	"Voluntary" restrictions on steel sales to the United States. Also, a system of "reference" prices that trigger extra duties on imported steel (first imposed in 1977).
Automobiles	Japanese firms are under "voluntary" restraints at 2.1 million cars per year.
Ships	Foreign-made ships cannot (1) ply U.S. coastal routes nor (2) get shipping subsidies.
Cotton	Restrictions are negotiated by governments. Japanese sales have dropped 60 percent.
Sugar, wheat, cotton	Restricted.
"Buy American"	Excludes foreign suppliers in a range of major industrial products.

classic effects of trade barriers, with large costs for consumers, high profits for producers, but little net gain of efficiency for the economy.

2. Antitrust Exemptions

Among the many departures from antitrust, two stand out: labor unions and military buying of weapons. But first, several lesser ones are presented.

Agricultural Cooperatives. These dominate the trade in most crops and livestock. Some of them are big businesses and hold a high degree of market power. A wave of mergers during the 1970s increased concentration among them further, and some have moved into large-scale production of fertilizers and chemicals. The Capper-Volstead Act exempts cooperatives from antitrust. In the most basic agricultural goods, they usually have little market power. However, where producers are geographically concentrated—as they are in fruits, vegetables, nuts, and milk—a cooperative may possess much market power. In some cases, cooperatives equalize the bargaining powers of sellers and buyers, but in others they are simply a license to monopolize.

Newspapers. These are another major exemption from antitrust. In recent decades, their numbers have been dwindling, partly because the economies of scale in production and distribution have risen. (Also, the profit gains from increasing the share of local advertising have risen.) In 1970, after a series of adverse court decisions against newspaper mergers, the newspapers succeeded in getting Congress to pass an act exempting joint arrangements between pairs of papers for mutual printing and business organization of newspaper production. This is, in effect, a large special application of the failing-firm criterion (recall Chapter 8). Genuine economies of scale (plus the gains from monopolizing advertising) might lead to a virtually complete situation of one-paper cities throughout the country. Therefore, the exemption may marginally promote variety and competition. Yet it does acquiesce in an extraordinary degree of monopoly in most newspaper markets.

Milk. Markets for milk are essentially the areas around the largest 60 or so cities in the United States. Each is limited by local health laws and price controls authorized by the U.S. Department of Agriculture. There are usually only a few milk suppliers, competing by brands and service rather than by price. A complicated set of formulas is applied in fixing local milk prices, involving discrimination as well as cartel results.

In 20 states, prices paid to milk producers are fixed by public agencies. Covering intrastate markets, they are generally similar to federal controls but tighter. Resale prices are fixed for milk under the laws of 15 states. Sales below cost are forbidden by the laws of 10 other states. They, too, restrict sales and raise prices.[25] Distributors' margins are also protected by regulations that restrain competition.

These official cartels have cost consumers over $500 million per year, at a net social costs of $200 million per year.[26] They could be replaced by free market processes, giving a much more efficient outcome.

---

[25]U.S. Department of Agriculture, Economic Research Service, *Government's Role in Pricing Fluid Milk in the United States,* Agricultural Economic Report no. 152 (Washington, D.C.: U.S. Government Printing Office, 1968).

[26]Reuben A. Kessel, "Economic Effects of Federal Regulation of Milk Markets," *Journal of Law and Economics* 10 (1967), pp. 51–78; and Richard A. Ippolito and Robert T. Masson, "The Social Cost of Government Regulation of Milk," *Journal of Law and Economics* 21 (April 1978), pp. 33–66.

Price Controls. Formal price controls have been tried in the United States mainly during World War II, the Korean War, and 1971–74.[27] Many U.S. economists have been part of the effort, and most of them regard it as frustrating and only partially successful. Since 1955, there have been many informal "jawboning" attempts—and quasi-formal "wage-price guidelines"—to abate price rises.[28] Expert opinion is divided on the issue. Some economists regard controls as worth trying, at least during crisis periods. Others liken them to bandages applied to cure a fever.

Four basic lessons hold: (1) Controls work best during a crisis, especially in war when loyalty is high and the situation seems to be temporary; (2) price-wage controls fail when any important groups (especially upper groups: top executives, capital-gains receivers, speculators) are exempted from controls, while ordinary citizens are made to sacrifice; (3) controls are most effective on major concentrated industries; and (4) price-wage controls are cumbersome, costly, and unfair to some groups.[29] Inspired leaders can minimize these flaws.

Labor Unions. Policy toward industrial labor evolved slowly, but then in the 1930s unions were largely removed from antitrust limits, under the Wagner Act. However, legal exemption from antitrust came slowly. In fact, the first use of the Sherman Act was to help break the Pullman strike in 1892. In the *Danbury Hatters'* case in 1908, the Court awarded damages to an employer who had been injured by a secondary boycott. This led to the inclusion in the Clayton Act of a section providing that unions, as such, shall not "be held or construed to be illegal combinations or conspiracies in restraint of trade." The courts also began in 1940 to permit unions to act in concert with others to enforce boycotts and controls on prices.[30]

Barriers to Certain Occupations. Next, consider various restrictions of "professional" trades. These are entry barriers, formal rules against competitive practices, and informal limits or behavior.

---

[27]An excellent analysis of World War II experience is given in J. K. Galbraith, *A Theory of Price Control* (Cambridge, Mass.: Harvard Univ. Press, 1952).

[28]John Sheahan, *The Wage-Price Guidelines* (Washington, D.C.: Brookings Institution, 1968).

[29]See the revealing analysis of these defects by C. Jackson Grayson, the head of the Price Commission, and the excellent analysis by R. F. Lanzillotti, Mary Hamilton, and Blaine Roberts, *Phase II in Review: The Price Commission* (Washington, D.C.: Brookings Institution, 1975).

[30]*Apex Hosiery Co.* v. *Leader,* 310 U.S. 469; *Allen Bradley Co.* v. *Local Union No. 3.* 325 U.S. 797.

Entry into professions affecting public health and safety—medicine, nursing, pharmacy, and the like—has long been restricted by groups operating under state laws. Qualifications have been established, examinations given, and licenses required. Over the years, this form of control has gradually been extended until, today, there are as many as 75 trades where entry is restricted by law, including not only accountants, attorneys, chiropodists, dentists, embalmers, engineers, nurses, optometrists, osteopaths, pharmacists, physicians, and veterinarians, but also licensed barbers, beauticians, chiropractors, funeral directors, surveyors, and insurance and real estate salespersons. A number of states also license such tradespeople as plumbers, dry cleaners, horse-shoers, tree surgeons, automobile salespeople, and photographers. Altogether, there are more than 1,200 occupational license laws, averaging 25 per state. Every state has at least 10 licensing boards for such trades; some have as many as 45.

Most of these laws reflect self-regulation for self-interest. The boards that administer the laws are usually composed predominantly of members of the trades concerned. The main effect is to reduce entry and raise incomes.[31] Though competition is being injected into some professions by recent court rulings (recall Chapter 9), the main effect of the state laws continues.

III. SPECIAL SECTORS

Finally, three sectors have distinctive policy treatments. Military purchasing has tolerated—or actively encouraged—market power in a range of weapons industries. Farm policies have altered pricing and production in important agricultural markets, and natural resources pose distinctive questions about efficiency under competition.

1. Military Purchases of Weapons

The supply of weapons is an ancient and universal problem, which can be solved in many ways, none of them satisfactory.[32] The issues include

---

[31]One result is a "Cadillac effect," which provides high-quality service for those that can afford it but cuts out all "economy-grade," service. Stricter licensing forces more people into do-it-yourself plumbing and electrical wiring, often with increased danger. Licensing also excludes minorities and the poor by stressing written tests, rather than practical skills. It has been shown to raise the dental fees by about 15 percent. See Lawrence Shepard, "Licensing Restrictions and the Cost of Dental Care," *Journal of Law and Economics* 21 (April 1978), pp. 187–202. The net social cost may be $700 million per year.

[32]Good basic sources include M. J. Peck and F. M. Scherer, *The Weapons Acquisition Process* (Boston: Harvard University School of Business, 1962); C. J. Hitch and R. N.

monopoly, profitability, public subsidy, and the costs of innovation. The capacity for waste and damage is great, and so "correct" public policies offer high yields. Yet the degree of monopoly and inefficiency are actually high.

The Sector. The weapons trade is a major sector, in both the United States and the world economy. Since 1940, a large armaments sector has become established, with several score major suppliers plus thousands of smaller subcontractors relying on military orders.

Military supplies embrace a remarkable variety, from pencils, tomatoes, and uniforms to complex electronic defense and attack systems. Since 1955, large advanced systems have been a main focus. They involve (1) rapid development, even at high extra costs; (2) high degrees of discovery, innovation, and risk; and (3) rapid obsolescence and replacement with new systems. This attitude breeds a tolerance for waste and error, because speed and new technology appear to be worth great costs.

The flow of purchases is large, and its treatment has repercussions in many markets. Pentagon decisions set or eliminate competition, both in weapons and in adjacent markets. Many large firms are dependent on weapons orders (altogether, perhaps 15 major companies are primarily weapons producers).

Most military contracts are sought by at least several firms. For firms reliant on defense orders, the key economic fact is that their short-run *marginal* cost for new orders is quite low when the order backlog is small. Yet the revenue from contracts must eventually cover their average cost. Each supplier, therefore, tends to bid aggressively when short of orders but only nominally when its order backlog is long.

There is also a pooling of overhead costs among contracts. The larger defense firms often hold many research, development, and production contracts at any time in varying stages of completion. Often funds, staff, and facilities mingle among the projects, so that costs, deficits, and performance are hard to define.

McKean, *The Economics of Defense in the Nuclear Age* (Cambridge, Mass.: Harvard Univ. Press, 1960); Jacques S. Gansler, *The Defense Industry* (Cambridge, Mass.: MIT Press, 1980); and F. M. Scherer, *The Weapons Acquisition Process: Economic Incentives* (Boston: Harvard University School of Business, 1963). See also J. K. Galbraith, *The New Industrial State* (Boston: Houghton Mifflin, 1968) on the mutual process of military and industrial planning. On World War II, see J. P. Miller, *The Pricing of Military Procurement* (Cambridge, Mass.: Harvard Univ. Press, 1949).

The practical features of procurement are laid out fully in J. Ronald Fox, *Arming America: How the U.S. Buys Weapons* (Boston: Harvard Univ. Press, 1974).

Many markets for the larger weapons are tight oligopolies or virtual monopolies. This reflects several factors, including the willingness of military purchasers to deal with only a few firms.

Special Conditions of Purchasing Decisions. Weapons purchases are essentially made at the grass-roots level of the Pentagon, by middle-level officers who are intimately familiar with their suppliers. These people—working closely with company personnel—prepare the contracting information about needs, capabilities, and costs.

These officials have little conception of, or interest in, competition in the wider range of the economy. Indeed, broadening the field of suppliers mainly adds to their tasks and insecurities. If their decisions tend to foster monopoly, that is only of incidental importance to them. Also, their training and incentives favor high quality and maximum reliability as criteria, rather than minimum cost.

The competitive status of weapons contracting is indicated in Table 16–2 (patterns since 1967 are similar). Approximately two thirds of purchases occur under conditions with virtually no competition at all. The military mind usually prefers to pick out a preferred supplier and then work with it or to consider only several familiar candidates. The uncertainty and fluidity of competitive conditions are generally regarded as unreliable and troublesome.

The Antitrust Division and related agencies concerned with competition have had virtually no role in monitoring or influencing military procurement.

Economic Incentives. The basic economic objectives are part of a broad optimizing (1) to get the efficient balance among the performance criteria of *each* weapon system and (2) to evolve these into the optimal bundle of *all* weapons systems.

The main difficulty arises from the gap between marginal cost and average cost. This was noted earlier; firms hungry for new orders have low marginal cost, and they are, therefore, willing to bid at prices that they know are below their eventual average costs. The net effect is to reduce competition and cause a tendency for the "buying-in" of contracts. Firms bid knowingly below average costs—but at or above marginal costs—expecting to be able to push up the effective price at later stages. This creates illusions of low weapons costs at the time when contracts are prepared and let. It also prevents effective minimizing of costs. It encourages weapons markets to evolve a limited set of suppliers, each heavily reliant on weapons orders.

These special cost incentives interact with the basis on which suppliers are paid. This basis can be summed up in the following formula for the actual profit realized on a contract:

$$\text{Realized profit} = \text{Target profit} + \alpha\,(\text{Target cost} - \text{Actual cost})$$

Table 16–2 Competitive Status of Defense Contracts, 1967

		Basis of Contracting ($ millions)					
	(1)	(2)	(3)	Negotiated			Virtual Absence of Competition Type (4), (5), and (6) Contracts (percent)
				(4)	(5)	(6)	
	Competitive Bids	Price Compitition	Design and Technical Competition	Extension of a (2) Contract	Extension of a (3) Contract	Single Source	
Airframes	$ 65	$ 632	$ 330	$477	$2,394	$1,596	81%
Aircraft engines	1	183	68	42	921	332	84
Missile systems	34	153	183	11	1,652	1,678	90
Ships	960	59	33	1	33	425	30
Combat vehicles	149	42	—	—	20	230	57
Noncombat vehicles	351	157	12	1	—	63	11
Weapons	21	55	3	—	4	243	76
Ammunitions	146	575	32	85	12	2,177	75
Electronics communications	250	377	210	48	288	1,376	67
Total (these and other items)	$3,465	$4,713	$1,451	$747	$5,647	$9,632	62%

Note: All categories of contracts except (1) Competitive Bids are negotiated with supplies.

Source: Defense Department compilations, given in W. G. Shepherd, *Market Power and Economic Welfare* (New York: Random House, 1970), pp. 260–61.

The key element here is α.[33] When α is zero, the firm realizes the target profit regardless of the costs it incurs in supplying the weapons. At the other extreme, if α is 1, the firm keeps whatever cost saving it manages below the cost target, but it has to pay out of its own pocket any excess of actual cost over target cost. Therefore, α is the degree of incentive felt by the supplier in trying to minimize cost. Typically, α has been in the range of zero to 0.25. The strongest possible incentive is when α is 1. This is called a *firm fixed-price contract*. At the other extreme, the notorious cost-plus incentive basis tends to eliminate incentives for efficiency and may even induce a preference for higher costs.

Getting α right is, therefore, part of optimizing the trade-offs among the various performance criteria for each project. In fact, α has often not been set right, and a large majority of contracting has been done (and continues to be) essentially on a cost-plus basis. The natural result includes cost overruns, a degree of X-inefficiency, and an imbalance among weapons systems.

Yet it is not enough just to set α at a tight incentive level, because α is only one of the elements in the choices being made both by the buyers and the suppliers. If α is set higher (therefore putting stronger cost incentives on the supplier), then company effort will be shifted to getting the cost target itself higher, perhaps inflating it so as to enable illusory cost cutting.

Probable Costs. Altogether, the weapons sector is managed in ways likely to generate appreciable net costs. Inefficiency in production is substantial, probably on the order of 20 percent of costs for the more complex systems, and in some cases reaching much higher.

Further, weapons quantities and quality both tend to exceed the optimum. There is excess ordering of many items, in part because of the cost illusions fostered by underbidding. Also, armaments often embody service qualities that exceed the levels of efficient design. These added costs are likely to be on the order of 10 percent of actual costs.

More Competition. One long-standing proposal is to apply a greater degree of competition in contracting. Although at each juncture the contracting officials commonly believe that a more direct (that is, bilateral monopoly) approach is essential, in the long run, a reliance upon a more flexible and competitive range of suppliers would tend to correct much of the inefficiency.

Yet the corridors of the Pentagon are stony ground for cultivating more reliance on competition. Military officials profess uneasiness at having only one supplier, but they behave as if averse to having more

---

[33]This is explained in Scherer, *The Weapons Acquisition Process*.

than two or three. Past efforts have only brought competitive contracting up to minor levels (perhaps 15 to 25 percent of purchases). Further marginal increases will be difficult to get and are likely to remain on the fringe.

2. Farm Policies

Farm incomes are often unstable from year to year, for two main reasons. One is weather. Drought or hail can destroy a crop one year; good weather can give a bumper crop the next year. The second reason is the inelasticity of demand and supply for most farm products.

Programs. Everyone agrees that, ideally, farm incomes should be more steady. The first programs to stabilize farm incomes were started in the 1930s, using the logical idea of a buffer stock or "ever-normal granary." Thousands of storage bins were built in the farming areas for use as reservoirs. The long-run equilibrium prices and quantities were estimated. In good years, the government bought and stored enough crops to keep prices up to the long-run level. In bad years, the bins were emptied of enough crops to make up the gap, thereby holding the price to the long-run equilibrium level. The cost of the bins and storage was small compared to the benefits of stabilizing farm incomes. The program worked well for grains, powdered milk, eggs, and several other crops.

However, the program was then altered to serve another purpose: *raising and holding the price above the long-run equilibrium level.* The "price supports" raised farmers' incomes by increasing their total and net revenues, but they also hurt consumers by raising the long-run prices that they would have to pay for the foods, clothing, and other products made from farm outputs. By raising prices above equilibrium cost levels, the price-support program caused inefficient allocation.

Besides being inefficient, the programs were also inequitable because they mainly benefited the farmers with the largest levels of output. The higher crop price is multiplied by the quantities sold. Since small farmers produce less, they also benefit less, even though they are the truly needy farmers. The benefits have flowed mainly to the big, already-prosperous farmers. Altogether, price supports have reflected political clout, rather than the use of clear, rational economic tools.[34]

Effects. This perversion of the original programs from *income stabilizing* to *price raising* has had several predictable economic effects. *First,*

---

[34]For a thorough treatment of these issues, see Geoffrey S. Shepherd and Gene Futrell, *Marketing Farm Products,* 7th ed. (Ames, Iowa: Iowa State University Press, 1982).

the higher price has led farmers to produce more over the long run and consumers to buy less. The resulting physical surpluses were enormous in the 1950s and 1960s. The Agriculture Department has had large surplus stocks, at high yearly costs for storage, spoilage, and interest.

A *second* effect has been to raise the price of farmland. By making crops more valuable, price supports have made the land itself more valuable. These benefits are strictly a rise in economic *rent,* which farmers get for doing nothing more than their normal work. The benefits have gone to the land or to land ownership, not to farmers as such, and they have gone mainly to large-scale farmers, most of whom were already prosperous.

In the 1950s, farmers were paid to take some of their land out of cultivation and put it in a "land bank." This was costly—more so because farmers naturally set aside their worst land. Moreover, they tilled the remaining land more intensively because their other inputs (equipment, labor) were little changed. Accordingly, total production was little reduced. The land bank, a clear case of economic waste and a costly failure, was abandoned in the 1960s.

Surpluses also were channeled into school milk programs and giveaways to needy foreign countries. However, such "Food for Peace" types of foreign aid depressed farm prices and farm incomes in those countries receiving the foods, thus harming farmers and undermining the prospects for agricultural progress in those countries.

Certain farm prices were also raised indirectly. For example, the land permitted for growing tobacco has been rigidly limited since 1938. That has raised tobacco prices and enriched landowners by raising the price of the land far above its economic value. The same is true of peanut acreage. About 40 other crops (from dates and grapes to California oranges) are under "marketing orders." When their prices threaten to fall below target prices in bountiful crop years, the Agriculture Department buys the surplus and destroys it.

Direct Payments. The efficient treatment would simply identify the needy farmers and raise their incomes by direct payments. The payments would, flow mainly to small-scale farmers, as in Appalachia and parts of New England.

Being relatively focused, the payments would be much less costly to the public purse than programs based indiscriminately on prices and outputs. They would avoid enriching already-rich farmers and would not raise farm prices. They would also avoid needless economic rents and windfall gains from rising land prices.

On the other hand, direct payments might encourage people to stay on farms that are too small and/or barren, or both, to justify farming. Thus this treatment could encourage a permanent class of small operators on inefficient farms.

Table 16–3   The Main Types of Natural Resources

Nonrenewable
  Fuels (coal, oil, gas), land, ores, chemical deposits
Replaceable at great cost
  Soil, wilderness, certain rivers and lakes
Renewable
  Other rivers and lakes, urban fresh air
Self-renewing
  Forests, fisheries, other "crops"
Virtually inexhaustible
  Rural fresh air, solar energy

Yet, this mistake could easily be avoided. The direct payments could be kept low enough to encourage inefficient farmers to migrate to towns. Alternatively, specific relocation grants could be provided to encourage marginal farmers to shift toward more productive jobs and locations.

3. Natural Resources

Natural resources come in many kinds, as Table 16–3 shows. Some are abundant, like sunlight and seawater. Others are renewable and can be efficiently harvested virtually forever—forests and farm crops, for instance. Still other resources, such as oil, ores, and coal, are strictly exhaustible. Once used, they are gone forever.

Should the exhaustible resources be saved, rather than used? If they should be used, how rapidly? Such issues appear to be complicated, involving many special features. No single best rate of use applies to all kinds of natural resources. Each one needs careful study.

Conservation: Reaching the Optimum Rate of Use. The term *optimum* here implies *social* efficiency: the best net use of resources for society as a whole, over the relevant span of time. The economic aim is to use efficiently—and equitably, both *within* each generation of people and *among* generations as the decades and centuries pass—each physically limited, depletable resource. Efficient use will yield the maximum net value for the resource over time. Equity involves difficult problems because the resources used up by present generations are denied to future generations. Since the future inhabitants of the world are not here now to urge that resources be saved for their use, present generations may selfishly consume these limited resources too rapidly.

Yet the hoarding of resources for future use can err on the other side, toward too slow a rate of use. The goal is to strike the right balance between present and future. Physical *preservation* is only one alternative among the ways to conserve a resource. The efficient use of a natural resource often requires that it be used up. The economic task is to define the efficient rate of usage.

Private Markets. Now return to the general case of a resource that is privately owned. Economists offer a clear, optimistic lesson about the conservation of privately owned resources: Private markets operating with reasonably complete knowledge and rationality can meet the social criteria for conserving resources over time. The owners will be guided both by their profit-maximizing motivations and by the objective conditions prevailing in financial and industrial markets.

This result holds only for competitive markets. Monopolists usually will hold the rate of resource utilization *lower,* by restricting output and raising price in the present. That will lean toward too-slow use, rather than toward using resources too quickly. Yet, because even monopolists will want to maximize the value of resource use in the long run, the restrictive effect may distort their choices only slightly.

Altogether, then, when there are rational choices in private markets, the prices of natural resources will tend to anticipate future scarcities. If people's expectations about future prices should rise, they will quickly bid up the capital value of the resource. Prices rise in anticipation of coming shortages. This price increase acts, in turn, to reduce the usage of the resource, if demand is at all elastic.

To this degree, the owners and users of resources will act in accordance with the genuine social costs of their use of resources. This will occur spontaneously, without conscious or detailed social planning.

Limitations and Biases. However, this optimum result depends on strict conditions, which may not be met.

1. Common-Property Resources. Some resources are not individually owned. Thus, no price for using them can be levied by a specific owner. As a result, they are available at a zero price to whoever captures them. This can lead to competitive overuse and destruction, as each user maximizes its own profits by taking the resource rapidly. Fish are one example. Oil and gas in an oil field that can be tapped by different landowners who own plots of land above the oil field are another. Each user is oblivious of the total use of the resource. Since the competitive user considers only its own interests and is aware that the resource will dwindle, the incentive for rapid removal is increased.

The net effect is often a race to capture the resource. If the resource is harvestable, as fish are, the process will exceed the optimum rate and possibly reduce the total catch or even render the species extinct.

If the resource is a fixed stock, such as oil, the current rate of extraction will be raised well above the optimum.

The corrective to this problem is to create a monopoly—to so unify the control of each such resource in one owner that the optimum technical pattern and rate of usage can be designed and applied. Here, monopoly is clearly preferable to competition.

2. *Discounting and Myopia*. The private rate of discount may be too high. This encourages a current rate of use *above* the optimal rate. The high rate of discount gives more weight to the present generation's interests than to those of future generations.

3. *Inadequate Forecasting*. Present users may simply fail to foresee future developments. This may reflect insufficient research or an inability to discern future change. There may be close interactions among the uses of resources that are not presently apparent to the various users.

4. *Political Influences*. Specific taxes and other incentives may encourage an overly rapid use of resources. In fact, the use of almost every resource is affected by artificial incentives. There are special tax provisions for the extraction of almost all natural resources, such as oil and ores. Maritime policies affect the exhaustion of oceanic fish resources. These incentives often induce a more rapid use of resources, even to the point of extinction.

5. *External Effects*. There may be important externalities in the uses of many resources, so that private users ignore major social costs of their actions. This affects both the rate of withdrawal of natural resources and the degree to which the common environment of air, water, and habitat is degraded.

QUESTIONS FOR REVIEW

1. "If inventions are mostly induced then a patent system will have little value." True?

2. "The optimal patent life will differ among inventions, rather than be the same for each." True?

3. "Patents are generally appropriate for really big or really little inventions, not the medium range of new ideas." True?

4. "Tariffs and quotas reduce competition by reducing the 'entry' of imports." True?

5. "Labor unions have had little clear effect on wage rates, but professional 'unions' are able to raise their members' incomes appreciably." True?

6. "Military goods often involve many dimensions, of which cost is only one." True?

7. "To get the maximum incentive effect for efficient supply of weapons, α should be set at 1." True?

8. "The bulk of military purchases is made under conditions that are basically noncompetitive." True?

9. "Conservation may involve strict physical preservation or it may require using a resource up." True?

10. "Private markets usually optimize the use of resources except where (*a*) there is multiple access, (*b*) private forecasts are wrong, (*c*) external effects are absent." Which?

11. "Competition in fishing is destructive because each operator has incentives to take out too much." True?

12. Which trade barriers are probably justified?

13. What professions should have licensing restrictions?

14. How could you make "renegotiation" of military contracts work well? Is it bound to be futile?

15. Which resources are probably being too rapidly exploited? What do you compare in reaching such judgments?

ANSWERS TO SELECTED REVIEW QUESTIONS

Chapter 2
1. True **2.** True **3.** True **4.** True **5.** Not true **6.** Not true **7.** True
8. True

Chapter 3
1. Not true **2.** True **4.** Not true

Chapter 4
1. True **2.** Not true **3.** Not true **4.** All **5.** True **6.** Not true
7. True **8.** Not true **9.** Not true

Chapter 5
1. Not true **2.** Not true **3.** True **4.** All **5.** Not true **6.** Not true
7. Not true **8.** Not true **9.** (d) **10.** True **11.** Not true **12.** True

Chapter 6
1. Not true **2.** Not true **3.** Not true **4.** Not true **5.** True **6.** Not
true **7.** True

Chapter 7
1. Not true **2.** Not true **3.** True **4.** True **5.** Not true **6.** Not true
7. Not true **8.** True

Chapter 8
1. Not true **2.** True **3.** True **4.** Not true **5.** Not true **6.** Not true
7. True **8.** True

Chapter 9
1. True **2.** True **3.** Not true **4.** Not true

Chapter 10
1. Not true **2.** True **3.** Not true **4.** True **5.** True **6.** True **7.** True

Chapter 11
1. Not true **2.** Not true **3.** Not true **4.** True

Chapter 12
1. True **2.** Not true **3.** True **4.** Not true **5.** Not true

Chapter 13
1. Not true **2.** True **3.** True **4.** True **5.** Not true **6.** True **7.** Not
true **8.** True **9.** True **10.** True **11.** True

Chapter 14
1. True   **2.** True   **3.** True   **4.** True   **5.** Not true   **6.** Not true   **7.** True
8. True   **9.** True   **10.** True   **11.** True   **12.** True   **13.** True   **14.** True

Chapter 15
1. True   **2.** True   **3.** True   **4.** Not true   **5.** True   **6.** True   **7.** True   **8.**
Not true   **9.** True   **10.** Not true   **11.** Not true   **12.** Not true   **13.** Not
true   **14.** True

Chapter 16
1. Not true   **2.** True   **3.** Not true   **4.** True   **5.** True   **6.** True   **7.** True
8. True   **9.** True   **10.** a and b   **11.** True

CASE INDEX

NAME INDEX

A

Abromeit, Heidrun, 344 n, 410 n
Acs, Zoltan, 111
Acton, Jan Paul, 376 n, 377 n
Adams, Walter, 75 n, 79 n, 111, 138 n, 190 n, 212, 213, 214, 215 n, 217 n, 322 n, 325 n
Adams, William James, 148 n, 170 n
Adelman, Morris A., 230 n, 275 n, 284 n
Agnew, John, 234 n, 254 n
Aharoni, Yair, 386 n, 410 n
Aigner, Dennis J., 377 n
Akers, John, 73 n
Allen, F. L., 210 n
Areeda, Philip, 154 n, 157 n, 274 n, 276, 277
Armentano, Dominick T., 4 n, 30 n, 31 n, 111
Arnold, Thurman, 15, 125, 180 n, 183
Arrow, Kenneth J., 23 n
Averch, H., 340 n

B

Bailey, Elizabeth E., 80 n, 84, 85 n, 112, 228, 314 n, 340
Bain, Joe S., 41 n, 61 n, 237 n, 239 n
Baldwin, William L., 76 n, 415 n
Bane, Charles A., 246 n
Baratz, Morton, 408 n
Barnekov, Christopher C., 321 n
Bauer, John, 354 n
Baumel, C. Phillip, 321 n
Baumol, William J., 4 n, 19 n, 31, 68 n, 84, 85 n, 228, 273 n, 277 n, 278 n, 310 n, 371, 372 n, 386 n
Beckenstein, Alan, 61 n
Beesley, Michael, 343 n, 410 n
Berg, Sanford V., 372 n
Berle, A. A., 24 n

Bishop, Robert L., 154 n
Bisson, T. A., 205 n
Blair, John M., 71 n
Blair, Roger D., 216 n, 230 n
Boeckh, A., 397 n
Bonbright, James C., 330 n, 350 n, 359 n, 366 n
Borkin, Joseph, 205 n
Bork, Robert H., 4 n, 19, 30 n, 31 n, 111, 215 n
Bowman, Ward S., Jr., 252 n
Boyer, Kenneth D., 154 n, 320, 321 n
Bradburd, Ralph M., 216 n
Braeutigam, Ronald, 306 n, 351 n
Brandeis, Justice, 340
Branfman, Eric J., 138 n
Breit, William, 112, 137 n, 300 n
Brennan, Timothy J., 194 n
Brenner, Melvin A., 80 n, 87 n, 314 n
Breyer, Stephen, 306 n
Brock, Gerald W., 74 n, 111, 188 n, 199, 325 n
Brock, James W., 60 n, 212, 213, 214, 217 n
Brodley, Joseph, 261 n
Brozen, Yale, 4 n, 30 n
Bullock, Charles J., 61 n
Burch, Philip H., Jr., 24 n
Burger, Justice, 249 n
Burns, Malcolm R., 280 n
Burstein, M. L., 170 n
Bush, George, 5, 116, 199, 226, 228, 310
Bussing, I., 354 n

C

Calvani, Terry, 154 n
Campbell, J. S., 233 n
Carlton, Dennis W., 342 n, 343 n, 371 n
Cassell, F., 87 n
Caves, Richard E., 19 n, 23 n, 80 n, 81 n, 314 n, 320 n, 409–10 n

SUBJECT INDEX

M–N

O–P